KOHELETH — THE MAN AND HIS WORLD

KOHELETH—THE MAN
AND HIS WORLD

A Study of Ecclesiastes

Robert Gordis

Third Augmented Edition

SCHOCKEN BOOKS • NEW YORK

For our sons

ENOCH, LEVI and DAVID

PREFACE

The book of Koheleth, better known as *Ecclesiastes*, is one of the most remarkable works in world literature, all the more striking in its impact because of its place within the canon of Holy Writ. Countless generations of students and general readers have been intrigued by this deeply human book, which half reveals and half conceals the fascinating yet enigmatic personality of its author.

My own interest in Koheleth was first aroused during student days by my teacher, the late Professor Max Leopold Margolis of Dropsie College, and its spell has grown deeper with the passing years. During the past two decades I have carried on detailed researches in various aspects of its background, style and content. These studies have laid the foundation for a new approach to Koheleth, who speaks to the modern age across an interval of two thousand years with the immediacy of contact of a contemporary. The results of these investigations are incorporated in a series of technical studies which have appeared in the scholarly journals of our day. All these papers were intended as *Vorstudien* to the present comprehensive work, the completion of which was delayed much too long by the pressure of other activities. As a result, it seemed wise to present my conclusions for the general public in brief, popular form, without scholarly documentation. The wide interest in the subject led to the publication of a small volume, which appeared in two editions, one American, the other British (*The Wisdom of Ecclesiastes*, Behrman House, New York, 1945; *The Wisdom of Koheleth*, East and West Library, London, 1950).

It is a source of profound thanksgiving to have been able to complete this present work over a period of years, in spite of the numberless distractions of a harried communal career. The book was written in the hope that it would prove of interest to the general cultivated reader who wishes to understand the complex cultural and intellectual background of ancient Palestine and the Near East, upon which Koheleth drew and in terms of which he formulated his world-outlook. The new translation which follows is intended to make Koheleth speak for himself to the reader of today. Accordingly, I have relegated to the footnotes virtually all technical material, such as the references to the scientific literature and the detailed documentation for the views expressed in the text. Only Chapter XV, which is concerned with the Hebrew text and the Ancient Versions, may be omitted by the non-technical reader. This chapter, together with the second half of the volume, which includes the Hebrew text and the philological and exegetical Commentary, is intended for the student of Hebrew and Biblical literature.

Strange as it may seem to the uninitiated reader, even exegesis has its fashions. In the past, the practice was to write voluminous commentaries which registered almost every conceivable view and emendation on every passage. As a reaction against this method, which is basically compilatory in nature, Biblical commentators today tend to be brief, which is surely no vice, and dogmatic, which is scarcely a virtue. As a rule, they present merely their own standpoint, without troubling to discuss contrary views or to cite their predecessors, even when they are indebted to them for their conclusions. As a result, the student is entirely at the mercy of the particular work he has in hand.

To be sure, a commentator has the duty to adopt a definite point of view on the issues before him, but this is not his whole duty. The cause of truth is served far better by assembling all the relevant and significant data on complicated questions, so that the reader can judge for himself, than by ignoring all possible alternatives and setting forth one view with a dogmatic assurance generally not shared by succeeding students.

My procedure has therefore been to present, as effectively as possible, what I regard as the best view of each passage. Since, however, I have not persuaded myself that ultimate truth has been achieved, other views that I felt had merit and deserved consideration have been quoted. Conscious, too, of the scholar's toil and of his meager reward, I have tried to do justice to earlier workers in the field, mindful of the Rabbinic dictum, "He who cites a matter in the name of him who said it, brings redemption to the world."

A few words more are in order. For the Hebrew text, Paul Kahle's Masoretic text as published in Kittel's *Biblia Hebraica* (4th ed., Stuttgart, 1949) has been followed. While the traditional chapters and verses are indicated for purposes of reference, I have subdivided both the Hebrew original and the English translation into sections that do justice to the structure of Koheleth. In addition, the rhythmic passages of the book have been printed in a form to exhibit their metrical character. The footnotes in the Hebrew text are limited to the Qere readings of the Masorah and to the few emendations which, I believe, are called for, and the grounds for which will be found in the Commentary.

During the three decades that I have taught Bible at the Jewish Theological Seminary, I have had the opportunity of teaching the book of Koheleth to many generations of students. Quite appropriately, the first edition of the present work appeared in the series of *Texts and Studies of the Jewish Theological Seminary* in 1951. Because of the wide interest the work has evoked among scholars, students and general readers, an augmented edition containing supplementary material appeared in 1955 and again in 1962.

The appearance of the present paperback edition has afforded me the opportunity of including new material in the "Additional Notes on the Text of Koheleth" at the end of the volume. Without presuming to exhaust the subject, I have also added a new chapter, "Koheleth and Modern Existentialism." This brief statement seeks to underscore the fundamental difference in approach between the Biblical Wisdom writers and modern existentialism, in spite of some superficial resemblances between the two.

The present work from its inception owes an incalculable debt to many friends and members of my family who contributed of their energy, knowledge and interest to make the work possible. I single out my devoted friend Doctor Abraham I. Shinedling, who placed at my disposal his wide erudition and remarkable gift of accuracy in proofreading the entire manuscript, besides making countless valuable suggestions with regard to both form and content.

My sons also were most helpful in assisting with the complicated proofreading involved in this book. The debt I owe my wife for her unflagging interest I cannot fully express.

It is my hope that in its present form this volume will contribute to a deeper knowledge and a wider appreciation of Koheleth, which has been described as the most modern book in the Bible. In an age when life often appears chaotic and meaningless, Koheleth has a special message for us, being dedicated to teaching men to love life, accept its limitations, and rejoice in its blessings.

ROBERT GORDIS

Rockaway Park, N.Y.
June, 1967

TABLE OF CONTENTS

ON READING KOHELETH

"Like a great and dark riddle is this little book to us, from its first cry of victory over the nothingness of the world to the silent words of sadness at the end, the sadness of man at his own inevitable doom." In these haunting words a contemporary writer bears witness to the perennial appeal of the Book of Ecclesiastes, now imbedded in the pages of Scripture and thus fortunately preserved to us.

There will be times when it will not suit the temper of the age, but it will never be outmoded as long as the systole and diastole of human life survives, and men fluctuate between progress and reaction, growth and decline, hope and disillusion.

The Book of Ecclesiastes will always remain a supreme expression of a basic ever-recurring phase in the life of man. Since its composition, most of the significant history of the Western world has occurred. Classical civilization flowered and surrendered to decay; the Middle Ages laid their heavy hand on human life; the modern era of progress was ushered in — and is now battling desperately for its survival. Yet the enigmatic figure of the sage of Jerusalem still endures, the symbol of the ache of disillusion and of the peace that comes after. Whoever has dreamt great dreams in his youth and seen the vision flee, or has loved and lost, or has beaten barehanded at the fortress of injustice and come back bleeding and broken, has passed Koheleth's door, and tarried awhile beneath the shadow of his roof.

Men have paid willing tribute to the fascination of Koheleth as they wrestled with the enigma of his personality. They have been baffled by his place in the Biblical canon, wedged in among resplendent priests, ecstatic psalmists and implacable prophets. What was he doing in such company? Commentators were confused by the startling contradictions in which the book

3

abounded, the cool skepticism of one passage, followed by apparently unimpeachable orthodox sentiments in the next. Was he talking with his tongue in his cheek, or writing a Socratic dialogue? Or perhaps (that last resort of the troubled reader) there was no Koheleth, as there was no Homer: a dozen uninspired scribes had each written a few verses, and their pooled resources formed the book of Ecclesiastes. Centuries later a soul-brother of Koheleth unwittingly described the fate of the Hebrew sage at the hands of his readers and commentators:

> Myself when young did eagerly frequent
> Doctor and saint, and heard great argument
> About it and about — but evermore
> Came out by the same door where in I went.

As men wrote and argued and dissected, the elusive figure of Koheleth grew further away than ever. They succeeded merely in proving the truth of the words in the Epilogue to Koheleth:

> Of making many books there is no end,
> And much study wears one's strength away.

Koheleth himself would have seen in all the time and ingenuity spent on the interpretation of his tiny masterpiece one more example of the futility of human effort. For there is scarcely one aspect of the book, whether of date, authorship or interpretation, that has not been the subject of wide difference of opinion.

Its very title is an insoluble problem. The author effectively hid his identity under the strange name "Koheleth," apparently derived from the Hebrew word *kahal*, meaning "congregation" or "community." Very aptly the Greek translator utilized an equally obscure Greek term as an equivalent — "Ecclesiastes," a word which occurs only a few times in Greek literature and means "a member of the ecclesia, the citizens' assembly in Greece." In Christian times "ecclesia" became the regular designation for the Church. Basing themselves on both the Hebrew root and its Greek equivalent, some translators render "Koheleth" as "the Preacher." This has the advantage of being less ponderous than "Ecclesiastes"; but a less conventional preacher than our author would be hard to find!

Traditionally the authorship of the book is ascribed to Solomon because the opening sentence reads: "The words of Koheleth, the son of David, king in Jerusalem," and Solomon enjoyed a reputation for wisdom, perhaps not wholly unmerited. Yet the view that Solomon is the author has been universally abandoned today, with the growth of a truer recognition of the style, vocabulary, and world-outlook of Koheleth. Even with Solomon eliminated, the dates assigned to the book vary from the Persian period to the Greek age, while Graetz has placed it in the days of Herod. In other words, Koheleth may have lived anywhere between 500 B. C. E. and 100 C. E. — no less a span than six centuries.

While there may legitimately be differences of opinion regarding the date of a book where historical allusions are few and indefinite, it is striking that the very meaning and purpose of the work have been equally unclear. The earlier commentators, following the Jewish Midrashim and the Aramaic Targum, saw in it the penitent reflections of a Solomon grown worldly-wise and sorrowful in the evening of life, an interpretation not without a poetic charm all its own.

On the other hand, there were Church Fathers who found in the book definite teachings of the Trinity and the Atonement! This approach is far from being completely surrendered even today. One older commentator sees in Koheleth "a schoolmaster leading men to Christ" (Plumptre) because his book reveals how futile and vain life appears without Christian faith. A more recent student calls it the most moving Messianic prophecy in the Old Testament (Hertzberg), and quotes with approval the query of another (Vischer), "If the Preacher is not right that all is vanity and there is nothing new under the sun . . . why did Christ descend from God's throne, and die on the cross to redeem the whole world?" Doubtless it is in this spirit that Cornill is able to see in Koheleth the greatest triumph of Old Testament piety!

As a rule, modern students of Ecclesiastes have tended to

regard it as basically heterodox, if not as downright heretical. Yet there is no unanimity as to whether Koheleth teaches natural enjoyment or Epicurean license as the norm of human life. Opinions differ as to whether he is a gentle cynic or an embittered misanthrope, or whether, as Renan maintains, "Koheleth is the only charming book ever written by a Jew."

Most critical readers have been struck by the variations in mood and thought within the book. Some medieval commentators suggested that it was the unsystematic record of debates between men of varying temperaments — sensualists, refined worldlings, men of affairs, saints and sages.

Modern scholars have sought to explain the apparent incoherence in other ways. Thus Bickell has declared, with enviable omniscience, that the book was originally written on separate leaves, each containing about 525 letters. These leaves were disarranged and hence the book is incoherent and disorganized. His theory, it must be confessed, has won few adherents.

Other critics have preferred to assume composite authorship for the book, in line with similar tendencies in other branches of Biblical research. Tentatively advanced by Haupt, the theory of multiple sources was meticulously worked out by Siegfried, who divided the two hundred odd verses of the book among nine authors, at least one of whom represents an entire group.

Less extreme and more widely accepted is the theory that the writings of Koheleth were fundamentally heterodox and unconventional, but that they were subjected to wide and persistent interpolation by conventional readers, in an effort to tone down, or at least to dissent from, Koheleth's heresies. Part of the difficulties involved in this view may be gauged by noting that Jastrow finds over 120 interpolations in a book of 222 verses. Barton, who is more conservative, claims that at least two hands were at work on the book, besides the original author, one, a Hasid or pietist, the other a Hakam or conventional Wisdom glossator. Between them, they are responsible for 45 important changes, besides many lesser ones.

There are other difficulties involved in the assumptions of multiple authorship and of widespread interpolations, which will be discussed below. Of late, as new tendencies are making themselves felt in the field of Biblical scholarship, a reaction has been growing against these atomistic theories. Most recent studies accept the view that the book of Koheleth is essentially the work of a single author (Hertzberg, Galling, Weber), but there still is no consensus as to the exact extent of the book, its message or the personality of its author.

Other instances of radical divergences of interpretation are not lacking. The existence of Greek influence in Koheleth has been affirmed by some commentators (Pfleiderer, Siegfried, Haupt, Plumptre, Tyler), and denied by others (McNeile, Delitzsch, Nowak, Barton). One scholar (Dillon) claims Buddhist influence.

Some authorities (Zapletal, Haupt) have applied elaborate metrical theories to the book, in accordance with which they transpose and excise at liberty. Hertzberg modifies the text to demonstrate its rhythmic structure, while others (Genung, Barton) are equally convinced of its prose character.

An absolute solution of these problems may never be possible. Nonetheless, the means for a better understanding of the book and its message are now at hand. Koheleth can be comprehended only if approached with sympathy and insight. He must be studied in terms of the cultural milieu in which he lived, both the nearer environment of post-Exilic Jewish Palestine and the larger background of the entire Near East of the first millennium B. C. E. For Egypt, Syria, Palestine and Mesopotamia were not only linked together geographically as parts of the Fertile Crescent, but constituted the individual members of the more inclusive larger pattern of Oriental civilization. In sum, the book of Koheleth cannot be fully understood apart from its own time and place, although, as the superb expression of one enduring aspect of the human spirit, it belongs to all ages and all men.

I. THE LARGER BACKGROUND OF ORIENTAL WISDOM

The Hebrew Bible, which has become the cornerstone of two of the world's great religions, and has had an incalculable influence upon a third, has paid a penalty for its transcendental spiritual significance. All too often it has been regarded as a collection of edifying tracts, instead of being recognized as a national literature upon a religious foundation.[1] The Hebrew Scriptures contain all the extant literary and cultural remains of the Hebrew people from its origin in the second millennium B. C. E. until the threshold of the Maccabean age fifteen centuries later.

This activity was as varied as it was creative, falling into three main patterns. By a striking coincidence, the two prophets who were destined to be eyewitnesses of the burning of the First Temple and the destruction of the national life in 587 B. C. E., Jeremiah and Ezekiel, refer specifically to these three main strands of intellectual activity in ancient Israel. Ezekiel says: "Men shall seek in vain for a vision from the prophets, the law from the priest and counsel from the elders" (7:26). His older contemporary, Jeremiah, quotes his enemies as saying: "Law is not lost to the priest, nor counsel to the sage, nor the word to the prophet" (18:18). The references to Law (*Torah*), the province of the priest, and to the *Word* (*davar*) or *Vision* (*hazon*) of the prophet are unmistakable. Paralleling them was the *Counsel* ('*ētzāh*) of the Sage (*hakam*) or the Elder (*zākēn*) generally embodied in the proverb or parable (*mashal*).[2]

The Hebrew Bible clearly reflects this triple activity in the first two of its three divisions, the *Torah* and the *Prophets*. The third section, in which *Koheleth* or *Ecclesiastes* is placed, bears the more general name of "Kethubim," *Writings* or *Sacred Writings*, but is not so heterogeneous as would appear at first sight. As will be noted below, it is basically the repository of "Wisdom," the third type of intellectual activity.

Until almost the beginning of the present century, the Bible was virtually the only literature from the ancient Near East to reach the modern world. For this reason, and because of its unique religious significance, the Bible reposed in a kind of splendid isolation. The revolutionary progress in archaeology since the turn of the century in the lands of the Fertile Crescent, and the researches stimulated by these discoveries, have set the Bible within the framework of ancient Oriental culture. Our understanding of Biblical law has been immeasurably advanced by the discovery of other ancient law codes, Sumerian, Babylonian, Assyrian, Hurrian and Hittite.[3] Comparative religion and anthropology have contributed greatly to our knowledge of the origins of Israelite prophecy; its culmination in the great Hebrew prophets remains unique.

Nowhere, however, has the vastly broadened background contributed more significantly to our knowledge than in the domain of Wisdom Literature. From Babylonia and Syria, and above all from Egypt, significant literary documents have come to light which clarify untold aspects of Hebrew Wisdom, whether embodied in books, like *Proverbs*, *Ben Sira*, *Job*, *Wisdom of Solomon* and *Ecclesiastes*,[4] in Wisdom Psalms, like Ps. 37, 49, 112, 128 and others, or imbedded as fragments within the Bible[5] and the Apocrypha.[6] Over and beyond the light shed on details, Oriental Wisdom makes it clear that Hebrew *Hokmah* was part of the culture-pattern of the Fertile Crescent, which prevailed in Egypt, Babylonia, Syria, and Palestine during the second and first millennia B. C. E. This literary genre must now briefly engage our attention.

Greatest in extent and importance are the remains of *Egyptian Wisdom* which emanate from both the Old Kingdom (c. 3000–2500 B. C. E.) and the New, from the reign of Thutmose I (1555) to that of Sheshonk of Lybia (c. 945 B. C. E.).[7]

It is significant that these Egyptian writings, which bear the name *sbōyet*, "instruction," include two literary types: a) "discourses on worldly prudence and wisdom intended merely for schools"; and b) "writings far exceeding the bounds of school philosophy."[8] This two-fold character of Egyptian Wisdom, which has not been sufficiently appreciated, is to be met with in its Babylonian and Hebrew counterparts as well.

Practical advice on life is to be found in the very ancient *Instruction of Ptahhotep*, which claims to be the work of a vizier of King Issi (c. 2675). Though doubtless later in origin, it was already an old text and was re-edited in the Middle Kingdom (19th–16th century B. C. E.). It teaches such virtues as the proper attitudes toward one's superiors and inferiors, toward one's son, as a guest, with one's friends and with women, and it emphasizes the need for caution in speech and in contracting friendships. Similar maxims are contained in the *Instruction for Kagemni*.

The *Instruction of Duauf* (end of the Old Kingdom) discusses and dismisses various occupations in favor of that of the official, a theme which reappears in the schoolboy texts of the 19th dynasty.[9]

The *Instruction of King Amenemhet* (1995–1968 B. C. E.) recounts his experiences for the benefit of his son Sesostris I, whom he appointed as co-regent in the twentieth year of his reign. His description of his achievements recalls the narrative in Ecc., chaps. 1–2. The *Instruction for King Merikere* (interregnum between the Old and Middle Kingdom) uses the proverb-form and inculcates not only the practical qualities a ruler must possess, but various religious conceptions practically nonexistent in other works of the same class.[10] Yet even here, no clash is found between moral injunctions and the hard-headed realism of the counsel given the king to suppress possible rivals to the throne. The theme of loyalty to the king is emphasized in varying ways in the *Instruction of Sehetepibrē* (19th cent. B. C. E.) and in the *Lansing Papyrus* (12th century B. C. E.). The *Proverbs of Ani*, written for his son (New Kingdom), takes the form of a dialogue between father and son.

The most important extant work of Egyptian Wisdom is the *Teaching of Amenemope* (10th–7th century B. C. E.), which has marked affinities with the *Book of Proverbs* (22:17 to 23:14).[11] While the suggestion of a common Hebrew original for Proverbs and Amenemope has been made, and even of the derivation of the Egyptian text from the Hebrew,[12] the prevailing scholarly opinion today is that the Hebrew shows a direct dependence on the Egyptian sage.[13]

Besides these examples of practical Wisdom, Egyptian literature contains meditations and complaints against the suffering which may have been induced by the gods, or, more commonly, be caused by the cruelty and oppression of men. While Erman regards such a production as the *Dispute with his Soul of the Man Tired of Life* (Middle Kingdom) purely as a rhetorical composition, it does reflect the despair induced by the breakdown of society. *The Admonitions of a Prophet* (end of the Old Kingdom) consists of six poems, which depict the collapse of the established order and the transfer of power and wealth to upstarts, a theme which reappears in Biblical Wisdom as well.[14] Other works of this genre are not lacking, the most popular being the highly rhetorical *Complaint of the Peasant*, which narrates an alleged tale of oppression and fraud perpetrated upon a salt-field dweller in the Wadi Natrun, west of the Delta. The so-called *Song of the Harper* (Middle and New Kingdom)[15] is concerned with the transitoriness of existence, and urges the enjoyment of life, in a rhythmic form that recalls both the Hebrew and the so-called "Babylonian Koheleth."[16]

With regard to *Babylonian Wisdom literature*, it cannot be determined whether it was originally less extensive than its Egyptian counterpart or whether the fewer remains are purely a matter of accident. Nonetheless, even these fragments exhibit both aspects of Wisdom, practical instruction and philosophic "laments."[17]

The first category of practical guidance is exhibited in various *Proverb-Collections* which stress experience and common sense almost exclusively.[18] On the other hand, the so-called *Babylonian Book of Proverbs* (late 3rd or early 2nd millennium B. C. E.) blends religious and ethical motifs with more practical considerations,[19] like the Biblical book of this name. Thus the Babylonian sage warns against such vices as undue talk, slander and impulsiveness in oaths, taking counsel with fools, or getting embroiled in quarrels or lawsuits. He teaches the virtues of requiting evil with good, helping the poor, and showing consideration for one's servants. He urges avoiding involvement with harlots and sacred prostitutes. The virtues he stresses are loyalty to one's superiors, honesty with one's possessions, the practice of truth-telling, and the performance of one's duty toward the gods through prayer and offerings. The widely popular *Ahikar-Romance*, which is probably of Assyrian origin,[20] contains proverbs of both the practical and ideal types.

The second category of complaints on the limitations of life includes the so-called *Babylonian Job*,[21] which tells the tale of the suffering and restoration of an innocent man. The poem lays great stress upon the ritual punctiliousness of the hero, and makes frequent reference to gods and demons, elements which naturally have no counterpart in the Hebrew *Job*, with its exalted monotheistic faith. While the work cannot pretend to the profundity of the Biblical book, the better preserved passages have a moving eloquence all their own. *The Pessimistic Dialogue of a Master and his Slave* apparently emphasizes the uselessness of all human activity, by describing the changing moods and impulses of the master, ending in the decision to die. Not only does this theme recall the "Catalogue of Seasons" in Ecc. 3:1–9, but other subjects treated, such as the ultimate oblivion which overtakes earlier and later generations and the limitations of man's knowledge, are reminiscent of Hebrew Wisdom in general and of Ecclesiastes in particular.[22]

The Complaint of a Sage over the Injustice of the World (15th or 14th century B. C. E.), which has been aptly called the "Babylonian Koheleth,"[23] contains many lacunae that make the connection difficult to follow. The themes treated apparently include such ideas as that death destroys love and joy (lines 12 ff.), that even the rich and the powerful cannot presume upon the abiding favor of the gods (lines 60 ff.), that the decrees of God are incomprehensible (lines 80 ff., 220 ff.), and that murder and violence are triumphant in human affairs (lines 215 ff.). The author urges joy (lines 21 ff., 246), and closes with a petition for help to the gods. The similarity with Biblical Wisdom applies to the style as well as to the subject matter.

Particularly striking is the use of quotations to cite accepted ideas on which the poet comments from his own standpoint.[24]

In sum, Hebrew Wisdom did not arise in a vacuum. On the contrary, it was part of the culture-pattern of the ancient Near East. Like all great manifestations of the human spirit, Biblical Hokmah presupposes a long period of preparation and development until it reaches its apogee in the books of *Proverbs*, *Job*, and *Ecclesiastes*.

II. THE FRAMEWORK OF HEBREW THOUGHT

From the preceding survey it is evident that Egyptian and Babylonian Wisdom were both older than their Hebrew counterpart and other forms of culture in Israel. This is, of course, entirely natural, since the Old and Middle Egyptian Kingdoms and the First Babylonian Empire are older than the Hebrew nation, which did not emerge upon the stage of history until the second half of the second millennium B. C. E. Only the establishment of a strong centralized monarchy in the days of Saul, David, and Solomon (960 B. C. E.) provided the basis for the intensive cultivation of the national culture, the roots of which, to be sure, were considerably older.

Throughout the days of the First Temple, there was an active intellectual and spiritual life in Israel. Occupying a central position of authority was the hereditary priesthood, centralized largely in the Temple in Jerusalem, which preserved, interpreted and administered the Torah, or Law, recognized as the Revelation of God. It is likely that originally there were brief compendia, or handbooks, on specific topics, such as the various types of sacrifices and the diagnosis and treatment of disease, which were prepared for the training of the younger priests and for the guidance of their elders. So, too, the various sanctuaries, such as Beth-el, Shiloh and Gilgal, doubtless had their sacred *Toroth* by which their ritual was governed. The prophet Hosea may be referring to documents similar to these when he declares: "Though I write for him ten thousand *toroth*, they are considered alien unto him."[1] By and large they ultimately disappeared, though some of them became imbedded in the great Torah of Moses, which Ezra succeeded in having adopted as the basic law of the Second Commonwealth. Moreover, Ezra succeeded in transferring the spiritual leadership of the community from the *kohanim* (priests) to a non-hereditary democratic class of

Sopherim or scribes, who were the interpreters and expounders of the Law, "the Masters of the Book."

In the days of the First Temple, however, this hegemony was vested in the priests. Deriving their sanction from Moses, the giver of the Torah, they were concerned with transmitting the ritual and ceremonial regulations for the sanctuary at which they officiated, as well as with preserving the civil and commercial codes of society and the handbooks for the diagnosis of leprosy and other maladies, being judges and medical experts as well.[2]

Paralleling the priestly activity, and often in vigorous opposition to it, was the work of the Prophets. Arising from the lowly level of superstition characteristic of prophecy and divining everywhere in the world, the institution of the *Nabi* in Israel had developed into a mighty spiritual force.[3] The great literary prophets Amos, Hosea, Isaiah, Micah and Jeremiah set forth their conception of God and humanity, and envisioned for Israel a unique function, as the bearer of the great ideals of human brotherhood, justice, and peace. In Isaiah's words: "The result of justice shall be peace, and the reward of justice, quiet and security for ever" (32:17). With their ideals as a standard, they sought to regenerate the national life. When their efforts failed, and evil remained dominant in society, they did not abandon their faith in righteousness as a reality. On the contrary, their conception of the universe as grounded upon the principle of justice led them to foretell the doom of their own nation, which they had weighed in the scales of truth and found wanting. Their tragic prophecy became a reality with the destruction of the Northern Kingdom of Israel by the Assyrians in 721 B. C. E. and the burning of the Temple in Jerusalem by the Babylonians less than a century and a half later, in 587 B. C. E.

For all their striking divergencies in substance and temper, both Torah and Prophecy placed the nation in the center of their thinking. Both were concerned with the weal or woe of the people as a whole, depending on whether or not it fulfilled the will of God which the priest found embodied in the Law and the Prophet in the moral code. To be sure, it was the

individual who was adjured to obey, but only as a unit of the
larger entity, his destiny being bound up, indeed submerged, in
the well-being of the nation: "And it shall come to pass, if ye shall
hearken diligently unto My commandments which I command
you this day, to love the Lord your God, and to serve Him
with all your heart and with all your soul, that I will send
rain for your land in its due season, the first rain and the latter
rain, that thou mayest gather in thy corn, and thy wine, and
thy oil" (Deut. 11:13–14). This concern with the group was a
fundamental aspect of traditional Semitic and Hebrew thought.

Nonetheless, the individual could not be completely disregarded. His personal happiness and success, his fears and his
hopes, were by no means identical with the status of the nation.
The people as a whole might be prosperous and happy, while
the individual might be exposed to misery. On the other hand,
even if the nation experienced defeat and subjugation to foreign
masters, the individual would still seek to adjust himself to
conditions and extract at least a modicum of happiness and
success from his environment. The recognition of the individual
plays an enormous role in the Torah. Being a practical code
of life, it necessarily had to deal with his problems and conflicts,
as its civil and criminal ordinances abundantly attest.[4] Increasingly, too, the Prophets, whose basic concern was the
ideal future of the nation, became concerned with the happiness
of the individual: "Say ye of the righteous, that it shall be well
with him; for they shall eat the fruit of their doings. Woe
unto the wicked! it shall be ill with him; for the work of his
hands shall be done to him" (Isa. 3:10–11). With the later
prophets, Jeremiah and Ezekiel, the problem of the suffering of
the individual becomes a central and agonizing element of their
thought.[5]

Fundamentally, however, Torah and Prophecy remained
concerned with the group, its present duties and its future
destiny. It was the third strand of Hebrew culture, that of
Hokmah or Wisdom, which made the life of the individual its
exclusive concern. The connotations of the Hebrew term
Hokmah are far wider than the English rendering "Wisdom"
would imply. *Hokmah* may be defined as a realistic approach
to the problems of life, including all the practical skills and

the technical arts of civilization. The term *hakam*, "sage, wise man," is accordingly applied in the Bible to the artist, the musician, the singer. Bezalel, the skilled craftsman who built the Tabernacle and its appointments in the wilderness, as well as all his associates, are called "wise of heart" (Ex. 28:3; 35:31; 36:1). Weavers (Ex. 35:25), goldsmiths (Jer. 10:9) and sailors (Ez. 27:8; Ps. 107:27) are *hakamim*. The guilds of singers in the Temple, the women skilled in lamentation (Jer. 9:16), the magicians and soothsayers with all their occult arts, are described by the same epithet, "wise" (Gen. 41:8; I Kings 5:10–12; Isa. 44:25; Jer. 9:16). Skill in the conduct of war and in the administration of the state (Isa. 10:13; 29:14; Jer. 49:7) is also an integral aspect of Wisdom. In Rabbinic Hebrew, *hakamah* is also applied to the "midwife."[6]

Above all, the term refers to the arts of poetry and song, both vocal and instrumental. The song in ancient Israel was coextensive with life itself. Harvest and vintage, the royal coronation and the conqueror's return, courtship and marriage, were all accompanied by song and dance. The earliest traditions dealing with the exploits of tribal and national heroes were embodied in song. Snatches of these poems are preserved in the later prose narratives, some being explicitly quoted from older collections, like the *Book of the Wars of the Lord* (Num. 21:14) and the *Book of Jashar* (Josh. 10:13; II Sam. 1:18; I Kings 8:53 in the Greek).

This relationship of song and Wisdom was so close that often no distinction was drawn between the two.[7] Thus, in I Kings 5:10–12 we read: "And Solomon's wisdom excelled the wisdom of all the children of the east, and all the wisdom of Egypt. For he was wiser than all men, than Ethan the Ezrahite, and Heman, and Calcol, and Darda, the sons of Mahol; and his fame was in all the nations round about. And he spoke three thousand proverbs; and his songs were a thousand and five."[8] Ethan and Heman are the eponymous heads of the musical guilds mentioned in I Chr. 15:19, to whom Psalms 88 and 89 are attributed. Evidence from Ugaritic sources corroborates the Biblical tradition, previously dismissed as anachronistic, which declares that these guilds of singers are very ancient. In fact, they probably go back to the Canaanite period.[9]

All these phases of *Hokmah* have disappeared with the destruction of the material substratum of ancient Hebrew life. What has remained of Wisdom is its literary incarnation, which is concerned not so much with the arts of living, as with developing a sane, workable attitude toward life. To convey its truths, Wisdom created an educational method and its own literature, which is generally couched in the form of the *mashal*, the parable or proverb, brief, picturesque, unforgettable.[10]

It should be added that the practical and technical meanings of *Hokmah* are unquestionably primary, and that the more theoretical significance of the term to designate metaphysical and ethical truths is a later development. This semantic process from the concrete to the abstract, which is universal in language, is validated also for the Greek *sophia*, which is strikingly parallel in its significance. The basic meaning of the Greek word is "cleverness and skill in handicraft and art," then "skill in matters of common life, sound judgment, practical and political wisdom," and, ultimately, "learning, wisdom and philosophy."[11] The adjective *sophos* bears the same meanings, being used of sculptors and even of hedgers and ditchers, but "mostly of poets and musicians."[12] The substantive *sophistes*, "master of a craft or art," is used in the extant literature of a diviner, a cook, a statesman, and again of poets and musicians.[13] From Plato's time onward, it is common in the meaning of a professional teacher of the arts.[14]

The Hellenic culture-area serves as a valuable parallel, shedding light not only on the origin and scope of ancient "wisdom," but also, as will be noted below, on the development and function of the teachers and protagonists of the discipline (Hebrew *hakamim*, Greek σοφισταί). Hellas and Israel were by no means identical, yet in both civilizations there is a striking similarity in the character and class origin of Wisdom and, significantly, in its bifurcation into two varieties, one conventional and practical, the other unconventional and skeptical.[15]

When the full scope of Hebrew Wisdom is taken into account, it becomes clear that the third section of the Bible, the *Kethubim*, "Sacred Writings" or "Hagiographa," is not a miscellaneous collection, but, on the contrary, possesses an underlying unity,

being the repository of Wisdom. The Book of *Psalms* is a great
collection of religious poetry, most of which was chanted at the
Temple service with musical accompaniment. Both the composition and the rendition of the Psalms required a high degree
of that technical skill which is *Hokmah*. Moreover, in point of
content, many Psalms (like 37, 49, 112, 128) have close affinities
with the proverbial lore of the Wisdom teachers.

Three other books, *Proverbs, Job,* and *Ecclesiastes*, obviously belong in a Wisdom collection. So does *Ben Sira*, or
Ecclesiasticus, which was not included in the canon of Scripture,
because it clearly betrayed its late origin. *Lamentations* is a
product of *Hokmah* in its technical sense. The *Song of Songs*
is included, not merely because it is traditionally ascribed to
King Solomon, the symbol and traditional source of Hebrew
Wisdom,[16] but because these songs, whether sung at weddings
or at other celebrations, were also a branch of technical song.[17]
It has also been suggested that the *Song of Songs* entered the
Wisdom collection because it was regarded as an allegory of
the relationship of love subsisting between God and Israel.
From this point of view, it would be a *mashal*, which means
"allegory" or "fable" as well as "proverb." The Book of *Daniel*,
the wise interpreter of dreams, obviously is in place among the
Wisdom books.

The reason for the inclusion of *Ruth* and *Esther* is not quite
so evident. Perhaps they were included here because both
reveal practical sagacity, Esther in saving her people from destruction and Ruth in securing a desirable husband! The three
closing books of the Bible, which survey history from Adam to
the Persian period, are really parts of one larger work, *Chronicles-
Ezra-Nehemiah*. It is possible that they owe their position in
the Wisdom section to the fact that they were placed at the
end of the Bible as an appendix to the work as a whole. Another
explanation has also been advanced. It has been suggested that
Chronicles (with its adjuncts) is really an appendix to *Psalms*,
since one of its principal concerns is to describe in detail the
establishment of the Temple ritual.[18] *Ruth* may then have been
a supplement to the *Psalms*, since it concludes with the gene-
alogy of David, the traditional author of the Psalter, and

Esther may be an appendix to *Chronicles*, the style of which it seeks to imitate. These links, however tenuous they appear to the Western mind, will not seem far-fetched to anyone familiar with the Semitic logic of association, evidence for which is plentiful in the redaction of the Bible and in the organization of the Mishnah and the Talmud.

The extensive remains of Oriental Wisdom, Sumerian, Babylonian, and Egyptian, practically all of which antedate by centuries the emergence of Hebrew culture, make it clear that *Hokmah* in Israel was a very old intellectual activity, paralleling that of the priest and the prophet. Hence the tradition that King Solomon is the great Biblical author is no longer airily dismissed as a figment of the folk-imagination. There is every reason to believe that his reign marked the first Golden Age of Wisdom literature, and that his extensive contacts, political and commercial, with other lands, particularly with Egypt, provided the basis for close intellectual relations with the Nile Valley.[19] At the same time, the domestic prosperity and sense of national well-being of the country during his reign supplied the necessary background for literary creativity. The existence of an extensive Wisdom literature in Egypt surely served as a spur, even if not as a source for emulation.

That Solomon himself engaged in literary composition is doubtful. Royal authors have been few and far between, Marcus Aurelius, James I of England, and Frederick the Great of Prussia being rare exceptions to the rule. Here, too, Egyptian Wisdom suggests the source of the tradition. Scribes were accustomed to attribute their writings to the king under whom they worked, and in fact put their words into the king's mouth, as in the *Maxims of Merikere* and the *Wisdom of Amenemhet*.[20]

Biblical Wisdom is, however, no mere importation from foreign soil, but, as is to be expected, an indigenous development. This is clear from the fact that the Bible has preserved Wisdom fragments of the pre-Solomonic age. The unforgettable "Parable of Jotham" (Jud. 9:7 ff.), which compares the would-be king to a sterile thorn-bush, could not have emanated from a later period after the monarchy was well established.[21] In I Sam. 24:13 David quotes "an ancient proverb" (*meshal hakkadmōnī*),

"Out of the wicked cometh forth wickedness, but let not my hand be upon thee." The prophet Nathan's parable of the poor man's lamb (II Sam. 12:1 ff.) with which he indicts his royal master, David, constitutes another valuable remnant of ancient *mashal* literature.

A particularly significant passage for the development of Wisdom is in II Sam., chap. 14. Here we have a "wise woman" (*'issāh ḥākhāmāh*) whom Joab calls and probably pays to present an imaginary case to King David. She possesses dramatic skill as well as literary inventiveness. Thus she prepares herself for the role of a mourner (v. 2), and then presents her fictitious case as a *mashal*, a parable of the king's relationship to his son Absalom, the murderer of Amnon. Finally, she climaxes her appeal by a reference to the melancholy brevity of human life, and thus goes beyond the practical Wisdom to its more philosophic aspect: "For we must surely die and be like water poured out on the ground which is not gathered up and which no one desires" (v. 14).[22] The parable of Joash, king of Israel, in which he contemptuously dismisses Amaziah of Judah as a thistle by the side of a cedar (II Ki. 14:9) is post-Solomonic. By the very nature of the subject matter, parable and proverb are not easily datable.

Thus the evidence from both Oriental Wisdom and Biblical tradition generally indicates that Hebrew *Hokmah* was not a late development, but, on the contrary, was cultivated *pari passu* with the Torah of the priests and the Vision or Word of the prophets. Much in the Book of *Proverbs* is pre-Exilic,[23] and other Wisdom writings have no doubt been lost.[24]

Throughout the period of the First Temple, Wisdom was a well-recognized activity. Hence the prophets' vision of the doom of the nation and the collapse of its spiritual leadership necessarily included the cessation of Wisdom activity (Ez. 7:26). Like most other aspects of Hebrew life and thought, however, the destruction of the Temple and of the state represented not the end of Jewish life, but a new beginning. In fact, the Golden Age of Wisdom literature lay in the period of the Second Commonwealth, of which only a Deutero-Isaiah and an Ezekiel had dared to dream.

III. THE CONTENT AND SCOPE OF
HEBREW WISDOM LITERATURE

The Golden Age of Hebrew Wisdom did not come during the days of national well-being and independence of the First Temple. It coincided with the period of national humiliation and subjection to foreign powers, which marked the first half of the Second Commonwealth, roughly from the fifth to the second centuries B. C. E.

That Wisdom came to flower at this time was not accidental, but a direct consequence of the spirit of the age. This period, which followed the Babylonian Exile, was well described by an older contemporary as a "day of small things,"[1] with little to stir men's hearts either to ecstasy or to wrath. The great dreams of the Redemption had turned into the petty realities of the Return, and the resplendent visions of the fathers had become the tangible but colorless background against which the children lived. True enough, on the selfsame site where Solomon had built his Temple five centuries earlier, its successor now stood. But this Second Temple was only a modest imitation of the older structure, which continued to grow ever more glorious in the national consciousness, as it receded further into the past.

There was, to be sure, much to be grateful for. In the case of all other peoples, national exile, which included forcible separation from soil and shrine and the destruction of the state, constituted a death-warrant from which there was no reprieve. Only the Jewish people had survived the catastrophe of exile, and in fact had outlasted its conquerors. Many of the Jewish captives in Babylonia were absorbed by the surrounding population in Mesopotamia and elsewhere, but not all had succumbed to their foreign environment. They were sustained by prophets of great spirituality, like Deutero-Isaiah and Ezekiel, who fortified the solidarity of the dispersed people and painted a vivid picture of the glorious Restoration that awaited Mother Zion.

That Restoration had indeed come, but on a scale far removed from the prophetic visions. A small band of settlers had been allowed to return to Palestine by the magnanimous and far-sighted Cyrus, founder of the Persian Empire. Instead of a mighty nation holding sway over distant lands, as the prophets had foretold, the Jewish people in its own homeland was a tiny island in a heathen sea. Centered in Jerusalem, the new community enjoyed at best a precarious autonomy in the religious and cultural spheres, while being completely subservient, politically and economically, to the Persian overlords. The Jewish settlement was also imperilled by internal discord. Ezra felt impelled to employ stern measures in order to stem the tide of intermarriage which was particularly prevalent among the priests and other leaders of the community, and which threatened, if unchecked, to obliterate the Jewish identity completely within the space of a few generations. Moreover, there was the perpetual threat of enemies from without. Only the resourcefulness of the Jewish governor, Nehemiah, had succeeded in erecting a city wall around Jerusalem, in spite of the intrigues of the neighboring Ammonites, Samaritans and Arabs.

The next few centuries that followed Ezra and Nehemiah are among the most obscure in Jewish history. Only a few incidents are recorded by Josephus for the entire period, and these generally of the most disreputable kind. We hear of a high priest murdering his brother in the Temple precincts, and of the scion of an aristocratic family of Judea having an affair with a Greek dancer in Alexandria.[2] Thus the upper classes were already showing signs of the moral disintegration that led them a little later into wholesale surrender to the blandishments of the Hellenistic world and the virtual abandonment of the Jewish way of life.[3]

There were, in addition, deeper spiritual currents among the people, which, inchoate and unrecognized until hundreds of years later, escaped the vigilant eyes of the chronicler. Due to the chastening influence of the Babylonian Exile and the Return, the long campaign of religious and ethical education waged by the prophets and legislators of the First Temple period was finally crowned with success. Scorned and vilified in their own day, the Prophets had now attained to wide authority, and were more truly alive centuries after their death than in their own lifetime.

Perhaps even more significant was the achievement of Ezra, who succeeded in establishing the Torah, or the Five Books of Moses, as the basic law of Judaism. At a great assembly, participated in by the heads of every family in the newly constituted community, it was publicly accepted as binding for all time.[4] But the Torah, written in earlier days, could not become a living force in the new community without study and reinterpretation. This significant function was undertaken by the *Sopherim*, or Scribes, better rendered "the Masters of the Book." They expounded the letter of Scripture, amplified it where it was brief or unclear, and extended its provisions to meet new conditions as they arose. They not only preserved the Torah; they gave it new life.

The importance of their work can scarcely be overestimated. Their activity made the Bible relevant to the needs of new generations, and thus prepared it to serve as the basic law of Judaism. Their discussions and decisions were incorporated into the Oral Law, constituting the oldest part of the Mishnah and the Talmud. Thus the *Sopherim* laid the foundations of Rabbinic Judaism. They gave to Jewish tradition some of its most noteworthy characteristics, its protean capacity for adjustment and its fusing of realistic understanding and idealistic aspiration. These nameless Scribes thus contributed in no small measure to the survival of the Jewish people. But their significance is not limited to the household of Israel. The Christian world, too, owes them a deep debt of gratitude, all too often left unacknowledged. As founders of Pharisaic Judaism, they helped create the background from which Christianity arose, and formulated many of the basic teachings that both religions share in common.[5]

Thus the three strands of Hebrew cultural life in the First Temple now underwent a far-reaching transformation. Torah, now no longer the special province of the priest, entered a new phase of interpretation and growth, through the Oral Law. Prophecy, like the written Torah, had also passed its creative phase. It declined and finally ceased to function in the days of the Second Temple. Ultimately, the impulse reasserted itself in a strange, scarcely recognizable form, to produce the Apocalyptic literature.[6] Various factors contributed to the decline of prophecy in the post-Exilic period. Not only had Amos, Hosea, Isaiah, Jeremiah and Ezekiel done their work and done it well, but there remained little stimulus or need for the grand prophetic vision. The Jews were a struggling community under the domination of successive foreign rules, Persian, Greek, Egyptian and Syrian. The unyielding insistence of the prophets upon national righteousness as the basic premise of national well-being was now an accepted element of Jewish thought, but it was no longer novel or especially relevant to the problems of the hour. For there was little prospect of national greatness and power for the Jewish people either in the present or in the recognizable future.

A fundamental revolution in men's thinking now took place. The ancient Semitic outlook, which was shared by the Hebrews, had placed the well-being or decline of the group, the family, tribe or nation in the center of men's thoughts. This collective viewpoint now gave way to a heightened interest in the individual. Prosperity and freedom for a tiny weak people were not likely to be achieved in a world of mighty empires. All that remained was for each human being to strive to attain his personal happiness. What qualities were needed, what pitfalls had to be avoided by a man seeking to achieve success and a respectable place in society? These perennially modern and recurrent questions, which indeed had never been suppressed even during the pre-Exilic days of national independence, now became the pivot on which men's convictions and doubts revolved. To help the individual attain to well-being had always been the function of Wisdom. It now became a central element in the religio-cultural pattern.

As was the case in Egypt and Babylonia, the principal aspect of Hebrew *Hokmah* was the giving of practical counsel, not merely transmitting the technical skills, but, even more, inculcating the personal qualities required to achieve success and avoid failure.

This was the function of the main school of Wisdom, whose major documents are *Proverbs* and *Ben Sira*. Conventional in its methods and goals, it was concerned with the problem of training men, and particularly the youth, to live in a hard-headed, imperfect world, rich in pitfalls and temptations for the unwary.

Everywhere, Oriental Wisdom teachers were convinced that morality, if not carried to excess, was the best policy. In Israel, where the ethical emphasis on religion was overpowering because of the activity of the great Prophets, the stress upon virtue in Wisdom was even more dominant, as the books of *Proverbs* and *Ben Sira* abundantly attest. The Hebrew Wisdom teachers sought to inculcate the virtues of hard work, zeal, prudence, sexual moderation, sobriety, loyalty to authority and religious conformity — all the elements of a morality making for worldly success. Where, however, ethical imperatives ran counter to more mundane considerations, they did not hesitate to urge less positive virtues on their youthful charges, such as holding one's tongue or distributing largesse, as aids in making one's way:

> Where words abound, sin is not wanting,
> But he that controls his tongue is a wise man.
>   (Pr. 10:19)

> A man's gift makes room for him,
> It brings him before great men. (Pr. 18:16)

In brief, this practical Wisdom represented a hard-headed, matter-of-fact, "safe and sane" approach to the problems of living. It is, however, significant for the impact of Hebrew thought on Oriental Wisdom that Biblical Hokmah never developed the indifference to justice and mercy implicit in the advice of the Egyptian *Instruction for King Merikere* to destroy a vassal grown too powerful or too popular.

These teachers upheld morality because they were convinced that it was a more effective road to success than sin. They preached adherence to religion because of the same pragmatic viewpoint — it served to make men good, and by that token, happy. In no invidious sense, this school may be described as the *lower* or *practical Wisdom*.

It is true that the human impulse to pierce the veil of reality and grapple with the abiding mysteries of life could not be crushed even among these teachers of the tangible. At times they yielded to the metaphysical urge, and saw the Wisdom they taught as an imperfect human reflection of the Divine Wisdom, the plan of the universe, by which God had created the world:

> The Lord by Wisdom founded the earth;
> By Understanding He established the heavens.
>
> (Pr. 3:19)

Generally, they preferred not to inquire too closely into the details of the Divine plan, knowing the perils that lurked on the frontier where human reason met the unknown. Their standpoint was expressed by Ben Sira in words that later teachers of religion have repeated countless times:

> What is too wonderful for you, do not seek,
> Nor search after what is hidden from you.
> Seek to understand what is permitted you,
> And have no concern with mysteries.
>
> (3:20 f.)

This theme is the burden, too, of the Hymn to Wisdom incorporated in the Book of Job (ch. 28). With matchless skill, the poet pictures the exertions men undergo until at last they unearth precious stones in the bowels of the earth. But his refrain is: "Where is Wisdom (*hahokmah*) to be found, and what is the place of Understanding?" Its value is above pearls, and its hiding place is not known to the deep, to the birds of the air, or to any living thing. Only God knows the place of Wisdom, for He created it together with His universe. The poet concludes:

> But to men, He has said, the fear of God is wisdom,[7]
> And abstaining from evil is understanding.
>
> (28:28)

Faith and morality are all man can hope to attain. The propagation of these ideals is the purpose of the conventional Wisdom writers.

For a few bolder spirits within the schools of Wisdom, these goals were not enough. They had been trained to apply observation and reasoning to the practical problems of daily life. They would use the same instruments to solve the more fundamental issues that intrigued them, the purpose of life, man's destiny after death, the basis of morality, the problem of evil. When they weighed the religious and moral ideas of their time by these standards, they found some things they could accept, but much that they felt impelled to reject as either untrue or unproved. Hence the higher or speculative Wisdom books, particularly *Job*, *Ecclesiastes* and perhaps *Agur ben Yakeh* (Pr., ch. 30), are basically heterodox, skeptical works, at variance with the products of the practical Wisdom School.

But the relationship between the main school and the dissidents is far from being merely that of antagonism. The writers of *Job* and *Koheleth* were undoubtedly trained in the Wisdom academies, and perhaps taught there themselves. That conditioning would affect their style and thought-processes ever after. Thus they would naturally utilize the conventional religious vocabulary of the schools, the only one they knew, to express their unconventional ideas.[8] Frequently, they would draw upon the proverbs and gnomes of the schools, either because they agreed with them, particularly in practical matters, or because they wished to modify or oppose them. Hence these books cannot be properly understood until the use of quotations is recognized.[9] In sum, both the conventional and the unconventional teachers of Wisdom spoke the same language, reflected the same environment and shared a common outlook.

Fundamentally, Wisdom was the product of the upper classes in society, most of the members of which gravitated toward the capital, Jerusalem. Some were engaged in large-scale foreign trade, or were tax-farmers, like the Tobiades.[10] Many were supported by the income of their country estates, which were tilled either by slaves, or by tenant farmers who might have once owned the very fields they now worked as tenants.[11] This patrician group was allied by marriage with the high-priestly families and the higher government officials, who represented the foreign suzerain, Persian, Ptolemaic, or Seleucid.

As is to be expected, the upper classes were conservative in their outlook, basically satisfied with the status quo and opposed to change. Their conservatism extended to every sphere of life, and permeated their religious ideas as well as their social, economic and political attitudes. What is most striking is that *this basic conservatism is to be found among the unconventional Wisdom teachers as well.* Though they were independent spirits who found themselves unable to accept the convenient assumption of their class that all was right with the world, they reflect, even in their revolt, the social stratum from which they had sprung or with which they had identified themselves.

It is, of course, quite possible that these Wisdom teachers personally were themselves of lower-class origin. This might account for their greater awareness of social and moral evils. It is a common phenomenon for dominant groups in society to draw their intellectual leadership from gifted members of the lower classes. The opposite process is equally frequent, where the submerged groups draw their leadership from the aristocracy, Moses and the Gracchi being cases in point. On the other hand, the heterodox Wisdom writers may have differed from their more conventional colleagues merely in their more sensitive temperament. But whatever their personal origin, their writings reflect upper-class viewpoints. This conclusion may be validated, not only for *Proverbs* and *Ben Sira*, but also for *Job, Koheleth* and *Agur ben Yakeh.*[12]

In favor of this contention, for which only part of the evidence can be adduced here, is the analogy of classical Greece, which has already been invoked to shed light on the origins of Wisdom. It is not being argued that the two movements influenced each other. The principle being invoked is that similar material conditions in different societies will produce similar spiritual and intellectual tendencies, *mutatis mutandis.* It is noteworthy that the same technique of drawing an analogy from Greek to Hebrew religion is employed in another connection by one of the most acute contemporary students of Wisdom literature, O. S. Rankin.[13]

The differences between these two culture-areas are far-reaching. Hebrew life was permeated by a profound religious consciousness, a preoccupation with moral issues that even the most secular-minded groups could not escape. Greek life, on the other hand, especially in its higher manifestations, was predominantly humanistic, with the trend strongly secular. This was true, even when the ritual was observed, as by Socrates before his death. The sophists were polymaths, teaching all the arts and sciences known in their day, and this basic aspect of their activity has no parallel in the post-Exilic Jewish community.

However, these differences should not obscure the resemblances existing between the *hakamim* and the sophists in technique and in goal. In the Platonic dialogue that bears his name, Protagoras, the sophist, declares that his goal is to teach his pupils prudence in public and private affairs, the orderly management of family and home, the art of rhetoric and the ability to understand and direct the affairs of state.[14] With the exception of the forensic art, these are the avowed purposes of Hokmah, as is attested by such passages as Pr. 1:4–5; 6:24; 8:15 ff., and indeed by every line of the literature. Wisdom is essential in preparing the upper-class youth for administration and leadership:

> To give prudence to the simple,
> To the young man knowledge and discretion.
>
>   (Pr. 1:4)
>
> By me kings reign,
> And princes decree justice.
>
>   (Pr. 8:15)
>
> By me princes rule,
> And nobles, even all the judges of the earth.
>
>   (Pr. 8:16)

In the case of the sophists a good deal is known about the economic arrangements which governed their activities, so that there is no need of inferential reasoning to establish the fact that their clients were the youth of the upper classes. Protagoras and Gorgias demanded ten thousand drachmas for the education of a single pupil; Prodicus, more moderate in his fees, asked from one to fifty drachmas for admission to his courses.[15] Evenus of Paros was praised for demanding only five hundred drachmas for instruction in "human and political virtue." No such rates could possibly have been demanded in Palestine, but whatever fees were required could have been met only by youths of means and leisure.[16]

Finally, and most significantly, the sophists and the *hakamim* exhibit the same process of intellectual development. In the case of some members of the group, at least, the sophists progress from the teaching of the conduct of practical affairs toward speculative thought in a skeptical spirit. Protagoras, who declared that "man is the measure of all things" and "with regard to the gods, I know not whether they exist or not," Gorgias of Leontini, whose chief philosophical tenet was that nothing exists, or at least that nothing is knowable, Thrasymachus of Chalcedon, who identified might with right and remarked that the success of villains cast doubt upon the existence of the gods, and above all Socrates, who subjected all ideas and ideals to his skeptical analysis, all these,[17] for all the vast differences between the Greek and the Hebrew ethos, are brothers of the spirit to Koheleth, who maintained that God made the truth forever unknowable to man, and to Job, who doubted that justice operated in the world.

It is noteworthy that in developing skeptical tendencies, the Greek sophists continued to function in their more conventional and more lucrative role as teachers of the practical virtues. In precisely the same manner, the heterodox Wisdom books of *Job*, *Koheleth* and *Agur* contain much typical Wisdom material of the same kind as we meet in *Proverbs*. Hence, attempts to excise this material as interpolations or to atomize the text by assigning it to many hypothetical authors must be stigmatized as unnecessary and unsound. A more sympathetic insight into the personality of these sages will spare us the necessity of resorting to such violent and subjective procedures.

In sum, Greek *sophia* and Hebrew *hokmah* are strikingly parallel in their concern with the education of the youth for practical life and in their culmination in philosophical skepticism. These analogies strengthen the view that the latter, like the former, arose in the upper strata of society, which alone had need of that type of training and could afford to pay for it.

These Wisdom academies presuppose the existence of a leisure-class youth. The extant Hebrew text of Ben Sira offers the first known use of the familiar technical term *bet hamidrash*, "house of study," in his plea: פנו אלי סכלים ולינו בבית מדרשי, "Turn aside to me, ye fools, and tarry in my house of study" (51:23). The word *beni*, "my son," which occurs twenty-two times in *Proverbs*, reflects the same pedagogic approach.[18] The constant emphasis upon sexual morality in *Proverbs* and *Ben Sira*[19] implies that the students were not children but young men, and, what is more, that they had the opportunity and the means for personal indulgence. All these conditions prevailed only among the scions of the wealthy classes.

There are other general considerations that reinforce this view. It was observed long ago that Wisdom is the most secular branch of ancient Hebrew literature, being concerned with broadly human rather than with specifically Jewish problems.[20] *Job* actually treats the problem of human suffering through a gallery of non-Israelitish characters.[21]

The use of the Divine names in the Wisdom books is also highly instructive, being parallel to the development in Babylonian and Egyptian Wisdom, where the individual names of the gods do not disappear, but yield increasingly to general descriptions of "God" or "The Gods." The individual names tend to appear principally in traditional apothegms or in contexts concerned with the attributes of a specific god.[22]

The use of Divine names in Hebrew Wisdom is entirely similar. The oldest collections in *Proverbs* (10:1 to 22:16; 25 to 29), which are probably pre-Exilic, use JHVH, the national name of the Deity, exclusively. Yet even here, when JHVH does occur, it is often in stock phrases like "the fear of JHVH," "the blessing of JHVH," "the abomination of JHVH," "the knowledge of JHVH."[23] The higher Wisdom writers avoid JHVH almost entirely, in favor of the general names *'el, 'eloah, 'elōhīm, shaddai*. JHVH is virtually lacking in the poetry of *Job*, and *'elōhīm* is the exclusive designation of the Deity in *Koheleth*.[24]

This cosmopolitan character of Wisdom is likewise most

naturally explained in terms of its upper-class origin. Foreign contacts, opportunities for travel and trade, and a fondness for the culture and fashions of other lands have always characterized the aristocracy.[25] Ben Sira speaks of himself as having made many journeys, accompanied by danger (34:11 f.), and includes travel as an element in the life of the ideal scribe (39:4). Koheleth speaks of amassing "the treasures of kings and provinces" (2:8). On the other hand, the peasant, the petty merchant and the craftsman have neither the opportunity nor the penchant for such contacts.

The *environment* reflected in Wisdom is that of the wealthy classes. The striking emphasis upon abstaining from sexual liaisons outside the marriage bond is a case in point.[26] These women against whom the preceptor of youth warns are not the street walkers, who ply their trade among the poor, but the kept women, often married, whose homes are decked with tapestry, woven of Egyptian linen, and whose couches are richly perfumed (Pr. 7:16 ff.). The references to precious stones,[27] to meat,[28] to the dangers of wine-bibbing and gluttony,[29] all point in the same direction.

The *morality* inculcated in Wisdom is utilitarian, and that from the standpoint of the possessing classes, the chief virtues being diligence, prudence, restraint in speech, reliability, and loyalty to authority. The moral code includes giving charity to the poor,[30] but not going surety for one's neighbor![31] It should not be overlooked, however, that the high valuation placed by the Wisdom teachers upon economic prosperity does not betoken a surrender of moral values.

The *religious ideas* of Wisdom literature reflect the same conservative upper-class orientation. Basic to its world-view is the idea that virtue leads to well-being and vice leads to poverty and disaster. Wealth is a blessing of the Lord bestowed upon the upright and removed from the wicked.[32]

In its origin, this view was not the possession of a single group, but the standpoint of the entire nation, being a corollary of the traditional Hebrew faith in the moral government of the world. During the days of the First Temple, when clan solidarity was all-powerful and reward and punishment were referred to the nation as a whole,[33] its truth was rarely questioned. With Jeremiah and Ezekiel, however, the individual began to emerge as an independent personality demanding happiness for himself as an entity distinct from the family, clan or nation.[34] As a result, the problem of the individual's fate became the central problem of Jewish theology in the Second Temple period. That individual success is the seal of virtue and individual suffering the proof of sin could continue to be maintained only by the successful groups in society.

The lower classes, ground by poverty and oppression, were tormented by the problem of the prosperity of the wicked and the suffering of the righteous. Holding resolutely to their faith in God and divine justice, they were nevertheless unable to make their peace with the world about them. The solution they ultimately reached was the doctrine of another world where the inequalities of the present order would be rectified. Thus the idea of a future life became an integral feature of Pharisaic Judaism and of Christianity.[35]

The teachers of Wisdom, on the other hand, being representative of the affluent groups, felt no compulsion to adopt these new views. The sages of the conventional school maintained unchanged the old view of retribution here and now. Indeed they made it, as has been noted, the cornerstone of their teaching of the youth, the justification for observing the code of practical morality they inculcated.

The idea of a future life is passed over in silence in *Proverbs*, probably because of the early date of its material. It is explicitly negated in *Ben Sira*, *Job* and *Koheleth*.[36]

It is in their reaction to the agonizing problem of evil that the social background of *Job* and *Koheleth* is most clearly revealed. It has long been evident that their predominant temper is that of skepticism, an incapacity to accept conventional ideas, merely because of the pressure of the mass. But it has not been noted that there is another element in the constitution of a skeptic — a psychological inability to act so as to modify conditions. In other words, skepticism is a state of mind possible only for those who observe and dislike evil, but are not its direct victims. Those who are direct sufferers are impelled either to change the conditions or to seek escape from them, through one or another avenue of action. Thus the Hebrew prophets, oppressed by the social iniquity of their day, utilized elements of the folk religion to create the exalted conception of the "End-time," when the kingdom of God would be ushered in on earth and a just order established for men and nations. The teachers of Pharisaic Judaism and of early Christianity offered the hope of another world after death where justice would be vindicated. The mystics of all religions, faced by the same problem, have chosen another way out by taking refuge in a realm of the spirit, beyond the accidents to which flesh is heir. On the other hand, reformers and revolutionaries in all ages have striven to transform society in their own lifetime through legislation or reconstruction.

The teachers of Wisdom adopted none of these alternatives. Their failure to do so was due to the fact that they personally found life tolerable even under the conditions they deprecated, not being victims of social injustice themselves. When these two elements of skepticism are taken into account — an awareness of evil and an absence of compulsion to modify conditions — it becomes clear why skepticism is usually to be found among the more intelligent groups of upper-class society, rather than among the masses of the people.

Professor G. F. Moore's comment on the social origins of Buddhism may be applied to the teachers of unconventional Hebrew Wisdom as well:

> "It is a common observation that it is not the people whose life seems to us most intolerable that are most discontented with life; despair is a child of the imagination and pessimism has always been a disease of the well-to-do, or at least the comfortably well-off."[37]

That the Wisdom writers do not accept the nascent idea of life after death has, of course, long been noted, but it has usually been attributed to their general conservatism and fondness for the older ideas. But this explanation is inadequate, for we should then have expected to find in Wisdom an adherence to the older doctrines of the "day of JHVH," as expounded by Amos, Isaiah and Jeremiah,[38] or the conception of the "End-time," as developed by Isaiah, Jeremiah and Ezekiel.[39] *Actually the*

Wisdom writers, whether conventional or not, accept neither the older nor the newer views that run counter to their group-associations. The Messianic hope on earth and the faith in an after-life alike find no echo in their thought. Nowhere in the entire literature do we find the faith of the prophets in a dynamic world. The Wisdom teachers are preëminently guides to the status quo, in which they contemplate no alteration. Whether they accept their contemporary society as fundamentally just, or whether they have their inner doubts, their basic attitude is that it is worth preserving without serious change.

All in all, the religious ideas in Wisdom may be described as proto-Sadducean. This is eminently the case with regard to the maintenance of the idea of free will without modification,[40] the denial of the existence of Satan[41] and the inability to accept the idea of judgment in the after-life.[42] Equally characteristic is the conviction that the accepted ritual should be maintained, though with little fervor or religious ecstasy.[43]

The *social attitudes* of Wisdom literature exhibit the same pattern even more clearly. Labor and trade are treated with condescension, if not with contempt, the typical approach of landed gentry, who remain country gentlemen at heart, even when they move to the cities and become absentee-landlords.[44] Even the unconventional writers, acutely sensitive though they are to injustice, are at one with the dominant school in their opposition to social change. This is true even of Koheleth, who, with few illusions left about human nature, nevertheless regards "the fool" and "the rich" as opposites:

> Foolishness is set in the high places,
> But the rich sit in low estate.
>   (Ecc. 10:6)

The opposition to social change is also indicated, indirectly but unmistakably, in *Job.*[45]

So, too, the conservative *political ideas* of Wisdom stand in the sharpest possible contrast to the rest of the Bible. Here we find no denunciation of monarchy as in Samuel, no attack upon the crimes of royalty, as in Nathan and Elijah, no arraignment of the political status quo, as in Amos, Isaiah, Micah, Jeremiah and Ezekiel. On the contrary, the most conservative passage in the Bible, unparalleled elsewhere, occurs in Proverbs (24:21):

My son, fear the Lord and the king.
And do not become involved with those who seek change.

This naïve identification of God and the political status quo is not for Koheleth. But even he counsels submission to authority:

I counsel thee: keep the king's command, and that in regard to the oath of God (pledging loyalty to him).

But he then adds an after-thought:

For the king's word is all-powerful, and who can say to him, "What are you doing?" (8:2, 4)

In fine, the environment reflected in Wisdom, its religious and ethical attitudes and its social and political standpoint all point to its upper-class origin. This is true not only of conventional Wisdom, embodied in *Proverbs* and *Ben Sira*, but also of the unconventional books of *Job* and *Koheleth*.

Indubitably stamped by the Hebrew spirit, Hokmah is nevertheless part of the larger pattern of Oriental Wisdom, international in scope, secular in spirit, and practical in intent. This explains the absence in Hebrew Wisdom of some of the most characteristic insights of Biblical thought, such as the concept of God in history, the passion for justice, the union of national loyalty with the ideal of international peace, the recognition of freedom as an inalienable human right, and the unceasing dissatisfaction with reality because of the vision of the ideal society.

Yet the contributions of Wisdom literature to human thought are equally notable. *Proverbs* and *Ben Sira* are characterized by an exalted yet workable morality, a sagacious understanding of human nature, and an unabashed interest in the happiness of the individual here and now. *Job* and *Koheleth* are distinguished by their fearless use of reason in confronting the most fundamental issues of life, their refusal to pretend to certainty where none is to be had, and their unswerving allegiance to truth, whatever the cost. It is a striking paradox that Wisdom, which began with the most mundane of concerns, ended by grappling with the most abiding issues of life.

The sagacity and practical common sense of the lower Wisdom, like the moral passion of *Job* and the intellectual integrity of *Koheleth*, are set forth with the clarity and eloquence appropriate to the context. It is this union of content and form that gives these works their place among the treasured masterpieces of the human race.

It is obvious that their inherent worth is not diminished by the recognition of the social background of Wisdom literature, for while it has its roots in one class, its fruits belong to mankind. On the abiding issues of life, no one is granted more than fleeting and partial glimpses of the truth, and every insight is therefore precious.

When it is recalled that Pharisaic Judaism fought energetically against Sadducean tendencies and, quite correctly, suspected the temper of the Wisdom books, the canonicity of which was warmly debated,[46] we must be grateful for the fortunate accident that our book was attributed to Solomon. But that would not have sufficed to preserve *Koheleth*, as the fate of Jewish pseudepigraphic literature attests. A tribute is due to the creators of the Biblical canon, to whose tolerance and catholicity of taste we owe the preservation of this monument of man's striving after the good life.

IV. THE THEORY OF SOLOMONIC AUTHORSHIP AND KOHELETH'S PLACE IN THE CANON

According to the tradition of the Synagogue, the book of Koheleth is attributed to Solomon, son of David.[1] One Rabbinic source declares that he wrote the *Song of Songs*, with its accent on love, in his youth; *Proverbs*, with its emphasis on practical problems, in his maturity; and *Ecclesiastes*, with its melancholy reflections on the vanity of life, in old age.[2] Another, less popular, view places the order as *Proverbs*, *Song of Songs* and *Koheleth*.[3] A third tradition declares that the holy spirit did not descend on Solomon until his old age, when he composed the three books.[4]

The same tradition of Solomonic authorship lies at the basis of the oldest Rabbinic source on the subject, which does not, however, state explicitly that Solomon was the author of the book. In a very old Tannaitic source, the order of the *Kethubim* is given as *Ruth*, *Psalms*, *Job*, *Proverbs*, *Ecclesiastes*, *Canticles*, *Lamentations*, *Daniel*, *Esther*, *Ezra* and *Chronicles*.[5] That Solomon is regarded as the author of *Ecclesiastes* is clear from its position between *Proverbs* and *Canticles*, both of which are specifically attributed to Solomon in the superscriptions of the Biblical text itself (Can. 1:1; Pr. 1:1; 10:1; 25:1). This same view underlies a succeeding statement in the same Baraita which reads: "And who wrote them? . . . Hezekiah and his group wrote Isaiah, Proverbs, Song of Songs and Ecclesiastes."[6] The reference to Hezekiah and his group is unquestionably based on Pr. 25:1, "These too are the Proverbs of Solomon which the men of Hezekiah, king of Judah, copied out." That the national revival and the religious reformation of Hezekiah's reign would flower into literary activity is a perfectly reasonable development. The verb $he'^{e}th\bar{\imath}q\bar{u}$ in Pr. 25:1 refers, however, not to the process of original literary creation, but to compilation and transcription from one scroll to another.[7] On the basis of this notation, the Talmud assigns to Hezekiah and his group the "copying out" or editing of all of Solomon's books, i. e. *Song of Songs* and *Ecclesiastes*, as well as *Proverbs*, and adds *Isaiah* as being a work contemporary with Hezekiah.

Actually, the oldest source for the tradition of the Solomonic authorship of *Koheleth* is to be found in the Bible itself, in the superscription of the book which appears in our present notation as the first verse: "The words of Koheleth, the son of David, king in Jerusalem." This verse, like other Biblical titles, does not emanate from the author.[8] The book proper begins and ends with the keynote theme: "Vanity of vanities, all is vanity" (1:2; 12:8). It is worth noting that the author himself never specifically calls himself "the son of David." That phrase in the superscription (1:1) is an addition by the editor, who goes beyond the author's statement in 1:12, "I, Koheleth, was king over Israel in Jerusalem."

Had it been the author's intention to palm his work off as the work of Solomon, he would not have used the enigmatic name "Koheleth," but would have used the name "Solomon" directly,[9] as happened time without number in the *Pseudepigrapha*, roughly contemporaneous with our book.[10] Actually the author makes no effort to imply seriously that Solomon is the author. In one passage (1:12 to 2:20) he takes on the guise of "the son of David," but only in order to give substance to his argument. He is seeking to demonstrate that even the ultimate of wisdom and luxury possible to man has no absolute value or significance. What more effective device than to have this view of the vanity of life expressed by Solomon, who symbolized both these goals of human striving? Any lesser figure might be charged with being an incompetent witness. As the Midrash acutely remarks: "People might say, 'This fellow, who never owned two cents, presumes to despise all the good things of the world!'"[11] This is evidently the meaning of the difficult final clause in 2:12: "For of what value is a man coming after the king, who can only repeat what he has already done?"[12] This purpose accomplished, the role of Solomon is laid aside for the remaining five-sixths of the book, never to be resumed.

Far from pretending to be the work of a king, the book reflects the standpoint of the commoner at many points. Such are the lament on the oppression of the weak (4:1 f.), the sardonic comment on corruption in government (5:7), the sense of fear of the royal authority (8:2–5; 10:20), the resigned remarks on unworthy leadership (10:5 ff.), and the complete absence of any national motif in the book. Even in the opening section, where "Solomon" is speaking, the author does not disguise the fact that a long line of kings had preceded him in Jerusalem.[13]

Nonetheless, the intention of the author aside, there was sufficient basis for the growth of a tradition of Solomonic authorship. Undoubtedly, this attitude was the prime factor for the admission of Koheleth to the Biblical canon and its retention there, for Rabbinic sources indicate how many and how strong were the reservations as to its sacred character.

The subject of its canonicity was one of the classic controversies between the schools of Hillel and Shammai, but ultimately the more liberal view of the Hillelites, that *Koheleth* "defiles the hands ritually," that is, is canonical, prevailed.[14] Yet even after its position in Scripture was officially recognized at the Council of Jamnia in 90 C. E., discussions as to its status continued. Many of the old arguments against its sacred character were constantly resuscitated, if only for theoretic purposes, since changes in the Canon were no longer possible.[15] It was criticized on many grounds. It bristled with contradictions, as in its attitude toward "joy" expressed in 2:2 and 7:3 against 8:15.[16] It consisted of mere "sayings" and was not to be regarded as Scripture.[17] It contained the wisdom of Solomon and was not Divine.[18] Most fundamental of all, it contained matters leading to skepticism and heresy.[19]

That all these doubts were brushed aside and a place given the book in Holy Writ is surely to be credited to the august authority of Solomon. Had it been believed that the work originated in the period of the Second Temple, it would have been excluded on the basis of date alone, aside from its contents, exactly as happened with the much less objectionable book of Ben Sira, which was declared to be uncanonical, because it clearly indicated its late date, when the period of Divine inspiration was over.[20]

Other factors of lesser moment also played a part in rescuing the book from the *genizah*, which would have spelled ultimate destruction for the book. The Epilogue (12:9–14), particularly in its two closing verses, ends on an unimpeachable note of orthodoxy: "In sum, having heard everything, fear God and keep His commandments, for that is man's whole duty. For God will bring every deed to judgment, even everything hidden, whether it be good or evil."

Many other passages in the book seemed to convey traditional ideas (cf. 2:25–26; 8:4a), especially since "the will to believe" the Solomonic tradition was there. The homiletic interpretation of "difficult passages," as embodied in the Targum and the Midrash,[21] did the rest.

That Solomon was the symbol of Wisdom and, as such, the reputed author of *Proverbs*, with which Koheleth has many affinities, served to buttress the tradition all the more firmly. That the book possesses a highly individual style, that the traditional ideas in the book may be quotations with which the author might disagree in greater or lesser degree, or that Koheleth might be using a traditional religious vocabulary in an unconventional manner, were critical considerations which would naturally not occur to ancient readers.[22]

One other factor must have played a part, though it doubtless operated on the unconscious level. The book must have exercised an undeniable fascination upon the people and their spiritual leaders, as evidenced by their unwillingness to surrender it. The persistent efforts to justify its retention in Scripture argue a recognition of its unconventional character, just as the secular theme of *Song of Songs* was clearly reckoned with.[23] But these efforts to preserve the book, it seems clear, would not have been undertaken, and, if undertaken, would surely not have succeeded, without the prior assumption that an author of Solomon's stature could not have been guilty of heterodoxy.

The history of literature knows of many unfortunate accidents which led to the loss of masterpieces. Koheleth provides a happy exception to this rule. The Solomonic tradition guaranteed the book a place in the canon of Scripture, and thus preserved it for posterity. It is not always a tragedy that *habent sua fata libelli*.

V. KOHELETH AND HEBREW LITERATURE

Koheleth was a writer of striking originality, both as to form and content. Hence his identifiable literary sources are few. Nonetheless, they are highly significant for indicating his spiritual development, as well as for helping to fix his period, as will be noted below.

Whatever its previous history, the Pentateuch in its present form was already in Koheleth's day recognized as the authoritative Torah of Moses. He himself utilizes classic passages from both *Genesis* and *Deuteronomy*. What is most characteristic of Koheleth is his *creative use of traditional material*, his giving to the time-hallowed texts a meaning congenial to his own unconventional religious outlook. This same procedure he adopts with the traditional Wisdom apothegms that he cites, for which we have no other extant literary sources.[1] His reminiscence of Gen. 3:19 does not differ strikingly from the original, because *Genesis* itself sadly reflects on the brevity of human life and the inevitability of death.

> *Gen. 3:19* For dust art thou, and unto dust wilt thou return.
> *Ecc. 12:7* The dust returns to the earth as it was.

On the other hand, Koheleth utilizes the passages in *Deuteronomy* which stress the immutability of the Law in order to express man's helplessness before an unknowable and uncontrollable universe:

> *Deut. 4:2* Ye shall not add unto the word which I command you, neither shall ye diminish from it, that ye may keep the commandments of the Lord your God which I command you.
> *Deut. 13:1* All this word which I command you, that shall ye observe to do; thou shalt not add thereto, nor diminish from it.
> *Ecc. 3:14* I know that whatever God does remains forever — to it one cannot add and from it one cannot

                subtract, for God has so arranged matters that men should fear Him.

With regard to vows, the substance of Koheleth's thought is virtually identical with that of *Deuteronomy*, but the two books are worlds apart in temper and spirit:

> *Deut. 23:22–5* When thou shalt vow a vow unto the Lord thy God, thou shalt not be slack to pay it; for the Lord thy God will surely require it of thee; and it will be a sin in thee. But if thou shalt forbear to vow, it shall be no sin in thee. That which is gone out of thy lips thou shalt observe and do; according as thou hast vowed freely unto the Lord thy God, even that which thou hast promised with thy mouth.

> *Ecc. 5:3 f.* When you make a vow to God, do not delay paying it, for He takes no pleasure in fools; what you vow — be sure to pay! Better not to vow at all, than to vow and fail to pay. Do not let your mouth bring punishment upon your body and do not tell the messenger, 'It was a mistake.' Why should God be angry at your voice and destroy the work of your hands? With all the dreams, follies, and idle chatter, this remains: Fear God!

It is also possible that Ecc. 5:5 may be based on a reminiscence of Lev. 5:4.

Another example of Koheleth's creative use of traditional material is afforded by Ecc. 7:20, which recalls a passage in the "Prayer of Solomon" (I Kings 8:46 = II Chr. 6:36):

> *I Kings 8:46* For there is no man that sinneth not (*yeḥᵉṭā'*).
> *Ecc. 7:20* There is no man on earth always in the right (Hebrew *ṣaddik*) who does the proper thing and never errs (*vᵉlo yeḥᵉṭā'*).

The verse in Koheleth need not be a direct borrowing from the passage in Kings; it bears the earmarks of a generally accepted apothegm that was utilized in the "Prayer of Solomon." What is most significant is the original use that Koheleth makes of the traditional phraseology. For him, the verse refers not to the accepted religious views of righteousness and sin, but to the Wisdom concept that equates goodness with good sense (cf. 7:16a, b, 17a, b) which Koheleth naturally interprets from his own standpoint. This is made abundantly clear by the context.

Another case in point is probably afforded by Ecc. 4:16b, which resembles the classic passage I Sam. 15:22 in form and content, but not in spirit:

> I Sam. 15:22c Behold, to obey ($š^e m\bar{o}'a$) is better than sacrifice (zebaḥ).
>
> Ecc. 4:17b It is better to understand ($liš^e m\bar{o}'a$) than to offer sacrifices (zebaḥ) like the fools (lit. than the fools' offering sacrifices).

Samuel is urging the prophetic doctrine that righteousness is better than ritual adherence. Koheleth is stressing the need of understanding rather than conforming piety, which he attributes to fools.

On the other hand, many of the parallels adduced by the commentators are doubtful.[2] There are no grounds for assuming that Koheleth is referring specifically to the patriarch Job in his comments on the tragedy of the prosperous man who fails to enjoy life (5:12 to 6:9)[3]; he is commenting on the fate of men in general. He may, however, have been familiar with the great Wisdom masterpiece which probably preceded him by a century.[4] The passage Ecc. 5:14 does not necessarily depend on Job 1:21; on the contrary, both verses seem to rest on a familiar folk saying. Kamenetzky's claim that the author of Koheleth "rolled through the relevant sections of the scroll of Chronicles"[5] is declared by Hertzberg to be "exaggerated"; it is actually without foundation.[6] It is, or should be, a truism of scientific method that the evidence for borrowing by one writer from another requires, not merely a similarity of theme or even of standpoint, but the same sequence of ideas, an unusual point of view, or a striking mode of expression in both literary documents.

It is, perhaps, not accidental that no clear-cut reminiscences of the Latter Prophets are to be met with in Koheleth, though such a passage as 4:1 demonstrates that the Prophets' cry against

injustice had left its mark upon him. It is entirely in keeping
with Koheleth's standpoint of adherence to the accepted Temple
ritual (cf. 4:17 ff.) and his affiliations with Wisdom that only
the two strands of Torah and Hokmah are clearly recognized
in his literary background.

*   *   *

Koheleth in turn served as a source for two important Apocryphal books, *Ben Sira* and *Wisdom of Solomon*, which thus
supply a *terminus non post quem* for the date of Koheleth.
Here, as so often everywhere, the quest for "parallels" has
been carried on with more enthusiasm than caution.

When the criteria cited above are applied to the parallels
generally adduced by scholars,[7] many items on their lists must
be discarded. No true dependence is proved by reflections on
such common themes as the brevity of existence,[8] the duty to
enjoy life,[9] the greatness of God's work,[10] the conviction that
evil recoils on the head of the evil-doer,[11] or the ultimate vindi-
cation of the righteous.[12] Nor is there any real relationship in
the treatment by both writers of such topics as the avoidance
of overlong prayers,[13] the lack of respect accorded the words of
the poor,[14] the meaninglessness of dreams,[15] and the duty of
paying one's vows.[16] In addition, many of the alleged parallels
between Koheleth and Ben Sira bear little or no resemblance
either in form or in substance.[17]

On the other hand, there are several striking phrases in both
books which do demonstrate that Ben Sira knew the book of
Koheleth intimately.[18]

Ecclesiastes	*Ben Sira*
4:8 ולמי אני עמל ומחסר את נפשי מטובה	14:4 מונע נפשו יקבץ לאחר ובטובתו יתבעבע זר
6:2 כי איש נכרי יאכלנו	33:14 f. (Greek)
7:14 ביום טובה היה בטוב וביום רעה ראה גם את זה לעמת זה	Over against evil stands the good, and against

Ecclesiastes   *Ben Sira*

עשה האלהים על דברת שלא
ימצא האדם אחריו מאומה

death, life. Likewise over against the godly, the sinner. Even thus look upon the works of God, each different, one the opposite of the other.

3:11   את הכל עשה יפה בעתו   39:16   מעשי אל כלם טובים וכל
צורך בעתו יספיק

The existence of a direct relationship is particularly clear when Ben Sira interprets a phrase in a sense which differs somewhat from its meaning in *Koheleth*:

3:15   והאלהים יבקש את נרדף   5:3   [19]כי ייי מבקש נרדפים

8:1   חכמת אדם תאיר פניו ועז פניו ישנא   13:24   לא אנוש ישנא פניו

7:16   ואל תתחכם יותר   32:4(35:4)   ובל עת מה תתחכם

A particularly noteworthy parallel, all the more striking because of the divergences, is afforded by B. S. 26:19 f.:

My son, keep thyself healthy in the flower of thine age,[20]
And give not thy strength unto strangers.
Having found a portion of good soil out of all the land,
Sow it with thine own seed, trusting in thine own good birth.

Ecc. 11:6, 9 reads:

Therefore in the morning sow your seed,
And in the evening do not be idle,
For you cannot tell which will prosper,
Or whether both shall have equal success.

Rejoice, O young man, in your youth;
And let your heart cheer you in your youthful days,
Follow the impulses of your heart
And the desires of your eyes;
And know that for all this,
God will call you to account.

In spite of the striking resemblance of phrasing, Ben Sira, the moralist, urges restraint where Koheleth preaches the duty of joy. Moreover, "sowing," which has a literal meaning in the passages in *Koheleth*, is used metaphorically in *Ben Sira* of sexual relations,[21] coinciding exactly with the Midrashic interpretation of the Biblical verse.[22]

Similarly, Koheleth's generalized condemnation of all womankind, which is climaxed by his statement in 7:26:

> He who is favored by God will escape her,
> But the sinner will be trapped by her

has its sting removed by Ben Sira's limiting the punishment to the *evil* woman in 26:23:

> A godless woman shall be given to the man who regards not
>   the Law as his portion,
> But a devout woman is given to him who fears the Lord.

Cf. also B. S. 9:3 f., another example of this transformation. So, too, Koheleth's realistic advice to courtiers to exercise patience and tact (8:5) is paraphrased into conventional religious doctrine in B. S. 15:15, a process probably induced by Koheleth's phrase "he who keeps the command" (*šōmer miṣvāh*).

There are also many casual phrases used in difficult contexts in both books, which, in view of the decisive evidence already adduced, may be due to Ben Sira's familiarity with the work of the older sage.[23]

Ben Sira is the assiduous and admiring, though not altogether comfortable, reader of *Koheleth*, very much like the anonymous author of the Epilogue (Ecc. 12:9 ff.).[24] Another apocryphal writer has no such ambivalent attitude, but is definitely opposed. The author of the *Wisdom of Solomon* set out to combat the skeptical attitudes prevalent among a section at least of his contemporaries, both in Palestine and in Egypt. As a believing Jew of the Pharisaic school, he might well be offended by the absence in Koheleth of any national feeling as well as of such basic religious attitudes as Israel's place in God's plan, the doctrine of judgment after death and the idea of resurrection. On the other hand, Koheleth's continued emphasis upon the enjoyment of life as the highest good might well seem to a traditional believer to be an implied justification, or at least an acceptance, of the oppression of the weak by the powerful and wealthy. It need not be added that Koheleth espouses no such view anywhere.

There were doubtless other books of skeptical tendencies current at the time.[25] Most scholars, however, have recognized in *Wisdom of Solomon*, ch. 2, a polemic against Koheleth, though there are no direct verbal reminiscences.[26]

In a highly eloquent passage *Wisdom* restates the ideas to which he is so passionately opposed:

For they said in themselves, reasoning not aright,
    Brief and sorrowful is our life,
Yea in the end of a man is no cure,
    And none was ever known that returned from Hades.

For at random were we begotten,
    And hereafter we shall be as though we had not been;
For smoke is the breath in our nostrils,
    And our reason but a spark in the beating of our heart,
Which being quenched, the body shall turn into ashes,
    And the spirit be dispersed as empty air;

And our name shall be forgotten in time,
    And none shall call to remembrance our works;
Yea, our life shall pass away as the traces of a cloud,
    And as mist shall it be dispersed,
Chased by the sun's rays,
And weighed down by his heat.

For our life is the passing of a shadow,
    And there is no prevention of our end,
    For it hath been sealed and none reverseth it.

Come then, let us enjoy the good things that are,
    And eagerly use creation like youth;

Let us be filled with costly wine and perfumes,
    And let not the flower of the spring pass us by;

Be we crowned with rosebuds ere they fade away,
   And let there be no meadow uncoursed by our debauch.

Let none of us go without his share in our insolent revelry;
   Leave we everywhere the tokens of our joy;
   For this is our lot and our portion is this.

Let us oppress the poor righteous man by our might.
   Spare we not the widow,
   Nor reverence the old man's grey hairs full of years.

Be our strength the rule of our justice,
   For weakness is approved to be unprofitable.

And let us lie in wait for the righteous, for he serveth not
     our turn,
   And he is opposed to our doings;
Yea and reproacheth us with our breaches of the law,
   And denounceth to us our breaches of discipline.

For he professeth to have knowledge of God,
   And calleth himself the Lord's child.

Later reminiscences of Koheleth, including such medieval works as Samuel Hanagid's *Ben Koheleth*, would take us too far afield. It is clear that our book is in the mainstream of Jewish literature, drawing upon the past and contributing to the future.

VI. THE RELATIONSHIP OF KOHELETH TO GREEK AND EGYPTIAN THOUGHT

The skeptical and non-traditional character of the book of Koheleth is today generally accepted, as is the fact that it was written after the conquest of Alexander the Great, so that it falls within the Hellenistic Age.[1] Many scholars have therefore been led to search for traces of Greek influence in the book, both in its language and its thought. Increasingly, however, it is being recognized that the linguistic argument[2] does not stand up under examination, all alleged Graecisms having their analogies in authentic Hebrew and Semitic usage.[3]

Even more persistent have been the varied efforts to find the sources of Koheleth's thought in Greek philosophy. Virtually every school of Greek thought has been laid under contribution.

The suggestion has been made that the "Catalogue of Seasons" (3:1–9) betrays the influence of Heraclitus,[4] or that 7:19 is an echo of Euripides.[5]

Traces of Aristotelian influence have been sought in Koheleth as well. The passage 7:27 has been taken to reflect the "inductive method," and 2:3 the philosophic quest for the *summum bonum*. This approach, however, means the introduction of formal categories of thought, which are entirely foreign to the unpretentious reflections of Koheleth. It is true that the "golden mean" is urged in 7:14–18, but from a vantage-point uniquely characteristic of our author, and in a spirit entirely remote from the ethical considerations of the Greek philosopher.[6] The idea of the "golden mean" was doubtless familiar throughout the Hellenistic world, aside from its inherent appeal, and its presence in Koheleth does not prove the Stagirite's influence.[7]

A more generally propagated view was that Koheleth was influenced by the Stoics.[8] This theory, however, rests not upon a correct exegesis, or interpretation of the written text, but upon a forced *eisegesis*, a reading into the text of extraneous ideas. That the "Catalogue of Seasons" (3:1–9) teaches the Stoic doctrine that one should live according to nature is as far-fetched as the idea that it expresses the Heraclitan concept of the eternal flux of events. In this passage, Koheleth is emphasizing the predestined character of all events, so that all human activity, including the search for ultimate truth, is useless. He therefore urges man to enjoy life to the utmost, as the only sensible goal of existence. The Stoics, like most philosophic thinkers since their time, accepted the principle of determinism, but they were far from sharing Koheleth's conviction that the truth was forever unknowable to man, or that pleasure is the only ideal of human conduct.

Nor does Chapter One reflect the Stoic theory of cycles. There is no hint here of the Stoic conception of repetitious world cycles, at the end of which everything will be destroyed, only to be recreated, with the process starting again.[9] As Barton points out, the dogmatic assurance of the Stoics as to the future course of events is at the farthest remove from one of the fundamental postulates of Koheleth's thought — the inability of man to know the future or the meaning of life.[10] Such basic Stoic ideas as the concept of God as pure reason, of the absolute good, and of the wise man as the only perfect man, all find no echo in Koheleth.

Another theory holds that the book of Koheleth manifests the influence of the diatribes of the Cynic-Stoic schools.[11] To be sure, some literary traits of the diatribe do have analogies in Koheleth. Such are the use of antithesis, rhetorical questions, the use of quotations, the repetition of characteristic words and phrases, the use of concrete illustrations to make a point and the setting forth of a conclusion through a question or a maxim. However, none of them are the result of a consciously adhered to literary genre, but rather the free expression of an informal style. Actually, all these elements, and many other stylistic traits of Koheleth, have a long background of usage in Biblical and Oriental Wisdom literature.[12] Most significantly, the chief characteristics of the Cynic-Stoic diatribe are lacking. These include the use of dialogue, the rhetorical use of the imperative, the device of personification and the aggressive polemic tone directed personally against the antagonist, which has made the term "diatribe" a synonym in all modern languages for an unbridled attack.

In sum, the divergences between our book and the Greek diatribe rule out any relationship, while the similarities are largely accidental and are to be expected in literary treatments of philosophic themes. The effort to equate the characteristic vocabulary of Koheleth with Cynic-Stoic terminology has also proved unsuccessful.[13] Neither does Koheleth agree with Democritus the Cynic that since all things are vain, men's goal should be the absence of desire, and hence the avoidance of disappointment and grief.[14]

Koheleth's standpoint is much nearer to that of Aristippus of Cyrene, though there is no evidence of any direct dependence.[15] The random agreement with one or two ideas of the Cyrenaics is not enough to demonstrate any relationship, in view of the larger divergences. Admittedly, Koheleth is much less concerned with the problem of injustice, which troubles the author of *Job*, than with the problem of truth, with which Job was not concerned at all.[16] But Koheleth never adopted the position of Theodoros the Cyrenaic, that spoliation of the sanctuary, stealing and adultery were not crimes "as of nature."[17] Nor was Koheleth "consistent" enough to argue, as did Ariston of Chios, that since all external things are worthless, it is impossible to set forth a moral law binding upon the wise man.[18] As the Hebrew Prophet did not speculate on the meaning of justice, so the Hebrew Sage did not question the existence of right and wrong. He parted company with the Prophets only with regard to their faith in the inevitable triumph of the right.

No more successful has been the quest for traces of Epicurean thought in Koheleth.[19] Unlike the Epicurean school, Koheleth expresses no dogmatic denial of immortality in 3:18–22, but rather his doubts as to this concept, which was beginning to make its way in Israel. The same hesitation with regard to the hope for immortality, which Koheleth voices sardonically, is given wistful expression in *Job* (14:7 ff., 10, 14). This attitude is entirely explicable in terms of the social milieu of Wisdom literature, and flows directly out of the indigenous spiritual development of Israel, without the assumption of foreign influence.[20] Nor does the indeterminism of Epicurean philosophy agree with the inexorable determinism of Koheleth. As for the enjoyment of life, which Koheleth urges as the *summum bonum*, this universally human attitude is consistently expressed in Oriental Wisdom literature. Perhaps the most striking parallel is afforded by the so-called "Babylonian Koheleth"[21]:

> Since the gods created man,
> Death they ordained for man,
> Life in their hands they hold.
> Thou, O Gilgamesh, fill indeed thy belly,
> Day and night be thou joyful.
> Daily ordain gladness,
> Day and night rage and make merry,
> Let thy garments be bright,
> Thy head purify, wash with water,
> Desire thy children which thy hand possesses,
> A wife enjoy in thy bosom,
> Peaceably thy work (?) . . .

This passage from Babylonian literature demonstrates what could have been maintained even without it, that the achievement of happiness, immediate and actual, was adopted as the goal of life by men who had never heard of Epicurus.

That thinking men in different cultures, possessing similar temperaments, will develop parallel attitudes on the basic issues of life is so self-evident a truth that it should have been a truism in Biblical scholarship.[22] Hence, the theory of Buddhist influence on Koheleth has rightly won few adherents.[23]

Over and beyond divergences in detail between Koheleth and the Greek philosophical schools is a world of difference in temper and attitude. He is by no means a Hebrew sage seeking to harmonize his Hebrew heritage with the Greek ideas of his time.[24] Koheleth is poles apart from Philo of Alexandria and the later medieval Jewish philosophers in almost every respect. Podechard's succinct statement: "L'Ecclésiaste observe; les stoiciens dogmatisent,"[25] may be generalized beyond the limits of one school to include the difference between Koheleth and all formal philosophical viewpoints.

Actually, Koheleth's world-view builds upon authentic Biblical thought, as even some of the proponents of Greek sources for Koheleth have recognized.[26]

His complete acceptance of an all-powerful God rests upon the traditional belief in the Living God holding sway over the universe, master of the seasons, the mighty sea and all the phenomena of nature.[27] Man, too, is under the power of God, even his thoughts and actions being determined.[28] Later Rabbinic thought sought to save the freedom of man[29] by postulating an exception to God's omnipotence: "Everything is in the hand of God except the fear of God,"[30] or by boldly seizing both horns of the paradox, as in Akiba's formulation: "Everything is foreseen, though freedom is given."[31] It is clear that Koheleth was not outside the Jewish tradition in stressing one aspect of the dilemma to the virtual exclusion of the other, and in making determinism a fundamental element of his thought. To be sure, in urging any course of conduct upon his readers, he was inevitably assuming man's freedom of choice as a practical procedure at least, but this is a contradiction to which all determinists are exposed.

So too, Koheleth's emphasis upon man's incapacity to penetrate to the absolute truth is an extension of the deeply-rooted Biblical conception of the distance between man and his Maker.[32] As for Koheleth's insistence upon joy as a divine command, this is, as will be indicated below, not merely a consequence of his own concept of God, but rests solidly upon the traditional Hebrew acceptance of life and its blessings as good. This view of life is enunciated in the opening chapter of Genesis, "And God saw all that He had made, and behold, it was very good," and is reiterated by the Prophet, "God has not created the world for chaos, but for human habitation."[33] Even Koheleth's modes of expression are paralleled in Oriental Wisdom and traditional Jewish sources.

Basically, Koheleth represents, as Barton correctly has noted, "an original development of Hebrew thought, thoroughly

Semitic in its point of view."[34] Only his final phrase that Koheleth is "quite independent of Greek influences" is open to important qualifications.

In Koheleth's day, Greek culture was an aggressive world-view, which exerted powerful attraction on the finest minds of the Mediterranean littoral. Palestine was particularly susceptible to Greek influences from two directions, Syria and Egypt.[35] As has been indicated, the various efforts to make Koheleth out to be a disciple of one or another Greek philosophical school contradict each other and must be pronounced failures, especially since there is no evidence that Koheleth knew Greek. But it would be strange indeed if a mind as vital and alert as Koheleth's had been completely insulated from the Greek ideas that permeated the atmosphere.[36] Hence it is not strange to find a resemblance in ideas between our author and such a Greek gnomic writer as Theognis of Megara (6th cent. B. C. E.), or the considerably later Marcus Aurelius (d. 189 C. E.)[37] On the other hand, the differences in outlook on many points and the complete lack of verbal similarity preclude any literary relationship between Koheleth and Theognis.

Though Koheleth was not a formal adherent of Greek philosophy, it is to be expected that he would be familiar with the catchwords and popular doctrines of the schools which were part of the intellectual climate of the age. One need not be an assiduous student of the writings of Marx, Veblen, Freud or Adler today, in order to be familiar with such concepts as the class struggle, the dictatorship of the proletariat, conspicuous consumption, the subconscious mind, and the inferiority complex.

This expectation is not disappointed, when we turn to Koheleth's book itself. What is most striking, however, is not his familiarity with some popular ideas drawn from Greek philosophy, but his *completely original and independent use of these ideas to express his own unique world-view*, the same procedure he adopts with regard to the ideas of Wisdom and traditional Judaism generally.[38]

Thus, as was recognized by the medieval commentator Abraham Ibn Ezra, the passage 1:2–11 which speaks of the earth, the sun, the wind and the sea is a restatement of the

Greek concept of the four elements, earth, water, heat and air, out of which the world was created.[39] But Koheleth is not interested in cosmogonic speculation; he employs this familiar idea of his time to emphasize the ceaseless and changeless cycles of nature, which possess neither goal nor meaning, and viewed against which all man's striving is folly.

In 7:14–18, Koheleth favors "the golden mean," the avoidance of the extremes of saintliness and wickedness, and urges his readers to learn to take both good and evil in their stride, since both are the consequences of the will of an inexorable and inscrutable God. The "golden mean" here is not a principle of ethics, as expounded by Aristotle. In insisting that "man grasp the one and hold fast to the other, for he who reverences God will do his duty by both," Koheleth is graphically expressing the conviction that in an uncertain world, moderation is a counsel of good sense as well as of safety.

As Egyptian Wisdom has been increasingly studied, the effort has been made to establish Koheleth's dependence upon Egyptian literature of this genre.[40] As has been made clear above,[41] Hebrew Hokmah is part of the larger area of Oriental Wisdom, and it is therefore to be expected that Koheleth will share some literary usages and viewpoints with other writers in the same field of interest.[42]

On the other hand, a general resemblance of ideas is insufficient to prove any dependency, unless there be some unusual correspondence of content or form. Men of similar temperaments or backgrounds will naturally develop similar viewpoints under like conditions. Moreover, many elements which, it has been arbitrarily argued, must be Egyptian borrowings, may be validated as authentically Hebrew[43] and indigenous to Palestine.[44]

None of the alleged parallels adduced are sufficient to prove that Koheleth was directly familiar with Egyptian literature, that he drew upon Egyptian ideas, or that he ever had travelled to Egypt.[45] His matter-of-fact references to rainfall,[46] like his mention of the Jerusalem Temple, presuppose the background of Palestine.[47]

* * *

Koheleth has two fundamental themes — the essential unknowability of the world and the divine imperative of joy. His
unique achievement lies in the skill and the sensitiveness with
which he presents his world-view. He has attained to his plane
of vision principally through his ancestral Hebrew culture, modified by some general contact with Greek ideas. But above all,
his book bears the stamp of an original observer, a wise and
fearless lover of life.

VII. THE LANGUAGE OF KOHELETH

The tradition of Solomonic authorship, which, as has been noted, possesses only symbolic value, and to which we owe the admission of Koheleth to the canon and hence its preservation, has been surrendered today by all scholars. As Delitzsch declared a century ago, "If Koheleth was written in Solomon's day, a history of the Hebrew language is impossible."[1] The language and style of Koheleth represent the latest stage in the development of Hebrew to be found in the Bible and the closest approximation to Mishnaic Hebrew.

Linguistic considerations, applied to questions of date, are generally cumulative in character. A few scattered phrases possessing parallels in Aramaic might be explained as examples of the North-West Semitic vocabulary, originally common to both Aramaic and Hebrew, some of which became frequent in Aramaic and remained rare (or poetic) in Hebrew.[2] Or they might reflect Aramaic influence on Northern Israel during the pre-Exilic period,[3] which was undoubtedly considerable, especially during the heyday of the Syrian kingdom. Similarly, stray resemblances in vocabulary to Mishnaic Hebrew might be interpreted as the fortuitous survival of old words which had otherwise been preserved only in the Mishnah.[4]

In the case of Ecclesiastes, however, the *abundance* of evidence points overwhelmingly to a period when Aramaic was becoming the dominant language of Western Asia and exerting an ever more pronounced influence on Hebrew.[5] That the Persian period is the terminus *non ante quem* for Koheleth is, moreover, rendered certain by the occurrence of two Persian words.[6] Koheleth contains a plethora of Aramaic words, forms and constructions.[7] The book is replete with forms and words which may occur sporadically in earlier Hebrew, but which become more common and familiar in the Mishnah.[8] Late morphological developments, which may have been induced by

Aramaic, are also common.[9] Late syntactic usages are also frequent.[10]

A striking phenomenon of style is the irregular use and absence of the definite article. This usage, however, is not so erratic as has been sometimes assumed, for generally Koheleth follows the rules for its use in Biblical and Mishnaic Hebrew,[11] from which parallels may easily be adduced. Nonetheless, the usage seems to reflect Aramaic influence, where the determinate status (with the article) became indistinguishable in meaning from the indefinite status (without the article) and ultimately replaced the latter almost completely. Because of these Aramaisms and parallel usages, the effort has recently been made to argue that our present book is a translation.[12] All the evidence proposed has been subjected to careful analysis, and it is our conviction that it fails to demonstrate an Aramaic original. On the contrary, there are instances in the forms[13] and in the semantics[14] of the book which prove that Koheleth stands midway between classical Biblical Hebrew and the Mishnaic idiom, though he is closer to the latter.

As for the examples of alleged "mistranslations" of the Aramaic original which have been put forth as the "strongest proof" of the theory, they also fail to stand up under examination. In many instances, the difficulty is exaggerated or largely imaginary, and can be met by a proper exegetical and grammatical approach.[15] In others the problem is real enough, but it remains precisely as before, with the translation-hypothesis contributing nothing significant to a solution,[16] at times even creating new difficulties.[17]

Moreover, if we are to assume that the author wished his book to be regarded as the work of Solomon, he would surely have written it only in Hebrew, the language of the great king.

There is a more fundamental objection, however, to the widely-held theory that a difficult text *ipso facto* presupposes a translation from another language.[18] Actually, the logical conclusion is directly contrary. A translator faced by a difficult original may misread it, because he lacks an adequate knowledge of the vocabulary and misconstrues the grammar. He may tacitly emend the text, read irrelevant matters into it and generally fail to penetrate its meaning. But ultimately he decides upon some view of the passage, which he then expresses in his idiom. If he commands his own language at all, his translation will be clear and intelligible, indeed far more so than the original, even if incorrect. For all the difficulties and possible alternatives posed by the original will have been solved, ignored or obscured in the process of translation. One has only to compare a difficult verse in the Hebrew of *Hosea, Ezekiel* or *Job* with any English version to see how the manifold difficulties of the Hebrew "disappear" in the smooth English renderings. *Other things being equal, it may therefore be maintained that a difficult text may be presumed to be the original rather than a translation.*

The abundance of Aramaisms in Koheleth is precisely what we should expect in the work of a Hebrew writer of the Second Temple period, particularly a prose writer[19] who would be very familiar with Aramaic and would be strongly influenced by it, especially because of its closeness to Hebrew. It is noteworthy, too, that Koheleth does not really include Aramaic words, but rather their Hebrew or Hebraized parallels.[20] Moreover, the Aramaisms in the book are only part of its linguistic affinities with Mishnaic Hebrew; others represent indigenous Hebrew developments in morphology, syntax and semantics, as already noted.[21]

A translator is always conscious of the distinctions between the two languages on which he is engaged, for that is the essence of his task. But a creative writer, familiar with two closely related tongues, and struggling to express his original thought, might unconsciously employ a word, or even a usage, from the other language. Thus, the *fluctuations* in the use or absence of the article tend to prove the existence, not of a translation, but of a Hebrew original. To be sure, the author was familiar with Aramaic and hence might at times use either the determinate or the indeterminate form, especially because he was so largely concerned with general truths, which might be expressed in either form. *Koheleth was written in Hebrew, by a writer who, like all his contemporaries, knew Aramaic and probably used it freely in daily life.*

Reconstructions of alleged mistranslations will be limited only by the ingenuity of scholars and may be argued pro and con.[22] But one additional fact, out of several objective considerations, may be cited here.[23] All the evidence points to Koheleth's having been written not earlier than 275 B. C. E. and probably about 250.[24] Ben Sira, who utilizes the Hebrew text of Koheleth on a par with other reminiscences of Biblical books,[25] wrote in 190–180 B. C. E. The hypothesis of an Aramaic original for Koheleth must therefore postulate: a) the writing of the book; b) its dissemination and popularity; c) its supplementation by one Epilogist or, successively, by two; d) its translation into Hebrew; e) the wide dissemination of the Hebrew version; f) its acceptance into the Biblical canon; and g) subsequently, its utilization by Ben Sira — and all seven stages, it must be assumed, took place within five, or at most, seven decades. In combination with other grave disadvantages under which it labors, the translation theory of Koheleth must be declared unconvincing.

A few decades ago, when the theory was widely held that Koheleth was a disciple of Greek philosophy,[26] linguistic parallels from the Greek were often proposed.[27] Closer study of both the substance and the form of the book has made it clear that there are no indubitable Greek constructions or idioms in the text[28] and not a single instance of a Greek word.[29]

It is clear, therefore, that Koheleth knew Aramaic but not Greek, and that his literary medium was the Hebrew of Second Temple Palestine,[30] in a form which was beginning to approximate the Hebrew of the Mishnah.

VIII. THE DATE AND PROVENANCE OF KOHELETH

The date of Koheleth, within fairly close limits, may be determined on the basis of evidence, both internal and external. Several of the more general considerations have already emerged in the previous discussion of the Wisdom background of Koheleth and his relationship to the cultural influence of his age. These factors, cumulatively viewed, together with more specific data now to be set forth, constitute the basis for the dating of the book.

1. The entire development of Wisdom literature, with its emphasis upon the individual and his destiny, reaches its apogee in the first half of the Second Temple period, roughly between the 5th and the 2nd century B. C. E. In the case of our book, several aspects buttress this conclusion. The thoroughgoing monotheism which is taken for granted throughout the book represents a later period than the sixth-century Deutero-Isaiah, who still must polemize vigorously against polytheism and dualism.[1] On the other hand, the doctrine of an after-life and of judgment beyond the grave had already taken hold of the masses, so that Koheleth, like the author of *Job*, is familiar with the doctrine. Like all the Wisdom writers, however, who represented the conservative standpoint of the well-established groups in society, he feels no inner compulsion to accept it, and expresses his skepticism with an ironic shrug of the shoulders.[2]

2. The degree to which Koheleth has been influenced by Greek ideas narrows the *terminus a quo* even further. The penetration of Greek culture into Asia opens with the meteoric conquests of Alexander the Great (died 323 B. C. E.), but its influence could not have become significant until at least several decades had elapsed.[3] It should be kept in mind that it is intellectual influence with which we are concerned. Commercial relations were much older. Greek trading-posts existed along

the Mediterranean littoral in the 6th century B. C. E. Recent archaeological discoveries have brought to light Ionian and Attic black-figured pottery and Attic red-figured ware at Tell en-Nasbeh emanating from that century. Attic coins were virtually standard currency in Palestine a century and a quarter before Alexander the Great. However, commercial contacts always precede intellectual influences, so that time must be allowed for the penetration of Hellenistic civilization before Koheleth's period of activity.

Moreover, granted that the counsel of submission to "the king" was a common element of Oriental Wisdom,[4] Koheleth was too original a writer to recapitulate stock formulas, if they were irrelevant to his life and thought. His description of a powerful and despotic ruler, whose whims must be obeyed without the illusory hope of a change for the better,[5] reflects the political conditions that prevailed after the death of Alexander the Great.

When Alexander's generals, the Epigonoi, carved out kingdoms for themselves, Palestine, lying between Seleucid Syria and Ptolemaic Egypt, constituted a permanent bone of contention.[6] It remained a province of Ptolemaic Egypt from the time of the Battle of Ipsus (301 B. C. E.) until 249, when Antiochus II of Syria received it as part of his dowry upon his marriage to Berenice of Egypt. When this marriage proved a failure, hostilities broke out anew. These lasted beyond the battle of Raphia (217 B. C. E.), when Palestine reverted to Egypt. The resounding victory of Antiochus III at Panium (198 B. C. E.) definitely transferred Palestine to Syrian rule, where it remained until the Maccabean Wars (168–165 B. C. E.).

Objectively viewed, Koheleth's observations on the state might be a reflection of the political situation under either the Seleucids or the Ptolemies. However, the impression of stable, apparently permanent conditions is more in keeping with the status prevailing during the first half of the 3rd century, when Ptolemaic Egypt was the suzerain, rather than the later period, during which the country changed hands three times (249, 217, and 198 B. C. E.) within fifty years. The evidence from Ben Sira, to be discussed below, also favors the earlier date.

3. Pointing in the same direction is another consideration. Since Koheleth is a Wisdom writer, broadly human interests predominate in him over specifically national concerns, to be sure. It is, however, inconceivable that an upheaval like the Antiochian persecutions or the Maccabean revolt would have left no mark upon Koheleth, had he lived during or after this period of storm and stress.

4. As virtually all students have recognized, Koheleth represents the latest Hebrew in the Bible, the closest approximation to Mishnaic Hebrew. At the same time, it is not identical with the latter, but represents an intermediate stage of development.[7]

5. Two passages in particular have been frequently invoked in fixing the date of Koheleth. The first passage is 4:13–14: "Better a lad of poor birth than an old king who is a fool, and can no longer take care of himself. For from the prison-house he came forth to rule; though he was born poor in his kingdom."

Beginning with the Midrash, which equated the old king and his youthful successor with Nimrod and Abraham, each commentator has proceeded to identify the reference, manifesting an assurance not shared by other students. Thus, to cite only those relevant to the Hellenistic period, the pair has been equated with the high priest Onias and his nephew Joseph the Tobiade, Ptolemy III and Seleucus II (Levy), Antiochus III and Ptolemy Philopator (Hertz.), Ptolemy IV and Ptolemy V (Barton), Antiochus Epiphanes and either Demetrius I or Alexander Balas (Winckler, Haupt), or Herod and his son Alexander (Graetz).[8]

Each of these suggestions suffers from weighty objections. Thus, Barton's view[9] that the "old and foolish King" is Ptolemy IV Philopator, who died in 205, while the "poor and wise youth" would be Ptolemy V Epiphanes, who was five years old when he came to the throne, proves untenable when examined. It is not likely that Ptolemy IV would be called "foolish" on the simple ground that, according to *III Maccabees*, he persecuted the Jews, while Ptolemy V would qualify as "wise" because the Jews had great hopes for him. Moreover, he was not "poor" in any sense, nor did he emerge from "a prison-house."[10]

In sum, if the passage were intended as a reference to an actual event, it might have been clear to Koheleth's contemporaries; it surely does not suit any historical figures known to us, and cannot be utilized to date the book.[11]

The second passage generally cited as a historical allusion is 9:14–15: "A small city there was, with few people in it; and a great king attacked it, besieging it and building breastworks against it. But there was found in it a poor wise man, who saved the city by his wisdom; yet no one remembered that poor man."

Here, too, there has been a plethora of proposed identifications. Thus Hitzig identifies the city with Dora, which Antiochus the Great besieged unsuccessfully in 218 B. C. E., but there is no "poor man" in the incident.[12] Neither the deliverance of Abel-Beth-Maacah (II Sam. 20:15 ff.) by a "wise woman" (Wright), nor the Athenians' treatment of Themistocles (Ewald), nor the action of Archimedes at Syracuse (Friedlander), conforms to the incident as described in *Koheleth*. As Levy has acutely observed, had the incident been remembered, it would have totally disproved the author's contention that the virtues of the poor are forgotten![13]

As a matter of fact, these two passages are not references to historical events at all. They exhibit a characteristic Oriental literary device, where an incident, typical rather than actual, is introduced, in order to drive a point home.

The first passage is actually introduced by the phrase *tōbh*, "better," which is frequently used in Wisdom literature to make a generalization, Koheleth in particular being fond of this usage.[14] But even when the passage is couched in narrative form, Oriental literary usage makes it clear that no actual incident is intended. Thus the Egyptian *Admonitions of a Prophet* contains a series of varied comments and poems, one section of which begins: "There was once a man that was old and stood in the presence of death and his son was still a child and without understanding."[15] In the *Instruction for King Merikere*, the advice to the young ruler-to-be is largely in the form of admonitions, but we find this incident: "There rose up one, a ruler in the city, and his heart was oppressed by reason of the Delta."[16] The similarity of style and theme to the passages in *Koheleth* is obvious.

This use of incidents, real and imaginary, characterized the Cynic-Stoic diatribe as well.[17] The parables in the Gospels and in Talmudic literature offer countless familiar instances of this literary usage. But whether these passages are rhetorical devices, as seems certain, or enshrine actual historical allusions, they cannot be utilized for dating the book.

6. The *terminus non post quem* is fixed even more definitely than the *terminus a quo* by Ben Sira's familiarity with Koheleth, the evidence for which has already been indicated. The Preface to the Greek version of *Ben Sira*, which was prepared by his grandson, indicates that the translator came to Egypt in the thirty-eighth year of King Ptolemy, who can be identified only with Euergetes II (Physcon). Hence the translation is dated at approximately 132 B. C. E., and the Hebrew original at about 190–180 B. C. E. This conclusion agrees with the fact that *Ben Sira*, like *Koheleth*, contains no echo of the Antiochian persecutions and of the Maccabean wars.

If we allow a minimum of fifty years for *Koheleth* to attain to sufficient popularity to be accepted within the corpus of Scripture and thus to be utilized by Ben Sira, its latest possible date would be the middle of the 3rd century B. C. E. Nor can its date be much earlier, since time must be allowed for the penetration of Greek ideas into Jewish Palestine.[18] The date of composition of the book of *Koheleth* may accordingly be set at about 250 B. C. E.[19]

As for the geographical provenance of the book, the effort has been made to find references to Egyptian weather conditions in 1:5–7, but on unconvincing grounds.[20] Nor do the comments on absolute monarchical rule in 8:2; 10:4 prove that the author lived in Alexandria,[21] for Palestine was a province of the same Ptolemaic empire.

On the other hand, the absence of any knowledge of Greek rules out the likelihood that the author was an Alexandrian Jew.[22] Hence there is no need to discount or reject the reference to Jerusalem (1:12; 2:9) and to the house of God where sacrifices are offered (4:17). The Oniade Temple at Leontopolis in Egypt was not built until 160 B. C. E., which is much too late for Koheleth. Moreover, the magnificent picture of the cistern falling into disrepair (12:6) reflects conditions in Palestine, where rain-water was carefully saved, rather than the Egyptian locale, which depended upon the inundations of the Nile.[23]

The conclusions that have thus far emerged may now be summarized. The Book of *Koheleth* was written in Hebrew by a Jew in Jerusalem, who knew Aramaic but no Greek, though he was familiar with basic Greek ideas. The date of his book, which coincided with the last years of his life, falls in the middle of the 3rd century B. C. E.

We may now turn our attention to his career, personality and world-view.

IX. THE INTEGRITY OF THE BOOK

Almost from the beginning, readers of Koheleth were troubled by the inconsistencies and contradictions in which the book apparently abounded. In the Rabbinic discussions as to its canonicity, the objection was raised that "its words contradicted one another."[1] Thus the book declares, "Better sorrow than laughter" (7:3), and "Of laughter I said, it is madness, and joy, of what good is it?" (2:2), and then opposes it by saying: "And I praised joy" (8:15).

The method preferred by the ancients for reconciling these differences was principally that of allegory and hermeneutic interpretation, by means of which the work emerged as a series of pious reflections on the vanity of all earthly desires and the abiding worth of faith and morality.[2] Thus the laughter that is condemned is God's temporary favoring of the wicked in this world as a prelude to their punishment in the world to come, while the joy that is praised is His abiding delight in the righteous of the world. The Midrash lays down the principle, "Wherever eating and drinking are mentioned in Koheleth, the reference is to the enjoyment of Torah and good deeds."[3]

Syntax and context were, of course, no obstacle to the interpreters. Thus the skeptical query in 3:21, "Who knows whether the spirit of man goes upward, and the spirit of the beast goes downward to the earth?" is boldly turned into a triumphant affirmation of man's immortality by the Septuagint: "The spirit of man *does* ascend, etc."

A large portion of Koheleth, of course, offered no problem to the pious reader, notably the proverbial material in the book, as well as Koheleth's frequent use of religious vocabulary, such as *tōbh liphᵉnei hā'elōhīm*, "the one pleasing to God"; *ḥēt*, "sin"; *ḥākhām*, "wise"; *mitzvāh*, "command." That these and other terms had a unique, unconventional meaning for Koheleth was naturally not even suspected by his ancient readers.

These methods of interpretation are dominant in the Midrashim, of which Koheleth Rabba is the most extensive, and in the Targum, which is virtually an Aramaic Midrash. They occur to a lesser degree in the Vulgate and Peshitta, and to some extent even in the Septuagint, which is extremely literal in *Koheleth*.[4] Similar methods were employed by Jewish and Christian homiletic interpreters in medieval and even modern times.[5] Often ingenious, sometimes even diverting, these techniques have only historical interest today.

The literal interpretation of the text, which had its origins in the Ancient Versions, underlay even the Midrash and became a canon of exegesis in the Talmud, which declared, in theory at least, that: "The Biblical text must be interpreted according to its simple, literal meaning."[6] With the development of medieval Hebrew grammar and scientific exegesis, countless difficulties emerged in *Koheleth*. These were met in a variety of ways. Several of the Church Fathers and many medieval exegetes, both Jewish and Christian, explained these contradictions as due to the debate of academies of wise men, or as a dialogue between men of varying standpoints, including a cynical worldling, a worldly sage and a pious believer.

In the 19th century, Bickell proposed the view that the book originally consisted of leaves of about 525 letters each which were disarranged. This theory never won many adherents because of its psychological improbability, as well as because of the fact that Hebrew texts were written on scrolls, not on sheets, as the newly discovered Ain Feshka scrolls, which have been dated roughly a century after Koheleth, demonstrate anew.[7]

The Documentary Hypothesis of the Pentateuch, which analyzed the Five Books of Moses into diverse and ever more numerous sources, influenced the study of Koheleth as well. Siegfried divided the book among nine sources (Q1, Q2, Q3, Q4, Q5, R1, R2, E1, E2). Nonetheless, he himself recognized that the uniformity of style which pervades the entire book constituted a basic weakness for his view. The idea that a book of such small size is to be assigned to nine authors, several of them representing an entire school, never won wide acceptance. As for the alleged contradictions of standpoint which the division of sources is intended to explain, many are exaggerated, others represent normal variations of mood, while others are explicable in terms of Koheleth's unique style, as will be indicated below.

At the end of the nineteenth century and the first decades of the twentieth, critical students of the book by and large tended to regard the work as consisting of an original nucleus of heterodox, skeptical material, which had then been extensively glossed by readers in an effort to make it palatable to the orthodox and thus find a place for it in the canon. Even this more moderate approach, however, bristles with difficulties that have been generally ignored. In the entire book, which consists of only 222 verses, Jastrow assumes 120 interpolations; Barton, who is more conservative, follows McNeile in the main, and finds two glossators or schools at work on the book, one a Hakam, who added proverbs of a conventional cast, the other a Hasid, who added pious sentiments. Podechard assumes two Epilogists, one a pupil of Koheleth, the other a Hasid, in addition to a Hokmah glossator and two more interpolators, to whom a total of 85 verses are to be assigned.[8]

None of these scholars seeks to explain why the book was deemed worthy of this effort to "legitimatize" it, when it could so easily have been suppressed. There were many other works written in this period, now known as the Apocrypha and Pseudepigrapha, all attributed to ancient worthies, which were far less objectionable to the alleged orthodox sentiment of the time. If it was clear that a given book had been compiled after prophecy had ceased in Israel, or if it contradicted traditional Halachah, or if it contained apocalyptic visions of "last things" or other doctrines upon which normative Judaism frowned,[9] no elaborate effort was undertaken to counteract its heterodox features by glosses and interpolations, as is assumed for *Koheleth*. Instead, such works were withdrawn by the authorities from public use, by being stored away in the *genizah*, and thus consigned to oblivion and ultimate destruction.[10] As a result, many, if not most, of these pseudepigraphical writings were lost altogether. A few managed to survive by accident in Greek, Latin, Syriac, Ethiopic or Slavonic translations, largely because of the interest of the Christian Church in their preservation. That a passage here and there might have been added in *Koheleth* is at least a possible view. But that the book was

subjected to thoroughgoing elaboration in order to make it fit
into the Biblical canon is an assumption for which no real
analogy exists, indeed is contradicted by the history of the
Apocrypha and the Pseudepigrapha after their composition.

Moreover, the theory of tendentious additions to Koheleth
raises extensive problems of chronology. It is difficult to believe
that in the ancient Orient, where time moved slowly, and changes
were few, so many steps in the process could have been consum-
mated in a comparatively short time. The critical view must
assume that the book was written, that it attained to wide
popularity and therefore sustained systematic interpolation at
the hands of various schools of readers, the conventional believers, or Hasidim, and the Wisdom teachers, or Hakamim.
Thereafter, these glosses were universally accepted as part of
the original, and the composite product was admitted into the
canon of Scripture, either because of the intrinsic interest of the
book or its attribution to Solomon. This complicated literary
history must all be compressed into a period of three centuries
or less. For toward the end of the first century of the Christian
era (90 C. E.), its place in the Biblical canon could still be theoretically discussed in the Academy at Jabneh, but was no
longer open to dispute.

The problem of chronology becomes virtually insuperable,
if we recognize that by the time of Ben Sira (190 B. C. E.),
the book of *Koheleth* had attained to at least quasi-canonical
status.[11] Its popularity by the beginning of the 2nd century
B. C. E. is clear from Ben Sira's utilization of phrases from
Koheleth in the same manner as he used other Biblical allusions.[12]
Perhaps the most striking borrowing from *Koheleth* in *Ben Sira*
is כי ייי מבקש נרדפים (B. S. 5:35), which is based on והאלהים יבקש
את נרדף (Ecc. 3:15), a passage generally regarded by critics as
a Hasid's gloss! Hence the complicated process of writing,
popularization and widespread interpolation must be contracted
still further, into a period of about a century or less (275-190
B. C. E.).[13]

Problems such as these impelled so consistent an advocate
of the source-analysis school as Kuenen to confess in the heyday
of the Documentary Hypothesis: "It may be hard to demonstrate

the unity of Koheleth; but it is even harder to deny it." Twentieth century Biblical scholarship is increasingly motivated by a general reaction against the extremes of nineteenth century Higher Criticism in general. In growing measure it is being recognized that the atomization of Biblical books is an unnecessary hypothesis and, by that token, untrue. For though unconscionably neglected in Biblical studies, William of Occam's principle remains fundamental to the scientific method: *Entia non sunt multiplicanda praeter necessitatem.*

In the study of Koheleth, the last few decades have introduced a growing recognition among scholars of its basic unity.[14] Only the Epilogue (12:9–14), which speaks of Koheleth in the third person and reflects a conventional and partly critical attitude toward Koheleth, is manifestly from another hand.[15] The first verse, which is really the title, emanates from the editor,[16] as is the case in the titles of the Prophetic books. It is possible that the phrase "says Koheleth" in 1:2; 7:27; 12:8 goes back to the same hand.[17]

With regard to the book as a whole, the assumption of wholesale interpolation, like the older theory of multiple authorship, is being surrendered more and more. Only a detailed study of each of the passages in question can indicate how this approach is at best needless and at worst fatal to an understanding of the book. The various Hakam glossators and Hasid interpolators are merely figments of the scholarly imagination.[18]

Instead, there is need to reckon with the full and complex spiritual background in which Koheleth lived and functioned. Being a teacher of Wisdom, he would naturally compose original proverbs and be in the habit of citing maxims with which he was familiar as a result of his professional activity. The author of the Epilogue, probably a younger contemporary of Koheleth, declares that he "weighed, searched out and fashioned many proverbs" (12:9). He thus offers welcome direct testimony that Koheleth himself wrote and contributed to gnomic literature, couching his maxims in rhythmic form.[19] The intermingling of conventional and unconventional Wisdom in one literary unit, with traditional proverbs being imbedded in original material, is not only thoroughly comprehensible in terms of

Koheleth's personality, but is amply attested in Babylonian and Egyptian Wisdom as well.[20]

As for the so-called pious sentiments which critics have attributed to the Hasid glossator, these need to be understood in terms of Koheleth's style. Reared in the bosom of Jewish tradition, and seeking to express in Hebrew a unique philosophic world-view possessing strong overtones of skepticism, Koheleth falls back upon the only abstract vocabulary he knows, that of traditional religion, which he uses in his own special manner.[21]

Moreover, in many instances, both the proverbs and the apparently pious sentiments to be encountered in the book are to be recognized as quotations by Koheleth, cited for the purpose of discussion. This use of quotations is not limited to *Koheleth* or even to Wisdom literature, but is an important stylistic feature of Babylonian, Egyptian, Sumerian and Jewish Rabbinic literature generally.[22]

Buffon's judgment that "le style, c'est l'homme même" is nowhere truer than of Koheleth. An appreciation of his personality is impossible without a comprehension of his style, and, conversely, his style cannot be evaluated without an understanding of the man. When these essential factors are present, the book emerges as a literary unit, the spiritual testament of a single, complex, richly endowed personality.

X. KOHELETH THE MAN

No other book within the Bible and few outside of it in world literature are as intensely personal as Koheleth. To be sure, he can be properly understood only within the framework of the intellectual life of ancient Israel, which is itself a distinctive part of the larger culture-pattern of the ancient Near East. Nonetheless, his vision of life is definitely his own, the reaction of his personality to the world about him, individual in content and unique in expression.

Modern psychological, economic, and social studies have shed valuable light on the factors entering into the thought-processes of men.

Unfortunately, this development has often been carried to extremes and the study of the genesis of an idea has tended to replace the evaluation of its truth and significance. All too often one encounters the tendency to interpret the world-view of thinkers almost exclusively in terms of their personal idiosyncrasies or of their social backgrounds and economic interests.

As though anticipating this development, and seeking to forestall, or at least hinder, this process, the Biblical writers generally give us little information about themselves and their times. The few details we have about Isaiah and the somewhat ampler information we possess about Jeremiah are revealed to us incidentally, in the course of the prophet's career. As a result, the message of the Prophets, rooted though it be in their life and age, confronts the modern man in universal form, as though beyond the limitations of time and space.

In this sense, too, Koheleth was a son of his people. His brief book gives tantalizingly few hints about his personal life, and these have been seized upon and elaborated variously by his readers. Some have regarded the detailed description of luxury in Chapter Two as autobiographical, and accordingly have pictured him as an extremely wealthy aristocrat, if not as a king.¹ In that passage, however, Koheleth is merely adopting the role of King Solomon as a literary device, in order to use the career of the great king to emphasize his conclusion as to the inadequacy of wealth and wisdom as absolute goals.²

The book of Koheleth is not a pseudepigraph, seeking to masquerade as the authentic work of Solomon. If that were the author's intention, he would have adopted the name "Solomon" outright, instead of inventing the enigmatic name of "Koheleth," which suggests the identity only by indirection.³ It should be remembered, too, that he does not call himself "son of David"; this phrase occurs only in the opening verse, which is the title of the book and emanates from an editor. That this identification played a large part in gaining admission for the book into the canon is one of the fortunate accidents of literary history, but does not gainsay the fact that it does not go back to the author.⁴

It has been inferred, on the basis of the difficult passage 5:8, which seems to glorify agricultural pursuits, that Koheleth was a country gentleman. Even if the meaning of the verse were certain, it would be merely a conventional tribute to country life, in which Koheleth is reflecting the standpoint of the conservative upper-classes. For the aristocracy of the ancient world, who lived in luxury in the great urban centers of Jerusalem, Alexandria or Rome, largely on the income they derived from their country estates, which were tilled by tenant farmers, liked to regard themselves as country gentlemen, and looked down upon the artisans and merchants of the cities.⁵

While these and similar deductions about Koheleth's personal life seem unwarranted, a few facts may be derived from his book. All signs point to the fact that Koheleth lived in Jerusalem.⁶ The sophistication which characterizes the book is best sought for in a great cultural center like the capital city. The references to the Temple and the sacrificial cult (4:17 f.) as being close at hand, and his matter-of-fact familiarity with the corruption of government (5:7), lend credence to the repeated mention of Jerusalem (1:12; 2:9; cf. 1:1) as the seat of Koheleth's activity. Evidence for the Palestinian locale of the book has already been indicated.⁷

The content and form of his book make it clear that Koheleth

was a teacher in one of the Wisdom academies in Jerusalem, which
served the educational needs of upper-class youth. The internal
evidence is buttressed by the testimony on Koheleth's calling
which is to be found in the Epilogue (12:9–14). These verses
were written not by Koheleth,[8] but by a contemporary, probably a colleague, who knew him personally:[9]

> Not only was Koheleth a sage himself, but he also taught
> the people knowledge, weighing and searching and fashioning
> many proverbs. Koheleth tried to find attractive words
> and honestly to set down the truth.

> The words of the wise are like goads, and like well-fastened
> nails are the collected sayings, coming from one Source.

> Furthermore, my son, be warned: of making many books
> there is no end, and much study wears one's strength away.

From this contemporary source we learn that Koheleth did not
limit himself to his professional activity as a Wisdom teacher
(*hakham*), but carried on literary activity, collecting (*ḥikker*, lit.
"search out") extant proverbs, and composing (*tikken*) original
material as well, being concerned not only with the truth of his
teaching (*dibhrē 'emeth*), but with an attractive literary form
(*dibhrē ḥefeṣ*).

As a Wisdom teacher Koheleth was closely identified with
the upper-class groups of Jewish society by vocation.[10] It is, of
course, possible that he was of lowly origin, and had won his
place among the successful groups by his superior abilities, but
we should then have expected, in one as sensitive as Koheleth,
a greater degree of reaction to social injustice and oppression
than we find in this book.[11] It therefore seems most probable
that Koheleth belonged to the upper classes by birth and position, for we find no indications that he ever suffered poverty
and want. Apparently he enjoyed the benefits of travel and
other opportunities that were denied to the poor.

While his range of knowledge may not have equalled that
of the author of *Job*, who has been described as the most learned
ancient before Plato, he was cultured and well-informed. He
was able to draw upon history, contemporary affairs, and the

science of his day, in order to express his own world-view. His familiarity with at least some of the fundamental ideas of Greek philosophy, like the four elements and the doctrine of the golden mean, as well as his creative use of these concepts in his own world-view, has already been discussed. In the same original manner he utilizes some basic formulations in the Pentateuch and the Historical Books.[12]

Only a few other facts may be inferred regarding his personal history. Koheleth was a bachelor, or at least a man without children. For he is considerably exercised over the fact that when a man dies he must leave his wealth to "strangers" who never labored to achieve it,[13] and he betrays no sentiment for kith and kin, even when he speaks of the family.[14]

That Koheleth is writing as an old man is clear from the deeply felt Allegory of Old Age in ch. 12. The same vantage-point is reflected in his nostalgic stress upon the joys of youth and upon man's obligation to do all things with might and main before it grows too late forever.[15]

Nothing more is known definitely of the external events of his life.[16] Fortunately, his book permits us to reconstruct the principal phases of his spiritual odyssey, for each of them left his impress upon his philosophy of life. Koheleth entered the world richly endowed in spirit. From earliest youth his intellectual and emotional faculties were exceptionally keen, and they determined the entire course of his development. Fundamental in the boy and the man was a passionate love of life, the universal heritage of the healthy mind and the healthy body. He loved the tang of living. The sight of the sun, the breath of the wind, the good things of the world held him enthralled:

> Sweet is the light, and it is good for the eyes to see the sun.
>
> (11:7)

The experience of life thrilled him to the core. Women he loved deeply, and even in old age he well remembered the world of sensation to which they beckoned:

> Enjoy life with the woman you love. (9:9)

Nor was he a stranger to other sources of material comfort and beauty. The cool spaciousness of gardens and orchards, the nobility of fine houses, the cheer of good food and fine wine, the charm of music and the grace of the dance — Koheleth savored them all. Even after his joy in life had been tempered by later experiences, he still felt that merely to be alive was a boon:

For surely a live dog is better than a dead lion. (9:4)

Had Koheleth possessed no other elements in his spiritual constitution than his love of life, he would have been happy. Possessing the means of gratifying his desires, he might have spent his days in carousing and feasting or in the subtler forms of sensual enjoyment. He could have been a Philistine or an esthete, but in any event a happy man. That happiness eluded him was the result of other facets in his personality.

As a Jew, Koheleth had naturally been reared in the rich religious tradition of Israel, embodied in the books of the Torah and the Prophets, which were in his day already recognized as Sacred Scriptures. These educative influences brought to bear upon him were no mere historical memories. For the teachings of the Torah were being practiced in the Temple cult by the priests, and were being expounded in the academies by the Scribes. As for the Prophets, though their greatest period was over, their teachings were now accepted as integral to Judaism. Moreover, the creative impulse of Prophecy was not altogether spent, expressing itself in the strange, submerged patterns of Apocalyptic literature.[17]

In spite of their varying emphases, both Torah and Prophecy were concerned with justice, the latter with its triumphant enthronement in society, the former, as the social legislation of the Pentateuch indicates, at least with the minimizing of social oppression and want.

The third spiritual current, that of Hokmah, richly creative and deeply influential in Koheleth's age, was less passionate on this score, but it also was permeated by the Hebrew quest for righteousness.[18] It is noteworthy that the Prophetic concept of history is most comprehensively stated in the book of *Proverbs* (14:34): "Righteousness exalts a people, but sin is the disgrace of nations." Were this religio-ethical standpoint lacking in Wisdom, it could never have been identified with Torah in the synthesis which was later to produce normative Judaism.[19]

Thus the zest for justice, the hallmark of the spirit of Israel, was early brought to bear upon Koheleth, and he was never again the same carefree, lusty youth. He was too clear-sighted to overlook the widespread scars of suffering on the body politic of society, and too sensitive to remain callous to human misery, merely because he himself was not directly affected. The beauty of nature and the luxury of wealth could not blot out the marks of man's injustice to his fellows:

> Furthermore, I saw under the sun, in the place of judgment, there was wickedness, and in the place of righteousness, wrong. (3:16)

Superimposed upon his innate love of life, there had now come a second great motive power, the love of justice. But there was a cruel difference between the two. While the first could easily be gratified, he was doomed to failure in the second. As he grew older, and became aware of the tragic distance that yawned between the prophetic ideal and the real world, something snapped within him. The magnificent audacity of the Prophets, their unshakable faith in the ultimate triumph of the right, these were not for him. He was too realistic, too sober, perhaps too narrow, for that. Too many years had elapsed since the Prophets had foretold the doom of evil and folly, and still the wicked prospered, while folly sat enthroned in the high places:

> I have seen everything during my vain existence, a righteous man being destroyed for all his righteousness, and a sinner living long for all his wickedness. (7:15)

> Folly is often enthroned on the great heights . . . I have seen slaves on horses, while lords must walk on foot like slaves. (10:6a, 7)

Nor did Koheleth possess the spiritual energy to grow indignant and reprove his God, as did the author of *Job*. At the spectacle of injustice, the Prophets had thundered and pleaded and proclaimed the day of doom, but Koheleth merely smiled. Wrong and corruption, he felt, were eternal, inherent in the scheme of things:

> If you observe the despoiling of the poor and the perversion of justice and right in the state, do not be astonished at the fact, for each guardian of the law is higher than the next, and there are still higher ones above them! (5:7)

Yet Koheleth did not react with a cheap and easy cynicism to human suffering. On other themes he might be light or sarcastic, but here he was in deadly earnest, with a fervor almost prophetic in its intensity:

> Again, I saw all the acts of oppression that are done under the sun. Here are the tears of the oppressed, with none to comfort them; and power in the hands of their oppressors, with none to comfort them. So I praise the dead who have already died, more than the creatures who are still alive.
> (4:1, 2)

He was yet to encounter other sources of frustration, but none except injustice possessed the power to evoke so bitter a denunciation of life. Henceforth the happiness of a carefree and joyous existence was evermore beclouded for Koheleth by the vision of a world in agony. Koheleth became a cynic, not because he was indifferent to human suffering, but, on the contrary, because he was acutely sensitive to man's cruelty and folly.

But Koheleth had not yet plumbed the full depths of the despair that life was to breed in him. Stronger even than his love of justice was his love of truth. Possessing a keen mind and a lively curiosity, he eagerly sought after the profounder *Hokmah*, the fundamental insight into the world and its meaning. It was the Wisdom hymned by the Sage, after which Koheleth strove:

> The Lord by Wisdom founded the earth;
> By Understanding He established the heavens. (Pr. 3:19)

Koheleth sought to probe these mysteries, which the more matter-of-fact Ben Sira had advised leaving alone, perhaps because he knew of the perils that lurked in the quest:

> What is too wonderful for you do not seek,
> Nor search after what is hidden from you.
> Seek to understand what is permitted you,
> And have no concern with mysteries.   (B. S. 3:20 f.)

Job, too, had sought this wisdom in vain:

> Where is Wisdom to be found?
> And where is the place of Understanding?   (Job 28:20)

Yet in this very unknowability of the world, Job had found an anodyne for his suffering, a token that there was a rational and just world-order, though on a scale incomprehensible to man. For Job, the grandeur and harmony of the cosmos, created by Divine Wisdom, were signs pointing toward an equally pervasive moral universe, founded on Divine justice. But that faith was not for Koheleth. His fruitless search for justice in human life had grievously wounded his personal happiness. Now came the tragic realization that the all-inclusive Wisdom of the universe was also unattainable:

> I saw that though a man sleep neither by day nor by night, he cannot discover the meaning of God's work which is done under the sun, for the sake of which a man may search hard, but he will not find it; and though a wise man may think he is about to learn it, he will be unable to find it.
> (8:17)

A deep woe now settled upon the youthful enthusiast, when the futility of his aspirations was borne in upon him. Justice he had sought, but it was nowhere; wisdom he had pursued, but the phantom had vanished. All life was meaningless and futile, and his judgment upon it was devastating:

> Vanity of vanities, says Koheleth,
> Vanity of vanities, all is vanity.   (1:1; 12:8)

> Hence I hated life, for all the work that is done beneath
> the sun seemed worthless to me, and everything vanity
> and a chasing of wind.   (2:17)

As the spectacle of human cruelty and suffering was revealed
to him, he despaired of life:

> More fortunate than both the living and the dead is he who
> has not yet been born and so has never seen the evil deeds
> that are being done under the sun.   (4:3)

Three great ideas had lighted his way in the world. The
love of life was rich with promise of happiness, but the yearning
for justice and wisdom had brought him only sorrow and
disillusion.

For a space, one can live in a state of complete intellectual
nihilism, without values or activities. Few men, however — and
Koheleth was not among them — can abide that emptiness
indefinitely. The quest for certainty is not abandoned merely
because two of its roads have proved blind alleys. Koheleth
had to discover some definite basis for belief, or at least some
rationale of action, if his life was to go on. It could not be
wisdom or justice, for these had been weighed and found wanting.
He had to retrace his steps to the first great principle of his
life, the only law that had not brought him to grief.

So Koheleth returns to his first love, but with a difference.
The whole-hearted, instinctive gladness of youth is gone. His
love of life is now the result of reflection, the irreducible minimum
of his life's philosophy. In the striving for happiness lies the
only reasonable goal for human existence. He chants a hymn
of joy, but there are overtones of tragedy, the sad music of the
inevitability of old age, the echo of the cruelty and ignorance
of mankind:

> For if a man live many years, let him rejoice in them all,
> and remember that the days of darkness will be many, and
> that everything thereafter is nothingness.   (11:8)

So I saw that there is nothing better for man than to rejoice in his works, for that is his lot, and no one can permit him to see what shall be afterwards. (3:22)

Koheleth sets up the attainment of happiness as the goal of human striving, not merely because he loves life, but because he cannot have justice and wisdom. Joy is the only purpose that he can find in a monotonous and meaningless world, in which all human values, such as wealth, piety, and ability, are vanity, where all men encounter the same fate and no progress is possible.

To set forth these basic attitudes toward life, the implications of which will be presented below, Koheleth writes his book in old age, recapitulating the stages of his spiritual history in the process. As he contemplates his past career, he has no personal complaint to make; on the whole, life has been good to him. He has been spared the degradation of poverty and the terror of insecurity, nor has he ever had to taste the bitterness of personal tragedy. His charm, insight and skill have doubtless made him a successful teacher in the Wisdom academies and brought him tangible as well as intangible rewards. The competence he has acquired now makes it possible for him to enjoy the amenities of life — a fine house in Jerusalem, a sense of independence, and the blessing of unworried leisure. Thus he sits in the sunset hours of his life, a tiny island of ease and contemplation within the whirling currents of life in the capital city.

His is a comfortable old age, but there is a quiet loneliness about it. He has no wife to share either the simple happenings of ordinary existence or the rare moments of deeper experience. His home has never reëchoed with the voices of children at play. He has never been stirred to ecstasy by their laughter or driven to distraction by their tears. But perhaps, he muses, it is better so, as he recalls the fine brave rapture of youth and the febrile ambitions of maturity, all now revealed as emptiness and chasing of wind.

From time to time, his former pupils visit him, for Judaism declares it a duty to pay respect to one's former teachers by

calling on them.[20] He looks into the faces of these lads who
have since gone forth to positions of prominence and dignity
in the practical world. Some are important government officials,
others are Temple dignitaries, while others have far-flung economic interests as merchant princes or landed gentry. As his
wise, understanding eyes scan their faces, he notes that they
have paid a high price for success. The shining, carefree counte-
nances of youth, the sparkling eyes brimful with mischief, are
gone. In their stead are worn faces, some drawn, others grown
puffy with the years, and tired, unhappy eyes sagging beneath
the weight of responsibility. Time was when his pupils were
young and he was old, but now the tables are turned. True,
Koheleth is a few paces before them in the inexorable procession
toward the grave. But in a deeper sense, he is young and they
are prematurely old. He knows what they have forgotten,
that men's schemes and projects, their petty jealousies and
labors, their struggles and heartaches, all are vanity and that
joy in life is the one divine commandment.

Before it is too late, he takes pen in hand to transmit the
truth, as he sees it, concerning the incomprehensible and in-
describably precious blessing called life. For it is his secret
wish that men after him, whom his living voice will never
reach, may face life with truth as their banner and with a song
in their hearts.

> Go, then, eat your bread with joy,
> And drink your wine with a glad heart,
> For God has already approved your actions.
> At all times let your clothes be white,
> And oil on your head not be lacking.
>
> Enjoy life with the woman you love
> Through all the vain days of your life,
> Which God has given you under the sun,
> Throughout your brief days,
> For that is your life's reward
> For your toil under the sun.

Whatever you are able to do, do with all your might, for there is neither action nor thought nor knowledge nor wisdom in the grave towards which you are moving. (9:7–10)

Doubtless Koheleth would have been the first to confess that in taking such pains to urge the enjoyment of life upon man, at a time when he himself had already passed his prime and reached the days in which there is no pleasure, there lurked more than a little of vanity — in both senses. Fortunately, however, the need for self-expression triumphed over the dictates of consistency and so a masterpiece was born.

XI. THE STYLE — HIS RELIGIOUS VOCABULARY

One of the principal obstacles to the understanding of *Koheleth* has been its unique style, for which readers have not been prepared, particularly since the book is in the Bible. Because of its place in the sacred canon, most readers turn to it with more devoutness than alertness, expecting to be edified rather than stimulated by its contents.

The time is long overdue for recognizing, as Ehrlich observed, that the Bible is not a collection of religious texts, but rather "a national literature upon a religious foundation."[1] Only from this point of view can the reader savor fully the vitality, color and broad humanity of the Bible and appreciate the variety in outlook, temperament and mode of expression to be found within its pages. Priest and prophet, sage and psalmist, legist and poet, rationalist and mystic, skeptic and believer, all have found their place in the Bible. The canon of Scripture was created not by a religious sect of like-minded believers, but by a people sharing a common historical experience.[2] The Librarian of the Synagogue was therefore capable of being hospitable to contradictory and even to extreme viewpoints, with which traditional Judaism might wrestle, but which it would never obliterate.[3]

For the religious spirit, the Bible is eternally the Revelation of God, but in no superficial and mechanical sense. The Bible must be approached in the spirit of the profound Rabbinic comment on two rival schools, "Both these and the others are the words of the Living God."[4]

Koheleth is the product of Hebrew life and thought and must be viewed against that background, but he represents a definitely individual interpretation of the tradition he inherited, and so cannot be understood purely in terms of parallels. His style reflects the elements both of similarity and of difference which mark his relationship to his contemporaries.

The impact of Aramaic upon the syntax and vocabulary has already been discussed,[5] while other elements of his style will be analyzed below. At the very outset it must be borne in mind that Koheleth was a linguistic pioneer. He was struggling to use Hebrew for quasi-philosophic purposes, a use to which the language had not previously been applied. A thousand years later, medieval translators like the Tibbonides, who rendered Saadiah, Maimonides, Judah Halevi and other Jewish philosophers into Hebrew, still found that the language had not yet fully developed the flexibility, precision and vocabulary necessary for the treatment of philosophic themes. Koheleth's comparative success in this respect is not the least element of his literary skill.

His task was rendered still more difficult by a third factor. Biblical Hebrew has a deceptively simple syntax, as far as the forms are concerned. But as a result, each available device possesses a large number of uses and nuances. Perhaps the principal syntactic trait of Hebrew is that it uses parataxis almost exclusively, as against the hypotaxis preferred in Indo-European languages. A study of the luxuriant variety of shades of meaning of the Biblical connective *Vav*, "and," proves highly instructive in this respect.[6] Hence, the interpreter must often use a large variety of subordinate clauses, where Hebrew uses a simple co-ordinate clause. Nor can he always be sure that he has gauged the author's intent correctly. Another difficulty inheres in the fact that the old Semitic mood endings had all but disappeared in Biblical Hebrew, with the result that the mood of verbs can only be inferred from the context.

Classical Hebrew had only two tenses, the perfect and the imperfect, and both were concerned not with the time of the action, which might be in the past, present or future, but with the extent to which the action was looked upon as completed.[7] As a result, the perfect was generally used to denote past action and the imperfect, future action, but this was far from universally the case. In the latest stage of Biblical Hebrew, represented by *Esther*, *Ezra-Nehemiah-Chronicles*, and *Koheleth*, the participle was increasingly used as a present tense, often with progressive force, a usage which became regular in Mishnaic and modern

Hebrew. The infinitive was likewise utilized in a variety of ways. The vigor and succinctness of Biblical Hebrew is in large measure due to the relative paucity of adjectives and adverbs — it is preëminently a language of nouns and verbs. All these aspects of Biblical Hebrew complicate the understanding of a text in which exactness is essential. But they do not exhaust the problems of Koheleth's style, which possesses several special features.

Like other writers since his time, who were raised in a religious tradition from which they later broke away in whole or in part, Koheleth uses the language in which he was reared, and incidentally, the only one he knew, to express his own individual viewpoint. The contemporary reader will think of Ernest Renan, Anatole France and George Santayana in modern times as offering a partial analogy.

A very remarkable parallel, *mutatis mutandis*, is afforded by the philosopher Spinoza, who lived nineteen centuries after Koheleth. One of the profoundest contemporary students of Spinoza, Professor H. A. Wolfson of Harvard,[8] demonstrated that Spinoza's *Ethics* has been widely misunderstood because of the failure to reckon with the author's practice of using the traditional philosophical vocabulary of his time to express his own individual and heterodox concepts. In Wolfson's words, "The *Ethics* — contrary to the generally accepted opinion — is primarily a criticism of the fundamental principles of religious philosophy which at the beginning of the Christian era were laid down by Philo and were still in vogue at the time of Spinoza in the seventeenth century. This criticism is constructed according to an old forensic device which may be described as 'yes' and 'but.' The 'yes' part is an expression of Spinoza's assent to the external formulation of some of the principles of traditional religious philosophy. The 'but' part is a statement of the special sense in which he himself is willing to use that formulation . . . It is for this reason also that the *Ethics*, in my opinion, has so often been misunderstood and so often misinterpreted." Wolfson proceeds to point out that such standard elements of the philosophical vocabulary as "substance," "mode," "attribute," "thought," "extension," "body," "soul," and "freedom," are all affirmed by Spinoza, but in senses widely at variance with those of conventional theologians and philosophers. For example, "Spinoza has no objection to adopting the vocabulary of his opponents and describing the human soul as being of divine origin."[9]

To be sure, Koheleth was far from being a systematic thinker and technical philosopher like Spinoza, but both men had undergone a strikingly similar development. They had both been reared within the Jewish tradition, which had indeed grown in extent in the intervening centuries, though remaining basically the same — a faith in a Creator ruling His world in justice and mercy. Both thinkers had broken with this all but universally accepted pattern of belief in many respects and had developed an original world-view. Because of their background and inclination, however, both preferred to express their ideas in the terminology to which they were accustomed. As might have been expected, Spinoza even accepted certain elements of traditional beliefs, which were not a direct and logical consequence of his thought.[10] In sum, both the skeptic of the 3rd century B. C. E. and the heretic of the 17th century C. E. retained not only the language and the modes of expression characteristic of their traditional upbringing, but part of its thought-content as well.

Another striking instance of the unconventional use of traditional vocabulary is afforded by Goethe's *Faust*. In lines 328 f. the poet writes:

> Ein guter Mensch in seinem dunklen Drange
> Ist sich des rechten Weges wohl bewusst.

Literally rendered, the passage reads: "A good man in his vague striving is quite conscious of the right way." Yet as all commentators on the passage have recognized, *ein guter Mensch* and *des rechten Weges* are used not in their ordinary moral sense, but in a Goethean sense as "one who has ideals and seeks to realize them, or in other words, possesses that 'good will' which Goethe calls 'the foundation of right conduct.' "[11]

In the ancient world of Koheleth, the world-view of traditional religion was, of course, infinitely more pervasive and compelling than in Spinoza's or Goethe's time. Hence Koheleth could not dispense with such conventional religious and ethical terms as "sinner," "fool," "good (before God)," "the gift of God," "God's favor, gift or will." Nor was it merely a matter of terminology. His entire world-view found expression within this same frame-work.

A few instances of this tendency may be cited. Traditional morality declared that he who fulfilled God's will would be happy. Koheleth declares that he who is happy is fulfilling God's will:

> Indeed, every man to whom God has given wealth and possessions and granted the power to enjoy them, taking his share and rejoicing in his labor, that is the gift of God . . . for it is God who provides the joy in a man's heart. (5:18 f.)

The conventional Wisdom teachers call the sinner a fool. So does Koheleth, but he reserves the right to define his terms. A sinner is he who fails to work for the advancement of his own happiness. The Book of *Proverbs* promises that the righteous will ultimately inherit the wealth of the evildoer:

> He who increases his wealth by usury and interest is gathering it for him who befriends the poor. (Pr. 28:8)

Koheleth promises the same to the man who is "pleasing to God," the man who obeys God's will, and seeks to achieve joy:

> To the man God favors, He gives wisdom, knowledge and joy, but to the sinner, He assigns the task of gathering and amassing, only to hand it over at last to the man who is pleasing to God. (2:26).

The Prophets, with unfailing insistence, call upon the people to hear the word of God. So does Koheleth. He, too, calls upon his reader to remember God and His purpose for man, before old age sets in and the time for joy is past:

> Remember your Creator in the days of your youth,
> Before the evil days come and the years draw near,
> Of which you will say, "I have no pleasure in them." (12:1)

This clothing of the hedonistic principle in religious guise is not without analogy in Hebrew literature. The book of *Proverbs* counsels:

> Hear, my son, and be wise,
> And walk in the ways of your heart.   (23:19)

Ben Sira, whose general moral system is conventional, makes' the enjoyment of life a duty:

> My son, if you have the means, treat yourself well,
> For there is no pleasure in the grave,
> And there is no postponement of death.   (14:11)

The same theme is stressed elsewhere in his book (14:15–19; 30:21–23). Even more striking are the words of the Babylonian sage, Samuel, of the 3rd century, cited in the Talmud:

> Seize hold and eat, seize hold and drink, for this world whence we depart is like a wedding feast.   (B. Erub. 54a)

Samuel's great contemporary, Rab, expresses the same sentiment in typically religious language:

> Every man must render an account before God of all the good things he beheld in life and did not enjoy.
>   (Jerusalem Talmud, *Kiddushin*, end)

No more perfect analogy could be found to Koheleth's words:

> Rejoice, young man, in your youth,
> And let your heart cheer you in your youthful days.
> Follow the impulses of your heart
> And the desires of your eyes,
> And know that for all this,
> God will call you to account.   (11:9)

The resemblance of language is striking. The Rabbi uses the traditional term *din vᵉḥešbōn* (lit. "judgment and reckoning"), Koheleth, the Biblical word *mišpāṭ* (lit. "judgment"). Similarly, when Koheleth says, "Go, then, eat your bread with joy and drink your wine with a glad heart, for God has already approved your actions" (9:7), he is expressing his philosophy

of life in a religious vocabulary congenial both to his own temper
and to the spirit of his age. Koheleth's insistence that man's
failure to enjoy life's blessings is a sin in the eyes of God has its
parallel in the Talmudic discussion on the Nazir, the ascetic in
Biblical times who took a vow to abstain from wine and to let
his hair grow long. In explaining the Biblical provision which
enjoined him to bring a sin-offering at the close of his Nazirate
period (Num. 6:14), the Talmud declares: "Whoever deprives
himself of wine is called 'a sinner,' " adding a further generalization, "If the Nazir, who deprived himself only of wine, is called
'a sinner,' how much more so he who deprives himself of every
blessing!"[12]

The same attitude of opposition to asceticism is reflected in
the deeply moving story attributed to Koheleth's contemporary,
the High Priest Simon the Just, who never ate the "guilt-offering"
of a Nazir who had been defiled, except in one special instance.
This was the case of a handsome, curly-headed youth who,
feeling that he was in danger of falling into sin because of his
own beauty, became a Nazir and dedicated his locks to God.[13]
Talmudic Judaism was all but universally opposed to the
institution of the Nazir because of its own wholehearted acceptance of life's blessings.[14] Koheleth's insistence upon the enjoyment
of life flowed from a tragic realization of the brevity of life,
rather than from an optimistic joy in a world governed by a
good God, as taught by the Rabbis. But his stylistic usage is
illumined by theirs.[15]

Moreover, Koheleth's highly personal use of conventional
religious terminology rests upon a solid foundation in Biblical
Hebrew. The key word is ḥāṭā', which originally meant "miss
(the goal or way), go wrong,"[16] as the Semitic cognates clearly
indicate.[17] This non-moral meaning of the root ḥāṭā', "miss,"
it is interesting to note, is preserved primarily in Wisdom
literature.[18] The more frequent meaning "sinner" is a secondary
development from "miss the path of duty, or of God, hence, sin."
Finally, in accordance with a widespread semantic process, the
nouns ḥēṭ', ḥaṭṭ'āth, "sin," develop the connotation of "the
consequence of sin," hence "punishment."[19]

In Koheleth, ḥōṭē' in its common sense of "sinner" does

occur, but in each instance its meaning is made clear by the juxtaposition of *rāshā'*, "wicked," or *ṣaddīḳ*, "righteous" (7:20; 8:12; 9:2). The meaning "punishment" occurs verbally in 5:5.[20] Its earlier but rarer meaning occurs in 9:18, where it is synonymous with "fool."[21] Two more passages remain, 2:26 and 7:26, which have been widely regarded as pious interpolations, because in them Koheleth foretells suffering to the "sinner." It is significant, however, that in both these passages the *ḥōṭē'* is contrasted, not with *ṣaddīḳ*, but with a characteristic term of his own, *tōbh liphᵉnei hā'elōhīm*, literally, "he who is good before God." Actually *ḥōṭē'* in these passages is used both in its non-moral sense of "fool, one who misses the right path," and in its religious connotation of "sinner," as Koheleth understands it, the man who violates God's will by failing to enjoy the blessings of God's world, as in the Talmudic parallels adduced above.

On the other hand, other words, which from their origin lack the purely intellectual non-ethical meaning which inheres in the root *ḥāṭā'*, are used by Koheleth exclusively in their conventional moral meanings. This is true of *rāshā'*, "wicked;"[22] *resha'*, "evil doing;"[23] and *ṣaddīḳ*, "righteous."[24]

Closely similar to Koheleth's use of *ḥāṭā* in terms of his own world-view is his employment of the traditional idiom *yārē' elōhīm*, "fearing God," which is frequent elsewhere in the Bible in the connotation of observing the moral law as the will of God.[25] The phrase occurs in the book of Koheleth four times.[26] The last of these is in the Epilogue, which does not emanate from our author, and so it is used here in the conventional sense. In 8:12, which is a quotation or a restatement of a conventional utterance, Koheleth uses it in its accepted meaning, and makes his meaning clear by using it in direct contrast with *rāshā'* in the next verse. In the two remaining passages, 5:6 and 7:18, Koheleth uses the idiom in perfect consistency with his viewpoint — "he who fears God" is he who obeys God's will by avoiding foolish actions and their consequent penalty.

An understanding of Koheleth's unique vocabulary is an essential key to the book and its message.

XII. THE STYLE—HIS USE OF QUOTATIONS

The second important characteristic of Koheleth's style, which has not been adequately noted in the past, with disastrous results for our understanding of the book, is his use of proverbial quotations. Sumerian, Egyptian and Akkadian literature, like the Bible and the Talmud, affords an impressive array of examples of quotations cited by writers for a variety of purposes.[1] These quotations have been generally overlooked or misunderstood because they are cited without any introductory formula indicating their true relationship to the literary document in which they are imbedded; that no such device as quotation marks was available to the ancient writers is self-evident. To complicate matters still further, their uses fall into no less than ten categories,[2] which are, however, related developments of the same basic technique. That any given passage is indeed a quotation must be understood by the reader, who is called upon in Semitic literature to supply not only punctuation but vocalization as well.

This widespread use of quotations is entirely comprehensible in the ancient world, in which the tradition of the past was omnipresent and age and wisdom were regarded as synonymous. Hence quotations are to be met with even in the Prophets, in spite of the fact that prophetic inspiration is essentially a unique and personal quality, the product of direct ecstatic communion with God. Though the prophet's message is not the result of study and argument, and needs no logical demonstration, for it bears its inner assurance of truth in the conviction that "thus saith the Lord," he, too, is conscious of the traditions of his predecessors.

It is, however, in Wisdom literature that quotations play the most fundamental role. Here there is no supernatural revelation, merely patient observation used as the basis of reasonable

conclusions. Each generation of Sages finds in the extant proverbial literature of the past a body of truth, created by their
predecessors, whose observations on life have approved themselves to their colleagues.

In particular, the unconventional Wisdom writers, to whose
ranks Koheleth belonged, would have occasion to use this literary
device, since their ideas were an outgrowth of the accepted
doctrine of the schools and their careers continued to be closely
associated with practical Wisdom. It must constantly be kept
in mind that the relationship of these unconventional Wise Men
to the culture of their day was essentially complex. Within
their world-view were elements of the completely conventional,
the modified old, and the radically new. They doubtless accepted
many aspects of the practical Wisdom as expounded in the
schools where they were educated and in which they themselves
taught. As teachers of Wisdom they would have occasion to
quote conventional proverbs or compose original sayings of their
own, which were not different in form or spirit from those of
their more traditionally minded colleagues. Especially in the
realm of practical affairs, their standpoint would resemble that
of the schools. In other areas of thought, there would be ideas
that they could accept in modified form, while still others they
would oppose entirely. These might be cited, as in *Koheleth*, in
order to serve as the text for an ironic or negating comment, or
they might occur as in *Job*, where the speaker cites the words
and sentiments of his opponents in order to demolish them, or
quotes the utterances of the Lord in order to submit to Him.[3]

Before the evidence for this usage in Koheleth is set forth,
several points should be made clear. The term "quotations,"
as used here, refers to *words which do not reflect the present sentiments of the author of the literary composition in which they are
found, but have been introduced by the author to convey the standpoint of another person or situation.* These quotations include,
but are not limited to, citations of previously existing literature,
whether written or oral. In sum, the term refers to passages
that cite the speech or thought of a subject, actual or hypothetical, past or present, which is distinct from the context in which
it is embodied.

The abundance of material not only demonstrates the validity of the usage postulated for the Bible, but sheds welcome light on the variety of techniques employed. Of the ten categories of quotations noted, several do not appear in Koheleth and therefore need not be discussed here.

As a point of departure for this usage, Ecc. 4:8 may be cited: יש אחד ואין שני גם בן ואח אין לו ואין קץ לכל עמלו גם עינו לא תשבע עשר ולמי אני עמל ומחסר את נפשי מטובה גם זה הבל וענין רע הוא. It is obvious that the words ולמי אני עמל ומחסר את נפשי מטובה are not the words of the author, but rather a citation of a hypothetical speech and thought, an idea that *might or should have* occurred to the subject. Needless to add, a *verbum dicendi* (or quotation marks) must be supplied, and, what is more, the verb must be made to reflect the required mood:

> Here is a man alone, with no one besides him, neither son nor brother. Yet there is no end to his toil, nor is his eye ever satisfied with his wealth. *He never asks himself*, "For whom am I laboring and depriving myself of joy?" Yes, it is vanity, a bad business.

In interpreting the passage in Song of Songs 1:7 f., it has been very plausibly suggested that the second verse is a hypothetical quotation. If the beloved is forced to ask after the whereabouts of her lover, the other shepherds will try to persuade her to forget him.

הגידה לי שאהבה נפשי   איכה תרעה איכה תרביץ בצהרים
שלמה אהיה כעטיה על עדרי חבריך:
אם לא תדעי לך היפה בנשים
צאי לך בעקבי הצאן   ורעי את גדיתיך על משכנות הרעים:

Tell me, O you whom I love,
Where do you feed and rest your flock at noon?
Why should I be a wanderer (?)
Among the flocks of your friends,
Who would mock me and say, if I asked about you:
"If you do not know, fairest among women,
Go forth in the tracks of the flocks
And feed your kids near the shepherds' tents."

A similar view has been proposed for Job 22:4 f., the second verse being regarded as a hypothetical formulation by Eliphaz of the reproof God could address to man, were He minded to do so:

המיראתך יכיחך   יבוא עמך במשפט:

הלא רעתך רבה   ואין־קץ לעונתיך

> Will God reprove you because of your piety,
> Enter into argument with you,
> *For God could say to man:*
> "Indeed your evil is great,
> And there is no end to your sins!"

The identical usage is often to be met with in Rabbinic literature, particularly in legal argumentation, where hypothetical considerations are frequently invoked:

Keth. 13: 3 בנכסים מועטים הבנות יזונו והבנים יחזרו על הפתחים אמר

אדמון מפני שאני זכר הפסדתי.

When an inheritance is small, the daughters are to be supported and the sons are to go begging from door to door. Admon says, *A son might argue under these circumstances,* "Shall *I* suffer because I am a male?"

Baba Metzia 35a ונהמניה לוה למלוה נמי בהא כמה היה שוה לא קים

ליה בנויה.

Let the borrower believe the lender on this point too, as to what the pledged object is worth. "No," *the borrower could say,* "*The lender is an honorable man,* but he is not familiar with its true value."[4]

Passages such as these are not, however, quotations in the usual sense of the term, that is to say, these passages did not have an independent literary existence before they appeared in their present context.

Quotations of the more usual form are also frequent in Koheleth, who would have occasion to utilize brief, pithy and widely familiar proverbs. This trait is undoubtedly the result of his background and occupation as a Wisdom teacher. His

speculations on life did not lead him to abandon his interest in
the mundane concerns of the lower Wisdom; he merely went
beyond them. As he continued to teach the practical Wisdom
to his pupils, he doubtless contributed to its literature, most
of which was couched in short, pithy maxims of a realistic turn.
Hence, maxims similar in both form and spirit to those in the
Book of *Proverbs* are common in *Koheleth*. These are not interpolations by more conventional readers, as had been assumed.
They belong, as MacDonald has well noted, to the author's
method of keeping connection with the past, while leaving it
behind.

Koheleth's quotations of proverbs vary in method and purpose. The several categories, which constitute one of the most
characteristic marks of his style, must now be described. In
each case, parallels in Biblical and extra-Biblical sources will
be cited in the notes.

I. *The straightforward use of proverbial quotations*, cited to buttress an argument and therefore requiring no expansion or comment, because the writer accepts them as true.[5]

How citations of this kind blend with the author's own words
is illustrated in B. Erub. 54a, where Ben Sira 14:11–12 is cited,
again without any external mark:

בני אם יש לך היטיב לך שאין בשאול תענוג ולא למות התמהמה ואם תאמר
אניח לבני חוק מי יניד לך בני אדם דומין לעשבי השדה הללו נוצצין
והללו נובלין.

While there is no formal indication, Rab begins this counsel
to Rab Hamnuna with a quotation from *Ben Sira* to which he
appends his own comments:

"My son, if you have the wherewithal,
Do good to yourself,
For there is no pleasure in the grave,
And no postponement of death."
And if you say, Let me leave a portion for my son,
Who can tell you in the grave (what will happen to it)?
Men are like the grass of the field,
Some sprout and others decay.

The stichs in quotation marks are cited from Ben Sira 14:11–12; the remainder is Rab's own, except for the last stich, which is a free paraphrase of Ben Sira 14:18b.

This straightforward use of quotations is common in Koheleth. Even the most unconventional thinker will recognize the value of practical counsel, such as is given in the Book of *Proverbs*. The most confirmed cynic will agree that

> Through sloth the ceiling sinks,
> And through slack hands the house leaks.
>
> (Ecc. 10:18)

Or he will suggest that it is wise to diversify one's undertakings:

> Send your bread upon the waters,
> So that you may find it again after many days.
>
> (Ecc. 11:1)

Exactly as in any other Wisdom book, like Proverbs and Ben Sira, the notebook of Koheleth registers these and others of a conventional mould. That these are generally excised by modern scholars like Siegfried, McNeile, Haupt and Barton, though with no unanimity, is due to a rigid view of his personality, which declares that if Koheleth be unconventional, he must be an iconoclast throughout, perpetually at war with conventional ideas.

Whether Koheleth is quoting proverbs already extant, or composing them himself, is difficult to determine. Thus in his learned and stimulating work, *The Proverb*,[6] Archer Taylor observes: "We shall never know, for example, which of the Exeter Gnomes in Old English poetry are proverbial and which are the collector's moralizing in the same pattern . . . . In a dead language the means which are available are various, but not always effective or easily applied. A passage, when it varies grammatically or syntactically from ordinary usage or from the usage of the context, can be safely declared to be proverbial." He also cites countless examples of the difficulty in distinguishing folk sayings and the work of individuals,[7] and he remarks: "Of course an individual creates a proverb and sets it in circulation. The inventor's title to his property may be recognized by all

who use it or his title may be so obscured by the passage of time
that only investigation will determine the source of the saying."
Especially pertinent is his statement: "Biblical proverbs, and
among them perhaps even those which we have discussed, may
have been proverbs before their incorporation into Holy Writ."[8]

Particularly congenial to the pessimism of Koheleth would
be a statement like 7:3, which he inserts in his notebook:

> "Sorrow is better than joy, for through sadness of counte-
> nance the understanding improves."

II. At times, Koheleth appears to buttress his argument with
*a proverb, part of which is apposite, while the rest of the saying,
though irrelevant, is quoted for the sake of completeness*, a literary
practice common to writers in all ages. The use of quotation
marks will serve to make the matter clear.

אל תבהל על פיך ולבך אל ימהר להוציא דבר לפני האלהים כי האלהים
בשמים ואתה על הארץ על כן יהיו דבריך מעטים: כי בא החלום ברב
ענין וקול כסיל ברב דברים:

Do not hasten to speak, nor let yourself be rushed into
uttering words before God; for God is in heaven and you
are on earth — therefore let your words be few. For "as
dreams come with many concerns, so the fool speaks with
many words." (5:1–2)

The same usage occurs in Egyptian literature. In the
Admonitions of a Prophet, which probably emanates from the
end of the second millennium, we have a graphic description
of the widespread destruction sweeping over the social order,
with the lowly attaining to wealth and importance. In the
"Second Poem," each stanza begins with the refrain, "Behold,"
a characteristic rhetorical device. Part of this section reads as
follows:

> Behold, he that had no bread now possesseth a barn; (but)
> that wherewith his storehouse is provided is the poverty
> of another.
> Behold, the bald head that used no oil now possesseth jars
> of pleasant myrrh.

Behold, she that had no box now possesseth a coffer.
She that looked at her face in the water now possesseth
a mirror.

(A verse left incomplete.)
Behold, a man is happy when he eateth his food:

"Spend thy possessions in joy and without holding thee
back! It is good for a man to eat his food, which
God assigneth to him whom he praiseth. . . ."

The last two sentences, as Erman notes, are "a quotation
from an old book."[9] They have been introduced to buttress
the argument. Actually they are not altogether appropriate.
For while the author is describing the lot of a man formerly
poor, who is now happy to have something to eat, the proverb
urges the enjoyment of life. But the use of quotations only
partly relevant to the context is usual with writers everywhere.

As Taylor has indicated, only where a characteristic fillip
of style occurs is it possible to determine whether the proverb
is a quotation or indubitably original.

Thus 11:4 seems a typical quotation, but all the earmarks
of Koheleth's personality are to be seen in the ironic comment
that precedes it (v. 3). His thought seems to be that the events
of nature will take place without man's assistance, and that
there is therefore no justification for idle gazing:

If the clouds are filled with rain, they will empty it upon
the earth; if a tree is blown down by the wind in the south
or in the north, wherever it falls, there it lies. Therefore
on with your work, for he who watches the wind will never
sow and he who gapes at the clouds will never reap.

(Ecc. 11:3–4)

Incidentally, the unity and integrity of the passage seem
clear from its chiastic structure, for 3a and 4b deal with cloud
and rain, while 3b and 4a are concerned with the wind uprooting
a tree.

Other examples of the straightforward use of proverbs in

Ecclesiastes are to be found in the collection 10:2 to 11:6, all of which may be original epigrams of Koheleth.

III. Particularly characteristic of Koheleth is *the use of proverbial quotations as a text*, on which he comments from his own viewpoint. While the Commentary should be consulted for a full discussion of all such passages, a few instances may be adduced here.

Ecc. 7:1–14 is a collection of seven Hokmah utterances, expressing conventional Wisdom teachings and linked together by the opening word *tōbh*.[10] Each proverb is amplified by a comment bearing all the earmarks of Koheleth's style and viewpoint. Thus a typically abstemious and moralizing doctrine is sounded in Ecc. 7:2a:

> Better to go to a house of mourning
> than to go to a banquet hall . . . .

a proverb, warning against the revelry and immorality of the house of mirth.[11] But Koheleth gives it a darker undertone:

> For that is the end of all men,
> And the living may take the lesson to heart. (Ecc. 7:2b)

Examples of this use of proverb as text with ironic comment are plentiful. Thus a proverb extols the virtues of cooperation. Koheleth approves the sentiment, but for reasons of his own:

> Men say, "Two are better than one, because they have a reward in their labor." True, for if either falls, the other can lift his comrade, but woe to him who is alone when he falls, with no one else to lift him. Then also, if two sleep together, they will be warm, but how can one alone keep warm? Moreover, if some enemy attack either one, the two will stand against him, while a triple cord cannot quickly be severed. (Ecc. 4:9–12)[12]

The teachers of morality emphasized that love of money does not make for happiness. This idea is expanded by Koheleth through the characteristic reflection that strangers finally consume the substance of the owner, an idea to which he refers again and again (cf. 2:18 ff.; 4:7 ff.):

"He who loves money will never have enough of it and he who loves wealth will never attain it"[13] — this is indeed vanity. For as wealth increases, so do those who would spend it, hence what value is there in the owner's superior ability, except that he has more to look upon?   (Ecc. 5:9 f.)

The Book of Proverbs counsels submission to political authority:

Fear, my son, God and king, and meddle not with those who seek change.   (Pr. 24:21)

Koheleth repeats this idea, but with his tongue in his cheek:

I say: keep the king's command, because of the oath of loyalty,

submit to the king because of your oath of fealty, but also, he adds as an afterthought:

Since the king's word is law, who can say to him, "What are you doing?"   (Ecc. 8:2-4) —

because the king is powerful enough to crush you.

Similarly, to maintain oneself in an atmosphere of political tyranny and intrigue requires skill in choosing the proper occasion. That idea Koheleth appends as a comment to a perfectly moral utterance about the virtue of obedience:

"Whoever keeps his command will experience no trouble," for a wise mind will know the proper time and procedure. For everything has its proper time and procedure, man's evil being so widespread.   (Ecc. 8:5 f.)

In addition to these examples, which mirror the political conditions of Koheleth's time, we find several interesting instances of his use of conventional *Hokmah* material in the field of religious and philosophic speculation.

For example, Koheleth is not disposed to deny altogether that retribution overtakes the sinner. But, he insists, this takes place only after a long delay, which affords the wrongdoer the opportunity and the incentive to sin.

These two limitations on Divine justice are referred to in an interesting passage, 8:11–14, the center of which (vv. 12b, 13) is a quotation of the traditional view, from which Koheleth dissents:[14]

> Because judgment upon an evil deed is not executed speedily, men's hearts are encouraged to do wrong, for a sinner commits a hundred crimes and God is patient with him, though I know the answer that "it will be well in the end with those who revere God and fear Him and it will be far from well with the sinner, who, like a shadow, will not long endure, because he does not fear God."

> Here is a vanity that takes place on the earth — there are righteous men who receive the recompense due the wicked, and wicked men who receive the recompense due the righteous. I say, this is indeed vanity.

Koheleth would undoubtedly agree with the common view that life on any terms is preferable to death. Yet his general intellectual conviction as to the futility of living impels him to a comment, which ostensibly justifies, but actually undermines, the entire proposition:

> "He who is attached to the living still has hope, for a live dog is better than a dead lion!" The living know at least that they will die, but the dead know nothing, nor have they any reward, for their memory is forgotten. Their loves, their hates, their jealousies, all have perished — never again will they have a share in all that is done under the sun.
>   (Ecc. 9:4–6)

This usage of a quotation cited by the author and then refuted, or at least discussed, occurs several times in the Babylonian *Complaint on the Injustice of the World*, the so-called "Babylonian Koheleth."[15] Thus the author explicitly cites two conventional proverbs on the well-being of the righteous, which he does not accept, as the succeeding comment indicates (ll. 69–71):

A saying I wish to discuss with you:

"They go on the road to fortune, who do not think of
    murder."
"More than a mere creature is the weak one who prays
    to God."
More than any other child of man, have I been troubled
    about God's plan.

Another quotation without an introductory formula occurs
in ll. 215 ff. The poet laments the prosperity and success of
the wicked. He then cites the conventional proverbs which
urge obedience to the god as the secret of well-being, but he
then refutes them by emphasizing the unpredictability and
transitoriness of God's favor:

Without God, the rogue possesses wealth,
For murder as his weapon accompanies him.
"You who do not seek the counsel of the God, what is your
    fortune?"
"He who bears the yoke of God, his bread is provided!"
No, seek rather a good wind of the gods.
What you have destroyed in a year, you restore in an
    instant,
Among men I have set offerings, changeable are the
    omens.

The lines in quotation marks are not indicated externally as
such, but are evidently citations of accepted ideas, with which
the melancholy poet is in disagreement. That lines 217 f. constitute a quotation is recognized by Ebeling, who adds the comment, "So sagen die Leute," the precise formula required in all
the instances cited above.

That Sumerian Wisdom literature, still awaiting investigation, will disclose a similar use of proverbs as quotations
has been affirmed by a leading Sumerologist.[16]

This literary technique has persisted from the dawn of civilization in Egypt and Mesopotamia through ancient Palestine
down to modern America. We encounter it in the work of a
contemporary poet, who uses a quotation, usually associated

with a sentimental context, and follows it up with a blunt comment of his own.[17]

IV. *Contrasting proverbs* offer another way of contravening accepted doctrines. As is well known, proverbs frequently contradict one another, since they express the half-truths of empirical wisdom. "Fools rush in where angels fear to tread" is opposed by the saw, "He who hesitates is lost." The beautiful sentiment, "Absence makes the heart grow fonder," is bluntly denied by the saying, "Out of sight, out of mind."

The compiler of *Proverbs* was aware of this tendency when he quoted these two maxims in succession:

> Answer not a fool according to his folly, lest thou also be
>   like unto him.
> Answer a fool according to his folly, lest he be wise in his
>   own eyes.   (Pr. 26:4–5)

Both *Job* and *Koheleth* use the same device, but for their own purposes. They quote one proverb and then register their disagreement by citing another diametrically opposed thereto.[18]

No theme was dearer to the hearts of the instructors of youth than that of the importance of hard work.[19] Koheleth expresses his doubts on the subject by quoting the conventional view and following it with another proverb of opposite intent:

> "The fool folds his hands and thus destroys himself."
> "Better is a handful acquired with ease, than two hands full
>   gained through toil and chasing after wind."   (Ecc. 4:5, 6)

That Koheleth favors the second view is proved by its position as a refutation after v. 5, by the characteristic phrase "vanity and chasing after wind," and by his oft-repeated view of the folly of toil in a meaningless world.[20]

Like all the Wise Men, conventional or otherwise, Koheleth has a prejudice in favor of wisdom as against folly. He himself tells how the wisdom of one poor man proved more efficacious than a mighty army. Yet he knows, too, how little wisdom is honored for its own sake, and how one fool can destroy the efforts of many wise men. These ideas seem to be expressed in some reflections, consisting of brief proverbs contradicted by others:

> "Wisdom is better than strength" but "the poor man's wisdom is despised and his words go unheeded."
>
> "Wisdom is better than weapons," but "one fool can destroy much good."   (Ecc. 9:16, 18)

Here, the latter proverbs, in which Koheleth expresses his own standpoint, are undoubtedly of his own composition. The former proverbs, from which he dissents, may be quotations, or, as seems more probable, original restatements by Koheleth of conventional *Hokmah* doctrines.

Koheleth's *unconventional use of a religious vocabulary* and his frequent *citation of proverbial lore* for his own special purposes are among the most unique elements of his style. Other stylistic features may be noticed more briefly.

XIII. OTHER STYLISTIC FEATURES

As a teacher of Wisdom, Koheleth naturally uses many of the literary forms characteristic of *Hokmah*.[1] The varied use of proverbs has already been discussed. Many of his comments are in the second person.[2] These *"Thou" passages* are not necessarily addressed to a special pupil,[3] but are rather part of the Wisdom style, which was basically pedagogic in origin. Even more common in a book of reflection are the *"I-passages"*[4] which also have their origin in the lectures of the master before his pupils.[5] That Koheleth has generalized these pedagogic forms and has a reader rather than a pupil in mind is clear from the fact that the usage *b^eni*, "my son," which is common in Proverbs,[6] does not occur in his writings.[7]

Two extended *proverb collections* occur in Koheleth (7:1–25 and 10:2 to 11:6). The material in the second collection, like the book of *Proverbs*, consists of separate maxims having little unity of thought, except that they deal largely with the virtues making for success. The first collection, on the other hand, is linked together in typically Semitic fashion.[8] It consists of seven utterances, each of which begins with *tōbh*, "good." That both these collections are authentically Koheleth's is clear from the characteristic commentary he adds to many of the sentiments expressed.[9]

Other stylistic features in Koheleth have their origin in the *parallelism* characteristic of Biblical verse. The usual types of parallelism, synonymous, antithetic and complementary, which occur in the book, do not call for special comment; only a few rarer verse-patterns should be noted. These usages are not merely matters of variation in form, such as a poet might employ, but rather modes of logical expression. Thus Biblical prosody includes chiastic parallelism, in which four stichs are arranged so that *a* is parallel to *d*, and *b* to *c*.[10] This structure occurs in Koheleth several times, with c giving the reason for b and d for a.[11]

Another usage in Biblical parallelism is "alternate structure," with stich a parallel to c, and b to d.[12] These usages are not limited to poetry. They occur even in legal sections of the Pentateuch.[13] Koheleth also uses this alternate structure, with c giving the reason for a, and d for b.[14]

The Masorah divides the book into four sections[15] which manifestly do not adequately represent the variety of themes in the book. Even the medieval division of the book into 12 chapters does not generally coincide with the thought-sequences into which the book falls.[16]

The true dimensions of each section in Koheleth must be discovered by an intensive study of the contents. Our own research divides the book into eighteen sections, aside from the Epilogue.[17] Whatever Koheleth's subject, be it wisdom, wealth or corruption, the end of a section in the book can often be told by his returning to one of his basic themes — *the tragedy of man's ignorance of ultimate truth*[18] and, consequently, *the vanity of all his efforts*,[19] and *his God-given duty to achieve happiness*.[20] Since these ideas are organically related, the discussion closes at times with a combination of two of these fundamental attitudes.[21] Uniquely passionate is Section IV, in which Koheleth speaks with unwonted bitterness of the injustice prevalent in the world, which makes life itself seem hateful.[22]

From all that has been said, it is clear that the Book of Koheleth is not a debate, a dialogue, or a philosophical treatise. It is best described as a *cahier* or notebook, into which the author jotted down his reflections during the enforced leisure of old age. They differ in mood, in style, and in length. Hence there is no logical progression of thought to be found in the book, and efforts to find it lead to a far-fetched exegesis.[23] Nor can the book be regarded as concerned with a single topic.[24] Its unity is not one of logical progression, but of mood and world-view. Like so much of Jewish literature, it is organic, not syllogistic in structure.[25]

Koheleth's medium is basically prose,[26] with an admixture

of passages in verse.[27] Proverbs and apothegms are naturally couched in the rhythmic parallelism characteristic of gnomic literature.[28] When Koheleth grows impassioned, he develops a subtle inner rhythm, as in the majestic opening section of Chapter 1. This rhythmic prose may go over into a regular metric line, which then, quite as naturally, may revert to prose.[29] This usage meets us in the Hebrew Prophets and Egyptian Wisdom literature as well.[30]

In the unforgettable "Allegory of Old Age" (11:7 to 12:8), which is the climax and conclusion of the book, the beat is very pronounced, so that it may fairly be described as formal poetry. That the book opens and closes with rhythmic sections and these the most eloquent in the book, is scarcely accidental, especially in view of the fact that the theme "vanity of vanities, all is vanity" occurs at the beginning and the end (1:2; 12:8). It indicates that Koheleth's notebook was more than a random collection and that Koheleth himself is responsible for the organization of the material. Its informality of tone and casualness of utterance are far from being accidental achievements, easily attained. On the contrary, as every creative writer can attest, knowing how to conceal the scaffolding in the beauty of the structure is a mark of the highest art.

XIV. KOHELETH AND MODERN EXISTENTIALISM

In recent years it has been suggested that there are important affinities between Biblical Wisdom and modern existentialism. Some writers have gone further and maintained that the authors of *Job* and *Koheleth* are actually precursors of existentialism. These comparisons are relatively easy to make and correspondingly difficult to evaluate because "existentialism" represents a wide spectrum of differing and even contradictory viewpoints.

Thus, one of the most perceptive students of existentialism writes, "Existentialism is not a philosophy but a label for several widely different revolts against traditional philosophy. Most of the living 'existentialists' have repudiated this label, and a bewildered outsider might well conclude that the only thing they have in common is a marked aversion for each other. To add to the confusion, many writers of the past have frequently been hailed as members of this movement, and it is extremely doubtful whether they would have appreciated the company to which they are consigned. In view of this, it might be argued that the label 'existentialism' ought to be abandoned altogether."[1]

Another authoritative statement on the movement also recognizes "the varying and conflicting thought of important existentialists like Sören Kierkegaard, Karl Jaspers, Martin Heidegger, Gabriel Marcel and Jean-Paul Sartre," and finds the nexus of the movement in its being "centered on the individual and its relationship to the universe or to God."[2] Even this generalization, however, is too broad, in view of the fact that many, if not most of the influential exponents of existentialism have been atheists or agnostics. Even those who accept some concept of God, like Paul Tillich, often have little in common with traditional theism and its attitude toward the universe as embodied in Judaism and Christianity.

Kaufmann declares that the heart of existentialism lies in "the refusal to belong to any school of thought, the repudiation of the adequacy of any body of beliefs whatever, and especially of systems, and a marked dissatisfaction with traditional philosophy as superficial, academic and remote from life."[3] With varying degrees of consistency and passion, the spokesmen for existentialism deny the validity of reason. Like Kierkegaard, they tend to echo Luther's famous dicta: "Whoever wants to be a Christian should tear the eyes out of his reason" and, "You must part with reason and not know anything of it and even kill it; else one will not get into the kingdom of heaven" and, "reason is a whore." In a striking phrase, Jaspers declares that "true philosophizing begins only after reason has suffered shipwreck."

For Sartre, who is, incidentally, the only self-declared existentialist among its major thinkers, the central idea of all existential thought is that existence precedes essence. There are no fixed elements in human nature or abiding ethical norms that can determine the decision the individual must make for himself at each moment of his existence.

From the varying formulations of existentialism extant, its essential features may be set forth as the distrust of reason and the placing of individual existence at the center of its world view. It is, however, not so much its doctrine—or its hostility to doctrine—that has made it influential today. Basically its impact derives from its preoccupation with failure, dread, and death. Hence, existentialism tends to approach life not in joyous anticipation but in "fear and trembling," which is, incidentally, the title of one of Kierkegaard's best-known works. In existentialism "individuality is not retouched, idealized, or holy; it is wretched and revolting, and yet, for all its misery, the highest good."[4]

It is obvious why existentialism appeals so powerfully to the modern temper. Our age has been marked by massive chaos and mass brutality unexampled in history. As a result, tremendous numbers of sensitive men and women have been persuaded of the meaninglessness of life and the lack of purpose in the universe. Existentialism offers a basis for abandoning all abstract theory, which seems to have been weighed in the scales of experience and found tragically wanting.

It would be misleading to say that the various manifestations of culture we call "modern" are all derivatives of existentialism. It would be more accurate to regard modern art, music, and literature as parallel reflections of the same "modern spirit" that nurtured existentialism. At least one factor in the development of the various schools of modern painting and sculpture has been the effort to depict the broken, misshapen character of existence, as modern men often encounter it. The atonality of modern music does not arise from a desire to shock the sensibilities of the traditional listener. Undoubtedly the creative desire to explore new, unheard dimensions of sound plays an important role. But avant-garde music in all its stages is also a reflection of the disordered and chaotic pattern of our urbanized, technological lives, disaster-ridden and death-laden.

In contemporary literature, the stream-of-consciousness technique is a direct consequence of psychoanalytic insights into the nature of man. In their works, modern novelists and dramatists express the conviction that the rational aspects of life are of little consequence by the side of the subconscious channels of feeling which rarely come to the surface. Such currently influential writers as Franz Kafka and Albert Camus stand four-square within this highly untraditional tradition. In drama, the "theater of the absurd" and the "theater of cruelty," as exemplified by such varied figures as Edward Albee, Harold Pinter, and Peter Weiss, reflect this feeling of the absence of significance in human life. Nevertheless, it is true that existentialism has had a more powerful impact on contemporary literature and drama than on music and art. This is largely due to the fact that some of the leading advocates of existentialism, like Jean-Paul Sartre, have not limited themselves to philosophic or anti-philosophic works, but have written novels and plays themselves.

As existentialism has gained in influence, a natural tendency has arisen to seek its forerunners. The great works of unconventional Biblical Wisdom, like *Job* and *Koheleth*, which found it impossible to accept on faith the teaching of traditional religion concerning God and man,[5] express a position that seems closely akin to that of existentialism. In *Job*, the suffering hero challenges the accepted doctrines of religion with regard to the purpose of life and the meaning of human suffering, not by juxtaposing a theory of his own but by confronting it with his own raw and bleeding experience.[6] Job has therefore seemed to many modern writers to be the "existential hero *par excellence.*" Koheleth, too, it is argued, refuses to go beyond the testimony of his own observation and experience and hence he rejects the conventional religious ideas of his day. The conclusion at which he arrives is therefore "vanity of vanities, all is vanity."[7]

It is often maintained in current treatments of the subject that both Koheleth and the existentialists see the world as absurd and incomprehensible, with nothing in life truly significant or worthwhile. As a result, it is argued, both Koheleth and the modern existentialists exhibit a feeling of psychological nausea or dread in the face of reality, a feeling of despair in the face of man's inevitable annihilation.

To question the validity of this comparison between *Job* and *Koheleth* on the one hand, and existentialism on the other, is not to belittle the significance of the movement, both in its own right and as a corrective to older tendencies characteristic of the classic schools of philosophy. Existentialism has made a valuable contribution in reminding men of the limitations of reason, for which too much was claimed on too little evidence. For in the past, philosophy in large measure was cultivated by thinkers who regarded themselves as rational but in truth were merely rationalists.

Another abiding value in existentialism has been its insistence that the heart of ethics—and of wisdom—lies not in the theoretical analysis of the good or in the passive contemplation of the eternal, but in making a concrete decision in each critical hour of existence. When existentialism came upon the scene, philosophy was pursued along one of two lines. The traditional philosophers were engaged in abstract theorizing and the formulation of lifeless systems of thought. Their positivist opponents, who rejected this approach, became immersed in the minutiae of linguistic analysis instead. As against both schools, existentialism has insisted that man must grapple with the abiding issues of human life with which classical philosophy at its greatest and Biblical thought at its deepest are concerned. It may be true that in its attack upon the "beautiful whore," reason, existentialism threw the baby out with the bath. Nonetheless, its contributions are very real and valuable.

It is, however, necessary to point out that there is a fundamental difference between existentialism and Biblical Wisdom, which is far more significant than any superficial similarity. It is true that Koheleth

is deeply pained by the realization that man cannot understand the
purpose of the universe, a theme to which he returns again and again.[8]
But because he is a Hebrew living within the Jewish tradition, a world
without God is impossible for him, because the existence of this world
testifies to its Creator. Hence Koheleth does not doubt for a moment
that there is such a purpose, known to God, though unknown to man:

> I know the concern which God has given men to be afflicted with.
> Everything He has made proper in its due time, and He has also
> placed the love of the world (*'olam*) in men's hearts, except that
> they may not discover the work God has done from beginning
> to end.[9]

No matter how the difficult word *'olam* is interpreted,[10] Koheleth
recognizes that everything in the world is *yapheh bᵉ 'itto* (lit. beautiful, proper in its time"). To be sure, the meaning of reality is veiled
from man, *but the meaning exists*. This conviction makes it possible
for Koheleth to constantly exhort his readers to enjoy the world, because its blessings are willed by God and granted by Him:

> Here is what I have discovered: it is meet and proper for a man
> to eat, drink and enjoy himself in return for the toil he undergoes
> under the sun in the scant years God has given him, for that is
> man's portion, and not long will he remember the days of his
> life. Indeed, every man to whom God has given wealth and pos-
> sessions and granted the power to enjoy them, taking his share and
> rejoicing in his labor, that is the gift of God, for it is God who
> provides him with the joy in his heart.[11]

Similarly, the author of *Job* is unable to accept the neat theories
regarding the problem of suffering expounded by the Friends as the
exponents of conventional religion. In the speeches of "The Lord Out
of the Whirlwind" (Job 38-41), the poet presents what he regards as
man's truest response to the problem of suffering—the realization that
man is not the center of the universe around which all else revolves,
but that, on the contrary, the universe in its entirety, and therefore its
purpose and meaning, are beyond man's grasp. This insight the poet
validates in magnificent nature poems that are more than paeans of
praise to nature.

Can Job comprehend, let alone govern, the universe that he weighs
and now finds wanting? Earth and sea, cloud and darkness and dawn,
sleet and hail, rain and thunder, snow and ice, and the stars above—all

these wonders are beyond Job. The lion and the mountain goat, the wild ass and the buffalo, the ostrich, the wild horse, and the hawk, all testify to the glory of God. Now these creatures glorified by the poet are not chosen at random. For all their variety they have one element in common: they are not under the sway of man, nor are they intended to serve his purpose. The implication is clear: the universe and its Creator cannot be judged solely from the vantage point of man, and surely not from the limited perspective of one human being.

The first speech of the Lord has glorified creatures that were not created for man's use, but nevertheless possess a beauty and grace that man can appreciate. The poet now goes a step further. The hippopotamus and the crocodile can lay no claim to beauty, but on the contrary, are physically repulsive and even dangerous to man. When the poet glorifies these beasts, he is calling upon us to rise completely above the anthropocentric point of view which, however natural for man, distorts his comprehension of the world. Precisely because they are unbeautiful by human standards, these monstrosities, fashioned by God's hand, are a revelation of the limitless range of God's creative thought. Since His ways are not man's ways, how can man's thoughts grasp God's thoughts—and, what is more, pass judgment upon Him?[12]

In these chapters the author of *Job* has not given us a catalogue of natural phenomena, but a vivid and joyous description that underscores one additional and basic truth: nature is not merely a mystery but also a miracle, a cosmos, a thing of beauty. From this flows the poet's basic conclusion: just as there is order and harmony in the natural world, though imperfectly grasped by man, so there is order and meaning in the moral sphere, though often incomprehensible to man. This, the heart and essence of the God-speeches, is made by implication, but nonetheless effectively.[13]

In sum, the Biblical Wisdom teachers find themselves unable to accept the easy answers offered by conventional religion to the perennial issues: the purpose of life, the meaning of suffering, the nature of death. With all their heart and soul the Biblical sages yearn to penetrate to the ultimate truth of reality. But that there *is* a purpose and meaning in the world they do not doubt for a moment. Hence the characteristic stigmata of existentialism are lacking in their writings. There is pain and passion, even resignation, before the Unknown and the Unknowable in *Job* and *Koheleth,* but no nausea or despair, no disgust or dread, no fear of failure. In a moment of bitterness or frustration Koheleth may say, "Therefore I hated life" (2:18), but it is not his dominant mood, which is an affirmation of life. In the depth of his misery, Job may picture his loneliness (19:13ff.), but he never succumbs to a sense of permanent alienation from mankind, whose sorrows he has made his own and in whose name he demands justice from God. The ultimate stance at which both writers arrive is positive acceptance, not permanent rebellion. Koheleth urges the enjoyment of life as the fulfillment of the Divine purpose in the world, to the degree to which that purpose is known to us. The author of *Job* exults in the beauty of the universe and therein finds an anodyne to suffering.

The medieval Jewish philosopher Moses Maimondes stood in the mainstream of Biblical Wisdom when he declared that "we cannot ask what is the purpose of the creation of God." In spite of apparent Biblical support for the idea, he denied that "the universe was created for the sake of man's existence that he might serve God."[14] On the contrary, Maimonides declared, "the universe does not exist for man's sake, but each being exists for its own sake, and not because of some other thing."[15] This idea is again expressed with philosophic deliberateness by Maimonides: "It is not unreasonable to assume that the works of God, their existence and preceding non-existence, are the result of His wisdom, but we are unable to understand many of the ways of His wisdom in His works."[16]

A modern scholar has given an excellent summary of Maimonides' view in these words: "Having affirmed design in the universe he is careful to assert that the character of the design remains unclear. It eludes human understanding. We may, in other words, render the position of Maimonides thus: the character of the universe is such that we cannot consider it the work of a blind force, operating without design or will. . . . But the principles of that rule, the ultimate nature of the design—the ultimate final cause of things—we do not know. But, added Maimonides, neither do the naturalists know the ultimate meaning of things."[17]

Justice Oliver Wendell Holmes, who was probably unfamiliar with Maimonides' views, expressed the same point of view when he declared, "We are all soldiers in a great campaign, the details of which are veiled from us. But it is enough for us to know there is a campaign." That he, too, was deeply influenced by Biblical Wisdom is clear from another passage in his writings, which not only quotes from *Koheleth* but epitomizes its essence: "The rule of joy and the law of duty seem to me all one. I confess that altruistic and cynically selfish talk seem to me about equally unreal. With all humility, I think 'whatsoever thy hand findeth to do, do it with thy might' infinitely more important than the vain attempt to love one's neighbor as oneself."[18]

The deep gulf separating Biblical Wisdom from modern existentialism becomes clear in the differing attitudes toward life which each school of thought engenders. Whether a man will approach existence with nausea or dread, or will face life with joy, depends in large measure on whether he regards the world as possessing no meaning, or believes that it does possess a meaning, though known only imperfectly to man. The quietism and the defeatism flowing out of the existentialist's confrontation of life undoubtedly require courage, but it is a courage born of desperation. It is poles apart from the courage of joyous acceptance derived from the Biblical sage's vision of the world.

This divergence in outlook between Biblical Wisdom and modern existentialism with regard to the meaning of life is of basic importance. It has its root in the Biblical faith in God which is superficially similar to the existentialist stance, but fundamentally different from it. As Harvey Cox has perceptively written:

> There have always been important similarities between biblical faith and atheism, as contrasted, for example, with belief in demons and spirits. But in our time this similarity has produced a rather novel heresy.... This curious phenomenon is made possible by the fact that the biblical doctrine of the hiddenness of God comports so very well, at one level at least, with contemporary atheism or, better, "nontheism." The two can easily be confused unless real care is used. Thus the hidden God or *deus absconditus* of biblical theology may be mistaken for the no-god-at-all of nontheism.
>
> This biblical God's hiddenness stands at the very center of the doctrine of God. It is so commanding that Pascal was echoing its intention when he said, "Every religion which does not affirm that God is hidden is not true." It means that God discloses himself at those places and in those ways he chooses and not as man would

want. And he always discloses himself as one who is at once different *from* man, unconditionally *for* man, and entirely unavailable for coercion and manipulation *by* man."[19]

In sum, Koheleth does not claim to have penetrated to the secret of the meaning of life. Nor, strictly speaking, does the author of *Job* offer a justification for suffering from man's point of view. But they have done far more. They have demonstrated that it is possible for men to bear the shafts of evil that threaten the human condition if they cultivate a sense of reverence for the mystery and miracle of life and strive to discover intimations of meaning in its beauty.

Like modern existentialism, Biblical Wisdom speaks to the modern mind because it rejects the unsubstantiated claims often advanced by conventional religion as well as the lifeless systems to be found in the accepted schools of philosophy. Both Wisdom and existentialism insist instead upon the irrefragable testimony of each man's experience here and now, as an indispensable instrument for understanding man's place in the universe.

But Biblical Wisdom offers modern man a *via tertia,* distinct both from the superficial and comfortable affirmations too often preached in the name of traditional religion and from the shattering negations of life and its meaning propounded by existentialism. Thornton Wilder concludes his haunting novel *The Eighth Day* with a paragraph that sets forth the options open to modern man in contemplating a world he never made:

> There is much talk of a design in the arras. Some are certain they see it. Some see what they have been told to see. Some remember that they saw it once but have lost it. Some are strengthened by seeing a pattern wherein the oppressed and exploited of the earth are gradually emerging from their bondage. Some find strength in the conviction that there is nothing to see. Some

The basic approach of existentialism is spelled out in the last choice given by Wilder: "Some find strength in the conviction that there is nothing to see." There is, however, one attitude missing from his list of options. Perhaps the author hints at it in his final, unfinished and unpunctuated sentence. It is the outlook of the Biblical Wisdom teachers who point the way to a world view that can sustain man's spirit without demanding the abdication of his mind. That man counts in this mysterious universe, that life has meaning and can be endowed with joy—even if the meaning is often veiled from man and the joy must be achieved in the face of frustration and pain—these convictions are possible for the Biblical sages, who look upon the world clear-eyed and unafraid and refuse to accept cant or convention. For they hold fast to the central faith of the Biblical world view: "In the beginning, God ..." Is there any better way for modern man?

XV. THE WORLD VIEW OF KOHELETH

I

The reconstruction of the precise stages in Koheleth's spiritual odyssey that we have proposed is confessedly an act of the imagination, rooted though it be in the facts before us. On the other hand, the conclusions at which he ultimately arrived are clear, for he set them forth in the book he left behind him. Personal experience or reflection, most probably both, had robbed him of the traditional Jewish faith in the triumph of justice in this world, preached by the Prophets, or in the redress of the balance in the hereafter, as affirmed by the forerunners of Pharisaic Judaism, who were his contemporaries. Moreover — and this was a deprivation he felt even more keenly — he had lost the assurance that man could fathom the meaning of life.

The modern reader might expect that Koheleth would be led by his views to deny the existence of God, but that was impossible to an ancient mind, and especially to a Jew. Even the Epicureans, who denied the gods' intervention in human affairs as a fundamental element of their outlook, did not deny their being. In the ancient world, atheism, the denial of God, referred to the view that the gods did not intervene in human affairs.[1] Koheleth, a son of Israel, reared on the words of the Torah, the Prophets and the Sages, could not doubt the reality of God for an instant. For him, the existence of the world was tantamount to the existence of God.

It was on the question of God's relation to men that Koheleth parted company with the conventional teachers of his time. For all the barrage of platitudes of the Wisdom teachers, there was not a shred of proof that God wished to reveal the true Hokmah, the secret of life, to men. Similarly, there was tragic evidence to contradict the confident assertion of the moralists:

> Say to the upright that it shall be well with him, for he shall eat the fruit of his doings. Woe to the wicked!

It shall be ill with him, for the reward of his hands shall be given him. (Isa. 3:10, 11)

The Psalmist had sung:

> I have been young, and now am old, yet I have never seen an upright man forsaken, and his offspring begging bread.
> (Ps. 37:25)

His words might be a prayer or a pious hope; they were scarcely the result of empirical observation!

With justice in human affairs an illusion, and truth unattainable, Koheleth is left with very little upon which to build. All that is certain is that man has an innate desire for happiness. Since God has created man, He has also created this impulse. It thus becomes clear that God's fundamental purpose for mankind is the furthering of man's pleasure.

We may put it another way: Koheleth's metaphysics postulates the existence of God, coupled with His creative power and limitless sovereignty. But beyond these attributes, Koheleth refuses to affirm anything about his God, except that He has revealed His will to His creatures by implanting in man an ineradicable desire for happiness. Koheleth's morality accordingly recognizes the pursuit of happiness as the goal. His religion is the combination of his theology and his ethics.

In substance, this is Koheleth's world-view, but setting it forth in systematic abstract categories gives it a lifelessness and a dogmatic cast that are completely alien to Koheleth's personality. For it robs the book of its most attractive qualities, the informality and tentativeness with which the author sets forth his ideas, his amused doubts even with regard to skepticism, his insights into human nature with all its weaknesses and pretenses, and his basic sympathy for men in their lifelong quest for happiness, elusive and fleeting at best. Above all, there is the haunting sadness of one who in earlier years had known and shared larger hopes for man upon earth.

The contradictions that troubled earlier readers are, in part, normal variations in temper and mood and, in part, the consequence of his clearsighted recognition that no one, not even

he, has a monopoly on truth. These contrasting passages are
not among the least of Koheleth's charms.

Thus the basic theme of the book is its insistence upon the
enjoyment of life, of all the good things in the world. There
is the love of woman — and the singular is noteworthy —

> Enjoy life with the woman whom you love
> Through all the vain days of your life,
> Which God has given you under the sun,

but the counterpoint of melancholy is never absent:

> Throughout your brief days,
> For that is your life's reward
> For your toil under the sun.   (9:9)

With a moving sense of the transitoriness of life, he calls for
the vigorous and full-blooded enjoyment of all it affords, food
and drink, oil and fine clothes, beautiful homes and music:

> Whatever you are able to do, do with all your might, for
> there is neither action nor thought nor knowledge nor wisdom
> in the grave toward which you are moving.   (9:10)

In practice, Koheleth advocates a moderate course, not very
different from the attitude of the Rabbis of the Talmud:

שלשה דברים מרחיבין דעתו של אדם בית נאה אשה נאה וכלים נאים
> Three things bring a sense of ease and contentment to a man:
> a beautiful home, an attractive wife, and fine clothes.
>   (Ber. 57b)

What set his standpoint apart from theirs was that his attitude
stemmed not from a full-hearted acceptance of the world, as
preached by religion, but from a sense of frustration and
resignation, induced by his philosophy.

For Koheleth, nothing really counts if truth and righteousness
cannot be attained. Yet man lives and God rules, and God's
manifest will is man's happiness, not that it matters overmuch,
but this at least is certain.

II

In Koheleth, form and substance are so closely interwoven that any restatement becomes a distortion. His view of life is best gathered from his own words, or at least from a summary of the book as he wrote it.

The work opens and closes with his fundamental judgment, "Vanity of vanities, all is vanity" (1:2; 12:8). In the opening section, Koheleth declares that the natural world about us presents a changeless cycle without novelty or progress. The four elements of the universe, the earth, the sun, the wind and the sea, repeat their monotonous courses interminably. Against this background, man's petty strivings are folly (I, 1:2–11).

Koheleth then takes on the role of King Solomon, and tells how he had experimented with wisdom and wealth, goals for which men are wont to struggle and squander their lives. Truth he found unattainable, and wisdom a source of misery. As for physical pleasure, it may offer a temporary satisfaction, but it is not an absolute or enduring good. Nonetheless, it is God who has endowed man with the desire for happiness; to enjoy life is therefore the only commandment of which man can be certain; to fail to obey it is to be a sinner before God (II, 1:12 to 2:26).

Not only are the processes of nature beyond man's power to contravene, but even human actions are preordained. All human activity is useless, above all the search for truth. Only joy remains for man as the gift of God (III, 3:1–15).

Bitterly, Koheleth condemns the world in which the powerful are unjust and the weak victimized. Nor can one be certain of a just retribution in the hereafter, as some would believe. Only joy is a sensible goal in life (IV, 3:16 to 4:3).

A favorite doctrine of the preceptors of youth is the value of diligence and hard work. Analysis reveals, however, that the reasons usually advanced for these virtues are worthless. The creative skill in which men glory is largely a disguise for their desire to compete with and outstrip their fellows (4:4). Some men claim to toil for the sake of their families, the advantages of which, Koheleth finds, are much overrated, being largely physical (4:9 ff.). As for the desire for fame, "the last infirmity of noble minds," that is the greatest illusion of all, for all men are quickly forgotten (4:13–16). The conclusion is inescapable — hard work is folly and only ease is sensible (V, 4:4–16).

A few brief comments now follow on the basic institutions of society. Religion is part of the accepted order, and a sensible man should do his duty to the Temple. He should visit the sanctuary at proper intervals, offer his brief prayers, and pay his vows by which the ritual is maintained. Koheleth scorns the religious ecstatic, but even more, the man who evades his obligation (VI, 4:17 to 5:6). He then turns to the political scene and finds that corruption is inherent in the very nature of government, with its endless hierarchy of officials. In a difficult verse, he seems to pay tribute to agriculture as the basic pursuit of society (VII, 5:7–8).

He now turns to a basic drive in the lives of men. Few vices are more widespread than the lust for wealth, and few bring less genuine satisfaction. Diligence and thrift are hardly more than expressions of greed. Men struggle and toil to amass riches, finding only that the dependents and parasites about them augment their responsibilities, but bring no increased pleasure in life. Greed often drives men into ill-starred ventures that wipe out overnight the patient accumulation of a lifetime. Even if a man does not lose all his fortune, some one else will inherit it all, after he goes down into silence. Whoever his heir, be it his child or kinsman, fundamentally he is a stranger to him (6:2). Hence it is better to seize joy before it is too late forever (VIII, 5:9 to 6:9).

Man remains incapable of changing the predetermined character of events or even of penetrating the mystery of existence — that is the fundamental tragedy (IX, 6:10–12).

There now follows a collection of proverbs dealing with the good life, linked together by the opening word *tōbh*, "good." These traditional apothegms are made to serve Koheleth's outlook. Man must not expect too much from life in order to avoid disappointment. Since life is unchanging, it is as foolish to weave elaborate hopes for the unborn future as to glorify the dead past. Good and evil are both to be accepted as part of the pattern ordained by God (X, 7:1–14). Man should avoid extremes, whether of saintliness or of wickedness, and strive after "the golden mean." In a world where nothing is predictable to man, hewing close to the center is the safest course (XI, 7:15–25).

Koheleth has little confidence in the character of men. Upon women, however, he pours out the vials of his bitterness and wrath — testimony that he had loved them and lost (XII, 7:26–29).

With regard to the political status quo, Koheleth urges submission to the king, not merely because of the oath of allegiance that he exacts from his subjects, but because of the royal power. The unpredictability of events and the perils of life in a mysterious universe are reflected and heightened in a royal court, where the ruler's caprice and the intrigues of the courtiers make survival, let alone advancement, a difficult and risky art (XIII, 8:1–9).

Noting how successful evil-doers are often eulogized as public benefactors in their last rites, Koheleth turns to the problem of reward and punishment. He does not altogether deny the principle of retribution. However, the long delays that occur before God metes out punishment to the sinner and the numerous cases where there is no discernible difference between the lot of the righteous and that of the evil-doer, act as a stimulus for men to do wrong. Hence, the quest for justice is futile — only joy remains (XIV, 8:10 to 9:3). This latter theme is then expanded in an eloquent call to man to enjoy life with all the zest at his command, before unknown perils crush him and death ends all sensation and activity (XV, 9:4–12).

Though Koheleth cannot overcome his natural bias for the wise man as against the fool, he knows how slight is the respect that wisdom commands and how easily all its achievements can be negated by stupidity (XVI, 9:13 to 10:1).

Another proverb collection, miscellaneous in character, now follows. Koheleth urges the same practical virtues as the conventional Wisdom teachers, but generally on more realistic grounds that are in harmony with his basic viewpoints — man's inability to know the future and his duty to enjoy life while he can (XVII, 10:2 to 11:6).

In the closing sentences, Koheleth rises to eloquent heights. Joy is God's great commandment for man. The time for joy is youth, the period of vigor and zest. Koheleth, from the vantage point of his own experience, calls upon the youth to "remember his Creator" before the shadows begin to lengthen and presage the end. With the unforgettable "Allegory of Old Age," Koheleth sounds the note of man's inevitable dissolution and death. Vanity of vanities, all is vanity (XVIII, 11:7 to 12:8).

The Epilogue, consisting of the six concluding verses of the book (12:9–14), are an addition by an editor, who knew Koheleth as a Wisdom teacher and a collector and composer of Hokmah literature. Fascinated by the book, the editor is fearful lest the reader be led away from the eternal verities and he calls upon him, having heard everything, to fear God and keep His commandments.

III

From this summary it is clear that Koheleth does not present a systematic philosophy in the grand manner of Aristotle, Spinoza, Hegel or Kant, but that is less of a defect than may appear.[2] For nothing is as certain as the fact that the elaborate systems of philosophers upon which they spend their life's energies ultimately pass away, and only scattered insights, minor details in their patterns of thought, become abiding elements in man's approach to reality. Only the flashes of illumination endure to light up men's path in a dark and mysterious world.

Basic to Koheleth, as we have seen, is the skeptical outlook, which, rooted in his temperament, was nurtured also by his position among the well-to-do classes of society. Essentially, a skeptic is one who refuses to be convinced without proof; concerning the shape of things to come, where such evidence cannot be forthcoming, he remains without faith. The skeptic finds it possible to be suspended in a state of perpetual doubt with regard to the future, because as a rule he finds his lot in the present not unbearable. Being generally a beneficiary and not a victim of the status quo, he feels no powerful urge to achieve or even to envisage a better world. That drive tends to arise among the submerged groups in society, who find existence intolerable without the hope of a change. Koheleth, on the other hand, rejects the older prophetic faith, which expressed itself in such concepts as the End-Time and the Messianic Age. At the same time, he is unable to accept the newer Pharisaic doctrine of life after death or the Apocalyptic faith in the imminent end of the world through a Divine cataclysm. He is, of course, at the farthest remove possible from the mystic, the social reformer or the revolutionary.

Undoubtedly, Koheleth's failure to respond actively to social injustice and political tyranny constitutes a crucial defect, so that our age cannot find in him the motive power toward the building of a better world that is so abundant in the Hebrew prophets. In the face of the towering evils of our own day coupled with the breath-taking vision of a more abundant life for all men, now for the first time within realization, Amos and Isaiah are incomparably more inspiring guides than the disillusioned sage of Jerusalem.

Yet for all Koheleth's remoteness from the fever and the fret of the world and his apparent lack of concern with social problems, his view of life does furnish a basis, at least, for men's age-old struggle against any order in which "man has power over his neighbor to do him harm." For Koheleth, joy is God's categorical imperative for man, not in any anemic or spiritualized sense, but rather as a full-blooded and tangible experience, expressing itself in the play of the body and the activity of the mind, the contemplation of nature and the pleasures of love. Since he insists that the pursuit of happiness with which man has been endowed by his Creator is an inescapable sacred duty, it follows that it must be an inalienable right.

To be sure, Koheleth never drew the implications of these premises, in facing the social, economic, and political ills of his day. His conservatism was, as has been noted, an amalgam of intellectual, temperamental and social factors. But had he been

confronted by the logic of his position, we may well believe that
he would have been too honest to deny the conclusion that a
system of society which denies inalienable rights to men is
not God-ordained, and that men have the duty as well as the
right to change it. He lacked the Prophets' faith that right
would triumph, but at least he shared their conviction that it
should. His passionate outcry against life because of human
oppression (4:1 ff.) should guard us against imagining that he
was complacent in the face of oppression. If, as a rule, he
deprecated where he should have condemned, he never committed
the blasphemy of regarding the status quo as the acme of
perfection. He was no apologist for folly enthroned in high
places and did not hesitate to call evil by its right name.

Koheleth's principal value, however, lies not in this implication for the social scene, but in his explicit concern with the
individual. The temperamental difference between Koheleth
and the Prophets must not blind us to the guidance he offers
men in meeting those ills that must be transcended because
they cannot be transformed. It is true that nowhere does
Koheleth preach the virtue of courage in so many words. For
him courage is not a conscious ideal, nor even an idea — it is
far more, an inborn, pervasive quality. Every line in his book
is instinct with the spirit of clear-eyed, brave and joyous
acceptance of life, for all its inevitable limitations.

And these limitations *are* inevitable, however unwilling a
youthful and activistic generation may be to confess it. However
successful men may become in moulding the pattern of the
world nearer heart's desire, they will still encounter pain and
frustration in life, in meeting which they will require dignity
and courage and the saving grace of good humor. The mounting
doubts, fears and tensions of our own day, carried to unconscion-
able lengths though they may be, have served at least to remind
us of this truth.

This need for resignation is independent of any given set of
political, social and economic conditions. It inheres in the
character of the universe and the nature of man. For he is a
creature whose reach is always greater than his grasp, with a
boundless imagination weaving hopes and desires far beyond the

capacity of his brief, earth-bound existence to fulfill. As Koheleth observes, "All a man's toil is for his wants, but his desires are never satisfied." In teaching men to taste life's joys without self-deception and to face its sorrows without despair, Koheleth performs an everlastingly significant function.

The several factors that played their part in gaining admission for the book of Koheleth to the canon of Scripture have been discussed above.[3] Undoubtedly the tradition of Solomonic authorship and Koheleth's unique style, particularly his un-conventional use of a religious vocabulary and his citation of proverbs for his own special purposes, proved decisive factors.

Yet with it all, there was much in the book that was a stumbling-block to the devout. That it was never dislodged may be due in part to the naïveté and lack of historical per-spective of many of its readers. But, basically, its preservation is a tribute both to the fascination of the book and to the catholic taste of the creators of the Biblical canon, who saw in every honest seeker after truth a servant of the one source of truth.

Moreover, ancient and medieval readers were not so naïve as their modern successors are wont to believe. That the basic theme of the book was *simḥah*, the enjoyment of life, was clearly recognized by Jewish religious authorities[4] who thus explained the custom of reading *Koheleth* in the synagogue on the Feast of Tabernacles, the Season of Rejoicing.[5] But whatever the motives that led to the preservation of the book, we cannot be too grateful.

Koheleth would have been shocked, even amused, to learn that his notebook was canonized as part of Holy Scripture. But the obscure instinct of his people was building more truly than it knew when it stamped his work as sacred. Two millennia after Koheleth's day, a pietistic movement arose in Eastern European Jewry at the farthest possible remove from the temper of the ancient sage of Jerusalem. Yet a classic tale of the Hasidic tradition reveals a remarkable affinity with Koheleth. One day, Rabbi Bunam of Pshysha found his beloved disciple Enoch in tears. The Rabbi asked him, "Why are you weeping?" and Enoch answered, "Am I not a creature of this world, and am I not made with eyes and heart and all limbs, and yet I do not know for what purpose I was created and what good I am in the world." "Fool!" said Rabbi Bunam. "I also go around thus." Thus Koheleth, too, went about, seeking the purpose of life and lamenting his ignorance. His book is the record of his wandering and his sorrow, and of the peace he finally attained.

In the deepest sense, Koheleth is a religious book, because it seeks to grapple with reality. The Psalmist had sung:

> A broken and contrite heart,
> O God, Thou wilt not despise.   (Ps. 51:19)

This cry of a sensitive spirit wounded by man's cruelty and ignorance, this distilled essence of an honest and courageous mind, striving to penetrate the secret of the universe, yet unwilling to soar on the wings of faith beyond the limits of the knowable, remains one of man's noblest offerings on the altar of truth.

XVI. TEXT AND VERSIONS

A. The Hebrew Text.

The Hebrew text of Koheleth, which has reached us through
the Masorah, has been edited by Baer, C. D. Ginsburg, S. R.
Driver and F. Horst.[1] In eleven passages the Masorah registers
Kethib-Qere readings[2] none of which are "corrections" of the
text, all being ancient manuscript variations.[3] Of these the
Kethib is somewhat to be preferred in one instance,[4] the Qere
definitely in two,[5] while either reading is possible in seven
others.[6] In one instance, the Kethib itself represents a conflate
of two readings, of which the Qere reproduces one.[7] The Oriental Masoretes record three additional Kethib-Qere variants, of
which only one affects the sense.[8]

S. Euringer has collected all the variations between the Ori-
entals and Occidentals,[9] none of which are of any real consequence. In an appendix to his work,[10] he has also set out all the
variant readings in the *Babylonian* and *Palestinian Talmud*,
the *Tosefta*, the Tannaitic *Midrashim*, *Pesikta de Rab Kahana*
and *Bereshith Rabba*. The popularity of Koheleth is attested by
the fact that no less than 122 verses out of 222 are quoted in
the Rabbinic sources, in whole or in part.

A careful analysis of these Rabbinic variations makes it
abundantly clear that the Rabbis tended to cite Scripture from
memory, especially since manuscripts were rare and often in-
accessible. Moreover, their concern was not the meticulous reproduction of the text to meet scholarly requirements, but its
free use for religious and ethical purposes. For both these reasons, their citations are often inaccurate in details. Particularly
widespread is the process of "levelling" the text, so as to make
abnormal features conform to the more usual pattern.[11]

The Rabbinic variants may be classified as follows:

1) *Orthographic*, plene spelling appearing in the unvocalized Rabbinic text for the defective spelling of the Biblical original, as e. g. בירושלים in 1:1 (B. Sanh. 20b) and שיעמול in 1:3 (B. Shab. 30b); this type of spelling may be the work of the printers.

2) *Vav* omitted when only part of the verse is cited, e. g. אין כל חדש in 1:9 (B. Ber. 59a; Shab. 30b); החוט המשלש in 4:12 (B. Keth. 62b).

3) *Vav inserted*, e. g. ומתת אלהים היא in 3:13 (Mid. Bereshith Rab., sec. 65) and והחכמה תעז in 7:19 (*Mekilta*, p. 26b, ed. Friedmann; Mid. Ber. Rab., sec. 34); the asyndetonic form is cited in Mid. Ber. Rab., sec. 39.

4) Phrase inverted, due probably to citing from memory, עת לשחוק ועת לבכות in 3:4 (Tos. Ber. 5:18).

5) "Levelling" to the more common form, e. g. האסורים in 4:14 (Mid. Ber. Rab., sec. 89); את added in כל זה נסיתי in 7:23 (*Pesikta de Rab Kahana*, 33b, ed. Buber) or את dropped to make the construction parallel, e. g. reading בבקר זרע זרעך ולערב אל תנח ידיך in 11:6 (B. Yeb. 62b); similarly עד ש... instead of עד אשר in 12:1, 6 (Shab. 151a).

6) Instances attributable to faulty memory, e. g. 4:15, ראיתי את הכל החיים (Mid. Ber. Rab., sec. 89), though this ungrammatical form may go back to the printers.

7) Free citation, e. g. שחיבל את מעשה ידיך in 5:5 (J. Hag. 77b), though וחבל is correctly quoted in Kallah 51a.

8) "Contamination" of two passages, as e. g. when 9:14 is cited as ובנה עליה מצודים וחרמים in B. Ned. 32b, a mixture of 9:14 and 7:26.

Purely homiletic in character and therefore offering no testimony as to a variant text are the passages cited with the אל תקרי formula:[12]

1) B. Taan. 7b citing 8:1. ועז פניו ישנא אל תקרי ישנא אלא יְשַׁנֵּא.

2) B. Git. 26b citing 8:10 אל תקרי קבורים אלא קבוצים אל תקרי וישתכחו אלא וישתבחו.

The latter passage is particularly instructive. The change of וישתכחו to וישתבחו has commended itself to scholars on its own merits, but the Talmud is not citing an old text here, as the other "variant" indicates — it is simply modifying the *textus receptus* for homiletic purposes.

All in all, the Masoretic text of Koheleth was the only one known to Rabbinic literature. Similarly, the variants collected by Kennicott and de Rossi in the 18th century, as well as those assembled by C. D. Ginsburg in the 19th, contain few significant readings.

B. The Ancient Versions

The most important witness to the Hebrew text in its pre-Masoretic form is the *Septuagint*, which is a collective title for a translation made over a considerable number of years by many hands.[13] The LXX on Koheleth has many striking peculiarities which recall the literalistic Greek Version of the Bible made by Aquila, a native of Pontus, who was converted to Judaism in the first half of the 2nd century C. E.[14]

At the behest of his master, Rabbi Akiba, Aquila prepared a remarkable translation of the Hebrew Bible to replace the Septuagint, which had become the official Bible of the Christian Church, and which now diverged considerably from the accepted Hebrew text.[15] Intended for the use of Greek-speaking Jewish communities, his work sought to reproduce the Hebrew text in Greek, as far as possible. Of his stylistic characteristics, perhaps the most noteworthy is the frequent rendering of את, the sign of the accusative, by the Greek preposition σύν.[16]

The Septuagint version of Koheleth renders this Hebrew particle by σύν no less than 32 times, besides exhibiting other "Aquilan" stylistic traits. Hence, Graetz suggested that the LXX of Koheleth is actually a translation of Aquila.[17] As a matter of fact, Jerome has occasion to speak of an *editio secunda* of Aquila.

Several objections were lodged against this view. First, our present LXX text of Koheleth does not coincide with the fragments of Aquila that have survived.[18] Second, it renders את by σύν in only 32 out of 72 cases. Moreover, Jerome refers to a "second edition" only in connection with *Jeremiah*, *Ezekiel* and *Daniel*, and it is not known whether it extended over the other Biblical books. Dillmann therefore argued that our Greek Version is actually the LXX, which was corrected in the manner of Aquila.[19] But this latter theory was answered effectively by McNeile,[20] who pointed to the psychological improbability of such a process in the early Christian centuries.

Another alternative theory has since been proposed — that our Greek version of *Koheleth* represents a new, highly literalistic translation-technique, of which Aquila's version of the entire Bible was the most ambitious and extensive example, while our Greek version of Koheleth constitutes an additional, though independent instance of the process.[21] Such a theory, however, requires the assumption of a special translation-method, of which no other examples have survived outside of Aquila.

We believe that all the relevant data are best explained by the theory that our present LXX is the "first edition" of Aquila's translation of *Ecclesiastes*, and that the extant fragments belong to Aquila's second edition.[22] That an Aquilan version of *Ecclesiastes* might enter the Septuagintal canon has its analogy in the official LXX of *Daniel*, which is basically the rendering of *Theodotion*. Moreover, Jerome reports that Aquila's "second edition" was described by the term κατ' ἀκρίβειαν "thoroughly accurate."[23] This phrase suggests that Aquila's "first edition" was tentative and that the literalistic principles of his translation were not consistently applied in it, hence the absence of σύν in half the examples. The Masorah affords countless examples where given principles operate in only part of the available passages. Moreover, when the first Aquilan version of Koheleth became part of the Septuagint, it would be a natural tendency for Greek scribes, who knew no Hebrew, to drop the preposition in passages where it was meaningless.

In addition to the "Aquilan" LXX and the fragments of *Aquila* that have survived, remnants of two other Greek translations have been preserved. They are the translations of *Theodotion*, who, as Swete says, "seems to have produced a free revision of the LXX rather than an independent version," and of *Symmachus*, the most periphrastic of the Greek versions.

Secondary versions made from the Septuagint, and generally attesting to our present Greek text, are the *Coptic*[24] and the *Old Latin*.[25]

Two highly important Versions, the Syriac and the Latin, stand midway between the Hebrew text, on which they are principally based, and the LXX, which exerted considerable influence upon them. As is the case in most Biblical books, the precise relationship of the *Peshitta* and the *Vulgate* to the Hebrew and the Greek texts is a moot question among scholars.

The *Syriac Peshitta* was written during the early centuries of the Christian era. While, on the one hand, it is obviously based on the Hebrew text, and Rabbinic tradition is imbedded in it at countless points,[26] in other instances it shows the marked influence of the LXX, a fact which may be either the cause or the effect of its becoming the official text of the Syriac Church. A detailed study of the *Peshitta* on *Ecclesiastes* was made by A. I. Kamenetzky.[27] He concludes that the Syriac was translated directly from the Hebrew, to which it is closer than is the LXX, but that it has been influenced by the LXX or revised in accordance with it. The results of our own study of the relationship of the Peshitta to the Masoretic text and the Septuagint are given below.

The Latin Version, called the *Vulgate*, was prepared between 383 and 420 C. E. by Jerome, who sought to translate the *Hebraica veritas* for the Roman Church and thus replace the *Old Latin* Version, which was a rendering of the LXX and therefore varied from the Hebrew text at many points. This ambitious project Jerome carried through in varying degrees in different books.

Another version made directly from the Hebrew is the *Aramaic Targum*. In their present form, the Targumim to the Megilloth are not earlier than the Middle Ages, since the oldest reference to them is in the *Arukh* of Nathan ben Jehiel of Rome, completed in 1101 C. E. It is, however, certain that the material imbedded in the Targum is in large degree considerably older than the date of its redaction, since these Aramaic versions served as repositories of Rabbinic lore, to which material continued to be added for centuries.[28] The strongly periphrastic and tendentious character of the Targum at many points, which makes it virtually an Aramaic Midrash, coupled with its late date, reduces its value as a witness to the text.[29] Nonetheless, there are times, even when dogmatic difficulties exist, when the Targum contains literal renderings, particularly when these are conflated with late, periphrastic interpretations.[30] When utilized judiciously in conjunction with the testimony of other versions, the Targum proves a valuable aid in several difficult passages.[31]

The *Arabic Version*, published in the Paris Polyglot of 1630 and in the London Polyglot of 1656, may be the work of the Gaon Saadiah ben Joseph (882–942), though this is highly doubtful.[32]

The text-critical study of Koheleth and the Ancient Versions makes it clear that the Hebrew text has suffered little corruption and has reached us basically in its original form.[33] This is in large measure due to the late date of its composition and to the rise of "proto-Masoretic" activity relatively soon thereafter. For the evidence makes it increasingly clear that the process of preserving the Biblical text, which was the fundamental purpose of the Masorah, began before the destruction of the Temple in 70 C. E. and that shortly thereafter a *textus receptus* was established.[34] It was this accepted text which served as the common source and basis of the hermeneutic methods of the Tannaitic schools of Rabbis Akiba and Ishmael in the 1st half of the 2nd century. Thus less than three centuries elapsed from the composition of the book to its receiving its present textual form, with the result that errors had less chance of multiplying than in the case of older Biblical writings.

There is no evidence that tendentious changes were made either in the vocalization or in the consonants of the text.[35] Only in a very few passages need the vocalization or the consonants be corrected. Fundamentally, however, we read Koheleth today in the form in which it left its author's hands.

TABLE A.

The Masoretic Text of Koheleth

Only in the following passages is there need of modifying the Masoretic Text, either with regard to a) the vowels; or b) the consonants.

a)	1:13	for	נַעֲשָׂה	read	נַעֲשָׂה (not certain)
	1:17	for	וָדַעַת	read	וָדַעַת
	2:12	for	עָשׂוּהוּ	read	עָשָׂהוּ
	3:18	for	וְלִרְאוֹת	read	וְלָרְאוֹת
	3:19	for	מִקְרֶה בני האדם וּמִקְרֶה הבהמה	read	מִקְרֶה
	5:9	for	תְבוּאָה	read	תְבוֹאָהוּ
	5:19	for	מַעֲנֶה	read	מַעֲנֵהוּ
	6:3	for	לֹא	read	לֹא (the second)
	10:3	for	וְאָמַר	read	וְאָמַר
	12:10	for	וְכָתוֹב	read	וְכָתוֹב (doubtful)
b)	1:15	for	לְהִמָּנוֹת	read	לְהִמָּלוֹת
	2:24	for	בָּאָדָם שֶׁיֹּאכַל	read	בָּאָדָם מִשֶּׁיֹּאכַל
	2:25	for	יָחוּשׁ	read	יָחוּשׁ (doubtful)
	2:25	for	מִמֶּנִּי	read	מִמֶּנּוּ
	7:27	for	אָמְרָה קֹהֶלֶת	read	אָמַר הַקֹּהֶלֶת
	8:10	for	קְבָרִים וָבָאוּ וְיִשְׁתַּכְּחוּ	read read	קָבָר מוּבָאִים וְיִשְׁתַּבְּחוּ
	11:5	for	כַּעֲצָמִים	read	בַּעֲצָמִים

Most of these minor changes are vouched for by the ancient versions, and only the smallest number are conjectural. For details, see the Commentary.

TABLE B.

Peshitta Agrees with LXX Against MT

1:10 Read text as יֵשׁ דְּבַר שֶׁיֹּאמַר

1:17 מתלא for הללות (inner Greek error). See Com.

2:2   Interpreted מָה אַתְּ עָשָׂה (2nd person)

2:3   שמשא for MT שמים (so V)

2:8   שדה ושדות (interprets like LXX)

2:12 Read עָשָׂהוּ with Vaticanus; הַמֶּלֶךְ interpreted as "counsel"

2:15 Addition in Peshitta

2:20 ליאש (interpretation)

2:25 For יָחוּשׁ rendered יִשְׁתֶּה (see Com.)

2:25 Read ממנו

3:18 Read וְלָרְאוֹת. Renders על דברת by מללו (Cf. LXX)

4:10 וְאִילוֹ = "Alas"

5:5   Read הַמֶּלֶךְ (God)

5:14 שֶׁיַּלֵּךְ (LXX, P read שֶׁיֵּלֵךְ)

5:15 וְכָעַס (Read as וְכַעַס)
       וְחָלְיוֹ (Suffix unexpressed)

5:19 מַעֲנֶה (Read with suffix, מַעֲנֵהוּ = מַעֲנָה, cf. Com. on 5:9 and ad loc.)

6:12 מה יותר לאדם (Attached to next verse)

7:2   והחי יתן אל לבו (Adds "good" as obj. of verb. Perhaps dittography from opening word of v. 3).

7:10 מחכמה (Rendered "in wisdom"; freely?)

7:24 רָחוֹק מֶשֶּׁהָיָה (LXX read רחוק מהישהיה; P: מֶשֶּׁהָיָה רָחוֹק = יתיר מן דהוא רחיקא)

7:25 רֶשַׁע כָּסֶל (P: "the wickedness of the fool," reading כָּסֶל or כְּסִיל; LXX: "of the wicked, the folly," reading רֶשַׁע).

7:27   אמרה קהלת (LXX read: אמר הקהלת; P read אמר masc.)

8:1   Read יִשְׁנֶא

8:3   אַל תִּבָּהֵל connected with v. 2

8:4   Read כַּאֲשֶׁר for בַּאֲשֶׁר

8:8   Read בְּיוֹם הַמִּלְחָמָה

8:11   Read פִּתְגָם מַעֲשֵׂי הָרָעָה

8:16   Read כַּאֲשֶׁר for בַּאֲשֶׁר

9:1   Read וְלִבִּי רָאָה for וְלָבוּר

9:2   Read הַכֹּל לִפְנֵיהֶם הֶבֶל (but P repeats הַכֹּל in addition!).
       Adds וְלָרָע after לַטּוֹב

9:3   Rendered וְאַחֲרֵיהֶם for וְאַחֲרָיו (See Com.)

10:3   Read וְאָמַר for וְאָמַר
       Read סָבָל for סָכָל

12:5   וְתֻפַר (LXX, P, "scatter")

TABLE C.

PESHITTA AGREES WITH MT AGAINST LXX

1:9   מַה שֶּׁהָיָה

1:16   עִם לִבִּי

1:18   רָב כָּעַס

2:3   בַּיַּיִן

2:21   וּלְאָדָם

3:16   הָרֶשַׁע (LXX הָרָשָׁע)

3:19   וּמוֹתַר הָאָדָם

5:11   הָעֹבֵד (LXX הָעֶבֶד)
       (לְהַעֲשִׁיר = לַעֲשִׁיר LXX; וְהַשֹּׂבַע לֶעָשִׁיר)

5:15   יֹאכֵל (LXX וְאָבַל; P renders both MT and P)

6:8   מַהֲלָךְ (LXX מַהֲלָךְ־נָפֶשׁ)

6:12   LXX adds a clause, a contamination from 8:7

7:7   מַתָּנָה (LXX: "vigor"; cf. Com.)

7:13 מַעֲשֵׂה (LXX, plural)

7:14 הָיָה בְטוֹב (LXX חַיֵּה)

7:17 סָכָל (LXX, freely: "cruel, wicked")

7:18 תַּנַּח (LXX μὴ μιανῇς, "pollute," inner Greek error for μὴ ἀνῇς, "remove"; so Sym.)

7:22 יָדַע לִבֶּךָ (LXX יֵרַע, rendered twice)

8:6 רָעַת הָאָדָם

8:9 עַת

8:12 מָאַת וּמַאֲרִיךְ לוֹ

8:13 כַּצֵּל

9:4 כִּי מִי אֲשֶׁר (relative clause; LXX interrogative; see V)

9:9 כֹּל יְמֵי הֶבְלֶךָ (see Com.)

9:10 בְּכֹחֶךָ (LXX כְּכֹחֶךָ)

TABLE D.

Peshitta Differs from Both MT and LXX

3:9 הָעוֹשֶׂה P; MT, LXX הַמַּעֲשֶׂה P

5:13 וְהוֹלִיד (P דאולד, inner Syriac error for ואולד)

5:17 קהלת added after אני

6:12 וַיַּעֲשֵׂם בְּצֵל (P read וַיַּעֲשֵׂם כַּצֵּל; LXX בְּצֵל)

7:11 עִם־נַחֲלָה (P, by contamination from 9:18: מבא הי חכמתא מן מאני זינא)

7:12 בְּצִלָּה הַחָכְמָה כְּצֵל (LXX read: בְּצֵל הַחָכְמָה בְּצֵל הַכָּסֶף; P read צֵל הַחָכְמָה כְּצֵל הַכָּסֶף; see Com.)

7:13 עִוְּתוֹ (P reading מדוד, inner Syriac error for מדור, also in 1:15)

7:15 מַאֲרִיךְ (P דאנד, inner error for דאנג)

8:7 שֶׁהָיָה P (so V); MT שֶׁיִּהְיֶה

11:7b Borrowed from 7:11b

12:2 וְהָאוֹר וְהַיָּרֵחַ (hendiadys; but see Com.).

TABLE E.

LXX Agrees with MT Against Peshitta

1:5 שׁוֹאֵף "drag" (P, V, "return")

1:13 שָׁמַיִם (P שׁמשׁא)

2:2 מהולל (מנא הנין P; see Com.)

2:24 שֶׁיֹּאכַל (P מֵיֹאכַל)

3:18 לְבָרָם

4:10 יִפֹּלוּ (P, freely)

5:8 מֶלֶךְ לְשָׂדֶה (P interprets)

6:7 לפיהו (P בפיהו)

6:8 מהיּוֹתֵר לחכם (P declarative מטל דאית יותרנא)

7:1 הִוָּלְדוֹ (LXX expresses suffix; not P)

9:18 וְחָטָא (P וחוטא)

10:2 לִימִינוֹ (P בימינו)

10:19 וְיַיִן (P adds ומשׁחא)

12:11 אֲסֻפּוֹת (LXX "collections"; P "thresholds")

ספר קהלת

THE BOOK OF KOHELETH, HEBREW TEXT
AND A NEW TRANSLATION

I

ON THE MONOTONY OF NATURE

*The processes of nature, holds Koheleth, are part of a
ceaseless and changeless cycle, without goal or meaning.
Nothing new ever happens. What appears to be new is*

The Words of Koheleth, son of David,
King in Jerusalem.

VANITY of vanities, says Koheleth, vanity of vanities,
all is vanity.

What profit has a man of all his toil beneath the
sun? One generation goes and another comes, but the
earth is forever unchanged. The sun rises and the sun
sets, breathlessly rushing towards the place where it is
to rise again. Going to the south and circling to the
north, the wind goes round and round, and then
returns upon its tracks. All the rivers flow into the
sea, but the sea is never full; to the place where the
rivers flow, there they continue to flow. All things
are tiresome, one cannot put them into words, and so
the eye is never satisfied with seeing nor the ear filled
with hearing.

What has been will be, and what has been done will
be done again; there is nothing new under the sun.
There may be something of which a man says, 'Look,
this is new!' It has already occurred in the ages before
us. For there is no recollection left of the earliest
generations, and even the later ones will not be remembered by those who come at the very end.

merely due to the fact that the past is quickly forgotten.
Viewed against the background of the universe, all man's
striving is folly.

(I. 2–11)

---

1 דברי קהלת בן־דוד מלך בירושלם: 1

2 הבל הבלים אמר קהלת   הבל הבלים הכל הבל:

3 מה־יתרון לאדם בכל־עמלו   שיעמל תחת השמש:

4 דור הלך ודור בא   והארץ לעולם עמדת:

5 וזרח השמש ובא השמש   ואל־מקומו שואף זורח הוא שם:

6 הולך אל־דרום וסובב אל־צפון   סובב סבב הולך הרוח
ועל־סביבתיו שב הרוח:

7 כל־הנחלים הלכים אל־הים   והים איננו מלא
אל־מקום שהנחלים הלכים   שם הם שבים ללכת:

8 כל־הדברים יגעים   לא־יוכל איש לדבר
לא־תשבע עין לראות   ולא־תמלא אזן משמע:

9 מה־שהיה הוא שיהיה   ומה־שנעשה הוא שיעשה
ואין כל־חדש תחת השמש:

10 יש דבר שיאמר ראה־זה חדש הוא כבר היה לעלמים אשר היה

11 מלפננו: אין זכרון לראשנים וגם לאחרנים שיהיו לא־יהיה להם
זכרון עם שיהיו לאחרנה:

II

THE TWIN EXPERIMENT

*Koheleth adopts the role of King Solomon in order to test
the value of wisdom and wealth, for both of which Solomon
was famous.*

*His first experiment is with wisdom. It leads him to
the conclusion that the search for truth is futile and
calculated only to make men miserable.*

*He then turns to physical pleasure, to the joys that
wealth can bring, spacious gardens and elaborate mansions
staffed with servants and the eternal triad of wine, women*

I, KOHELETH, was king over Israel in Jerusalem. I
applied my mind to search out and explore in my
wisdom all that happens beneath the sky — a sorry
business it is that God has given men to be afflicted
with. I have seen all the works that are done under the
sun and behold all is vanity and chasing of wind, a
crookedness not to be straightened, a void not to be
filled.

Said I to myself, 'Here I have greatly increased my
wisdom, beyond all those who were before me over
Jerusalem, for my heart has attained much wisdom and
knowledge.' But as I applied my mind, I learnt that
wisdom and knowledge are madness and folly. Yes,
I perceived that this, too, is chasing after wind. For
the more wisdom the more grief, and increasing one's
knowledge means increasing one's pain.

Then I said to myself, 'Come, let me try you out in
joy and enjoy pleasure,' but this, too, was vanity. Of
laughter I said, 'It is folly,' and of joy, 'What good is
it?' For I had explored the matter with my mind, by

and song. For a space, he finds satisfaction in the novelty
of sensation and the joy of activity, but it soon wears off.
He then discovers that pleasure is no more satisfactory
than wisdom as an attainable goal.

Koheleth concludes that the wise man has no advantage
over the fool, nor the diligent worker over the sluggard.
To cap it all, when a man dies, after a life-time of toil,
some stranger whom he may not even know inherits
after him. The only sensible goal that remains is the
quest for 'joy,' however inadequate it may be by any
absolute standard.

אני קהלת הייתי מלך על־ישראל בירושלם: ונתתי את־לבי   13-12

לדרוש ולתור בחכמה על כל־אשר נעשה תחת השמים הוא | ענין

רע נתן אלהים לבני האדם לענות בו: ראיתי את־כל־המעשים שנעשו   14

תחת השמש והנה הכל הבל ורעות רוח: מעות לא־יוכל לתקן וחסרון   15

לא־יוכל להמנות:

דברתי אני עם־לבי לאמר אני הנה הגדלתי והוספתי חכמה   16

על כל־אשר־היה לפני על־ירושלם ולבי ראה הרבה חכמה ודעת:

ואתנה לבי לדעת חכמה ודעת הללות ושכלות ידעתי שגם־זה הוא   17

רעיון רוח: כי ברב חכמה רב־כעס ויוסיף דעת יוסיף מכאוב: 18

אמרתי אני בלבי לכה־נא אנסכה בשמחה וראה בטוב והנה גם־   1   2

הוא הבל: לשחוק אמרתי מהולל ולשמחה מה־זה עשה: תרתי בלבי   3-2

(I. 12–II. 26)

פסוק 15: גרס לְהָמָלוֹת

פסוק 17: גרס וָדַעַת

stimulating my body with wine (while my mind was acting with wisdom) and by taking hold of frivolity, so that I might see what course is best for men under the sky during the brief span of their lives.

I acted in grand style, I built mansions for myself and planted vineyards. I laid out gardens and parks, and planted in them every kind of fruit-tree. I made pools of water, to water a forest of trees. I bought slaves, both male and female, though I already had a large household. I also owned much cattle and sheep, more than any who had been before me in Jerusalem. I also amassed silver and gold, and the treasures of kings and provinces. I acquired singers and song-stresses, all the delights of men, of mistresses a goodly number. So I grew great and added to my possessions beyond all who had been before me in Jerusalem, while my wisdom remained with me. Whatever my eyes desired, I did not deny them; I did not deprive myself of any pleasure — for my soul rejoiced in all my labour, and that was my reward for all my labour.

I then turned to observe all the work that my hands had done, and all the labour I had strained to perform, and lo, everything was vanity and chasing of wind, with no advantage under the sun.

Once again I saw that wisdom is but madness and folly, for of what value is a man coming after the king, who can only repeat what he has already done?

I have heard it said: 'Wisdom excels folly as the light is better than darkness'; 'The wise man has his eyes in his head, but the fool walks in darkness.' But *I* know that one fate overtakes them both! So I said to

למשוך ביין את־בשרי ולבי נהג בחכמה ולאחז בסכלות עד | אשר

אראה אי־זה טוב לבני האדם אשר יעשו תחת השמים מספר ימי

4-5 חייהם: הגדלתי מעשי בניתי לי בתים נטעתי לי כרמים: עשיתי לי

6 גנות ופרדסים ונטעתי בהם עץ כל־פרי: עשיתי לי ברכות מים

7 להשקות מהם יער צומח עצים: קניתי עבדים ושפחות ובני־בית

היה לי גם מקנה בקר וצאן הרבה היה לי מכל שהיו לפני בירושלם:

8 כנסתי לי גם־כסף וזהב וסגלת מלכים והמדינות עשיתי לי שרים

9 ושרות ותענוגת בני האדם שדה ושדות: וגדלתי והוספתי מכל שהיה

10 לפני בירושלם אף חכמתי עמדה לי: וכל אשר שאלו עיני לא אצלתי

מהם לא־מנעתי את־לבי מכל־שמחה כי־לבי שמח מכל־עמלי וזה־

היה חלקי מכל־עמלי:

11 ופניתי אני בכל־מעשי שעשו ידי ובעמל שעמלתי לעשות והנה

12 הכל הבל ורעות רוח ואין יתרון תחת השמש: ופניתי אני לראות

חכמה והוללות וסכלות כי | מה האדם שיבוא אחרי המלך את

13 אשר־כבר עשוהו: וראיתי אני שיש יתרון לחכמה מן־הסכלות כיתרון

14 האור מן־החשך: החכם עיניו בראשו והכסיל בחשך הולך וידעתי

15 גם־אני שמקרה אחד יקרה את־כלם: ואמרתי אני בלבי כמקרה

פסוק 12: נרס עָשָׂהוּ

myself, 'The fate of the fool will befall me too. Why, then, have I become so extremely wise?' and I said to myself that this, too, is vanity. For the wise man is no more remembered than the fool; in the multitude of coming days everything is forgotten. Yet how *can* the wise man die like the fool! Hence I hated life, for all the work done beneath the sun seemed worthless to me, and everything vanity and chasing of wind.

And I hated all my wealth on which I was toiling under the sun, which I must leave to the man coming after me, not knowing whether he would be wise or a fool. Yet he would rule over all my possessions, upon which I had spent my effort and skill under the sun. Indeed this is vanity! So I turned to rid my heart of any illusions concerning all the work on which I had laboured under the sun. For here is a man who has laboured with knowledge and skill, yet he must leave his portion to a man who has not toiled over it — surely that is vanity and a great evil. For what good does a man derive from all the labour and thought he expends under the sun? During all his days, pain and grief are his lot, and even at night his mind is not at rest — that too is vanity.

There is no greater good for man than eating and drinking and giving himself joy in his labour. Indeed, I have seen that this is from the hand of God, for who can enjoy a pleasure or abstain, except it be by His Will? To the man God favours He gives wisdom, knowledge and joy, but to the 'sinner' He assigns the task of gathering and amassing, only to hand it over at last to the man who is pleasing to God. Indeed, this is vanity and chasing of wind!

הכסיל גם־אני יקרני ולמה חכמתי אני אז יותר ודברתי בלבי שגם־

16 זה הבל: כי אין זכרון לחכם עם־הכסיל לעולם בשכבר הימים

17 הבאים הכל נשכח ואיך ימות החכם עם־הכסיל: ושנאתי את־החיים

כי רע עלי המעשה שנעשה תחת השמש כי־הכל הבל ורעות

רוח:

18 ושנאתי אני את־כל־עמלי שאני עמל תחת השמש שאניחנו לאדם

19 שיהיה אחרי: ומי יודע החכם יהיה או סכל וישלט בכל־עמלי

20 שעמלתי ושחכמתי תחת השמש גם־זה הבל: וסבותי אני ליאש את־

21 לבי על כל־העמל שעמלתי תחת השמש: כי־יש אדם שעמלו בחכמה

ובדעת ובכשרון ולאדם שלא עמל־בו יתננו חלקו גם־זה הבל ורעה

22 רבה: כי מה־הוה לאדם בכל־עמלו וברעיון לבו שהוא עמל תחת

23 השמש: כי כל־ימיו מכאבים וכעס ענינו גם־בלילה לא־שכב לבו

גם־זה הבל הוא:

24 אין־טוב באדם שיאכל ושתה והראה את־נפשו טוב בעמלו גם־

25 זה ראיתי אני כי מיד האלהים היא: כי מי יאכל ומי יחוש חוץ ממני:

26 כי לאדם שטוב לפניו נתן חכמה ודעת ושמחה ולחוטא נתן ענין

לאסוף ולכנוס לתת לטוב לפני האלהים גם־זה הבל ורעות רוח:

פסוק 24: גרס מִשֶּׁיֹּאכַל

פסוק 25: גרס מִמֶּנּוּ

III

THE FUTILITY OF HUMAN STRIVING

Like the events of nature, all human actions are prede-
termined by God. All man's activity is therefore useless —
including the search for ultimate truth, which God has
hidden from His creatures. Koheleth reverts to his main

EVERYTHING has its appointed time, and there is a
 season for every event under the sky.

There is a time to be born, and a time to die,
A time to plant and a time to uproot,
A time to kill and a time to heal,
A time to wreck and a time to build.
A time to weep and a time to laugh,
A time to mourn and a time to dance,
A time to scatter stones and a time to gather
  them,[1]
A time to embrace and a time to hold off embraces.
A time to seek and a time to give up,
A time to keep and a time to cast off,
A time to tear and a time to repair,
A time to be silent and a time to speak.
A time to love and a time to hate,
A time of war and a time of peace.

What profit then has the worker in his toil?

---

[1] A phrase having a sexual connotation.

theme — the only reasonable goal for man is the enjoy-
ment of pleasure, which is the gift of God.

(III. 1–15)

---

3 ¹   לכל זמן ועת לכל־חפץ תחת השמים:

ועת למות   ² עת ללדת

ועת לעקור נטוע :   עת לטעת

ועת לרפוא   ³ עת להרוג

ועת לבנות :   עת לפרוץ

ועת לשחוק   ⁴ עת לבכות

ועת רקוד :   עת ספוד

ועת כנוס אבנים   ⁵ עת להשליך אבנים

ועת לרחק מחבק: עת לחבוק

ועת לאבד   ⁶ עת לבקש

ועת להשליך :   עת לשמור

ועת לתפור   ⁷ עת לקרוע

ועת לדבר :   עת לחשות

ועת לשנא   ⁸ עת לאהב

ועת שלום :   עת מלחמה

⁹ מה־יתרון העושה באשר הוא עמל:

I know the concern which God has given men to be
afflicted with. Everything He has made proper in its
due time, and He has also placed the love of the world
in men's hearts, except that they may not discover the
work God has done from beginning to end.

I know that there is no other good in life but to be
happy while one lives. Indeed, every man who eats,
drinks and enjoys happiness in his work — that is the
gift of God. I know that whatever God does remains
forever — to it one cannot add and from it one cannot
subtract, for God has so arranged matters that men
should fear Him. What has been, already exists, and
what is still to be, has already been, and God always
seeks to repeat the past.

10-11 ראיתי את־הענין אשר נתן אלהים לבני האדם לענות בו: את־
הכל עשה יפה בעתו גם את־העלם נתן בלבם מבלי אשר לא־ימצא
האדם את־המעשה אשר־עשה האלהים מראש ועד־סוף:

12-13 ידעתי כי אין טוב בם כי אם־לשמוח ולעשות טוב בחייו: וגם
כל־האדם שיאכל ושתה וראה טוב בכל־עמלו מתת אלהים היא:

14 ידעתי כי כל־אשר יעשה האלהים הוא יהיה לעולם עליו אין

15 להוסיף וממנו אין לגרע והאלהים עשה שיראו מלפניו: מה־שהיה
כבר הוא ואשר להיות כבר היה והאלהים יבקש את־נרדף:

IV

THERE IS NO JUSTICE

The spectacle of wickedness in the seats of justice and the fruitless tears of the oppressed fill Koheleth's heart with despair. Nor can he find consolation in the shadowy

FURTHERMORE, I saw under the sun that in the place of judgment there was wickedness, and in the place of righteousness, wrong. I said to myself, 'Both the righteous and the wicked, God will judge, for there is a proper time for everything and every deed — over there!' I said to myself concerning men, 'Surely God has tested them and shown that they are nothing but beasts.' For the fate of men and the fate of beasts is the same. As the one dies, so does the other, for there is one spirit in both and man's distinction over the beast is nothing, for everything is vanity. All go to one place, all come from the dust and all return to the dust. Who knows whether the spirit of men rises upward and the spirit of the beast goes down to the earth? So I saw that there is nothing better for man than to rejoice in his works, for that is his lot, and no one can permit him to see what shall be afterwards.

Again I saw all the acts of oppression that are done under the sun. Here are the tears of the oppressed, with none to comfort them; and power in the hands of their oppressors, with none to comfort them. So I praise the dead who already have died, more than the creatures who are still alive. And more fortunate than both is he who has not yet been born and so has never seen the evil deeds that are being done under the sun.

doctrine of retribution in another world, which he dismisses
with a shrug of the shoulders. Only the pursuit of personal
happiness is a sensible goal for men.

(III. 16–IV. 3)

ועוד ראיתי תחת השמש מקום המשפט שמה הרשע ומקום 16

הצדק שמה הרשע: אמרתי אני בלבי את־הצדיק ואת־הרשע ישפט 17

האלהים כי־עת לכל־חפץ ועל כל־המעשה שם: אמרתי אני בלבי 18

על־דברת בני האדם לברם האלהים ולראות שהם־בהמה המה

להם: כי מקרה בני־האדם ומקרה הבהמה ומקרה אחד להם כמות 19

זה כן מות זה ורוח אחד לכל ומותר האדם מן־הבהמה אין כי הכל

הבל: הכל הולך אל־מקום אחד הכל היה מן־העפר והכל שב אל־ 20

העפר: מי יודע רוח בני האדם העלה היא למעלה ורוח הבהמה 21

הירדת היא למטה לארץ: וראיתי כי אין טוב מאשר ישמח האדם 22

במעשיו כי־הוא חלקו כי מי יביאנו לראות במה שיהיה אחריו:

ושבתי אני ואראה את־כל־העשקים אשר נעשים תחת השמש 4 1

והנה | דמעת העשקים ואין להם מנחם ומיד עשקיהם כח ואין להם

מנחם: ושבח אני את־המתים שכבר מתו מן־החיים אשר המה חיים 2

עדנה: וטוב משניהם את אשר־עדן לא היה אשר לא־ראה את־ 3

המעשה הרע אשר נעשה תחת השמש:

V

THE FOLLY OF HARD WORK

Koheleth discusses three reasons usually advanced for human effort and finds them all wanting. First is the joy of creation, which some call today the instinct of workmanship. This he dismisses as a thin disguise for the competitive spirit by which each man seeks to outstrip his neighbour and rival. Hence all preachments against laziness, to which youth is exposed, are foolish. The only

I SAW that all hard work and skill are merely one man's rivalry with his neighbour. This too is vanity and chasing of wind. Some men teach, 'The fool folds his hands and thus destroys himself.' But I declare: 'Better a handful acquired with ease than two hands full gained through toil and chasing after wind.'

I turned and saw another folly under the sun. Here is a man alone, with no one besides him, neither brother nor son. Yet there is no end to his toil nor is his eye ever satisfied with his wealth. He never asks himself, 'For whom am I labouring and depriving myself of joy?' Yes, it is vanity, a bad business.

Men say, 'Two are better than one, because they have a reward in their labour.' True, for if either falls, the other can lift his comrade, but woe to him who is alone when he falls, with no one else to lift him. Then also, if two sleep together, they will be warm, but how can one alone keep warm? Moreover, if some enemy attack either one, the two will stand against him, while a triple cord cannot quickly be severed.

sensible course is to take one's ease, especially if one has no family ties, and so no responsibility for others.

Koheleth then comments sarcastically on the alleged benefits of family companionship, which he finds are almost entirely physical. That surely cannot justify hard and unremitting toil.

Finally, there is the argument that hard work and ability are the key to advancement and fame. Here Koheleth may be referring to a political occurrence well-known to his contemporaries. It is, however, more probable, in view of accepted literary usage, that he is inventing a typical incident to illustrate the transitoriness of fame. Even an illustrious deed is unknown in all the ages before and after the event.

(IV. 4–16)

———————

4 וראיתי אני את־כל־עמל ואת כל־כשרון המעשה כי היא קנאת־

5 איש מרעהו גם־זה הבל ורעות רוח: הכסיל חבק את־ידיו ואכל את־

6 בשרו: טוב מלא כף נחת ממלא חפנים עמל ורעות רוח:

8-7 ושבתי אני ואראה הבל תחת השמש: יש אחד ואין שני גם בן ואח

אין־לו ואין קץ לכל־עמלו גם־עיניו לא־תשבע עשר ולמי | אני עמל

ומחסר את־נפשי מטובה גם־זה הבל וענין רע הוא:

10-9 טובים השנים מן־האחד אשר יש־להם שכר טוב בעמלם: כי

אם־יפלו האחד יקים את־חברו ואילו האחד שיפול ואין שני להקימו:

12-11 גם אם־ישכבו שנים וחם להם ולאחד איך יחם: ואם־יתקפו האחד

השנים יעמדו נגדו והחוט המשלש לא במהרה ינתק:

———————

פסוק 8: עֵינוֹ קרי

'Better a lad of poor birth, who is wise, than an old king, who is a fool and can no longer take care of himself. For from the prison-house he came forth to rule, though he was born poor in the kingdom.' I have seen all the living who walk under the sun on the side of the lad, his successor, who appears on the scene in his stead. Yet there is no end to the people who lived before them both, nor will later generations find joy in the youth — indeed, this, too, is vanity and chasing of wind.

¹³ טוב ילד מסכן וחכם ממלך זקן וכסיל אשר לא־ידע להזהר

¹⁴⁻¹⁵ עוד: כי־מבית הסורים יצא למלך כי גם במלכותו נולד רש: ראיתי
את־כל־החיים המהלכים תחת השמש עם הילד השני אשר יעמד

¹⁶ תחתיו: אין־קץ לכל־העם לכל אשר־היה לפניהם גם האחרונים לא
ישמחו־בו כי־גם־זה הבל ורעיון רוח:

VI

ON RELIGIOUS ETIQUETTE

Koheleth's philosophy does not predispose him to excessive piety. Yet the Temple is part of the accepted order, and it is seemly to observe the precepts of religion. Prayer

WATCH your step when you go to the house of God, for it is better to understand than to offer sacrifice like the fools, who do not even know how to do evil! Do not hasten to speak, nor let yourself be rushed into uttering words before God, for God is in heaven and you are on the earth — therefore, let your words be few. For 'as dreams come with many concerns, so the fool speaks with many words.'

When you make a vow to God, do not delay paying it, for He takes no pleasure in fools — what you vow, be sure to pay! Better not to vow at all than to vow and fail to pay. Do not let your mouth bring punishment upon your body, and do not tell the messenger, 'It was a mistake.' Why should God be angry at your voice and so destroy the work of your hands? With all the dreams, follies and idle chatter, this remains — fear God!

should be brief, and vows should be few. No enthusiasm and ecstasy, only the performance of one's duties is required. Koheleth here reflects the background of the upper class, which later crystallized in Sadduceeism.

(IV. 17–V. 6)

שמר רגליך כאשר תלך אל־בית האלהים וקרוב לשמע מתת ¹⁷

הכסילים זבח כי־אינם יודעים לעשות רע:

אל־תבהל על־פיך ולבך אל־ימהר להוציא דבר לפני האלהים ¹ 5

כי האלהים בשמים ואתה על־הארץ על־כן יהיו דבריך מעטים: כי ²

בא החלום ברב ענין וקול כסיל ברב דברים: כאשר תדר נדר ³

לאלהים אל־תאחר לשלמו כי אין חפץ בכסילים את אשר־תדר

שלם: טוב אשר לא־תדר משתדור ולא תשלם: אל־תתן את־פיך ⁴⁻⁵

לחטיא את־בשרך ואל־תאמר לפני המלאך כי שגגה היא למה יקצף

האלהים על־קולך וחבל את־מעשה ידיך: כי ברב חלמות והבלים ⁶

ודברים הרבה כי את־האלהים ירא:

פסוק 17: רַגְלְךָ קרי

VII

ON THE POLITICAL SCENE

Koheleth ironically observes that oppression and injustice,
which it is the ostensible function of government to curb,

IF YOU observe the despoiling of the poor and the
perversion of justice and of right in the State, do not
be astonished at the fact, for each guardian of the law
is higher than the next, and there are still higher ones
above them!

The advantage of land is paramount; even a king is
subject to the soil.

are in reality increased because of the hierarchy of corrupt officials, who prey upon the people.

Then follows an enigmatic verse that apparently extols agriculture as the basis of national prosperity, a point of view reflecting the attitude of the wealthy absentee landowners, who fancied themselves country gentlemen, while they lived in the capital, enjoying a life of luxury.

(V. 7, 8)

אם־עשק רש וגזל משפט וצדק תראה במדינה אל־תתמה על־ ⁷

החפץ כי גבה מעל גבה שמר וגבהים עליהם: ויתרון ארץ בכל היא ⁸

מלך לשדה נעבד:

פסוק 8: הוּא קרי

VIII

THE SENSELESSNESS OF GREED

The lust for wealth can never be satisfied. Increased income brings increased demands for expenditure. Men have been known to deny themselves every pleasure, only to lose their hoarded wealth in some ill-starred venture, so that their children are penniless. Nor is it much better

HE WHO loves money will never have enough of it and he who loves wealth will never attain it — this is indeed vanity. For as wealth increases, so do those who would spend it, hence what value is there in the owner's superior ability, except that he has more to look upon? Sweet is the sleep of the toiler, whether he has eaten little or much, but the full stomach of the rich man does not let him sleep.

There is a crying evil that I have seen under the sun — a man's wealth hoarded up to his own hurt. His wealth may be lost in an unlucky venture and then he begets a son, for whom there is nothing. As he came forth naked from his mother's womb, so will he return, just as he came, and nothing that he can take with him will he carry off for his toil.

This, too, is a crying evil — as he came so will he depart, hence what advantage was there in labouring for the wind? All his days he eats in the dark and suffers much grief, sickness and anger. Here is what I have discovered: it is meet and proper for a man to eat, drink and enjoy himself in return for the toil he *to bequeath one's wealth to another, after a life-time of privation.*

God's will is that man find joy in life, before he goes down into eternal darkness. To Koheleth's keen eye, the virtues of diligence and thrift are hardly more than manifestations of greed — an observation uncomfortably close to the truth. (V. 9–VI. 9)

------

⁹   אהב כסף לא־ישבע כסף ומי־אהב בהמון לא תבואה גם־זה

¹⁰ הבל: ברבות הטובה רבו אוכליה ומה־כשרון לבעליה כי אם־ראית

¹¹ עיניו: מתוקה שנת העבד אם־מעט ואם־הרבה יאכל והשבע לעשיר

איננו מניח לו לישון:

¹² יש רעה חולה ראיתי תחת השמש עשר שמור לבעליו לרעתו:

¹³⁻¹⁴ ואבד העשר ההוא בענין רע והוליד בן ואין בידו מאומה: כאשר

יצא מבטן אמו ערום ישוב ללכת כשבא ומאומה לא־ישא בעמלו

שילך בידו:

¹⁵ וגם־זה רעה חולה כל־עמת שבא כן ילך ומה־יתרון לו שיעמל

¹⁶⁻¹⁷ לרוח: גם כל־ימיו בחשך יאכל וכעס הרבה וחליו וקצף: הנה אשר־

ראיתי אני טוב אשר־יפה לאכול ולשתות־ולראות טובה בכל־עמלו |

פסוק 9: גרס תְּבוֹאָהוּ

פסוק 10: רָאוּת קרי

undergoes under the sun in the scant years God has given him, for that is man's portion, and not long will he remember the days of his life. Indeed, every man to whom God has given wealth and possessions and granted the power to enjoy them, taking his share and rejoicing in his labour, that is the gift of God, for it is God who provides him with the joy in his heart.

There is an evil I have seen under the sun and it weighs heavily upon men. Here is a man whom God gives wealth, means and position, so that he lacks nothing he can possibly desire. Yet God does not let him enjoy it, for some stranger is destined to consume it — this is vanity, an evil plague. If a man begets a hundred children and lives many years, as many as his days may be, if he derives no pleasure from his wealth, even if he have an elaborate funeral — I say that the still-born child is more fortunate than he. Though it comes into the world in vain and departs into darkness, and in the gloom its name is hidden, never seeing or knowing the sun, its lot is happier than his. Even if a man lives a thousand years twice-told, but finds no joy in life — do not all go to the same place?

'All a man's toil is for his wants, but his desires are never satisfied.' What advantage then has a wise man over a fool, or a poor man, who knows how to meet the problems of life? Better a joy at hand than longing for distant pleasures — that, too, is vanity and chasing of wind.

שיעמל תחת־השמש מספר ימי־חיו אשר־נתן־לו האלהים כי־הוא

חלקו: גם כל־האדם אשר נתן־לו האלהים עשר ונכסים והשליטו ¹⁸

לאכל ממנו ולשאת את־חלקו ולשמח בעמלו זה מתת אלהים היא:

כי לא הרבה יזכר את־ימי חייו כי האלהים מענה בשמחת לבו: ¹⁹

6   יש רעה אשר ראיתי תחת השמש ורבה היא על־האדם: איש ²-¹

אשר יתן־לו האלהים עשר ונכסים וכבוד ואיננו חסר לנפשו | מכל

אשר־יתאוה ולא־ישליטנו האלהים לאכל ממנו כי איש נכרי יאכלנו

זה הבל וחלי רע הוא: אם־יוליד איש מאה ושנים רבות יחיה ורב | ³

שיהיו ימי־שניו ונפשו לא־תשבע מן־הטובה וגם־קבורה לא־היתה לו

אמרתי טוב ממנו הנפל: כי־בהבל בא ובחשך ילך ובחשך שמו ⁴

יכסה: גם־שמש לא־ראה ולא ידע נחת לזה מזה: ואלו חיה אלף שנים ⁶-⁵

פעמים וטובה לא ראה הלא אל־מקום אחד הכל הולך:

כל־עמל האדם לפיהו וגם־הנפש לא תמלא: כי מה־יותר לחכם ⁸-⁷

מן־הכסיל מה־לעני יודע להלך נגד החיים: טוב מראה עינים מהלך־ ⁹

נפש גם־זה הבל ורעות רוח:

פסוק 19: גרס מַעֲנֵהוּ

פסוק 3: גרס לֹא־הָיְתָה

IX

ON MAN'S IGNORANCE

Koheleth reverts to another of his basic themes — the predetermined character of events and men's helplessness

WHAT has been has already been determined, and it is known that man cannot argue with One mightier than himself. Many words merely add to the futility — what advantage does man derive from it? Who knows what is good for man in life, during the brief days of his vain existence, which he spends like a shadow? Who can tell man what will happen under the sun after he is gone?

before the mystery of the world, which is unrelieved by any knowledge of the meaning of life and the outcome of events.

(VI. 10–12)

---

10 מה־שהיה כבר נקרא שמו ונודע אשר־הוא אדם ולא־יוכל לדין

11 עם שהתקיף ממנו: כי יש־דברים הרבה מרבים הבל מה־יתר לאדם:

12 כי מי־יודע מה־טוב לאדם בחיים מספר ימי־חיי הבלו ויעשם כצל

אשר מי־יגיד לאדם מה־יהיה אחריו תחת השמש:

פסוק 10: שֶׁתַּקִּיף קרי

X

THOUGHTS ON THE GOOD LIFE

Though man cannot know 'the good' in any absolute sense, life must be lived and certain attitudes are better than others. These are expressed through a series of aphorisms that superficially seem to be examples of conventional proverb literature. Actually, however, by a characteristic comment or turn of phrase, Koheleth has made them his

BETTER a good name than good oil, and so the day of death rather than the day of one's birth.

Better to go to a house of mourning than to a banquet-hall, for that is the end of all men and the living may take the lesson to heart.

Better sorrow than laughter, for through sadness of countenance the understanding improves. Therefore wise men prefer the house of mourning and fools the house of joy.

Better to hear the reproof of a wise man than the praise of fools. For, like the sound of thorns crackling under the pot, the laughter of fools grates on the ear. But even the wise man's reproof may be vanity, for a gift turns the wise man into a fool and a bribe perverts the understanding.

Better to judge a matter at its end rather than at its beginning, hence patience is better than pride. Therefore do not be quick to rouse your temper, for anger lodges in the bosom of fools. Do not say, 'What has happened? The earlier days were better than these!' For not wisely have you raised the question.

*own, reflecting his basic conviction that one must not expect
too much from life to avoid tragic disappointment.*

*Extravagant hopes for the future as well as idealizations
of the past are alike foolish. Recognizing his ignorance
and powerlessness, man should learn to take good and
evil in his stride.*

*The bond of connection in this group of sayings is
typically Semitic. The collection contains seven utterances, each of which begins with the word* tob *('good').
These brief gnomic sayings are amplified by several
others, in which the connection is not always close, very
much as in the book of Proverbs. The section ends with a
characteristic reflection that man is unalterably ignorant
of the real meaning of events.*

(VII. 1–14)

---

7 ‏2-1‏   טוב שם משמן טוב ויום המות מיום הולדו: טוב ללכת אל־בית־

אבל מלכת אל־בית משתה באשר הוא סוף כל־האדם והחי יתן אל־

לבו:

‏4-3‏   טוב כעס משחוק כי־ברע פנים ייטב לב: לב חכמים בבית אבל

ולב כסילים בבית שמחה:

‏6-5‏   טוב לשמע גערת חכם מאיש שמע שיר כסילים: כי כקול

‏7‏   הסירים תחת הסיר כן שחק הכסיל וגם־זה הבל: כי העשק יהולל

חכם ויאבד את־לב מתנה:

‏9-8‏   טוב אחרית דבר מראשיתו טוב ארך־רוח מגבה־רוח: אל־תבהל

‏10‏   ברוחך לכעוס כי כעס בחיק כסילים ינוח: אל־תאמר מה היה

שהימים הראשנים היו טובים מאלה כי לא מחכמה שאלת על־זה:

Better is wisdom with an inheritance — an advantage to all who see the sun, for there is the double protection of wisdom and money, and the advantage of knowing that wisdom preserves the lives of those who possess it.

Observe the work of God, for who can straighten out what He has made crooked? In the day of good fortune, enjoy it, and in the day of trouble consider that God has set the one against the other, so that man may not discover anything that happens after he is gone.

11-12   טובה חכמה עם־נחלה ויתר לראי השמש: כי בצל החכמה בצל

הכסף ויתרון דעת החכמה תחיה בעליה:

13-14   ראה את־מעשה האלהים כי מי יוכל לתקן את אשר עותו: ביום

טובה היה בטוב וביום רעה ראה גם את־זה לעמת־זה עשה האלהים

על־דברת שלא ימצא האדם אחריו מאומה:

XI

THE 'GOLDEN MEAN'

Closely connected with the preceding collection comes Koheleth's reflection on the 'golden mean,' the Aristotelian principle of ethics with which Koheleth is familiar. He

I HAVE seen everything during my vain existence, a righteous man being destroyed for all his righteousness and a sinner living long for all his wickedness. Hence do not be righteous overmuch nor be overzealous for wisdom — why be left desolate? Neither be overly wicked, nor be a fool — why die before your time? Far better it is to grasp the one and hold fast to the other, for he who reverences God will do his duty by both! Be not a fool, for it has been well said, 'Wisdom gives a wise man strength greater than ten rulers who are in the city.' Nor be overly righteous, for it has been observed, 'There is no man on earth always in the right, who does the proper thing and never errs.'

Pay no attention to every word that is spoken, lest you hear your own slave reviling you. Besides, you know very well that many times you have reviled others.

All this I tested concerning Wisdom. I thought I could become wise, but it is much beyond me. Far away is all that has come into being and very, very deep; who can find it? With all my heart I turned to learn, explore and seek after wisdom and thought, and I saw that wickedness is foolishness, and folly is madness.

*urges it, however, from his own vantage-point: both ex-
tremes of saintliness and wickedness lead to unhappiness.*

*As always, the ideas are couched in typical religious
terminology. 'Reverencing God' means fulfilling His purpose, by seeking the happy life. Folly and wickedness are
synonymous for Koheleth, as for all the Wisdom teachers,
though his views of what folly means differ from theirs.
Reminding his readers that his conclusions are based on
experience and sound observation, and are therefore no
conventional platitudes, he repeats his conclusion that the
extremes of wickedness and folly lead to disaster.*

(VII. 15–25)

---

15 את־הכל ראיתי בימי הבלי יש צדיק אבד בצדקו ויש רשע

16 מאריך ברעתו: אל־תהי צדיק הרבה ואל־תתחכם יותר למה

17 תשומם: אל־תרשע הרבה ואל־תהי סכל למה תמות בלא עתך:

18 טוב אשר תאחז בזה וגם־מזה אל־תנח את־ידך כי־ירא אלהים יצא

19-20 את־כלם: החכמה תעז לחכם מעשרה שליטים אשר היו בעיר: כי

אדם אין צדיק בארץ אשר יעשה־טוב ולא יחטא:

21 גם לכל־הדברים אשר ידברו אל־תתן לבך אשר לא־תשמע

22 את־עבדך מקללך: כי גם־פעמים רבות ידע לבך אשר גם־את

קללת אחרים:

24-23 כל־זה נסיתי בחכמה אמרתי אחכמה והיא רחוקה ממני: רחוק

25 מה־שהיה ועמק | עמק מי ימצאנו: סבותי אני ולבי לדעת ולתור

ובקש חכמה וחשבון ולדעת רשע כסל והסכלות הוללות:

פסוק 22: אַתָּה קרי

XII

ON WOMEN

All the evidence points to Koheleth's having been a bachelor.
It has been noted that he says too much of women that is

I FIND woman more bitter than death, for her heart
is full of traps and snares, her hands are chains. He
who is favoured by God will escape her, but the sinner
will be trapped by her.

See, this I have found, says Koheleth, as I sought,
step by step, to reach a conclusion. This, too, I sought
but in vain, one man in a thousand I did find, but one
woman among as many I could not find. Besides, note
this that I have learnt: God has made men straightforward, but they have sought out many devices.

evil not to have loved them much. To which it may be
added that he loved them but did not trust them!

(VII. 26–29)

---

26 ומוצא אני מר ממות את־האשה אשר־היא מצודים וחרמים לבה

27 אסורים ידיה טוב לפני האלהים ימלט ממנה וחוטא ילכד בה: ראה

28 זה מצאתי אמרה קהלת אחת לאחת למצא חשבון: אשר עוד־בקשה

נפשי ולא מצאתי אדם אחד מאלף מצאתי ואשה בכל־אלה לא

מצאתי:

29 לבד ראה־זה מצאתי אשר עשה האלהים את־האדם ישר והמה

בקשו חשבנות רבים:

פסוק 27: גרס אָמַר הַקֹּהֶלֶת

XIII

LOYALTY TO THE KING

*Typical of the upper-class orientation of Wisdom litera-
ture is its preoccupation with training its youthful charges
for important careers at the royal court. To achieve and
maintain a position in the atmosphere of tyranny and*

Who is like the truly wise man,
And who can understand the meaning of events?
A man's wisdom lights up his face,
And the boldness of his countenance is transformed.

I say: Keep the king's command, because of the
oath of loyalty. Do not hasten to leave his presence,
but do not persist in a matter distasteful to him, for
he can do whatever he wishes. Since the king's word
is law, who can say to him, 'What are you doing?' He
who keeps his command will experience no trouble,
for a wise mind will know the proper time and procedure. For everything has its proper time and procedure,
man's evil being so widespread.

Indeed, man does not know what the future will be,
for when it happens, who will tell him?

Man is powerless over the spirit
To confine the spirit,
Nor has he any power over the day of death,
Nor any control over a battle,
And even wickedness cannot save the wrong-doer.

All this I saw, as I noticed the actions going on
under the sun, when men have power over their
fellows to harm them.

intrigue of an Oriental palace requires a variety of gifts, not all of the highest moral level — loyalty to the ruling power, the avoidance of both undue fearsomeness on the one hand and unbending obduracy on the other, a quick grasp of complex situations, a capacity to disguise one's feelings, patience to bide one's time and skill in selecting the proper means for reaching a given objective.

The conventional Wisdom writers moralize these qualities by conceiving of loyalty to the ruling power as a virtue — especially since an oath is involved. Koheleth urges the same qualities, but with his tongue in his cheek. Basically, men should be faithful to the king, because he is powerful! A sensible subject will obey the royal command, awaiting the proper time for every act, but this practical idea recalls to Koheleth one of the principal mainsprings of his melancholy — man knows nothing of the future nor is he master of his destiny.   (VIII. 1–9)

---

8 1   מי כהחכם ומי יודע פשר דבר חכמת אדם תאיר פניו ועז פניו

ישנא:

3-2   אני פי־מלך שמור ועל דברת שבועת אלהים: אל־תבהל מפניו

4   תלך אל־תעמד בדבר רע כי כל־אשר יחפץ יעשה: באשר דבר־

5   מלך שלטון ומי יאמר־לו מה־תעשה: שומר מצוה לא ידע דבר רע

6   ועת ומשפט ידע לב חכם: כי לכל־חפץ יש עת ומשפט כי־רעת

האדם רבה עליו:

7   כי־איננו ידע מה־שיהיה כי כאשר יהיה מי יגיד לו:

8   אין אדם שליט ברוח   לכלוא את־הרוח

ואין שלטון ביום המות   ואין משלחת במלחמה

ולא־ימלט רשע את־בעליו:

9   את־כל־זה ראיתי ונתון את־לבי לכל־מעשה אשר נעשה תחת

השמש עת אשר שלט האדם באדם לרע לו:

XIV

ON THE FAILURE OF RETRIBUTION

Koheleth notes how evil-doers, after long and successful careers of evil, are duly eulogized as benefactors of the community.

He is thus led to consider the entire problem of reward and punishment. Koheleth is not disposed to deny completely that retribution overtakes the sinner. Yet, in many

I HAVE seen wrong-doers being carried with pomp to their graves, and, as men return from the sacred ground, the evil-doers are praised in the city where they had acted thus. Indeed, this is vanity!

Because judgment upon an evil deed is not executed speedily, men's hearts are encouraged to do wrong, for a sinner commits a hundred crimes and God is patient with him, though I know the answer that 'it will be well in the end with those who revere God because they fear Him and it will be far from well with the sinner, who, like a shadow, will not long endure, because he does not fear God.'

Here is a vanity that takes place on the earth — there are righteous men who receive the recompense due to the wicked, and wicked men who receive the recompense due to the righteous. I say, this is indeed vanity.

Therefore I praise joy, for there is no other good for man under the sun but to eat, drink, and be joyful and have this accompany him in his toil, during the days of his life, which God has given him beneath the sun.

cases, the punishment is meted out after a long delay and,
all too often, the righteous and wicked are treated alike.
These failings and postponements in the process of retribu-
tion give men both the incentive and the opportunity for
wrong-doing.

The quest for justice is as fruitless as the search for
truth. Only personal joy remains for man.

(VIII. 10–IX. 3)

---

10 ובכן ראיתי רשעים קברים ובאו וממקום קדוש יהלכו וישתכחו

בעיר אשר כן־עשו גם־זה הבל:

11 אשר אין־נעשה פתגם מעשה הרעה מהרה על־כן מלא לב בני־

12 האדם בהם לעשות רע: אשר חטא עשה רע מאת ומאריך לו כי גם־

13 יודע אני אשר יהיה־טוב ליראי האלהים אשר ייראו מלפניו: וטוב

לא־יהיה לרשע ולא־יאריך ימים כצל אשר איננו ירא מלפני אלהים:

14 יש־הבל אשר נעשה על־הארץ אשר | יש צדיקים אשר מגיע

אלהם כמעשה הרשעים ויש רשעים שמגיע אלהם כמעשה הצדיקים

אמרתי שגם־זה הבל:

15 ושבחתי אני את־השמחה אשר אין־טוב לאדם תחת השמש כי

אם־לאכל ולשתות ולשמוח והוא ילונו בעמלו ימי חייו אשר־נתן־לו

האלהים תחת השמש:

פסוק 10: גרס קָבֶר מוּבָאִים, גרס וְיִשְׁתַּבְּחוּ

When I set myself to acquire wisdom and see all the activity taking place on the earth, I saw that though a man sleep neither by day nor by night he cannot discover the meaning of God's work which is done under the sun, for the sake of which a man may search hard, but he will not find it, and though a wise man may think he is about to learn it, he will be unable to find it.

All this I grasped and clearly understood, that the just and the wise, together with all their works, are in God's hands; men can be certain of neither God's love nor His hate — anything may happen to them. One fate awaits all men, one lot comes to the just and the unjust, to the good and pure and the impure, to him who brings his offerings and him who does not; as with the good man, so with the sinner; as with the man who swears lightly, so with him who fears an oath.

This is the root of the evil in all that happens under the sun — that one fate comes to all. Therefore men's minds are filled with evil and there is madness in their hearts while they live, for they know that afterwards — they are off to the dead!

¹⁶ כאשר נתתי את־לבי לדעת חכמה ולראות את־הענין אשר נעשה

¹⁷ על־הארץ כי גם ביום ובלילה שנה בעיניו איננו ראה: וראיתי את־
כל־מעשה האלהים כי לא יוכל האדם למצוא את־המעשה אשר
נעשה תחת־השמש בשל אשר יעמל האדם לבקש ולא ימצא וגם אם־
יאמר החכם לדעת לא יוכל למצא:

9 ¹ כי את־כל־זה נתתי אל־לבי ולבור את־כל־זה אשר הצדיקים
והחכמים ועבדיהם ביד האלהים גם־אהבה גם־שנאה אין יודע האדם

² הכל לפניהם: הכל כאשר לכל מקרה אחד לצדיק ולרשע לטוב
ולטהור ולטמא ולזבח ולאשר איננו זבח כטוב כחטא הנשבע כאשר
שבועה ירא:

³ זה ׀ רע בכל אשר־נעשה תחת השמש כי־מקרה אחד לכל וגם
לב בני־האדם מלא־רע והוללות בלבבם בחייהם ואחריו אל־
המתים:

XV

IN PRAISE OF LIFE

*For all its frustrations, life remains the central good in the
world. After death all activity and sensation are ended —*

HE WHO is attached to all the living still has hope, for
surely a live dog is better than a dead lion! The living
know at least that they will die, but the dead know
nothing, nor have they any reward, for their memory
is forgotten. Their loves, their hates, their jealousies,
all have perished — no longer have they a share in all
that is done under the sun.

> Go, then, eat your bread with joy,
> And drink your wine with a glad heart,
> For God has already approved your actions.
> At all times let your clothes be white,
> And oil on your head not be lacking.

> Enjoy life with the woman whom you love,
> Through all the vain days of your life,
> Which God has given you under the sun,
> Throughout your brief days,
> For that is your reward in life
> For your toil under the sun.

Whatever you are able to do, do with all your might,
for there is neither action nor thought nor knowledge
nor wisdom in the grave towards which you are moving.

Again I saw that beneath the sun the race is not to
the swift, nor the battle to the brave, nor is bread won
by the wise, nor wealth by the clever, nor favour by
the learned, for time and accident overtake them all.
Though man does not know his hour, like fish caught
in an evil net, like birds seized in a snare, so men are
trapped in an hour of misfortune, when it falls upon
them suddenly.

and even during life unknown perils lurk along the way.
All the more reason why man should enjoy life while he
can with all the vigour and zest at his command. This
section is closely connected with the preceding.

(IX. 4–12)

---

⁴ כי־מי אשר יבחר אל כל־החיים יש בטחון כי־לכלב חי הוא

⁵ טוב מן־האריה המת: כי החיים יודעים שימתו והמתים אינם יודעים

⁶ מאומה ואין־עוד להם שכר כי נשכח זכרם: גם אהבתם גם־שנאתם

גם־קנאתם כבר אבדה וחלק אין־להם עוד לעולם בכל אשר־נעשה

תחת השמש:

⁷ לך אכל בשמחה לחמך   ושתה בלב־טוב יינך

כי כבר רצה האלהים את מעשיך:

⁸ בכל־עת יהיו בגדיך לבנים   ושמן על־ראשך אל־יחסר :

⁹ ראה חיים עם־אשה אשר־אהבת   כל־ימי חיי הבלך

אשר נתן־לך תחת השמש   כל ימי הבלך

כי הוא חלקך בחיים ובעמלך   אשר־אתה עמל תחת השמש:

¹⁰ כל אשר תמצא ידך לעשות בכחך עשה כי אין מעשה וחשבון ודעת

וחכמה בשאול אשר אתה הלך שמה:

¹¹ שבתי וראה תחת־השמש כי לא לקלים המרוץ ולא לגבורים

המלחמה וגם לא לחכמים לחם וגם לא לנבנים עשר וגם לא לידעים

¹² חן כי־עת ופגע יקרה את־כלם: כי גם לא־ידע האדם את־עתו כדגים

שנאחזים במצודה רעה וכצפרים האחזות בפח כהם יוקשים בני

האדם לעת רעה כשתפול עליהם פתאם:

פסוק 4: יְחֻבַּר קרי

XVI

THE INADEQUACIES OF WISDOM

By training and temperament, Koheleth is prejudiced in favour of wisdom, but he is aware of how little genuine respect it commands. The wise man who lacks wealth

THIS also I saw as an instance of wisdom under the sun, and it seemed significant to me. A small city there was, with few people in it, and a great king attacked it, besieging it and building breastworks against it. But there was found in it a poor wise man, who saved the city by his wisdom, yet no one remembered that poor man. So I said, 'Wisdom is better than strength,' but the poor man's wisdom is despised and his words go unheeded.

It is said, 'The words of the wise spoken quietly are heard better than the ranting of the king of fools,' and 'Wisdom is better than weapons'; but I say, 'One fool can destroy much good,' and 'As dying flies befoul the perfumer's ointment, so a little folly can outweigh an abundance of wisdom.'

*and position is unhonoured in the society he has helped
to save. Moreover, the greatest achievement of wisdom
may be undone by a single act of folly.*

*Koheleth cites a series of proverbs, reflecting the conven-
tional adulation of wisdom. He proceeds to refute them
by maxims and comments of an opposite tenor.*

(IX. 13–X. 1)

13-14   גם־זה ראיתי חכמה תחת השמש וגדולה היא אלי: עיר קטנה

ואנשים בה מעט ובא־אליה מלך גדול וסבב אתה ובנה עליה

15 מצודים גדולים: ומצא בה איש מסכן חכם ומלט־הוא את־העיר

16 בחכמתו ואדם לא זכר את־האיש המסכן ההוא: ואמרתי אני טובה

חכמה מגבורה וחכמת המסכן בזויה ודבריו אינם נשמעים:

17-18   דברי חכמים בנחת נשמעים מזעקת מושל בכסילים: טובה

10 ¹ חכמה מכלי קרב וחוטא אחד יאבד טובה הרבה: זבובי מות יבאיש

יביע שמן רוקח יקר מחכמה מכבוד סכלות מעט:

XVII

THE VIRTUES THAT MAKE FOR SUCCESS

A collection of maxims dealing with the practical virtues, but with little organic connection among them, now follows. Warnings are sounded against foolishness, plotting to injure one's neighbour, indolence and excess in food and drink. Such virtues as prudence, energy and loyalty to the government are inculcated. Only at certain points

A WISE man's mind is his support, a fool's mind is his misfortune. Even on the road, as the fool walks, he shows a lack of sense, and proclaims to all that he is a fool!

If the ruler's anger rises against you, do not give up your post, for calmness can overcome the effects of grave offenses.

Here is an evil I have seen under the sun, indeed an error emanating from the ruler. Folly is often enthroned on the great heights, but the rich sit in the low places. I have seen slaves on horses, while lords must walk on foot like slaves.

He who digs a pit may fall into it, and he who breaks a fence down may be bitten by a snake. He who loosens rocks may be hurt by them, and he who cuts logs may be endangered by them.

If an axe is blunt, and a man does not sharpen it beforehand, he must exert greater strength to wield it, but it is an advantage to prepare one's skill in advance. For if the snake bites before it is charmed, there is no value in the charmer's art.

The words of the wise man's mouth win favour, but the lips of the fool lead to his undoing. For the be-

can these utterances be distinguished from the conventional
products of the Wisdom academies — either through a
characteristic trait of style or a special viewpoint. Such is
Koheleth's lament, typical of a conservative, on the fluctu-
ations of the social scene, or his praise of money as the
means for providing life's pleasures, or his caution against
disloyalty, because of the danger of being discovered and
punished.

Koheleth gives sound advice when he advises his reader
to diversify his business undertakings and work ener-
getically at his appointed tasks, without standing idly by,
to watch for wind and rain. But he bases these practical
suggestions on ideas uniquely his own. Man can never
tell when evil will descend upon him. Besides, the world
and its happenings remain forever unknowable to man.

(X. 2–XI. 6)

לב חכם לימינו ולב כסיל לשמאלו: וגם־בדרך כשהסכל הלך   3-2
לבו חסר ואמר לכל סכל הוא:

אם־רוח המושל תעלה עליך מקומך אל־תנח כי מרפא יניח   4
חטאים גדולים:

יש רעה ראיתי תחת השמש כשגגה שיצא מלפני השליט: נתן   6-5

הסכל במרומים רבים ועשירים בשפל ישבו: ראיתי עבדים על־   7
סוסים ושרים הלכים כעבדים על־הארץ:

חפר גומץ בו יפול ופרץ גדר ישכנו נחש: מסיע אבנים יעצב   9-8
בהם בוקע עצים יסכן בם:

אם־קהה הברזל והוא לא־פנים קלקל וחילים יגבר ויתרון   10

הכשיר חכמה: אם־ישך הנחש בלוא־לחש ואין יתרון לבעל הלשון: 11

דברי פי־חכם חן ושפתות כסיל תבלענו: תחלת דברי־פיהו   13-12

פסוק 3: כְּשֶׁסָּכָל קרי

פסוק 3: גרס וְאֹמֵר

ginning of his speech is folly, and its end, complete madness. Though the fool multiplies words, man does not know what is to be, and who can tell him what happens after his lifetime?

The efforts of the fool exhaust him, for he does not even know the way to town.

Woe to you, O land, whose king is a child and whose lords carouse into the morning. Happy are you, O land, whose king is nobly born, and whose lords feast in due season, in strength and not in drunkenness.

Through sloth the ceiling sinks, and through slack hands the house leaks.

Men make a feast for pleasure, and wine cheers the living, and it is money that provides it all!

Do not curse the king even in your thoughts, nor the rich even in your bed-chamber, for a bird of the air may carry your voice and a feathered creature betray the matter.

Send your bread upon the waters, so that you may find it again after many days. Divide your means into seven or eight portions, for you cannot tell what calamity will come upon the earth.

If the clouds are filled with rain, they will empty it upon the earth; if a tree is blown down by the wind in the south or in the north, wherever it falls there it lies. Therefore, on with your work, for he who watches the wind will never sow and he who gapes at the clouds will never reap.

As you do not know how life enters an embryo in the womb of a pregnant woman, so you cannot know the work of God who does everything. Therefore in the morning sow your seed and in the evening do not be idle, for you cannot tell which will prosper or whether both shall have equal success.

14 סכלות ואחרית פיהו הוללות רעה: והסכל ירבה דברים לא־ידע

האדם מה־שיהיה ואשר יהיה מאחריו מי יגיד לו:

15 עמל הכסילים תיגענו אשר לא־ידע ללכת אל־עיר:

17-16 אי־לך ארץ שמלכך נער ושריך בבקר יאכלו: אשריך ארץ

שמלכך בן־חורים ושריך בעת יאכלו בגבורה ולא בשתי:

18 בעצלתים ימך המקרה ובשפלות ידים ידלף הבית:

19 לשחוק עשים לחם ויין ישמח חיים והכסף יענה את־הכל:

20 גם במדעך מלך אל־תקלל ובחדרי משכבך אל־תקלל עשיר

כי עוף השמים יוליך את־הקול ובעל הכנפים יגיד דבר:

11 2-1 שלח לחמך על־פני המים כי־ברב הימים תמצאנו: תן־חלק

לשבעה וגם לשמונה כי לא תדע מה־יהיה רעה על־הארץ:

3 אם־ימלאו העבים גשם על־הארץ יריקו ואם־יפול עץ בדרום

4 ואם בצפון מקום שיפול העץ שם יהוא: שמר רוח לא יזרע וראה

בעבים לא יקצור:

5 כאשר אינך יודע מה־דרך הרוח כעצמים בבטן המלאה ככה

6 לא תדע את־מעשה האלהים אשר יעשה את־הכל: בבקר זרע את־

זרעך ולערב אל־תנח ידך כי אינך יודע אי זה יכשר הזה אורזה

ואם־שניהם כאחד טובים:

פסוק 20: כְּנָפַיִם קרי

פסוק 5: גרס בַּעֲצָמִים

XVIII

JOY — THE DIVINE IMPERATIVE

*In the closing section of his book, Koheleth rises to heights
of eloquence that equal and surpass the majestic opening.*

Sweet is the light
And it is good for the eyes
To see the sun!
For if a man live many years,
Let him rejoice in them all,
And remember that the days of darkness will be
     many,
And that everything thereafter is nothingness.

Rejoice, young man, in your youth,
And let your heart cheer you in your youthful
     days.
Follow the impulses of your heart
And the desires of your eyes,
And know that for all this,
God will call you to account.

Banish sadness from your heart,
And remove sorrow from your flesh,
For childhood and youth are a fleeting breath.

Remember your Creator in the days of your
     youth,
Before the evil days come and the years draw
     near,
Of which you will say, 'I have no pleasure in
     them.'

*In impassioned phrases he repeats that it is God's will
that man be happy. The time for joy is youth, when our
faculties are unimpaired. It is then that man must seek
his happiness, before old age sets in, with its burdens of
debility and failing powers.*

*The book closes with a moving 'Allegory on Old Age,'
in which the tragedy of man's progressive deterioration is
graphically described.*

(XI. 7–XII. 8)

לראות את־השמש:	וטוב לעינים	⁷ ומתוק האור
בכלם ישמח	יחיה האדם	⁸ כי אם־שנים הרבה
כל־שבא הבל:	כי־הרבה יהיו	ויזכר את־ימי החשך
ויטיבך לבך בימי בחורותיך		⁹ שמח בחור בילדותך
ובמראי עיניך		והלך בדרכי לבך
יביאך האלהים במשפט:		ודע כי על־כל־אלה
והעבר רעה מבשרך		¹⁰ והסר כעס מלבך

כי־הילדות והשחרות הבל:

עד אשר לא־יבאו ימי הרעה	12 ¹ וזכר את בוראיך בימי בחורתיך
אין־לי בהם חפץ:	והגיעו שנים אשר תאמר

פסוק 9: וּבְמַרְאֶה קרי

Before the sun grows dark,
And the light of the moon and the stars,
And the clouds return after the rain.

In the day when the watchmen of the house
    tremble,
And the strong men are bent.
The grinding maidens cease, for they are few,
And the ladies peering through the lattices grow
    dim.

When the doubled doors on the street are shut,
And the voice of the mill becomes low.
One wakes at the sound of a bird,
And all the daughters of song are laid low.

When one fears to climb a height,
And terrors lurk in a walk.
When the almond-tree blossoms,
The grasshopper becomes a burden,[1]
And the caperberry can no longer stimulate desire.
So man goes to his eternal home,
While the hired mourners walk about in the
    street . . .

Before the silver cord is severed,
And the golden bowl is shattered,
The pitcher is broken at the spring,
And the wheel is shattered at the pit.
The dust returns to the earth as it was,
And the spirit returns to God, who gave it.
Vanity of vanities, says Koheleth, all is vanity.

---

[1] Apparently an allusion to the decline of sexual vitality.

² עד אשר לא תחשך השמש   והאור והירח והכוכבים

ושבו העבים אחר הגשם:

³ ביום שיזעו שמרי הבית   והתעותו אנשי החיל

ובטלו הטחנות כי מעטו   וחשכו הראות בארבות:

⁴ וסגרו דלתים בשוק   בשפל קול הטחנה

ויקום לקול הצפור   וישחו כל־בנות השיר:

⁵ גם מגבה יראו   וחתחתים בדרך

וינאץ השקד   ויסתבל החגב   ותפר האביונה

כי־הלך האדם אל־בית עולמו   וסבבו בשוק הספדים:

⁶ עד אשר לא ירחק חבל הכסף   ותרץ גלת הזהב

ותשבר כד על־המבוע   ונרץ הגלגל אל־הבור:

⁷ וישב העפר על־הארץ כשהיה   והרוח תשוב אל־האלהים

אשר נתנה:

⁸ הבל הבלים   אמר הקוהלת   הכל הבל:

—————

פסוק 5: גרס יִירָא

פסוק 6: יֵרָתֵק קרי

XIX

EPILOGUE

The six concluding verses of our present book of Koheleth are the comments of an editor, who was both fascinated and troubled by its contents. He may have been a Wisdom teacher himself, but of a more conventional cast than Koheleth. He offers important biographical data on our author, whom he probably knew personally. The stim-

Not only was Koheleth a sage himself, but he also taught the people knowledge, weighing and searching and fashioning many proverbs. Koheleth tried to find attractive words and honestly to set down the truth. The words of the wise are like goads, and like well-fastened nails are the collected sayings, coming from one Source.

Furthermore, my son, be warned: of making many books there is no end, and much study wears one's strength away.

In sum, having heard everything, fear God and keep His commandments, for that is man's whole duty. For God will bring every deed to judgment, even everything hidden, whether it be good or evil.

ulating power of the book was undeniable, but so was the danger to faith of its sceptical temper. The editor would agree with the widow of the old Scotch minister who once told her husband's younger successor, 'You young men have too many books nowadays.' Speculations are interesting, but they must not be permitted to undermine the eternal verities of faith in God and the triumph of His justice!

(XII. 9–14)

---

9   ויתר שהיה קהלת חכם עוד למד־דעת את־העם ואזן וחקר תקן

10 משלים הרבה: בקש קהלת למצא דברי־חפץ וכתוב ישר דברי

11 אמת: דברי חכמים כדרבנות וכמשמרות נטועים בעלי אספות נתנו

12 מרעה אחד: ויתר מהמה בני הזהר עשות ספרים הרבה אין קץ

13 ולהג הרבה יגעת בשר: סוף דבר הכל נשמע את־האלהים ירא ואת־

14 מצותיו שמור כי־זה כל־האדם: כי את־כל־מעשה האלהים יבא
    במשפט על כל־נעלם אם־טוב ואם־רע:

סוף דבר הכל נשמע את האלהים ירא ואת מצותיו שמור כי זה כל
האדם:

סימן יתק״ק

פסוק 10: נרס וְכָתוֹב

COMMENTARY

Section I — Introductory Note

1:1. The earth, the sun, the wind and the sea cited here recall the four primal elements of creation according to Greek thought, earth, wind, fire, and water, as was noted by Ibn Ezra. Koheleth probably was familiar with this doctrine, but he used it not to expound a cosmological view but for a purpose uniquely his own, to emphasize the meaninglessness of nature and man's incapacity to effect any true progress or change.

The first section, consisting of verses 2–8, is written in rhythmic prose, the dominant meter being the four-beat stich (vv. 2, 5, 6). It is varied by the use of three-beat stichs (vv. 3, 4, 7) to create the 4:3 meter, a common type of the Kinah rhythm, and highly appropriate to the mood here. The passage then ends with the triple-beat stich (v. 8):

v. 2 — 4:4
v. 3 — 4:3
v. 4 — 4:3
v. 5 — 4:4
v. 6 — 4:4:4
v. 7 — 4:3 ‖ 4:3
v. 8 — 3:3 ‖ 3:3

In verse 3, בכל־עמלו must receive two beats, as the accents mark it, in spite of the Makeph; similarly, כל־הדברים in v. 8. In v. 6 על־סביבתיו also receives two beats; in all these cases because of the length of the words, like את־מוסרותימו in Ps. 2:3a (cf. MHHH, pp. 140 f.).

1:1. The name Koheleth remains as enigmatic today as ever before. Renan's guess that KHLT is an abbreviation for some unknown name, as RMBM stands for Maimonides, explains nothing. Jastrow's suggestion that Koheleth is a *nom de plume* for Solomon, arrived at by substituting the root *khl*, "assemble," for *šlm*, "complete," and having a Tav replace the He of *Šelomo*, is too ingenious to be convincing. Zimmermann's suggestion that the Aramaic "equivalent" כנשה is the numerical equal of שלמה is untenable, both on archaeological and other grounds. Nor does Ginsberg's proposed Aramaic קהלא(ה) solve the problem. For the reasons, see QHA.

From such proper names in late Biblical Hebrew as סֹפֶרֶת (Ezra 2:55; Neh. 7:57) and פֹּכֶרֶת הַצְּבָיִם (Ezra 2:57; Neh. 7:59), it becomes clear that the feminine participles were used to denote functionaries or officials and then became masculine proper names. As these names preserve some functional meaning, "scribe" and "binder of gazelles," so *Koheleth* still retains some of its original verbal force. Hence it occurs with the article in 12:8 and 7:27 (which should also be read אמר הקהלת). So, too, Arabic *bā'kraï*, "inspector"; *ḥā'līfa*, "successor, caliph." The Kal participle is used at times for verbs in the derived conjugations; cf. דּוֹבֵר, כּוֹזֵב, and perhaps מְאָן. קהלת is derived from קהל, "assemble," and is related to "voice, speech" (Arabic *Kā'la*, "speak." (On the relationship of ע'ו and ע'ה roots, cf. Heb. בוש, Aram. בהת; Heb. רוץ, Aram. רהט, etc.) Hence the Greek ἐκκλησιάστης, i. e. member of the *Ecclesia*, assembly or congregation. The meaning seems to be "speaker" or "assembler," but the word is best left untranslated.

The book of Koheleth is not a pseudepigraph, which the author seeks to attribute to Solomon, like "the Wisdom of Solomon." He impersonates Solomon only in the opening section because he wishes to prove that both wisdom and pleasure are worthless as goals in life (1:16–18; 2:1–12), and Solomon had the reputation of possessing both in superlative degree.

Verse 1 is a superscription by an editor, who may have believed that Solomon was its author. On the other hand, he may merely have followed out the suggestion of the first two chapters in this regard, and recognized the device as a literary fiction.

1:2. This verse sounds the dominant note of the book, and properly occurs here at the beginning and in 12:8 at the conclusion.

הבל is "breath, vapor" (Isa. 57:13 ‖ רוח, "wind"; Pr. 21:6, הבל נדף, "a driven vapor"). The noun occurs in Mishnaic Hebrew,

אין העולם מתקיים אלא בהבל פיהן של תינוקות של בית רבן .B. Shab)
119b), "The world endures only because of the breath of school
children," as does the verb in the Hiphil, מהביל, "create vapor"
(M. Shab. 1:6). The breath is a) unsubstantial and b) transi-
tory. Hence from a) הבל derives the meaning "vanity" (Ecc.
passim; Ps. 94:11), from b) the sense of "short-lived." This
latter sense is to be found in Ps. 144:4, "man is like a breath,"
and should also be recognized in Job 7:16, כי הבל ימי, "turn aside
from me for my days are but a breath." Failure to recognize
this nuance in Ecc. 11:10 has led scholars to excise the entire
stich כי הילדות והשחרות הבל as a tendentious gloss. The Midrash
Koheleth Rabba (ad loc.) interprets the word הבל even here
concretely: דוד אמר אדם להבל דמה לאיזה הבל אם להבל של תנור
של כירה יש בו ממש בא שלמה בנו ופירש הה"ד הבל הבלים, "David said:
'Man is like a vapor.' What kind of vapor? If it be the vapor
of an oven or the vapor of the hearth, it has some substance.
Then Solomon his son came and explained: Thus it is written:
'vapor of vapors!' "

1:3. The entire verse contains several stylistic favorites of
Koheleth. יתרון is probably a commercial term, the surplus of
the balance sheet (*Pl.*). תחת השמש, another characteristic of his
style, is taken by many as a Graecism: ὑφ' ἡλίῳ (*Pl.*), but cf.
תחת השמים in Ex. 17:14; Deut. 7:24; 9:14 etc., as well as Ecc.
2:3; 3:1, and the occurrence of our phrase in two Phoenician
inscriptions of Tabnith and Eshmunazar (3rd cent. B. C. E.;
cf. G. A. Cooke, *NSI*, pp. 26, 30; M. Lidzbarski, *Alt-semitische
Texte*, I, 1897, pp. 16, 18). עמל in late Hebrew means "laborious
toil, hard labor," as e. g. Ps. 105:44; 107:12; and Ecc. 2:11, 19–20
and *passim*.

1:4. עמדת means "to continue, endure," as in Ps. 19:10;
Lev. 13:5; Dan. 10:13.

1:5. שואף is rendered by LXX ἕλκω "drag, pull." It is
therefore clear that P, V, rendered MT freely by "return," but
did not read שָׁב. The emendation שָׁב אֶף (Gr. Gal.) creates the
difficult text אף זרח, and, in addition, is unnecessary. The root
שאף means "gasp, pant," a) either with desire (Ps. 119:131 ||
יאב; Job 7:2 || קוה), hence, in modern Hebrew, "aspire"; or
b) from weariness, as Isa. 42:14; Jer. 14:6 and here. Hence,

"the sun pants wearily towards the place where he rises." Cf. *equis anhelis*, "the panting steeds of the sun," Vergil, *Georgics*, I, 250. שׁוֹאֵף is to be read with מְקוֹמוֹ, against the accents, as the rhythm requires. The sun was regarded as making his way at night from west to east in most ancient mythologies, the Greek conception being best known. The Egyptians saw this nocturnal journey by the sun as in a ship (cf. K. Sethe, *SAB*, 1928, pp. 259 ff.). For the Psalmist who revels in his faith the sun rejoices like a hero to run his course ordained by God (Ps. 19:6); for the life-weary Koheleth, the panting sun has only a monotonous, exhausting task to complete, without joy or meaning. There is therefore no need to invoke the Akkadian *šīpu*, "go, march," as suggested by S. I. Feigin in a private communication.

1:6. V, T erroneously refer the first half of the verse to the sun instead of to the wind. East and west were implied in connection with the sun; here north and south complete the four directions; cf. Can. 4:16; B. S. 43:20. LXX κύκλοι κύκλων may have read סֹבֵב סָבִיב. MT should be perhaps revocalized: סָבִיב סָבִיב הוֹלֵךְ הָרוּחַ.

1:7. The verse is usually taken to mean that the channels flowing into the ocean accomplish nothing by their continuous activity. The idea is therefore similar to the expression used by Aristophanes (*Clouds*, l. 1248):

> "The sea, though all the rivers flow to it,
> Increaseth not in volume."

In the final clause, שׁוּב is an auxiliary verb meaning to "repeat, continue, do again"; cf. Gen. 26:18; Mi. 7:19. For this construction of a complementary infinitive with Lamed, cf. Deut. 30:9, כִּי יָשׁוּב ה' לָשׂוּשׂ עָלֶיךָ; Ez. 8:17; Ezra 9:14. Our clause is then to be rendered "thither they continue to flow" (*Jast. Wr. Ehr. Bar.*). While V (*unde*) and Sym. ("whence") may have read מִשָּׁם as a haplography from הֹלְכִים, more probably they so interpreted שָׁם. *Pl.* and *Jast.* interpret similarly "unto the place whence the rivers come, thither they return again," but this is not likely. T, followed by *Ra.*, *Ibn Ezra*, *Gins.* and *Levy*, renders "thence they return, i. e. (through subterranean channels)." Ibn Ezra more scientifically explains "through evaporation." This latter view has the advantage of suggesting a cycle for the sea, as for the sun and the wind. Linguistically, however, this is rather forced. *Hertz.* points out that Koheleth is not interested in the cycles but in the vanity and monotony of the world, and the picture of waters perpetually flowing and yet unable to fill the sea is admirably suited to his purpose. The first view is therefore preferable.

1:8. כל הדברים יגעים is rendered by LXX, *Pl.*, *Levy*, and *Hertz.* "all words are feeble, sc. to express the monotony of nature." It is better to interpret the clause as referring to the phenomena described above, "all things are tiresome," because they repeat themselves *ad infinitum* and *ad nauseam*. The word is a transferred epithet (cf. Horace's phrase *tarda podagra*, lit. "the slow gout; the gout that impedes the sufferer"). Hence there is no need to read מְיַגְעִים (Ehr.). Besides this primary sense, there is a suggestion in the choice of words that the phenomena are themselves weary of their unending and useless activity. Cf. note on v. 5. For stich b, Gal. reads: לֹא יִכְלֶה לָשׁוֹן לְדַבֵּר. מלא is usually governed by the accusative of material, but it occurs with Mem in Ez. 32:6.

1:9. מה שהיה הוא שיהיה, a late construction meaning "that which was, is." Cf. 6:10. It is identical with the Aramaic מה די, Dan. 2:20, 29, 45 and Ezra 7:18. Curiously, LXX and V interpret the phrase as an indefinite interrogative clause: "What is it that was? The same that will be!" This is obviously wrong.

1:10. יש דבר has the force of a protasis in a conditional sentence, and is equivalent to "If there be anything, it has already been, etc." יש is virtually equal to a participle, on the hypothetical use of which in conditional sentences see Gordis, JBL (49), 1930, pp. 200 ff. For יש דבר שיאמר, LXX reads ὅς λαλήσει καὶ ἐρεῖ, *P* כל דנמלל ונאמר, which do not go back to an original שֶׁיְדַבֵּר וְשֶׁיֹּאמַר (so *Kn. McN. Bar.*), which is impossible Hebrew and graphically remote from MT. Probably they read MT, which was misvocalized as יש דבר שֶׁיֹּאמַר. The subject of שיאמר is indefinite הָאוֹמֵר (Ra.). לעולמים = "worlds, periods, generations," αἰῶνες. Cf. Ps. 145:13; Sifre Deut. 25:5, אחיו שלא היה בעולמו (so *Ibn Ezra, Ehr.*). The singular verb היה in spite of the plural antecedent לעולמים (cf. also 2:7a) may be due to the neuter use of היה (cf. ועלטה היה, Gen. 15:17; ארבע הידות יהיה, Gen. 47:24; Ex. 12:49), or because of its attraction to אשר, which is construed as a singular relative pronoun governing a third person singular verb. Compare the common liturgical formula ברוך אתה ה', which takes a *third* person verb in the subordinate clause, after אשר, in spite of the *second* person of the main clause, as אשר יצר את האדם (Wedding Service), or אשר גאלנו וגאל את אבותינו (Passover Service, quoted in M. Pes. 10:5).

For מלפנו, the comparison with Isa. 41:26, "at the beginning" (*Sieg. Wr. Bar.*), is inappropriate, while the rendering "in a period that belongs to the periods that were before ours" (Ehr.) is too involved. The word is a late and inexact form for לפנינו. Cf. I Chr. 16:30, חִילוּ מִלְפָנָיו ‖ חִילוּ מִפָּנָיו, Ps. 96:9; I Chr. 16:33, ה' ‖ אז ירננו עצי יער מלפני ה' ‖ Ps. 96:12, 13: אז ירננו כל עצי יער: לפני ה'. Our phrase means simply "the ages that were before us." כבר is another characteristic usage. It is frequent in Mishnaic Hebrew, but rare in Targumic Aramaic. It occurs also in Syriac, where it usually means "perhaps," though it occurs as "already" in Mat. 11:21; Heb. 10:2 and in Mandaic כבאר. Its root is common in all Semitic languages in the meaning "be great," hence כבר = lit. "length of time," while כִּבְרָה is "length of land" (Gen. 35:16; 48:7; II Ki. 5:19).

1:11. This verse gives the reason for v. 10. Things appear new only because the past is forgotten (Levy) — an additional element in the vanity of human existence; not only can nothing be accomplished, but the memory of the effort is wiped out (Hertz.). זִכְרוֹן is best regarded not as a late form of the absolute state like יִתְרוֹן, כִּשְׁרוֹן (Del.), since it occurs everywhere else as זִכָּרוֹן, but as a construct before Lamed: זכרון = זכרון לראשונים הראשונים. On the construct before prepositions, cf. Ges.-K., sec. 130, and Hos. 9:6, מחמד לכספם; Ps. 58:5, חמת-למו; Pr. 24:9, ותועבת לאדם; I Chr. 23:28, ועל טהרת לכל קדש; Isa. 9:1, ישבי בארץ; Ps. 2:12, חוסי בו, as well as Mishnaic examples like הולכי לבית המדרש (Aboth 5:14). ראשונים and אחרונים refer not to "things early and late" (LXX, V, Ha.), for that would have been expressed by the feminine plural (cf. Isa. 42:9; 43:9, 18; 46:9), but to men, the early and the later generations (cf. Job 18:20). Hertzberg naïvely describes the desire to perpetuate one's identity as a Jewish trait, as proved by synagogue inscriptions! Evidently Egyptian, Greek and Roman monumental inscriptions have escaped his notice.

Section II — Introductory Note

1:12 ff. Koheleth assumes the role of Solomon only for his experiment with wisdom (1:12–18) and with pleasure (2:1–11). He is not writing a pseudepigraphic work and has no desire to convince the reader that he is Solomon. Hence his use of "Koheleth" and not "Solomon" son of David. For the same reason הייתי is to be rendered not "am" (Graetz) or "have been" (*Wr.* JPSV, etc.), but "was." This use of the perfect tense, implying that Koheleth no longer was king, served to create the later Jewish legend about the deposition of the arrogant monarch, his replacement on the throne by Asmodeus and his subsequent repentance and restoration (cf. Targum on Ecc. 1:12; *Pesikta de Rab Kahana*, ed. Buber, p. 169a; J. Sanhedrin 20c).

In accordance with a well-marked characteristic of Koheleth's style (see introduction), he gives the conclusion at which he arrived and then proceeds to recount the details of the experiment. Thus vv. 14 and 15 constitute a summary of the views Koheleth has finally attained.

1:13. נתן לב, lit. "set my heart" (cf. 1:17; 7:25; 8:9, 16), also שית לב (Ps. 48:14) in earlier Hebrew. The heart was conceived of as the seat of understanding, hence לב occurs as a synonym for "understanding" (Pr. 15:32; 19:8; Ecc. 10:3).

תור is not a Graecism (σκέψασθαι), but good Hebrew, being used of spies in Nu. 13:2, 16, 17 (*McN. Bar.*). דרש means "to penetrate to the root of a matter," תור to "investigate it from all sides." The former refers to searching the depths, the latter to exploring the breadth of a matter (*Del.*).

בחכמה cannot mean "to search *for* wisdom in everything done under the sun" (ag. Hertz.), but "through wisdom," with the organon of Hokmah as the instrument. LXX and V may have read נַעֲשָׂה, the participle, but the perfect of MT is safeguarded by

שנעשו in v. 14. The sense is general: "that has been done." For השמים P, V, T, and many manuscripts read השמש, but this is an example of "leveling." MT is preferable as the *difficilior lectio*. ענה occurs frequently in Biblical Hebrew in the senses a) "answer" and b) "be bowed down, afflicted." Koheleth uses a homonym, "be occupied with, busied with"; cf. Syriac ענא and Arabic عنى. The commentators naturally derive the noun ענין from the same root as the infinitive, and render: "a sore task to be exercised with." However, the *verb* occurs nowhere else in Biblical or Mishnaic Hebrew except here and 3:10, while the noun ענין is very common (2:23, 26; 3:10; 4:8; 5:2, 13; 8:16 and frequently in Mishnaic and medieval Hebrew). Hence it is better to interpret the verb here and in 3:10 as "be afflicted with" and to see in the clause a striking paranomasia, the sense being in thorough consonance with Koheleth's views on life. The Kal of ענה is used in this sense in Zc. 10:2; Ps. 116:10; 119:67; the Niphal in Isa. 53:7; 58:10, all late passages. Hence read with MT לַעֲנוֹת or לַעֲנוֹת (cf. Ex. 10:3), so Targum לאסתנפא.

1:14. The phrase רעות רוח (2:11, 17, 26; 4:6; 6:9), like רעיון רוח (1:17; 2:22; 4:16), is characteristic of Koheleth's style. Various meanings have been suggested: 1) from רעע, "break," hence "vexation of spirit" (T, V, P). 2) on the basis of Hos. 12:2, אפרים רעה רוח ורדף קדים, as "chasing of wind" (A. Th. Sym. *Ibn Ezra Pl.* AV). 3) as "desire, thought," from Aramaic רעא, "derive, take pleasure" ‖ Hebrew רצה (cf. רעו, Ezra 5:17; 7:18; רעיוניך, Dan. 2:29). *Bar.* points to "Phoenician inscriptions of the Piraeus and North Africa where רעת occurs," and then argues "that there is no reason to suspect Aramaic influences" (G. A. Cooke, *NSI*, pp. 97, 150). But it is not likely that the Hebrew רעות and רעיון are entirely distinct from the common Aramaic nouns of the identical forms, nor can Hos. 12:2 be left out of account. "Aramaisms" in Hebrew fall into 3 categories: 1) Words belonging to the Northwest-Semitic vocabulary, and hence common to both Hebrew and Aramaic. Those that became common in Aramaic and fell into disuse in Hebrew, except in poetic style, appear as Aramaisms. Such are אתה and הוה. 2) Words that entered Hebrew and Phoenician during the First Temple period, especially in the North, where there was close contact with the Arameans (cf. the Second Book of Kings, *passim*). 3) Words entering Hebrew during post-Exilic days, when Aramaic became the *lingua franca* of the Near East. רעה, "desire," may have entered Hebrew during pre-Exilic days, hence its occurrence in Hos. 12:2 and perhaps also in Ps. 37:3 and Pr. 15:14 ‖ בקש. In Ps. 139:2, 17 (רעיך) and in Koheleth, it retains its early meaning "desire"; for the later nuance "thought," cf. Dan. 2:29, 30; 4:16; 5:6, 10. In Pr. 15:28, לב צדיק יהגה לענות ופי רשעים יביע רעות, the last word may need to be emended to רעות, "thoughts" (cf. רֵעֶיךָ, רֵעִי, Ps. 139:2, 17), and the verse then rendered: "The heart of the righteous thinks before answering, but the mouth of the wicked expresses its thoughts." A similar broadening of meaning has taken place in Biblical and Mishnaic חֵפֶץ, from "desire" to "thing." See below on 3:1.

1:15. This verse is regarded by most commentators as an aphorism quoted by Koheleth as apposite to his theme (*Re. Pl. Wr. Bar. Hertz.*). Ehr. points out, however, that were it an independent verse, the subjects of the clauses, מעות and חסרון, would normally require the article, and he therefore takes it as an additional predicate to הבל in v. 14. See the trans. לתקן is the only instance of the Kal of this verb, which occurs in the Piel in 7:13 and 12:9 and frequently in Piel and Hiphil in Mishnaic Hebrew (as e. g. Aboth 4:21). Hence it is emended to לְתָקֵן (*Gr.*) or לְהִתָּקֵן (*Sieg. McN. Dr.*). Actually, no change is required, even though a passive sense, parallel to להמנות, is essential. Cf. 3:2, where the infinitive Kal ללדת (‖ למות) has the passive meaning "be born" (*Ibn Ezra, Ehr.*). להמנות, "be counted," is vouched for by LXX, V, P, T. Sym. reads לְהִמָּלות, "be filled," which is accepted by *Ew. Bar. Levy* and many others. Cf. Ber. 16b, המקום ימלא חסרונך, "May God fill your lack." *Ehr.* argues against the emendation on the ground that we have here a commercial idiom, meaning "the books cannot list all the deficiencies of life." For the figurative use of commercial idioms, see Aboth 3:20, הכל נתון בערבון . . . החנות פתוחה. The emendation is actually suggested in the Talmud; cf. Hag. 9b: אמר לו בר הי הי להלל האי להמנות להמלות מיבעי.

1:16. הגדלתי והוספתי are coordinates in form, but the second verb is modified by the first adverbially: "I increased greatly."

Cf. Hos. 1:6, לא אוסיף עוד ארחם, "I shall not have mercy again." There is no need to read נָרְלְתִּי with *Gr.* and *Ehr.*

על כל אשר היה לפני refers to more than one king, and not merely to David. There is no need, however, to go back to Melchizedek and the Jebusite kings. The phrase means "whoever ruled before me." Cf. I Chr. 29:25, where it is said of Solomon, "He set upon him the glory of kingship which had not been upon any king (כל מלך) before him over Israel." (Wr.)

This might refer to Saul as well as to David, but is more naturally taken in a general sense. Our verse, however, need not be precise. The author is assuming the role of Solomon for literary purposes only. Hence there is no real anachronism in the use of a phrase that betrays knowledge of a long line of kings in Jerusalem.

1:17. According to the Masoretic accentuation, ודעת is an infinitive governing הוללות ושכלות, exactly as לדעת governs חכמה: "To know wisdom and to know madness and folly." LXX, P, V, T, however, unite in seeing four nouns here, חכמה ודעת הוללות ושכלות, construing them all as objects of לדעת, a far more natural construction (so *Gr. McN. Bar.* and *Hertz.*). In spite of their apparent divergence from MT, the Vss. on careful examination all substantiate the wording of our text. Thus LXX παραβολάς, "proverbs," for הוללות does not go back to מְשָׁלוֹת (ag. *Gr.*) but is an inner Greek error, especially easy in the uncials, ΠΑΡΑΒΟΛΑΣ for ΠΑΡΑΦΟΡΑΣ, "errors" = MT! P מתלא merely follows LXX as it frequently does where the Hebrew text is difficult; cf. e. g. 2:8; 2:25, and ch. 15 above. T interprets והוללות as "confusion of the kingdom," which is the Rabbinic paraphrase of the Hebrew; cf. Midrash Lev. Rab., ch. 20, on Ps. 75:5, אמרתי להוללים אל תהלו אלו שלבן מלא חלחוליות רעות, and Midrash Koheleth Rabbah, הוללות זו הוללה של מלכות. שכלות, translated "understanding" by LXX, P and T, substantiates the Masoretic orthography with *Sin*, and may have been prompted by a desire to avoid imputing folly to Solomon. But cf., for this unusual spelling, משמרות in 12:11 and כעש in Job 5:2; 6:2, etc.

With MT validated, the difficulties of interpretation still remain, if we interpret that Koheleth sought "to know wisdom and knowledge, madness and folly." הוללות is typical of Koheleth's style (2:2, 12; 7:7, 25; 9:3; 10:13), and means "madness, mad revelry, wickedness"; cf. the Arabic هل and Akkadian 'alâlu "shout, rejoice"; Ps. 5:6; 75:5. But the experiments with pleasure are not described until ch. 2, and the next verse, v. 18, speaks only of חכמה and דעת, making no mention of הוללות. *Gins.* therefore omits הוללות ושכלות in v. 17 as an imitation of 2:12, while *Jast.* removes חכמה ודעת. *McN.* eliminates all of 17a, ודעת . . . ואתנה, and combines vv. 16 and 17b. *Ehr.* eliminates the entire verse 17, as do *Zap. Ha.*, the last two on metrical grounds.

Not only is MT validated by all the Vss., as has been noted, but such a violent procedure is unnecessary. The construction here is the use of a double object in the accusative after verbs of perception. This construction is very frequent in Arabic, علمت زيد جاهلا "I know that Zaid is a fool" (cf. Caspari-Mueller, *Arabische Grammatik*, 4th ed., 1876, sec. 389), but it occurs also in Hebrew. The second object may be a) an *adjective*, ומוצא אני מר ממות את האשה ותרא את המלך (Ecc. 7:26); b) a *participle*, אשר לא תשמע את עבדך מקללך דוד מפזז (II Sam. 6:16); (Ecc. 7:21); c) a *clause*, וירא אלהים את האור כי טוב אתה ידעת את (Gen. 1:3); דוד אבי כי לא יכל (I Ki. 5:17); or d) a *noun*, ולדעת רשע כסל (Ecc. 7:25), "to know that wickedness is folly." Thus practically each type of the double accusative occurs in Koheleth, undoubtedly constituting a characteristic of his style. Similarly, לדעת in our passage is a verb of perception governing a double object, each consisting of two nouns: "To know that wisdom and knowledge are madness and folly." This view is adopted also by Gal. ואתנה לבי לדעת, "I applied my heart to learn," is equivalent to "I applied my heart and learned," since clauses of purpose and result are grammatically and psychologically related.

Vv. 12–17 are now a well integrated unit. V. 16 deals with Koheleth's experiment with wisdom, while vv. 17–18 give his conclusions. See the trans. The v. is introduced by a Vav consecutive in order to express the idea that after years of experience, Koheleth one day decided to draw the logical conclusion (*Hertz.*). For a full discussion of this verse, cf. our paper in *JBL* (66), 1937, pp. 323–330.

1:18. This verse has the structure of a proverb, but is not to be excluded on that account (ag. Renan, Jast.) It may well be a quotation cited by Koheleth (cf. Intro. sec.), but it is organically related to verse 17.

יוֹסִיף is either a Kal participle, written plene = יֹסֵף (so substantially *Wr.*), or a participle Hiphil = מוֹסִיף (so Boettcher). Passages like Isa. 29:14; 38:5, יוֹסֵף; Ps. 16:5, תּוֹמָךְ = תּוֹמִיךְ, seem to strengthen the first view. It is, however, best taken with *Del. Bar. Ehr.* as an imperfect used as a substantive, in gnomic style, to express a permanent truth; cf. Pr. 12:17, יפיח אמונה יניד צדק.

2:1. אֲנַסְּכָה in the MT is derived not from נסך (V, Ibn Ezra), but from נסה, "test," with 2nd per. sing. suffix (LXX, P and most moderns). This plene spelling of the 2nd person suffix is frequent in the Dead Sea Scrolls, as e. g. בידכה, נפלאותיכה, etc. (cf. E. L. Sukenik, *Megillot Genuzot*, pp. 29, 31, 37, etc.). ראה = "to experience," applied to "the whole gamut of experience from life (9:9) to death (Ps. 89:49)" (*Bar.*). It is frequently followed by Beth (Gen. 21:16; 44:34; Jer. 29:32; Job 3:9). רְאָה is an imperative parallel to לְכָה. The final clause and the following verse present Koheleth's conclusion before giving details of the experiment. Cf. 1:13 followed by vv. 16 ff.

Harry Torczyner (N. H. Tur-Sinai) made the striking and attractive suggestion that the words ביין את בשרי ולבי נהג in v. 3 originally belonged in v. 1 after אנסכה. This solves the difficulty of אנסכה in v. 1 and למשוך ביין את בשרי in v. 3, besides doing justice to the parallelism of אחז and משך, both in form and meaning (see below on v. 3). Accordingly, Torczyner would read v. 1 as follows: לְכָה נָא אֲנַסְּכָה בַיַּיִן אֶת בְּשָׂרִי וְלִבִּי נֹהֵג בְּשִׂמְחָה וּרְאֵה בְטוֹב. It should be added that ולבי נהג should perhaps be better read ולבי ינהג, the Yod having fallen out through haplography. On the other hand, the MT ולבי נהג may be retained as a circumstantial clause. An essential change would be to vocalize וּרְאָה as an infinitive absolute consecutive וְרָאֹה, instead of the present imperative. If this emendation be adopted, v. 3 would read: תרתי בלבי למשוך בחכמה ולאחז בשמחה, and its translation would be as follows:

> V. 1. "Come, let me anoint my body with wine and let my heart act in joy and see pleasure."

V. 3: "For I had explored the matter with my mind, by grasping wisdom and taking hold of frivolity."

The Wisdom of Solomon, which polemizes against Koheleth, offers a striking parallel: "Let us *be filled* with costly wines and perfumes" (2:7), which sounds almost like a paraphrase of "let me anoint my body." The only substantial linguistic objection to the transposition is that נסך in Biblical Hebrew governs an accusative of material, like wine (Hos. 9:4) or water (I Chr. 11:18), and in one passage (Isa. 29:10) the "spirit of slumber," and that it means "pour out," not "be-pour, water," a meaning that the Arabic cognate *nasaka* originally possessed; cf. BDB, p. 650b. Hence the use of the Beth of material and the required meaning "be-pour, anoint" are unattested.

Moreover, the present text offers a more logical sequence of thought, 1:12–18 giving Koheleth's experience with Wisdom and 2:1–11 his experiment with pleasure. Torczyner's text would introduce "wisdom" into the second section as well. Because of this absence of evidence for the meaning and usage of נסך that would be required and the disturbance of the thought-sequence, we have retained the MT as the basis of our translation.

2:2. ל is "concerning," as frequently after *verba dicendi*; cf. Gen. 20:13; 26:7; Ex. 14:3 f. On מהולל, participle of the Polal = "mad," cf. on 1:13 above and I Sam. 21:14, ויתהלל, "he played the madman." LXX follows its usual practice of rendering this word in Koheleth as "error." The reading of P, מנא הנין, is usually translated "what do they avail?", הנין being construed as a participle from הני — "be useful," and the underlying Hebrew text is taken to be מה יועיל. This is much too distant graphically from MT. The reading of P is to be rendered "what are they?", הנין being the 3rd person pl. pronoun, and going back to the MT vocalized as the Mishnaic form מְהַלָל = מַה הַלָלוּ; cf. Ex. 4:2 Kethib מַזֶּה; Ez. 8:6 Kethib מָהֵם, and the usual Mishnaic form מָהוּ.

2:3. תור, "search, spy out, explore" (Nu. 10:33), is used of intellectual effort by Koheleth (1:13; 2:3; 7:25). למשוך is often rendered, on the basis of the context, "stimulate, refresh," though, it must be confessed, with no real parallels in Biblical or post-Biblical usage. In B. Hag. 14a: בעלי אגדה שמושכין לבו

שׁל או, the verb means "attract, draw men's hearts like water." Levy compares the Talmudic phrase אימשיך בתרייהו (A. Z. 27b), "he let himself be drawn after (sc.) wine and the bath, i. e. he gave himself up to them," and renders our Kal here, like the Aramaic Ithpe'el: "to give myself over to wine."

Jouon's emendation לְשַׂמֵּחַ (Biblica, 1930, p. 419), accepted by Gal., is linguistically possible, but not necessary, in spite of Ps. 104:15. ולבי נהג בחכמה is a parenthetical clause; it must be understood as describing the circumstances and indicating that his indulgence was part of his experiment, not a mere surrender to physical desires. Jouon's rendering, "My understanding remained master in Wisdom," is inferior to the common view "while my heart conducted itself with wisdom."

On the other hand, the parallelism of למשוך with לאחז is particularly striking; cf. Ex. 12:21, משכו וקחו. It led to Tur-Sinai's (Torczyner) suggestion that the words ביין . . . נהג belong in v. 1. For a discussion of this proposed text, see note on v. 1 above. On משך, cf. N. H. Tur-Sinai, Halashon Vehasefer, vol. 1 (Jerusalem, 5708), pp. 383 ff. סכלות, primarily "folly," develops the connotation of "sin, unrighteousness" (cf. 7:17, where it is parallel to רשע), on the basis of the equation by the Wisdom teachers, "wickedness is folly" (7:25). It also assumed the sense of "revelry, moral looseness." It thus shows a semantic progression opposite to הוללות, which develops from "revelry" (Arabic "shout," cf. Hebrew הלל, "praise") to "sin," and then to "folly." All these meanings must be understood in the English terms "fool" and "folly."

The LXX rendering of סְכְלוּת as "understanding" is either an interpretation of MT = שְׂכְלוּת (cf. on 1:17 above) or more probably an inner Greek error (εὐφροσύνη for ἀφροσύνη) induced by σοφία nearby.

LXX, P, V, but not T, read השמש for MT השמים. The latter is to be preferred as the difficilior lectio; the Vss. represent the "leveling" process. מספר ימי = "small number of days, brief span"; cf. Job 14:5, מספר חדשיו.

2:4. הגדלתי מעשי, "I did things on a grand scale." Pl. and Hertz. cite parallels to each of these acts referred to here from the activities of the historical Solomon (I Kings, chaps. 9 and 10), but there is no need to assure a slavish reproduction of those passages by Koheleth here.

The ethical dative לי, used here and in succeeding verses, and untranslatable in modern English, subtly conveys the sense of Koheleth's limitless capacity for activity, directed only to the end of his own pleasure.

2:5. פרדס is a loan-word from Persian *pairi-daêza*, "enclosure," whence the Greek παράδεισος. עץ כל פרי recalls the Genesis narrative (1:11, 29). Koheleth has at his command all the delights of Paradise (*Hertz.*).

2:6. The final word in the clause יער צומח עצים is not to be deleted (ag. Ehr.). It is an accusative of specification, the phrase meaning lit. "a forest growing, in respect to trees"; cf. כאלה נבלת עליה (Isa. 1:30); ועלתה ארמנתיה סירים (idem, 34:13).

2:7. מקנה here means "possession" (cf. Gen. 49:32) in its original meaning. The noun later developed the meaning of "cattle," the basic form of wealth in a nomadic society; cf. Latin *pecus* "cattle," *pecunia* "money," German *Vieh* "animal," English "fee." The Greek κτῆσις, "acquisition," on the other hand, usually refers to "farm land," a typical semantic development reflecting an agricultural society.

On the aberrant vocalization מִקְנֶה for the construct, in some mss., cf. מִקְרֵה בְּנֵי אָדָם, 3:19, etc. In ובני בית היה לי, the masculine singular verb is either used in neuter fashion (cf. Gen. 15:17, ועלטה היה; Ex. 12:49, תורה אחת יהיה לאזרח ולגר), or is the result of attraction to בית (Ges.-K., König, Bar.). As ordinarily rendered, "I bought servants and I had many slaves," the clause is both tautologous and meaningless. Hence Feigin suggests that through the marriage of slaves, he acquired a large household. It is best understood as a circumstantial clause of concession: "I bought additional servants, *though* I already had a large household." Cf. Gen. 18:12, ואדני זקן; idem 15:2, ואנכי הולך ערירי; Ex. 33:12, ואתה לא הודעתני; Isa. 53:4, ואנחנו חשבנהו נגוע; cf. BDB, p. 253b; Driver, *Hebrew Tenses* (Appendix I). Slaves were distinguished as "house-born" or "acquired" (Gen. 17:12). הרבה ... מכל = lit. "much had I, more than," etc. Hertz. reads שהיה for שהיו, an unnecessary change.

This verse offers an interesting example of a divergence

between the Masoretic vocalization and the accentuation. The vocalization with a *kameṣ*, וְצָאן, rather than וְצֹאן is probably pausal (only a few exceptions occur; cf. Ges.-K., sec. 104, 2e). Thus the caesura comes after וצאן. On the other hand, the accents of וצאן הרבה, Mahpakh and Pašta, link them together and place the caesura after בקר. Rhythmically the former division seems somewhat preferable. Besides, the phrase מקנה בקר וצאן is paralleled by ומקנה צאן ובקר (II Chr. 32:29) and מקנה צאן ומקנה בקר (Gen. 26:14; 47:17).

2:8. The omission and the use of the article in the phrase סגלת מלכים והמדינות led Delitzsch and Ehrlich to emend the last word to וַחֲמָדוֹת. The change is unnecessary. On the irregular use of the article in Koheleth, see 7:25 and OLQ, pp. 81 f. On the same phenomenon in Mishnaic Hebrew, see M. H. Segal, *Dikduk Leshon Hamishnah*, sec. 85–88. This is probably due to the influence of Aramaic, where the determinative status loses its significance and is equivalent to the undeterminative status. It offers no genuine support for the thesis that Koheleth is a translation from the Aramaic (ag. F. Zimmermann, in JQR, vol. 36, 1945, pp. 17–45). תענגות refers to sexual pleasure; cf. Can. 7:7, אהבה בתענוגים (Pl.). שדה ושדות must therefore refer to women, as nearly all interpreters since Ibn Ezra have recognized. Hence the suggestions that it means "wine, cup bearer" (LXX, P), "goblets," "pitchers" (V, T), "chariots" (Rashi; Boettcher), or "music" (Kimḥi, Luther) may be dismissed. The required meaning has been derived in various ways:

1) From the root *šdd* "seize," hence women captured in war (Ibn Ezra).

2) from the Arabic سلدیة "mistress"; cf. Spanish *Cid* from ساد *Mediae Vav* "lord, prince"; feminine "lady, milady, mistress" (Olshausen, Vollers). But the Masoretic vocalization implies a geminate root.

3) from the Akkadian *sadâdu* = "love" (Friedrich Delitzsch).

4) from שַׁד, "breast" — hence "concubine" (Pl.).

5) Levy regards שדה as the Aramaic equivalent of Hebrew יָרֵךְ (cf. Targum on Ex. 25:31; 37:17; Lev. 1:11, "side of candlestick and altar"). The word is also used for the privy parts, as in

oaths, Gen. 24:2; 47:29; and in Midrash Ex. R. 1:16, בשעה שכורעת
לילד ירכותיה מצטננות.

All in all, the derivation from šad, "breast," used synec-
dochically, as a part for the whole, hence "woman," is simplest.
On similar instances cf. רחם, "woman," Jud. 5:30; Mesha Inscription l. 17 and Ugaritic; מרחם (Isa. 49:15); cf. Louis Ginzberg
Jubilee Vol. I, p. 186; נקבה, "female," from נקב; צלע, "rib," hence
"wife" (Job 18:12); יד, "hand, hence offspring" (II Sam. 18:18;
Job 20:10); cf. Gordis, "A Note on Yad," JBL, 1943, vol. 62,
pp. 341 ff.

The use of the singular and plural שדה ושדות is correctly
understood by Ibn Ezra, who quotes the passage in Jud. 5:30,
רחם רחמתים, and adds והעניין שלא תאמר אחת בלבד כי אם הרבה.
Cf. also the Arabic usage مال واموال "abundance of riches."

2:9. אף, "in addition (to my wealth)." The phrase עמדה לי
is rendered "my wisdom stood by me, helped me" (Ew. Gr.
Hertz.); cf. the Hanukah prayer עמדה להם בעת צרתם and the Passover Haggadah והיא שעמדה לאבותינו ולנו. But the sense required
here is that all these projects were part of Koheleth's wise
design; cf. v. 3, ולבי נהג בחכמה. Hence the better rendering is "my
wisdom stayed with me."

2:10. אצל, "lay aside, withdraw"; cf. Gen. 27:36; Nu.
11:25; and our paper, "Studies in Hebrew Roots of Contrasted
Meanings," in JQR, 1936 (vol. 27), p. 48. The heart and the eyes
are the seat of desire; cf. Nu. 15:39.

2:11. פנה ב = "turn in order to observe"; cf. Job 6:28.
שעמלתי לעשות = lit. "that I did by dint of exertion." The complementary infinitive in Hebrew is frequently equivalent to an
adverbial modifier. Cf. Ges.-K., sec. 120, end, and such passages
as Hos. 1:6, לא אוסיף עוד ארחם, "I shall not pity again"; I Sam.
2:3, אל תרבו תדברו, "Do not speak proud talk exceedingly." In
Gen. 2:3 אשר ברא אלהים לעשות is to be rendered similarly, "which
God made creatively, as an act of creation" (Ew. Dill. Del.).

2:12. The usual rendering of the first half of the verse is
"I turned to see wisdom and madness and folly." There are two
considerations militating against this view: 1) The entire section (vv. 12 ff.) is concerned with the uselessness of "wisdom"
alone, whether abstract (vv. 13–16) or practical in character

(vv. 17–19). Koheleth is not observing "folly" here. 2) The clause is definitely reminiscent of 1:17, which has been rendered, on grounds set forth above, as "to know that wisdom and knowledge are madness and folly." Hence a similar meaning is required here. Hitzig recognized this in his translation: "I turned myself to behold wisdom and lo! it was madness and folly." Wr. properly objects that וְהִנֵּה would be required before הוללות, and he therefore emends accordingly. A simpler solution is to delete the copulative Vav in והוללות and render "and saw that wisdom was madness and folly." The construction of the double accusative after לראות being misunderstood (cf. 1:17 and 7:25), the three nouns were construed as parallel objects and a Vav connective was inserted before הוללות. Moreover, it is probable that even the Vav need not be deleted. The two Vavs may be coordinate, like the Arabic و ... و "both ... and."

This usage, though not frequent in Hebrew, does occur; cf. Gen. 34:28; Num. 9:14; Josh. 9:23; Isa. 38:15; Jer. 13:14; Job 34:29; Neh. 12:28; a. e., and see BDB, p. 253a. It has not been noted that Koheleth employs it again in 12:2: והאור והירח והכוכבים, "and the light both of the moon and the stars"; cf. Com. ad loc.

The clause is then to be translated, "I saw that wisdom is *both* madness and folly"; cf. note on 1:17 on this construction and on the force of the Lamed of לראות. Another possible, though less plausible, view of the passage is to render "to see wisdom in relation to madness and folly" (Zap. Gal.).

The second half of the verse is an ancient *crux interpretum*. LXX and P (so Ibn Ezra, Ehr.) render המלך from the Aramaic מלך, "counsel, advise," for which there is no warrant in Biblical Hebrew. Hitz. emends עָשׂוּהוּ to the infinitive עָשׂוֹהוּ, but the form with suffix is normally עֲשׂוֹתוֹ, not to speak of the absence of a finite verb in the clause. Del. and Wr. translate "the king whom they made long ago," which is entirely irrelevant. AV, Rosenmüller, Kn., JPSV, Levy, Hertz. render the verse as question and answer: "What can the man (do) who comes after the king? Even that which has already been done!" This is based on the first interpretation of Ibn Ezra, who regards עשוהו as impersonal, supplying העושים as subject. But the addition of "do" to the first half of the clause is unwarranted, and the assumption of a question and answer creates an exceedingly harsh construction. Gal. inserts the verb מה יעשה האדם. In spite of the textual difficulties, the idea is quite clear. Koheleth, in his assumed role of Solomon, wishes to assure the reader that he has experienced the ultimate in both wisdom and pleasure and that there is no need for any one else to repeat the experiment. Cf. Midrash Koh. Rabba on 3:11, אלו אמר אחר הבל הבלים הייתי אומר זה שלא קנה ב' פרוטות מימיו הוא מגנה ממונו של עולם, "If some one else (but Solomon) had said 'Vanity of vanities,' I should answer, 'This fellow who never owned two cents despises all the wealth of the world!' " To arrive at this needed meaning here, it is best to adopt the reading עָשָׂהוּ instead of עשוהו, which is found in 68 mss. and was apparently at the basis of V (cf. Kittel, BH²).

מה האדם is to be compared with מה אנוש (Ps. 8:5; Job 7:17); מה אדם (Ps. 144:3); כי מה עבדך (II Ki. 8:13), etc., and means "of what value is the man?" The verb יבוא governs את and means "come with, hence bring"; cf. MT in Deut. 31:7, כי אתה תבוא את העם הזה, and the parallel construction with *Beth* in בזאת יבוא אהרן (Lev. 16:3); אבוא ביתך בעולות (Ps. 66:13; 71:16); and Arabic أتى ب. On instances where the usages of את, עם and *Beth* coalesce, see BDB, s. v. Note the parallel use of both prepositions in Isa. 66:10, שמחו את ירושלם וגילו בה. Hence render: "Of what value is the man coming after the king with what he (sc. the king) has already done?", i.e. "what can he add to what I have already attempted?" An illuminating parallel, both as to content and form, occurs in the Egyptian *Instruction for King Merikere*: "I would fain see a brave man (i. e. a reference to his son and successor) that equaleth me therein and that doeth more than I have done" (cf. Erman, p. 80).

2:13-14. וראיתי אני introduces two statements of conventional Wisdom thought (vv. 13, 14), both couched in typical proverbial fashion. Following the presentation of the conventional teaching, Koheleth's own position is introduced by the emphatic וידעתי גם אני, "but *I* know." See the translation and introduction on Koheleth's use of quotations. There is therefore no need to excise vv. 13 and 14a as glosses. So, too, the harmonistic interpretation "though all is vanity, it is better to face reality intelligently" (Pl. Bar.) is unacceptable. Were this Koheleth's

theme, the order should have been reversed: vv. 13 and 14a
should have followed and not preceded 14b. That is the precise
thought-sequence in the beautiful Homeric passage (*Iliad*, XVII,
l. 647): "And if our fate be death, give us light and let us die."
Besides, this theme is irrelevant and even contradictory to
Koheleth's object here — the worthlessness of wisdom. Jast.
renders: "It seemed that *perhaps* wisdom was better," and
then he deletes 14a. Levy, Hertz. recognize v. 14 as a quotation,
but not v. 13. That they constitute a unit is clear from the
comparison of darkness and folly carried through in both maxims.

גם in an adversative sense is an earmark of Koheleth's style
(4:8, 14; 6:7; 8:17), though it occurs elsewhere (Jer. 6:15 = 8:12;
Ez. 16:28; 20:15, 23; Ps. 23:4; 95:9; 129:2; Neh. 5:8. See BDB,
s. v. גם, sec. 5, 6, and the parallel use of אף, sec. 1, end).

כלם means "both"; cf. 7:18 and note there.

2:15. יתר, "especially, very much." Cf. 7:16, ‖ הרבה and
equivalent to the Mishnaic ביותר, as e.g. Sifre Deut. 31, עלינו
הוחל שמו ביותר, "upon us His name rests especially." With the
Mem of comparison, it means "more than"; cf. יתר מהמה (12:12),
יותר ממני (Est. 6:6). Similarly הרבה מן = "much more than" (2:7).
אז is logical, not temporal, "then, therefore"; cf. Isa. 58:14;
Pr. 2:5; Job 9:31 and elsewhere.

The emendation אז אין יתרון (Jouon) is unnecessary, besides
being poor Hebrew.

2:16. עם = "on a par with"; cf. Ps. 106:6; Job 9:26; I Chr.
25:8 (where it is parallel to Kaph). כבר is frequent in Koheleth
and Mishnaic Hebrew in the sense "already"; שכבר occurs in the
meaning "inasmuch as"; cf. Git. 4:5, לישא שפחה אינו יכול שכבר
חציו בן חורין. בשכבר, however, is no analogy. It is best taken as
כבר with the prefix בְּשֶׁ equivalent to the earlier באשר, meaning
"inasmuch as, since." Cf. Gen. 39:9, באשר את אשתו; Gen. 39:23,
etc. Cf. BDB, s. v. Hence בשכבר = "since already." הימים הבאים
is an accusative of time; cf. the common use of היום, "on this day,"
also II Sam. 21:9 Kethib, קציר שערים תחלת; Jer. 28:16, השנה אתה
מת, and Ges.-K., sec. 118, 3. Koheleth complains that already
in the days that follow closely upon the life-span of the sage and
the fool, with no long interval of time elapsing, all is forgotten.
Hertz.: "denn längst in künftigen Tagen," ignores the article

of הימים and does not do justice to Koheleth's idea that almost immediately the sage is forgotten. JPSV, "seeing that in the days to come all will long ago have been forgotten," would have been ואיך ימות החכם עם הכסיל. באשר הימים הבאים הכל כבר נשכח is not the gloss of a pious commentator, but Koheleth's authentic cry of protest and anguish at the discovery that wisdom is unavailing and impermanent. In a passage such as this, and in 4:1, the cynic's pose of studied indifference falls away and the impassioned spirit of Koheleth, the idealistic seeker of truth and justice, is revealed. See Introduction.

On this rhetorical use of איך cf. Jud. 16:15; Isa. 14:12; 16:1; Jer. 2:23; Ez. 26:17; and the poetic איכה, Deut. 1:12; Isa. 1:21; Lam. 1:1; 2:1; 4:1.

2:17. The LXX text σὺν ὁ τὴν ζωήν shows Aquilan influence. רע על is a late idiom parallel to טוב על, Est. 3:9; שפרה עלי, Ps. 16:6; and the Mishnaic חביב על (Aboth 2:10, 12; 4:12), doubtless Aramaic in origin; cf. Dan. 4:24; 6:15, 24; Ezra 5:17; 7:18.

2:18. עמל means both "labor" and "that achieved by labor," a semantic development found also in יניע, כח, חיל, און (הון), which mean "wealth = that acquired by toil, strength or skill." In v. 21, the first meaning of עמל occurs; in v. 19, the second. In our verse, עמל may have either meaning. If taken in the sense of "wealth," שאניחנו means "which I must leave." If rendered "labor," שאניחנו must be understood as "because I shall leave it." For this use of ש as "because, inasmuch as," cf. Can. 1:6, 6, and for אשר used similarly, cf. Gen. 30:18; 31:49; and BDB, s. v. אשר and ש. The rendering "wealth" is preferable, since it supplies an antecedent for the suffix of אניחנו, which is lacking if עמל is interpreted as "labor."

2:19. שעמלתי ושחכמתי is a hendiadys = "I toiled wisely" (Zöck. Del. Bar.).

2:20. סבותי is equivalent to פניתי, "I turned." The MT reads either לְיַאֵשׁ (Piel with compensatory vowel under the Yod) or לְיַאֵשׁ (Piel with virtual doubling). Cf. בֵּאַר etc. The root יאש, "to despair", occurs elsewhere in the Bible only in the Niphal (I Sam. 27:1; Isa. 57:10; Jer. 2:25; 18:12; Job 6:26). But the noun derivative of the Piel and the Hithpael are frequent in Mishnaic Hebrew. Cf. יאוש שלא מדעת, "unconscious resignation of a lost object" (B. B. Metz. 21b); אל תתיאש (Ab. 1:7). Here עמל has both meanings, "toil" and "wealth." See above on v. 18.

2:21. כשרון, a mark of Koheleth's style, from the Aramaic, late-Hebrew root כשר, "be proper, succeed"; cf. Ecc. 2:21; 4:4, כשרון המעשה; 10:10; 11:6. The root occurs also in Est. 8:5 and in Ps. 68:7, בכושרות, which has mythological affinities with the Ugaritic god Kothar. In Koheleth the noun means "skill, ability," but includes also the related sense of "zeal, diligence" which the Syriac cognate כושרא possesses (H. Hirschberg). On 5:10 see below. The LXX inexplicably reads καὶ ἄνθρωπος in the nominative for ולאדם, perhaps an inner Greek error for ἀνθρώπῳ. P follows the MT exactly.

יתננו is rendered by both LXX and P = יתן לו. On the accusative personae after נתן, cf. Jud. 1:15 = Josh. 15:19, כי ארץ הנגב נתתני. חלקו is the direct object (Ibn Ezra). It is possible to regard חלקו as a predicate accusative (König, 340; Hertz.) and to give the suffix of יתננו the same antecedent as בו, namely עמל (v. 20). The clause would then be rendered "will he leave it as his portion." גם, as often in Koheleth, is an emphatic particle, "indeed, surely"; cf. 2:23, 26.

2:22. הוה is the less common cognate of היה. Since it occurs in the ancient poem in Gen. 27:29, הוה גביר לאחיך (and in Isa. 16:4), Bar. denies that it is an Aramaism. See, however, our discussion of Aramaisms in the note on 1:14. הוה, like אתה, מן, and the accusative Lamed, belongs to the common North-West Semitic vocabulary of Hebrew and Aramaic. While it became normal in Aramaic, it was retained in Hebrew only for poetical use. When Aramaic influence became stronger in the post-exilic period, הוה became increasingly common; cf. Neh. 6:6; Ecc. 11:3 (?) and in the Mishnah. The Mediae Vav root occurs in Hebrew only in the imperative הֱוֵי, הֱוָה, in the participle הֹוֶה (here and in Neh. 6:6), in the nouns הֹוָה, "desire, destruction," and הַוָּה, "ruin" (the Kethib היה in Job 6:2 being an error), and apparently in the Divine Name JHVH. In all these instances, the medial consonant occurs between two vowels, where phonetic changes from Vav to Yod, Yod to Vav, Yod to Aleph and Aleph to Yod are particularly common; cf. BTM, pp. 110–113. The

name JHVH probably derives from this root. ... ל הוה corresponds to ... ל יש, "has, acquires." עמלו ורעיון לבו, "labor and
thought" (cf. v. 19), the two ideals that Koheleth has tested and
found wanting as ends in themselves. On רעיון, originally
"desire," then "thought," cf. on 1:14.

2:23. Most interpreters render the first half "all his days
are pain, and vexation is his concern." This view suffers from
the difficulty that "the pain" is referred to "the days," while
"vexation" to the man himself (suffix of עניגו). It seems clear
that כל ימיו is parallel to בלילה and should therefore be taken as
an accusative of time; cf. note on הימים הבאים in 2:16 (so Hitz.
Gr. Ehr. McN. Hertz.). Hence render: "During all his days,
pain and grief are his lot." Hertzberg comments here: "The
problem of the eternal Jew stands behind this verse — the
characteristic restlessness, the lack of capacity of peaceful enjoyment, the need to be busily engaged, qualities marking the
Jew to the present!" But who can decide whether this describes
the Jew or modern man? Perhaps the publication date of
Hertzberg's commentary, 1932, the year before Hitler's assumption of power in Germany, is not altogether irrelevant in evalu-
ating the spirit of Hertzberg's remark!

2:24. It is evident that Koheleth is here urging the value
of physical enjoyment. There are differences of opinion, however, as to how this idea is to be derived from the clause אין
טוב באדם שיאכל:

1) Read it interrogatively, "Is it not good to eat, etc.?"
(V, Ra.).

2) Assume the absence of an excluding particle like אך or רק
(so Ibn Ezra, who compares כי אינם יודעים לעשות רע in 4:17, but
see our note). Professor Margolis compared the common Talmudic
idiom לא צריכא, "it is unnecessary," to which אלא ("except")
must be added. We might also compare Sifra 3:22, שאין תלמוד
לומר זכר אלא טומטום, "For the Biblical verse does not imply
[except] 'a male' but not 'a *tumtum*'." In paraphrasing this
cumbersome formula, Rashi adds אלא שאין ת״ל אלא להוציא טומטום
ואנדרוגינוס.

3) Most moderns assume an error of haplography and read
אין טוב באדם מִשֶׁיֹּאכַל on the analogy of 3:22 (Del. Ehr. Wr.).

This is the simplest procedure and is validated by the fact that
אין טוב is always followed by כי אם (3:12; 8:15) or מן (3:22).
גם is not adversative (ag. Del.), but emphatic (Hertz.).

Hertz. argues that in 2:1 ff. Koheleth objects to pleasures
created by man, while here he affirms the virtues of God-given
joys. This view fails to comprehend Koheleth's temperament and
overlooks the use of a religious terminology. For Koheleth, as
for Biblical writers generally, the physical pleasures of life were
divine in origin, as this verse eloquently attests. The association
of flesh with the Devil has no warrant in Hebrew thought.
Koheleth's thought is clear when late theological preconceptions
are not permitted to obscure it — he denies that pleasure is an
adequate goal in life, in the *absolute* or philosophic sense — but
it remains the only *practical* program for human existence. See
Intr. This sense was given, and perhaps this slightly modified
text was read, by LXX and P.

The sequence of perfect and imperfect tenses in שיאכל ושתה
והראה is equivalent to a present and expresses a universal truth.
גם זה ראיתי אני כי מיד האלהים היא is an example of "anticipation."
זה, the logical subject of the subordinate clause (כי . . . היא) after a
verb of perception (ראיתי), has been lifted into the main clause,
becoming the object of the verb. Hence it is equal to גם ראיתי
אני כי זה מיד האלהים היא. Cf. Ehr. on Gen. 1:4 and Job 11:8, and
the writer's paper, "A Note on Josh. 22:34," in *AJSL*, vol. 47
(1931), pp. 287 f.

2:25. יחוש has been generally interpreted as "feel, perceive,"
hence "experience, enjoy" (Del. Wr. Levy, Bar.). The cognate
roots חוש, חשש, however, which are common in Mishnaic Hebrew,
Aramaic and Syriac, are used only of feeling pain, suffering, as
in חש בראשו, "feel pain in the head" (B. Erub. 54a), or of fear
and apprehension, as in חיישינן, "we are concerned lest" (passim).
Levy, it is true, adduces Akkadian *hasâsu*, "be happy," and
אשקייה חד חמרא וחשו מבינתא דראשו (B. Shab. 14a), which the
Arukh interprets as "I enjoyed it greatly," but this is a free
rendering. Indeed, that Hebrew חוש could mean "enjoy"
has scarcely been proved. Moreover, v. 26, which gives the
reason for v. 25, speaks of enjoyment (שמחה) and of the failure
to enjoy (לאסף. לכנוס). יחוש should therefore have a significance

contrary to יאכל. Ehr. accordingly emends יָחוּשׁ to יָחוּשׁ and cf.
the Mishnaic idiom כחס על השמן, "refrains from using (lit. has
pity on) the oil" (Shab. 2:5). No emendation is, however,
required. The Arabic حشى VI means to "abstain from, refrain,"
and the common idiom حشا الله "Allah forbid!" The relationship of *Tertiae Yod* and *Mediae Vav* roots may be studied in this
very root, חשי and חוש (cf. the Talmudic lexicons), and in such
pairs as שרי — שוד, בזה — בו. Hence יחוש is "refrain." ממני
is to be emended to ממנו with 8 Heb. mss., LXX, P, and Jerome,
and practically all moderns. The suffix refers to God: — "All
enjoyment or its absence is a divine fiat, and obedience to God's
will is true religion!"

2:26. This verse is often eliminated (Bar. Wild. McN.
Haupt, Jast.) as the gloss of a pious commentator. It is to be
noted, however, that the verse speaks not of the צדיק and the
רשע, but of אדם שטוב לפניו and the חוטא, as in 7:26. This variation
in usage is most significant. Koheleth uses the conventional
terms צדיק and רשע to express the concepts of conventional
morality and piety, "the righteous and the wicked"; cf. 7:15 ff.,
20; 8:9 f., 13 (a quoted proverb; see note ad loc.); and 9:2. On
the other hand, חוטא, etymologically "the one who misses the
mark," has a richer semantic development. Koheleth rarely
uses the word in the conventional sense of sinner (8:12 is a cited
proverb, where incidentally it is explained by עשה רע, and in 9:2
its meaning is clear from the contrast with כטוב). As in Pr.
14:21; 19:2 and the Wisdom writers generally, חוטא occurs as
synonymous with "fool." In 9:18, where this meaning is clear
from the contrast with *hokmah*, it lends itself admirably to
Koheleth's conception that the man who misses God's purpose,
the enjoyment of life, is a "sinner" (2:26; 7:26), and this nuance
is indicated by the contrast with טוב לפני ה'. This last meaning
is related to the connotation "sin against oneself," hence "be
punished" (Pr. 20:2); cf. the parallel idiom *hōmēs nafšō* in
Pr. 8:36 and the use of *'āšam*, "sin, be punished" (Jer. 2:3;
Hos. 5:15; 14:1; Ps. 34:22 f. a. e.). The pious moralist declares
that the sinner suffers; Koheleth, that he who suffers is a sinner.
Conventional wisdom declares that the sinner is a fool; Koheleth

that the fool is a sinner. On this use of the conventional religious vocabulary in an unconventional manner, see Intr. Levy correctly recognizes that Koheleth equates sin with folly, but regards that as the result of a purely intellectual process, due to Greek Cynic-Stoic influence. He overlooks the spirit of Wisdom thought and the psychological factors involved, which require no assumption of Greek influence. Sieg. has already recognized that חוטא is not a sinner in the conventional sense, but one displeasing to God, the opposite of טוב לפני ה', and calls attention to I Ki. 1:21, והייתי אני ובני שלמה חטאים.

That this goal of pleasure represents for Koheleth resignation to the inevitable, rather than the cheerful contentment of a pious believer who sees God's will in his destiny, is clear from the closing formula: גם זה הבל.

Section III — Introductory Note

3:1-15. The famous catalogue of times and seasons has been variously interpreted:

1. Man must do everything in its proper time (Ibn Ezra, Pl.) or, in Stoic terms, live in accordance with nature (Tyl. Sieg.). But there is no evidence here of the idea of man's doing things in their appropriate time (note v. 11: "God has done"). V. 9 implies rather the uselessness of human activity and initiative.

2. Man's activities are limited to certain times and seasons, in which he goes his little round doing what has been done before him (Bar.).

3. Life is monotonous and all human acts are repetitious. This is the theme of the catalogue of Marcus Aurelius (*Meditations*, Bk. IV, 32).

4. All human activity is useless, since everything is predetermined by God (Levy).

While any of these interpretations is consistent with vv. 1–8, the key to the meaning Koheleth attaches to them is to be found in the verses following (9–15), which represent the conclusions to which he comes. Koheleth begins with noting an accepted datum of experience, that all actions have their proper time (3:1). He then draws two conclusions that go far beyond the practical utility of the observation:

a) all acts are predetermined and all human activity is therefore useless. This is stated explicitly in v. 9; and b) all events, even those which man regards as calamities, have their place in God's plan (11a). What oppresses Koheleth is that man is given no glimpse of that meaning. That is the sense of v. 11. What might have been a justification of the ways of God becomes a lament on the ignorance of man.

3:1. זמן is a late Hebrew word (Neh. 2:6; Est. 9:27, 31 etc., and frequently in Mishnaic Hebrew) meaning "time."

In Daniel 2:16 etc. it means "appointed time." חפץ is used practically in the Mishnaic sense of "thing." Cf. also the Arabic شَيْء "thing," from شاء "desire." In Rabbinic Hebrew חֵפֶץ is used of objects, here of a phenomenon; cf. 5:7.

The emendation of השמים to השמש is unnecessary (cf. e. g. Jer. 10:11; Lam. 3:66).

3:2. All attempts to transfer phrases in order to achieve logical coherence by our standards are foreign to the spirit of the book (so McN.). Most of the pairs are, however, logically connected within the verse. See below on v. 5. There are 7 verses, each consisting of 4 stichs, yielding 28 in all, which Levy regards as significant in astrology. This is far-fetched. The use of seven units or multiples thereof is a widely practiced usage of literary composition. Cf. Gen. 12:2 f.; Ecc. 7:1 ff., "the *tōbh* collection"; Amos, chaps. 1, 2 (7 nations); ibid. 3:3 ff. (7 examples). On this and other material from Biblical, Rabbinic and New Testament sources, cf. Gordis, "The Heptad As An Element of Biblical and Rabbinic Style," in *JBL* (1943), vol. 62, pp. 17–26; U. Cassuto, *Meadam ad Noah* (Jerusalem, 1944), pp. 4 f.; S. Spiegel, in *Ginzberg Jubilee Volume* (English part), p. 317; also Oskar Goldberg, in *Scripta Mathematica*, vol. 12 (1946), the material of which must be used, however, with caution.

3:3. There is no need to correct להרוג to להרוס, on the basis of I Ki. 18:30, וירפא את מזבח ד' ההרוס, in order to create a perfect parallelism with stich b. The change is unnecessary, since both vv. 2 and 3 now exhibit a, b, a, b, "alternate" parallelism (2a ‖2c; 2b ‖2d; 3a ‖3c; 3b ‖3d). V. 2 begins with a favorable event, in reverse order from v. 3, which begins with an evil act, but this is due, not merely to the logical necessity of placing birth before death, but principally to the desire to begin on a pleasant note. Similarly, 8c, d reverses the order of 8a, b in order to end on a favorable note (בכי טוב). Cf. the Masoretic rule of repeating the penultimate verse at the public reading of Isaiah, Malachi, Lamentations and Ecclesiastes, in order to avoid ending on a negative theme.

3:4. רקוד, "dance," may possibly have the significance of "sing," which Levy attributes to the verb in the Talmudic phrase כיצד מרקדין לפני הכלה (B. Keth. 76b, 17a). On the other hand, רקוד may have been chosen here for the antithesis as a *talḥin* for ספד, since ܠܡܐ in Syriac means "lament"; cf. P on Gen. 50:10.

3:5. Levy has demonstrated that 5a, b has an erotic significance and is parallel to stichs c, d. "To cast stones" is used symbolically of sexual congress; "gathering in stones" of abstinence. The Midrash (Koh. R. ad loc.) understood the passage clearly thus: עת להשליך אבנים בשעה שאשתך טהורה ועת כנוס אבנים בשעה שאשתך טמאה, "A time to cast stones — when your wife is clean (menstrually), and a time to gather stones in — when your wife is unclean." Cf. Ex. 1:16; Jer. 2:27; Mat. 3:9 and the Deucalion legend. For further examples of this symbolism in folk-lore and language, see Levy's interesting appendix to his Commentary (pp. 144–152). Hertz. is not justified in rejecting this interpretation in favor of a literal reference to stone-work.

Both the Kal of רחק (Ex. 23:7) and the Piel of חבק (Pr. 4:8; 5:20) are well attested, while LXX, V, P, T attest to the vocalization of stich d: "to be far from embracing." There is therefore no need to emend to לִרְחֹק מְחַבֵּק, "to keep the embracer afar off" (ag. Ehr.).

3:6. לאבד, a declarative use of the Piel, "to consider lost, give up for lost" — the opposite of לבקש (S. Bernfeld, Levy, Ehr., Vaih.); cf. טִהַר, טִמֵּא (Lev. 13:3, 6 and passim); cf. also König on וַיְכַל (Gen. 2:2), lit. "and God declared finished the work, etc."

3:7. The rending of garments (קריעה) is the ancient mode of mourning (Gen. 37:29; II Sam. 13:31). The next phrase may contain an allusion to the Jewish practice of sewing up the rent after the mourning period (אחוי הקרעים, so Kn. Levy). The silence (stich c) could likewise refer to the period of mourning (Lev. 10:3; Job 2:13), when speech was forbidden, and the speech (stich d) to the period after sorrow (Ps. 126:2). So the Midrash ad loc.: עת לחשות בשעת האבלות ועת לדבר אחר האבלות. Hertz. doubts that the custom of sewing up the rent existed as early as in Koheleth's day. However, mourning customs are very tenacious and may be more ancient than our sources permit us to know.

A reexamination of Biblical mourning customs is a desideratum. Thus Mi. 1:11, לא יצאה יושבת צאנן, may contain a reference to staying indoors during the mourning week, "sitting shivah" (cf. the parallel מספד בית האצל יקח מכם עמדתו). So, too, Ez. 24:17, 22, לחם אנשים לא תאכל, may be a reference to the סעודת הבראה, "the meal of recovery," which, according to Jewish law, should be supplied by strangers to mourners on their return from the funeral; cf. II Sam. 3:35 and Kimḥi ad loc. There is no need to emend the latter passage to לחם אונים. Cf. also Jer. 16:7, where it is better to correct the word להם to לחם, rather than insert לחם after להם (ag. LXX, Giese.). However, the interpretation of v. 7 as mourning is somewhat doubtful in view of the distance from 4c.

3:10. See note on 1:13.

3:11. The crux העלם has been rendered in many ways: 1) "eternity" (so LXX αἰῶνα, Ibn Ezra, Pl.). 2) From the root עלם = "hide" (so T = שמה רבה "the ineffable Name of God"), hence "ignorance" of the day of death (so Ra. Dill. Gr. Ha.); cf. the Talmudic phrase העלם אחד, Ker. 4:2 a. e., "in a single state of unconsciousness." 3) As the equivalent of the Arabic cognate علم "knowledge" (Hitzig). 4) In its later Hebrew meaning "world." So apparently V, *mundum tradidit disputatione eorum*, doubtless influenced by והמה בקשו חשבנות רבים, 7:29; Rashi: "wisdom of the world"; Ibn Ezra (2nd): "desires of the world." While this sense עולם = "world" is Mishnaic and not Biblical, it does occur in Ben Sira 3:18 in this very sense: מעט נפשך מכל גדולות עולם, "Restrain thyself from all the glories of this world" (so Levy). In addition, it is the only meaning of the noun attested to in any period of the language. Hence, it seems preferable to render העלם here as "the world, love of the world." מבלי אשר לא is a pleonasm. The double negatives strengthen the negative; cf. Ex. 14:11, המבלי אין קברים (Bar.).

3:12. בָּם is attested by LXX, P and V. The MT is best explained as = "in them, i. e. in life," חיים being plural. This is preferable to referring the suffix to the seasons (Rashbam, Tyl.) or men (T, Ra.). If בם is to be retained, בחייו must be rendered "in one's life, while one lives"; for the impersonal suffix, cf. בְחָמּוֹ, "when it is hot" (Job 6:17); הִוָּלְדוֹ (Ecc. 7:1), "one's birth." On the other hand, בם remains difficult both in itself and because of בחייו at the close of the verse. Bar. suggests that it is a corruption of לָם = "for them, i. e. = for mankind;" cf. לאדם (8:15) and באדם (2:24), which he regards as an error for לאדם.

The origin of בם in our text may be explained far more simply, the Beth as a dittography of the final letter of טוב and the Mem as a virtual dittography of the Kaph of כי, which it resembled in the old script. Cf. the "Table of Alphabets" in Cooke, *NSI* (Moabite and Siloam Inscriptions), and such examples ‚as Ez. 3:12, בָּרוּךְ כְּבוֹד ה' מִמְּקוֹמוֹ, where, as Luzzatto pointed out long ago, the correct reading is בְּרוּם; Josh. 19:30 וְעָמָה to be read וְעַכּוֹ (cf. LXX and Jud. 1:31); II Chr. 22:6, where כי should be מן (so LXX, P and the parallel in II Ki. 8:29); and I Ki. 1:47 (Kethib אלהיך; Qere אלהים); cf. also Fr. Delitzsch, *Schreib- und Lesefehler im A. T.* (Berlin, 1920), p. 114; J. Kennedy, *An Aid to the Textual Amendment of the O. T.* (Edinburgh, 1928), pp. 83 ff. The introduction of the square script was gradual, and far from complete in Koheleth's day; note the passage II Chr. 22:6 adduced above, the old script on the Hasmonean coins and L. Blau, *Einleitung in die Heilige Schrift* (Budapest, 1894), who adduces evidence from Rabbinic sources to show that the square script did not supplant the old until the 2nd century C. E. On recent paleographic evidence, cf. D. Diringer, *The Alphabet* (London, 1948); *idem*, in *BA*, 1950.

Whatever the process by which our MT emerged, it is clear that the deletion of בָּם creates a perfect text. לעשות טוב = "do good, i. e. enjoy oneself"; cf. ועשה רעה (II Sam. 12:18) = "be miserable." Hence the idiom is not the Graecism εὖ πράττειν (ag. Tyl. Sieg.).

3:14. The style here reflects both Koheleth's learning and his personality. The phrase is used of the Torah in Deut. 4:2; 13:1 (לא תספו . . . ולא תגרעו ממנו), and was familiar in this sense to every Jew. Koheleth utilizes it to express his sense of the immovable destiny of things. That men's future is both unknown to them and inevitable can be explained only by the desire of God to be feared of His creatures. "The jealousy of the gods" is a primitive religious concept widely held. It is reflected in the Garden of Eden tale (Gen. 3:22; see J. Skinner, *ICC on Genesis*, pp. 90 ff.; our paper "The Interpretation of the Paradise Myth," AJSL, 1936, vol. 52, pp. 86 ff.; ag. Cassuto, *Meadam ad Noah*, Jerusalem, 1945, p. 61) and in the Tower of Babel tale (cf. Gen. 11:6). Also the Greek concept of *hybris*, man's pride vis-à-vis the gods, is closely related. Later Biblical thought conceived of God as favorable to man. Only for Koheleth, who has been drained of faith in life's possibilities, does the primitive attitude reassert itself. This is not the only instance where the sophisticate reverts to the primitive, so that "les extrêmes se touchent."

3:15. The first half of this verse is taken as question and answer by Bar.: "What is that which is? Already it has been." This strange rendering is impossible. Such an idea would be expressed by מה שהיה. מה היה כבר היה can mean only: "That which has been," as in 1:9 and often in Mishnaic Hebrew. P seems to have placed the pause after כבר, rendering "what has already been." According to the accents and the requirements of the rhythm, the caesura comes after שהיה: "What has been already is." The first clause in the verse asserts the identity of past and present, the second, the identity of future and past — all time is the same, and all events repetitive and foreordained.

נרדף has been variously interpreted: 1) "the oppressed, poor" (LXX, P, T, Rashi, Ehr.), but this does not suit the context. It is therefore removed as a gloss or placed after v. 17 (Gr. Ha.). As a gloss it is meaningless here and it would destroy the structure of v. 17 (see there).

2) Levy points out that רדף and בקש are synonymous (Ps. 34:15; Zeph. 2:3, ‖ Deut. 16:20). Hence: "God keeps on seeking what He sought before — i. e. there is no novelty in life." On

the absence of the article after את, which, though irregular, is
met with elsewhere (Isa. 41:7; 50:4; Pr. 13:21; Job 13:25; Ecc.
7:7), cf. Ges.-K., sec. 116, 1, 2, and OLQ, pp. 81–83.

3) After the Arabic cognate مردف "analogous"; cf. the
Medieval Hebrew נרדף, "synonym." Hence נרדף here = "the
same." 4) = "what is driven away, i. e. the past, events that
vanish" (Tyl. Bar.). Cf. Ovid, *Metamorphoses*, XV, 179 ff.,
"Even time itself glides on with constant progress," etc. Hence,
each event chases the other in a circle. This meaning suits the
context best. This clause is cited in the Hebrew of Ben Sira 5:3,
אל תאמר מי יוכל כחו כי ייי מבקש נרדפים. In Ben Sira it does not mean
"God avenges the oppressor" (so Levy) since the following verses
demonstrate that stich b is a continuation of the sinner's speech,
and not a warning by the author:

אל תאמר חטאתי ומה יעשה לי מאומה כי אל ארך אפים הוא
אל תאמר רחום ייי וכל עונותי ימחה
אל סליחה אל תבטח להוסיף עון על עון.

This fact Noeldeke, Smend, Oesterley-Box and R. H. Charles,
Apocrypha (ad loc.), do not notice. For Ben Sira, the clause may
mean what Levy suggests: "God is seeking the circle of things
gone by," or as Del. interprets our passage in Ecc.: "God is
always seeking the same." On both views, the sinner is saying
that God has no interest in human affairs (cf. Ps. 94:6 f.; Job
22:12 ff.).

3:16. LXX vocalizes רָשָׁע in both instances (the reading
εὐσεβής the second time is obviously an inner Greek error for
ἀσεβής; so Euringer, ag. McN.). P, V, attest to MT, reading
an abstract noun both times. The repetition of the phrase
שמה הרשע has a somber power, reflecting the intensity of Koheleth's feeling on the subject. A similar repetition occurs at
the end of the section, ואין להם מנחם (4:1).

3:17. This verse, which appears to express a belief in future
retribution, has been widely deleted as the gloss of a pious reader
(Sieg. McN. Ha. Bar. Ehr. Jast.) or regarded as representing a
conflict of thought through which Koheleth is passing (Pl.).
Jast. recognizes that the style resembles that of Koheleth. He

is therefore driven to answer that the pious glossator has imitated the author in style!

Actually the verse bears an authentic stamp. The post-Exilic age was marked by the growth among the lower groups, the proto-Pharisaic elements, of a belief in life after death and in a judgment in the after-world. The doctrine became fundamental in Pharisaic Judaism, though the Sadducees never accepted it. Precisely because its Biblical origin was challenged, it attained virtually to the level of a dogma: הכופר בתחיית המתים מן התורה אין לו חלק לעולם הבא (Sanh. 10:1). Wisdom literature reflects the skepticism of Proto-Sadduceeism on this point. Thus Job is familiar with these new ideas but laments his inability to subscribe to them (14:7–14). Koheleth likewise rejects them in his own manner, by citing the theory with skeptical overtones.

The clue to the passage lies in שָׁם, which has been found difficult. It has been derived from the Mishnaic Hebrew verb שׁוּם, "estimate, judge" (Hertz.), or emended to שָׂם, "he sets" (Houb. Luz. Gr. Dr. Bar.). However, its position at the end of the verse makes the assumption of a verb very unlikely, as does the unanimous testimony of the Versions to the meaning "there." שָׁם is a reference to the other world, the period after death as in Job 1:21; 3:17, 19 (Ibn Ezra, Levy). Its intent here, however, as its position indicates, is satirical. For a striking parallel to this word-order and meaning, compare Euripides, *Medea*, l. 1065:

> "All good to you — but there!
> Here, it is stolen from you by your father!"

Our stich is to be rendered: "There is a time for every event and every deed — over there!"

On the use and absence of the article (המעשה, חפץ), see note on 2:8 and OLQ, pp. 81–83.

3:18. This difficult verse is basically substantiated by the Versions. עַל דִּבְרַת is a late phrase characteristic of Koheleth (7:14; 8:2, and occurring elsewhere only in Ps. 110:4), equivalent to על דבר or עַל דברי in earlier Hebrew (Gen. 20:11, 18 etc.; Deut. 4:21). In all Biblical passages the phrase means "because of, for the sake of"; and it is so rendered here (LXX, V, P, Ibn Ezra, Ehr. Jast. Bar.). There is no basis for the view of Levy, who translates: "I (originally) thought in the *manner* of men."

לברם is an ancient crux. It is usually interpreted 1) "to judge them" (LXX, Ibn Ezra, Gins.). 2) "to test them" (T, V, Ges. Pl. Wr. Jast. BDB). 3) "to sift them" (Bar. JPSV), from the late Hebrew ברר, "select," "choose" (I Chr. 7:40; 9:22; 16:41; Neh. 5:18; Mishnah Maas. 2:6, בורר ואוכל; B. Sanh. 45a, ברור לו מיתה יפה). The general meaning does not vary considerably. The form is regarded as the shorter infinitive, like לְרַד (Isa. 45:1) from רדד and שַׁךְ (Jer. 5:26) from שכך (Wr. Bar.). On this view, however, the clause lacks a finite verb. This difficulty is met by regarding האלהים after לברם as the subject of the infinitive, and the comparison made with להאיר עינינו אלהינו (Ezra 9:8), "that God may light up our eyes." The parallel, however, is not adequate, for there a main clause exists with a finite verb, היתה.

Ehrlich's brilliant emendation, לא בָרָם אֱלֹהִים, "God has *not* distinguished men," does not seem convincing in the absence of a negative in all the Vss.

We prefer to regard the prefix of לברם as the Lamed of asseveration. Cf. Isa. 32:1, וּלְשָׂרִים לְמִשְׁפָּט יָשֹׂרוּ, Akkadian *lu* and Arabic ل, used before both nouns and verbs (Caspari-Mueller, *Arabische Grammatik*, 4th ed., Halle, 1876, sec. 359, 389, note d). Ugaritic supplies many instances of the use of the emphatic *lu* prefixed to verbs (so vocalized by H. L. Ginsberg, *Kitbe Ugarit*, Jerusalem, 1936): לתתנו, "she will surely set" (ibid., p. 28, l. 20); לרגמת, "I have surely spoken" (ibid., p. 3–9, l. 24). Thus לברם would be the perfect of ברר with suffix, "He surely has tested them."

ולראות is vocalized וּלְהַרְאוֹת=וְלָרְאוֹת by LXX P, V, Gins. McN. Bar., while MT is preferred by Del. and Wr. Midrash Koh. Rabba reads both the Kal and the Hiphil: לראות ולהראות. Syntactically, the form is difficult. It is best taken as the infinitive consecutive, used instead of a finite verb, in a connected narrative, a usage particularly common in later Biblical Hebrew (cf. Ges.-K., sec. 113, 4a; 114, 2, 5). This use occurs with either the infinitive absolute (Gen. 41:43; Isa. 37:19; Jer.

14:5; 19:13; Est. 2:3; 9:6) or with the infinitive construct with
Lamed (cf. 7:25 [ולדעת]; 9:1 [ולבור]; Neh. 8:13 [ולהשכיל]; II
Chr. 7:17 [ולעשות]). The usage exists also in Phoenician, South
Arabic, and Ugaritic (cf. Ginsberg, *Kitbe*, p. 32). Levy construes
the form correctly, takes it as the continuation of אמרתי, then
renders it adversatively, "but I saw, etc." ולראות is, however,
too far distant from אמרתי to follow smoothly as an infinitive
consecutive, and the adversative sense should have been indicated more directly; cf. 2:13, 14, ראיתי ... וידעתי גם אני. Hence
ולראות (=ולהראות) is to be associated with the finite verb לברם
and means "and He has shown."

The final clause is often abbreviated by the deletion of the
last two words. It should be noted, however, that it is reproduced
in its entirety by LXX, though the translators could not interpret the clause and attached להם to the following verse: καὶ
τοῦ δεῖξαι ὅτι αὐτοὶ κτήνη εἰσίν καίγε αὐτοῖς κτλ. The last
two words in MT constitute a phonetic word play, designed to
emphasize Koheleth's conclusion. Ewald (sec. 315a) compares
the Latin *ipsissimi* and the German *hochselbst*. להם is taken by
Levy as an ethical dative, but it generally appears after a verb;
cf. Gen. 21:16; Ps. 120:6, etc. It seems better to regard להם
as = "*per se*, in themselves," and to compare Ps. 90:10, ימי שנותינו
בהם, "The days of one's years, in themselves, i. e. normally."
On the interchange in meaning and usage of Beth and Lamed,
cf. 2:24, אין טוב באדם; 3:12, אין טוב בם; Isa. 5:4, ולא עשיתי בו. The
phrase is best rendered: "they are nothing but beasts, *lit.* they
are beasts in themselves." The entire verse is to be rendered:
"I said to myself concerning men, 'Surely God has tested them
and He has shown that they are nothing but beasts in essence.'"

3:19. Though LXX and P do not reproduce the Vav before
מקרה אחד, it is not to be deleted. It is the equivalent of the
Arabic ف used to emphasize the predicate (cf. II Sam. 15:34;
Job 4:6, תקותך ותם דרכיך; 36:26, מספר שניו ולא חקר; Ehr. ad loc.;
Driver, *Hebrew Tenses*, sec. 185, who cites Ibn Ezra). The
clause is to be rendered literally: "For the fate of the children
of men and the fate of the beast — they both have one fate."

On מקרה with Seghol instead of Ṣere in the construct, cf.
note on 2:7, מִקְנֶה; Gen. 43:15; Jer. 17:18 (מִשְׁנֶה). In spite of the

aberrant vocalization, it is a construct and not a predicate nominative (ag. Pl. Wr., who render awkwardly "Chance are the sons of men").

רוח refers to the spirit of life.

3:21. הָעֹלָה and הַיֹּרֶדֶת are vocalized by MT with the full *kameṣ* and *pataḥ-dageš* respectively. But this is not an effort to give the passage an "orthodox" character by converting the interrogative *He* obviously demanded by the context into the definite article (ag. Geiger, Del. Levy). Not only is the unmistakably heterodox sentiment of v. 19 left untouched by MT, but P, V, and T render the words interrogatively. Finally, the evidence is clear that before Aleph and Yod, there was a tendency to vocalize the interrogative *He* with full vowels and dageš. Cf. הָאֶחָד, Gen. 19:9; הַיֵּיטַב, Lev. 10:19; הָאִישׁ, Nu. 16:22; cf. also Job 23:6, הַבְּרָב.

3:22. P adds בָּם after טוֹב as in 3:12, perhaps a dittography from טוֹב מֵאֲשֶׁר. אַחֲרָיו, usually given as "after him, after his death," is best taken as an adverb with petrified suffix, like יַחְדָּו (so also Levy); cf. 6:12; 7:14; and especially 9:3 (where the passage is in the plural); Jer. 51:46; also Neh. 3:16–31 (where it frequently follows a plural) (vv. 18, 23, 29, 30, 31 Qere; the Kethib אַחֲרֵי, to be read אַחֲרַי, is likewise a neuter adverb; cf. Gordis, *BTM*, p. 127 and note 242).

The pain of not knowing the future is a purely intellectual deprivation for Koheleth. For Job it takes on the warmer human note of the grief of a father who cannot know the fate of his children (cf. Job 14:21 f.). Here is another sign of Koheleth's lack of family ties.

4:1. The first העשקים is an abstract noun as in Am. 3:9; Job 35:9; the second is the passive participle (so LXX, P, comm.). ומיד עשקיהם כח is syntactically difficult. It is best connected with והנה and is thus a contrasting parallel to דמעת העשקים, lit.: "and behold power out of the hands of their oppressors." This is far preferable to supplying a non-existent verb and creating the independent clause, "power *went forth* from the hands of the oppressors" (McN., Bar.). The emendation of the second מנחם to מושיע (Gr.) or מציל (Oort), in order to avoid a repetition of the same word, is uncalled for, nor is it necessary to give the word a different nuance the second time (ag. Ha

Levy). The iteration "rings like a knell of doom" (Kirk.). Note, too, that the section begins with a repetition, שמה הרשע (3:16), and ends with one, אין להם מנחם (4:1). That parallel stichs may not at times employ the same word is a widespread assumption, but it is not valid; cf. Job 11:7; 12:23; 38:17, 22 and frequently elsewhere.

4:2. ושבח has been variously construed: 1) as a perfect (LXX, P), perhaps originally וְשִׁבַּחְתִּי (Dr.); 2) as a verbal adjective (Ibn E., Gins.); 3) as a participle with the Mem erroneously dropped (Ges. Del. Sieg.). It is best understood as an infinitive absolute consecutive used instead of a finite verb (Rashi, Mend., Ewald, Bar., Levy). The addition of a subject (here אני) occurs in Biblical Hebrew (cf. Ges.-K., sec. 113, end; Lev. 6:7; and Deut. 15:2, etc.) and in Phoenician, as in the Azitawadd text (JNES, 1949, vol. 8, pp. 112 f.). עֲדֶנָּה and עֲדֶן in the next v. are generally regarded as contractions of עַד הֵנָּה and עַד־הֵן (BDB). But the common Mishnaic עֲדַיִן, "yet," suggests rather that our spelling here is the old orthography for the *ai* diphthong in which the Yod was unexpressed (so also Ehr.); cf. *Mesha Inscription* (l. 10) קריתן and בת דבלתן (l. 30) and חורנן (l. 31) for Biblical קִרְיָתַיִם (Jer. 48:1) and בֵּית דִּבְלָתַיִם and חוֹרֹנַיִם (ibid., 48:22, 34); דֹתָן (Gen. 37:17) by the side of דֹּתָיְנָה; the old spelling ירושלם, and other examples adduced in Gordis, *BTM*, p. 100. The most pertinent evidence lies in II Ki. 14:2, where the Kethib יהועדין Qere יְהוֹעַדָּן reproduce exactly the Mishnaic and Biblical forms of the adverb in the last two syllables.

4:3. את אשר is not to be regarded as the accusative after ושבח, which is very awkward (ag. Wr. Sieg. König), but with LXX, P as the nominative, with טוב as the predicate. This usage of את אשר in the nominative is frequent in Mishnaic Hebrew, as Ehr. has pointed out; cf. Ber. 3:1; Demai 2:5; Shek. 8:7; Git. 9:5, את שהעדים נקרין בו כשר. In the one Biblical instance Ehr. adduces, Nu. 22:6, את אשר תברך מברך, we probably have an accusative. Note, however, Jer. 38:16 Kethib, חי ה' את אשר עשה לנו, which is thus not an error, but a variant construction, which became frequent later. נעשה was apparently read by LXX as a participle, rather than as a perfect, which is a preferable reading; cf. v. 1, נעשים.

Section V — Introductory Note

4:4–16. The unity and meaning of the entire section have been overlooked, largely because Koheleth's use of quotations to reproduce conventionally accepted ideas has not been noted. Thus Wright finds in vv. 9–12 a straightforward praise of companionship, but this is not in keeping with the spirit of Koheleth. Accordingly, these verses and v. 5 are deleted by Sieg. McN. Ha. Jast. and Bar. (doubtfully). However, this procedure deprives the book of a characteristic note. On the other hand, Levy sees 4:2 to 5:16 as a unified section concerned with the Greek doctrine of moderation, μηδέν ἄγαν, but this does not commend itself from a study of the text (see our note on v. 5, etc.). For our conception of the unity of the section see the Introduction to the translation and notes below. In this passage, Koheleth is concerned with refuting three arguments usually advanced in favor of hard work.

4:4. The opening clause is an instance of "anticipation": "Thus I saw all the hard work that it is rivalry, etc." = "I saw that all the hard work is rivalry." Cf. Gen. 1:4 and "Note on Josh. 22:34," AJSL, 1931, pp. 287 f. כשרון, "skill," a common word in later Hebrew and Aramaic, is restricted in Biblical Hebrew to Koheleth (2:21; 5:10; 10:10; 11:6), Esther (8:5) and Ps. (68:7, בכושרות, which has mythological affinities with the Ugaritic deity Kothar). קנאת איש מרעהו need not be rendered "envy caused by one's neighbor" (Ehr.) or even "rivalry over one's neighbor," with the Mem of comparison (Wr.). While קנא generally governs the acc. (Nu. 5:14), it occurs with Beth (Gen. 30:1) and with Lamed (Ps. 106:16 ויקנאו למשה). It may occur here with Mem; cf. ירא construed with acc. pers. (e. g. Nu. 14:9), with מן (e. g. Lev. 19:14, 32; Ecc. 12:5), with מפני (Deut. 5:5). Hence render: "a man's envy of his neighbor." On the nuance of קנאה as "rivalry," cf. Isa. 11:13 and the familiar Talmudic proverb קנאת סופרים תרבה חכמה (B. Bathra 21a), "the rivalry of scholars increases wisdom."

4:5. This verse and the following are diametrically opposed to each other. The problem is met in several ways: 1) Gins. takes v. 5 to mean "even the indolent fool eats his meat and

finds life more satisfying than the eager worker," but this is
far-fetched and irrelevant. 2) V. 6 is taken as the quotation of
the fool mentioned in v. 5, who says "Better a handful of quietness, etc." (V, Ibn E., Levy). But the fact that throughout the
book, and in this section in particular, Koheleth stresses the
folly of hard work precludes the idea that Koheleth would call
the man who takes his ease a fool. Moreover, the style of v. 6
is indubitably Koheleth's own. 3) V. 5 is omitted as a pious
gloss (Bar. Ehr. McN., Ha. a. o.) — an all too easy solution.

Actually, no such procedure is required. V. 5 is a conventional
quotation, which is refuted by a directly opposed quotation.
Of the two views, the latter is Koheleth's own, as is clear from
its coming at the end, as well as from the style and sentiment
expressed. See Intr. and notes on Ecc. 2:13, 14; 9:16–18, and
cf. Job 12:12 f. and Pr. 26:4, 5 for examples of contrasting
proverbs. The sense can be expressed in translation only through
adding introductory formulas, such as "some men teach" to
v. 5 and "But I declare" to v. 6.

חבק את ידיו (Kal part. for Piel) is a symbol of laziness; cf.
Pr. 6:10. אכל את בשרו, "consumes his own flesh, i. e. destroys
himself"; cf. Isa. 49:26, והאכלתי את מוניך את בשרם, and Mi. 3:3;
Ps. 27:2; Pr. 30:14 for related usages.

4:6. נחת and עמל ורעות רוח are undoubtedly adverbial accusa-
tives (Sym., T, Ibn E., Wr., Levy). The author declares that
one handful achieved through ease is better than two handfuls
won through exertion. The interpretation "one handful of rest
is better than two handfuls of labor" (Del., Sieg., Bar.) is self-
evident to the point of absurdity, for no one would deny that
rest per se is preferable to exertion. Besides, the verse would
then exhibit an excessively strained use of metaphorical language
(Tyler).

4:8. עינו, the sing. of the Qere, is followed by LXX, P, T;
עיניו, the plural of the Kethib, by V, Del., Ehr. The singular
occurs in Ecc. 1:8. The verse recalls the striking Talmudic
legend of Alexander the Great during his journeys of conquest
receiving a human eye, the symbol of desire. It proved heavier
than all the gold and silver that could be placed on the scales,
and finally was outweighed only by dust, the symbol of death

(B. Tamid 32b). ואין שני may refer to friend, servant or wife, probably the last (Ibn E.). The second half of the verse is a striking illustration of the use of a quotation without an introductory formula (see Intr.). Koheleth is citing the hypothetical argument that a man without family ties should have used. Hence we must supply: *"He never asks himself,* 'For whom, etc.' "

4:9. The entire passage, through v. 12, is eliminated by Sieg. McN. Ha. Ehr., but Bar. notes that the verses may have been introduced by Koheleth. Their association with the section is clear. Having spoken of the man without a family, Koheleth is led to point out that the vaunted advantages of family life are exaggerated. He does so obliquely, by citing a conventional proverb (v. 9) to which he adds an ironic comment, ostensibly validating, but actually undermining, the proposition by limiting the benefits of family life to a few minor physical advantages. On this use of proverbs see Intr. That the passage refers to friendship is highly unlikely, especially in view of v. 11 (ag. Pl. Wr. Levy).

אשר = "because"; cf. 6:2; 8:11–12; 10:15; Gen. 30:18.

4:10. אם יפלו is to be taken partitively: "If either of them falls"; cf. ויאמרו איש אל רעהו, Gen. 11:3; Jud. 6:29. It is this interpretation which lies at the basis of T, P, V rather than an assumed reading like אם יפל האחד השני יקים את' (Dr. in BH), which is much too distant graphically (ag. Bar.). Nor need השנים be inserted after יפלו (ag. Gal.). ואילו, "But woe to him!" (LXX, P, Rashi, Ibn E., Wr., Bar.); cf. 10:16, אי לך ארץ. This is preferable to reading the Mishnaic ואילו, "but, on the contrary" (Gr. Ehr.).

4:12. תקף, meaning "be powerful, mighty," is best taken here not as "overpower, prevail" (so Kn. Wr. Ha. Levy), for the following clause would then be meaningless, but "attack" (Rashi, Ibn E., Bar.); cf. the common Aramaic term in the Talmud, מתקיף, "raises a strong objection." This meaning is common in modern Hebrew. The subject of the verb is indefinite (cf. Gen. 48:1, 2, a. e.), while the suffix of יתקפו anticipates the object האחד, an Aramaic usage frequent in the Mishnah, but not without analogy in the Bible; cf. ותראהו את הילד (Ex. 2:6); יביאה

את תרומת ה' (Ex. 35:5); יתננו חלקו (Ecc. 2:21); and note Ges.-K., sec. 131 e, note 4, c.

החוט המשלש refers to the added advantage of a son in time of stress. Cf. Gen. 15:2; 30:1; Ps. 127:3 for the normal attitude of the Hebrews on children.

4:13. The word מִסְכֵּן, "poor," characteristic of Koheleth (cf. 9:15–16; Isa. 40:20, where the vocalization מְסֻכָּן is erroneous; Deut. 8:9, מִסְכֵּנֻת), has a fascinating international history. Derived from Assyrian *muskenu* "beggar," it has traveled through the Arabic مسكن into the Romance languages; cf. Spanish *mesquino*, French *mesquin*, Italian *meschino* (meaning "shabby, pitiful").

להזהר, "to be careful, take care of himself," another late Hebrew word occurring in Ez. 3:21; 33:4, 5, 6; Ps. 19:12 and Ecc. 12:12, and particularly frequent in Mishnaic Hebrew; cf. חכמים הזהרו בדבריכם (Ab. 1:11). The meaning of the word in our context is not certain. It is usually taken as "who does not know how to take advice" or "take care of himself" (Ehr.). The latter view seems preferable as a description of an old man in his dotage. The verse is apparently a proverbial saying extolling the virtues of energy and ability over entrenched position. Both this verse and the next, with which it is connected, are marked by sentiments and stylistic features characteristic of Koheleth (כי גם, אשר, כסיל, מסכן). Hence the passage seems to be his restatement of a conventional apothegm.

Virtually every commentator has felt impelled to identify the protagonists of the passage. The identifications include Abraham and Nimrod (Tar.), Joseph and Pharaoh, David and Saul, the high priest Onias and his nephew Joseph the Tobiade. Other suggestions are Herod and Alexander his son (Gr.), Antiochus III and Ptolemy Philopator (Hitz., Bar.), Antiochus Epiphanes and Demetrius I or Alexander Balas (Winckler, Ha.). Several of these are ruled out by the pre-Maccabean date of the book. What we have here, as in 9:13 ff., is probably not a historical reference, but a typical incident, invented by Koheleth to illustrate his point. On this usage in Egyptian Wisdom, see note on 9:13 ff. Contemporary American literary usage speaks of such themes as "success story" and "rags-to-riches."

If Koheleth was citing an actual event, it must have been clear
to his contemporaries, though it remains obscure to the modern
reader. The theme, however, is clear — the transitoriness of
fame. Granted that an able young man may supplant an old
fool and win the acclaim of his entire generation, yet oblivion
ultimately overtakes even the youthful successor — the countless
generations that follow know nothing of him. Hence, Koheleth
reasons, even the quest for fame is a hollow justification
for the exertion of labor and ability. It is in truth "the last
infirmity of noble minds" for "il n'y a pas d'homme nécessaire" —
no man is indispensable!

4:14. הָסוּרִים is not to be derived from סור, "rebel," a meaning
the root does not possess (ag. Ha. Bar.), nor is it to be rendered
"Syrians." The kameṣ beneath the *He* in MT implies a recognition of the loss of an Aleph, hence הָאֲסוּרִים=; cf. הָרַפִּים, II Chr.
22:5 ‖ אֲרַמִּים, II Ki. 8:28. כִּי גַם = "although"; cf. 8:12; BDB,
p. 169b.

Levy, followed in part by Gal., regards 14a as an explanation
of 13a, and 14b as explaining 13b, and reading יֵצֵא with LXX,
he renders —

> "For from the prison the lad can become a king,
>   While the old man in spite of his royal sway
>   will become a beggar."

While "alternate structure" does occur (cf. 2:24–26; 5:17–19),
this view, which is similar to Gins. Hertz., does not commend
itself on linguistic grounds. In spite of the Greek γίγνομαι,
there is no evidence that נולד can be used of something already
in existence to mean "become." The Mishnaic passages adduced
by Dr. and Gins. (see Bar., p. 122) prove nothing. Thus שנולד
להן מום (Temurah 3:5) does not literally mean "which became
crippled" but "in whom a defect was born." Obviously unacceptable is the rendering "while the old man is born poor in
understanding" (Ibn E., Ehr.). All in all, the generally accepted
view of the passage seems preferable, the verse referring to the
wise lad of v. 13 who is able to supplant the old king in spite of
his lowly origin — "from the prison-house he came forth to rule,
though he was born poor in his (i. e. the old man's) kingdom."

For another example of Koheleth's use of the third pers. masc. suffix to refer to an antecedent other than the subject of the clause, with the consequence of some ambiguity, cf. 5:15 and Com. ad loc.

4:15. The major difficulty lies in הילד השני. Does it imply another lad, in addition to the first and to the old king (so McN. Bar.)? To avoid this profusion of characters in the episode, many scholars delete השני (Bick. Sieg. Ha. Dr. Ehr.), or הילד (Gal.), but the entire phrase is vouched for by all the Vss. Levy's attempt to refer the ordinal to Ptolemy Philadelphus the Second is unconvincing. H. Hirschberg's emendation to יֶלֶד הַשְּׁבִי, "the captive lad," is also unnecessary, since a better solution is at hand. השני is to be construed as an apposition, "the lad, the second one, i. e. the old man's successor." Examples like יַיִן תַּרְעֵלָה (Ps. 60:5), "wine which is poison," מַיִם לַחַץ (I Ki. 22:27), "water which is oppression," which are cited as support by some scholars, are not parallel, since the second word is a noun, not an adjective. There is, however, an exact parallel, which has not hitherto been noticed. In Hos. 2:9, אלכה ואשובה אל אישי הראשון does not mean "let me return to my first husband," since for the prophet the adulteress had only one legitimate husband and the others were "lovers" (cf. מאהבי, Hos. 2:7). Hosea is too careful with the word 'iš (cf. 2:18) to use it loosely. Hence אל אישי הראשון can mean only "to my husband, who was first." Identically, הילד השני means "the lad, who was second." Hebrew lacks a word for successor like the Arabic *Khalifa*.

המהלכים תחת השמש = "those who walk beneath the sun, i. e. are now alive," a reference to their contemporaries. Cf. Ecc. 11:7. The verse describes how all men flock to the youth's banner, as he attains to power. אשר יעמד תחתיו = "who will come upon the scene, stand in his place" (cf. *BDB*, p. 764a, b). *Amad* is a late Hebrew equivalent for *qūm*; cf. Ps. 106:30; Est. 4:14; Dan. 8:22 ff.; 11:2 ff.; Ezra 2:63 = Neh. 7:65; Ben Sira 47:1, 12.

4:16. This verse is taken by Pl. Wr. Bar. to refer to the throngs whom the king rules. But the king is usually described as being "before his people" (cf. I Sam. 18:16; Ps. 68:8; II Chr. 1:10), not the people before the king. Besides, the plural suffix of לפניהם cannot refer to the young ruler. Finally, on this

view, האחרונים would have no meaning. Hence, Jast. deletes the
clause אשר היה לפניהם, while Ehr. eliminates the entire first half
of the v. The key to the meaning of the passage lies in grasping
the correct meaning of אשר היה לפניהם, which can mean only "who
lived before them (i. e. the old king and his young successor),"
exactly as in 1:10; 2:9, and which is contrasted with האחרונים
as in 1:11, to denote the earlier and the later generations. The
theme, too, is similar to the passage in chap. 1, though concretized
by a specific example. Great as is the present fame enjoyed by
the new, young king (v. 15), there is an endless number of men
who lived before them both (לפניהם) (the old king and the new)
and who therefore never knew his fame, and future generations
will likewise take no joy in the ability of the young monarch,
which won the throne for him. On Ki, cf. Com. on 5:6.

Exegetes have been led astray by the absence of a transi-
tional word at the beginning of v. 16, but such examples are not
uncommon; cf. 4:5 f.

Section VI — Introductory Note

4:17 to 5:6. This entire passage is deleted as a gloss by
McN. and Sieg., a position which Bar. correctly rejects. Koheleth reflects here the proto-Sadducean upper-class viewpoint,
which regards the Temple as essential to the accepted order,
and therefore required. Hence, vows of support for its maintenance should be fulfilled, especially since God's name has been
taken. Yet undue enthusiasm for the Temple, as manifested for
example by the Psalmists (27:4 ff.; 42:2 ff.; 84:11), is not "good
form." Conventional adherence to institutional religion has
always characterized the upper classes. That the passage is
authentically Koheleth's is clear, not only from the vocabulary
(בית האלהים, not ביתה, כסיל, למה) and from the characteristic
cynical attitudes expressed in 5:17 and 6:1, but also from the
use of a rhetorical question in 5:5 (cf. 7:16, 17). Vv. 5:3 f. reveals
a knowledge of Deut. 23:22 ff.

The "fear of God" has for Koheleth, as for more conventional
teachers, both a metaphysical and an ethical character, that is
to say, it embodies both a theory of life and a course of conduct.

From his standpoint, "to fear God" means to be conscious of
His limitless and unfathomable power and to be aware of the
uncertainty and brevity of life. Consequently to "do God's will"
is to enjoy life to the limit of one's capacity. See Intr.

4:17. The Kethib רגליך and the Qere רגלך are both satisfactory. "Do not run thoughtlessly and over-frequently to
the Temple." The sense is not very different from Pr. 25:17,
הוקר רגלך מבית רעך, which refers, of course, to a human friend.
The emendation רִגְלָיִךְ, "thy feasts" (Ehr. Jast.), is untenable.

קָרוֹב לִשְׁמֹעַ is taken variously as 1) an infinitive used as an
imperative — "Come near to listen" (Del. Wr.); or 2) as an infinitive — "to come near to listen is better," etc. (Del. König Bar.);
or 3) as an adjective meaning "better, more praiseworthy" (M.
Seidel, in *Debir*, vol. 1, Berlin, 1923, pp. 3 f.). This is based on
the sense Seidel assigns to the root קרב, "praise, glorify," as in
Ps. 75:2; 119:151; Job 17:12. He then interprets our passage:
"It is more excellent to listen than to offer sacrifice," comparing
I Sam. 15:22 for the sense. On this view, it is not necessary to
supply or understand טוב before מתת.

לִשְׁמֹעַ, "listen," is usually taken to mean "obey." More
probably it has the meaning here "to understand." Koheleth
is not interested in preaching religious obedience, but in contrasting the need of understanding with the conforming, empty
piety of those he regards as fools. On this meaning of the verb
cf. Gen. 11:7; 42:23; Deut. 28:49; II Ki. 18:26, etc. It is particularly common in Mishnaic Hebrew, where it develops the nuance
of "deriving a logical inference" in such phrases as שומע אני מ,
שמע מינה. This borders closely on the sense required here. Koheleth may well have had I Sam. 15:22 in mind: "to obey
(š°mō'a) is better than sacrifice (zebaḥ)," as Seidel suggests,
but he is using the traditional passage in a spirit far removed
from that of classic Hebrew prophecy. מִתֵּת הַכְּסִילִים זָבַח, lit. "than
the fools' giving sacrifice." כִּי־אֵינָם יוֹדְעִים לַעֲשׂוֹת רָע has occa-
sioned many forced interpretations: 1) "they do not know that
they do evil" (Ra. P). 2) "they do not know so that they do
evil" (Del.). 3) "when they do evil" (Kn.). Many emendations
have also been proposed: לעשות טוב ורע (Gr.), לעשות טוב או רע
(Levy), כי אינם יודעים מלעשות רע (Renan), כי אם לעשות רע (Sieg.

McN. Bar.), which is taken to mean: "they know only how to do evil." The last emendation is impossible Hebrew. T: טב לביש and P: טב, are efforts to interpret away the sense of the passage, not variant texts, as is clear from the fact that LXX and V support MT. All these views derive from an unwillingness to follow the "plain sense." Koheleth's contempt for the pious fools who run to the Temple and pay their pledges is expressed admirably by the given Masoretic text, literally rendered: "who do not know how to do evil." They are good — because they lack the brains to do evil!

5:1. בהל in the meaning "hasten" is late Hebrew, occurring only in Est., Chr. and Ecc. (cf. also Pr. 20:21 Qere). It is construed with a direct object (Est. 2:9; II Chr. 35:21), with Beth and noun (Ecc. 7:9), and with על here. The parallels adduced by Levy of על פי, על לשון and על שפתי are therefore irrelevant. That God was distant from the affairs of men and hence unconcerned with their fate was the characteristic form of unbelief in Israel (Ps. 14:1; Job 22:11–14), as it was in the doctrine of Epicurus, hence *epikorus* = heretic in Talmudic Hebrew.

5:2. On this proverb, which Volz eliminates unnecessarily together with v. 1, see Introduction. The second half is the relevant portion. החלום with the article is generic, referring to a class (Ges.-K., sec. 126 r).

ענין, "concern, occupation"; cf. note on 1:13.

5:3. חפץ, "delight, pleasure"; cf. Isa. 62:4. Ehr. may be right in seeing here a protest against the Pharisaic practice of the annulment of oaths (הפרת נדרים) and in finding in v. 5 a sarcastic reference to the scholars' search for a reason to have an oath abrogated (cf. Ned. 9:1).

5:4. A sharp restatement of the sentiments of Deut. 23:22 ff., which in turn is repeated by Ben Sira 18:21.

5:5. אל תתן, "do not permit" (Gen. 20:6 and elsewhere). להחטיא = לחטיא = "make your flesh sin, i. e. suffer the penalty of sin" (Rashi, BDB). Words meaning "sin" are frequently used for the consequence of punishment in Hebrew. Cf. חטאים, I Ki. 1:21. So, too, Lam. 3:39 f., מה יתאונן אדם חי גבר על חטאיו, which is to be rendered, "Why should a living man complain, a mortal, on his punishment? Let us search our ways, etc."

המלאך is referred by LXX and P to God, but this does not imply האלהים as an original reading (ag. Bar. Jast.). The MT = "the messenger of God" is precisely the term for the Temple emissary, coming to collect the unpaid pledges (Ra.), or, less probably, the Pharisaic scholar, who acts as God's representative in annulling the vow (cf. Ehr. Wr.). The term is applied to priests and to prophets (Hag. 1:13; Mal. 3:1). Koheleth may be using the term with a sarcastic overtone.

למה is equivalent to classical פֶּן (cf. 7:16, 17).

חִבֵּל = destroy (Can. 2:15).

5:6. The syntactic difficulties of this v. have not been solved by the comm. Bar. regards the first half as a proverbial interpolation, which has been corrupted. It is, however, difficult to see any remnant of a proverbial structure. He transposes והבלים and ודברים and then renders "For in a multitude of dreams and words are many vanities," but the copula in והבלים does not permit this rendering. Ehr. reads וּנְדָרִים for ודברים; Kit. emends drastically, reading ברב ענין חלמות והבלים בדברים הרבה, but this is questionable Hebrew. Jastrow combines the v. with v. 2 and eliminates most of it. Wr. (pp. 363 f.) surveys the efforts made to rearrange the nouns to create an independent clause, and finally chooses: "For in the multitude of dreams are also vanities and in many words as well."

Since no emendation commends itself, the MT must be the point of departure. As the text stands, חלמות, הבלים and דברים are identical in construction, and all efforts to make some the subject and others the predicate nominative violate the text.

A simple procedure is at hand. ברב is equivalent to "in spite of the multitude"; cf. Ps. 94:19, ברב שרעפי בקרבי תנחומיך ישעשעו נפשי, "In spite of the multitude of doubts within me, Thy consolations delight my soul."

On the concessive use of the Beth, cf. Ps. 46:3; Isa. 1:15; and see BDB, p. 91a. Thus our stich a is a concessive clause, and stich b is the principal one. כי is therefore the asseverative = "indeed" which occurs frequently in Biblical Hebrew (Gen. 18:20; Num. 23:23; Isa. 15:1; Amos 3:7; Ps. 16:8; 130:4; Pr. 30:2; Job 5:2; 22:2b; 28:1; 31:18; Ecc. 7:7) and is now familiar in Ugaritic as well (cf. for the older view *BDB*, 474a, and more recently H. L. Ginsberg, in *JRAS*, Jan., 1935, p. 56; C. H. Gordon, *Ugaritic Grammar* (Rome, 1940), p. 54; Gordis, in *JAOS*, vol. 63, 2, p. 176).

Hence the verse is to be rendered: "In spite of all the dreams, follies and idle chatter, indeed, fear God!" LXX, P and V seem to have vocalized אֵת as אַף.

The verse summarizes Koheleth's view on religion — in spite of all the follies that fools regard as religion, this principle remains — fear God!

5:7. The older view that שֹׁמֵר refers to God (Ra., Ibn E., Ew., Del.) has been abandoned by most moderns, who properly refer it to office-holders. For a similar use of the term, cf. Can. 3:3, where it refers to city watchmen, who correspond to our police officers.

5:8. An insuperable crux, yet LXX attests to MT completely, rendering the second clause as "the king of a tilled field." This militates against the interesting reading מֶלֶךְ לַשָּׂר וְלָעֶבֶד (Gal.). In order to create a context, Levy renders: "The profit (derived) from the land (is recognized) by all (the officials) to be king over tilled ground." Bar. interprets: "In spite of it all (i. e. the corruption of the state) an advantage to a country on the whole is a king — an agricultural land." Both these interpretations and others even less adequate are obviously unsatisfactory. Perhaps the best rendering is: "Agriculture has an advantage over everything else, for even a king is subject to the land" (Tar., Ibn E.). Not only is this view in harmony with the emphasis on agriculture in Josephus and Rabbinic literature, but it would anticipate the standpoint of the Sadducees, who identified themselves with the country party against the urban Pharisees (cf. L. Finkelstein, *The Pharisees*). Vv. 7 and 8 would thus constitute a brief if not fragmentary comment on the political and the economic system of the day.

Section VIII — Introductory Note

5:9 to **6:9.** This section is concerned with one of the two basic themes of the book — the duty to enjoy life and taste its pleasures to the full. Naturally the suggestion is relevant only for those possessing adequate material means. Koheleth warns against excessive greed, which simply leads to an increase of wealth without increasing its enjoyment, except for the greater opportunity for ostentation. We have here an interesting adumbration of Thorstein Veblen's idea of "conspicuous consumption" in his *The Theory of the Leisure Class.* Koheleth also ridicules miserliness, allied to greed, which ends in a man's leaving his fortune to "strangers."

5:9. This verse is a typical moralizing proverb which Koheleth utilizes as a text for his own purpose — incidentally a most instructive example of Koheleth's unique style. LXX testifies to MT (including the Beth of בהמון), with one interesting variation. Apparently it read לו instead of לא. Since אהב is never construed with Beth (in spite of the analogies of רצה and חפץ), the Beth of בהמון is to be deleted as a dittography. לא תבואה is generally rendered: "no income for him," with לו understood (Ehr., Levy). However, the noun means "grain, produce," not "income," and the parallelism requires a verb instead of the nominal form, as P recognized in its rendering: "will not acquire it." Hence, the form should be revocalized לא תבואהו = לא תבואֶה, "it will not come to him." The direct accusative with בוא occurs not only in poetry (Ps. 119:41, 77) but in folk-speech. Cf. Isa. 28:15, שוט שוטף כי יעבר לא יבואנו. The second clause is a conditional sentence: literally, "if anyone love wealth, it will not come to him." On this variety of conditional sentence which uses a participle in the protasis, see Gordis, *JBL*, vol. 49, 1930, pp. 200 ff., and cf. Gen. 4:15, כל הרג קין שבעתים יקם; I Sam. 2:13; Nu. 35:30, and other Biblical and Mishnaic examples there adduced.

המון = "wealth, abundance"; cf. Isa. 60:5; Ps. 37:16; I Chr. 29:16. תבואהו is in the fem. because המון is also feminine (cf. Job 31:34).

5:10. כשרון is not to be emended to יתרון or equated with it (ag. Bar.). Not only is the emendation uncalled for, but it would efface a significant idea. Koheleth, who has previously defined ability as a kind of envy of others (4:4), here notes that its only value is to increase the extent of the possessions a man can gaze upon, without enjoying, for lack of leisure and the proper attitude. מה כשרון לבעליה = "What value is there in superior ability for the owner?"; like מָה אָדָם, "What is man?"

The Kethib ראית = either רְאִית or רָאִית; the latter, a form parallel to the Qere רְאוּת, = "The mere sight of his eyes, i. e. what he can gaze upon." While this phrase also means "the enjoyment of the eyes" (cf. מראה עינים, Ecc. 6:9; 11:9), the parallelism favors the view here proposed. On this meaning of the phrase, cf. וראה בעיניך כי לא תעבר את הירדן הזה (Deut. 3:27); ועיניך ראות וכלות אליהם כל היום (Deut. 28:32); Deut. 28:34, 67; and especially J. Kidd., end: עתיד כל אדם ליתן דין וחשבון על כל מה שראתה עינו ולא אכל, "Each man is destined to account for all the joys he gazed upon in life without tasting," also the Talmudic interpretation of Ecc. 6:9, טוב מראה עינים באשה יותר מגופו של מעשה, "A man's joy in gazing at his wife, etc." (Yoma 74b).

5:11. LXX reads הֶעָבָד for הֶעָבֵד, and, failing to recognize the late genitive construction of הַשָּׂבָע לָעָשִׁיר — "the satiety of the rich" (cf. Ps. 123:4; 122:5) — vocalizes it as הַשָּׂבַע לַעֲשִׁיר, "He fills himself to grow rich!" For שבע as referring to a full stomach, cf. Pr. 25:16. הַנִּיחַ = "permit"; cf. Ps. 105:14; the classical Hebrew would have been לֹא יִתְּנֶנּוּ (Levy, Ehr.).

5:12. רָעָה חוֹלָה is a transferred epithet, lit. "a sick evil, hence, a sickening evil"; cf. on 1:8.

לְרָעָתוֹ, "for his hurt." The guarding of wealth entails anxiety and care. If no pleasure is derived from its enjoyment, the entire process is a minus and not a plus.

שָׁמוּר לִבְעָלָיו = not "preserved *by* the owner" (so Wr.), but "preserved *for* the owner," as the context requires; cf. I Sam. 9:24, כִּי לַמּוֹעֵד שָׁמוּר לְךָ. Hertzberg's rendering of עשֶׁר שָׁמוּר לִבְעָלָיו לְרָעָתוֹ as "wealth well-guarded becomes harmful to him who possesses it" is dictated by his metric theory, but it creates awkward Hebrew, both because of the word order and because of the absence of the copula הוא at the end of the clause.

5:13. עִנְיָן = "affair, venture." בְּיָדוֹ is generally rendered "in the hand of the father, i. e. for his son" (Bar.) or "in the hand of the son" (Levy, Hertz.). Perhaps בְּיָדוֹ is a phonetic misspelling of בַּעֲדוֹ = "for him" for which extra-Biblical evidence is to be found in Ugaritic and the Tel-el-Amarna Letters, as well as in the Bible. Cf. Ez. 37:19, בְּיַד אֶפְרַיִם; Isa. 64:6, בְּיַד עֲוֹנֵנוּ;

Job 8:4; 15:23; 27:11; and see Gordis, "A Note on Yad," JBL, vol. 62 (1943), pp. 341 ff., and the literature there cited. The last clause would then mean, literally, "and he begets a son and there is nothing for him."

5:14. The author may have had Job 1:21 in mind, but the idea is sufficiently general not to presuppose a reminiscence. Since the son has been introduced in v. 13, it seems best to regard v. 14 as a description of his lot. The entire passage would then exhibit a chiastic structure: v. 12 describes the unhappy rich man, v. 13 his son, v. 14 continues the description of the son, and v. 15 turns back to the sad fate of the father, and it thus underscores the basic thought of the folly of unremitting toil. See on v. 15.

כְּשֶׁבָּא emphasizes the comparison by its very repetition, "just as he came." ישוב ללכת, the complementary infinitive, is equal to an adverb, "will he go again"; cf. 1:7. It is impossible to revocalize שֶׁיַּלֵךְ as שֶׁיֵּלֵךְ (LXX, P, Sym.) without deleting בְּיָדוֹ, but this procedure, which Ehr. adopts, leaves the verse hanging in the air. The MT is superior. The last clause שילך בידו must modify מאומה, hence, "nothing that he can take in his hand will he carry off for his toil."

בעמלו is not the Beth of instrumentality (Bar.), but of price (so Hertz). The suffix of the noun must be referred to the father, in spite of the fact that the rest of the verse is best taken to refer to the son. See above and on v. 15. For another instance of Koheleth's use of a suffix to refer to an antecedent other than the subject of the clause, see 4:14 and note ad loc.

5:15. That this verse does not refer to the same subject as v. 14, and therefore deals with the father, is clear from the introductory phrase וגם זה רעה חולה. Not only is the father unable to provide for his son, but he himself can take nothing with him. . . . כל עמת ש is best regarded as a compound of כ, ל and עֻמַּת; cf. לְעֻמַּת, I Chr. 24:31; 25:8; 26:12; and מִלְעֻמַּת, I Ki. 7:20 (Kimhi; Geiger; Lambert, *REJ*, 1895 [31], p. 47; Gordis, *JQR*, vol. 40 [1949], p. 107). In that event, it should be vocalized with a Hireq, כִּלְעֻמַּת. The vocalization כָּל is an Aramaism, under the influence of . . . כל קביל ד; see Tar. ad loc. For other instances of Aramaisms in the vocalization, cf. וּמוֹצָא (Ecc. 7:26); וְחוֹטֵא

(9:18). Levy's attempt to make כָּל the subject of the clause is far-fetched. Whatever its derivation, the idiom means lit. "all the juxtaposition, hence, exactly."

5:16. בְּחֹשֶׁךְ need not be emended to בְּחֶסֶר, "in want" (ag. Ehr.). The word depicts vividly the parsimony of the miser. A happy household is marked by the light in the window; cf. Jer. 25:10, קול רחים ואור נר. Thus Rashi in his Talmudic commentary, B. Shab. 23b s. v. שלום ביתו, says, שבני אדם מצטערין לישב בחשך. Among the Arab *fellahin* in Palestine the phrase "to sleep in the dark" represents the ultimate of poverty (Benzinger, *Hebräische Archäologie*, 2nd ed., p. 97). In our passage, Koheleth pictures the stinginess of the man of means, who tries to economize on illumination at night. This literal view is preferable to taking the word metaphorically, as an allusion to bitterness and trouble, for which cf. Isa. 9:1 and for the reverse, Est. 8:16. LXX read וְאָבַל for יֹאכֵל. P renders בחושכא אכל וברוגזא סגיאא ובחמתא ואבלא וכורהנא, a conflate reading, based on an original translation from the Hebrew (אכל) which was then supplemented by the LXX rendering (ואבלא). This procedure is often characteristic of the P on Koheleth as a whole. See Intr. Instead of the MT וְכָעַס as a verb, LXX and P vocalized it as a noun, "vexation." Though adopted by many scholars (Gr. Levy, McN., Bar., Hoel.), this reading is ruled out syntactically. If, as Bar. maintains, we have a series of nouns governed by the Beth in בחשך, Hebrew usage would demand the repetition of the preposition — בכעס בחלי ובקצף. This usage is plentifully illustrated in Deut., chap. 28, which contains many series of nouns governed by Beth, Mem and Lamed; cf. v. 22, בשחפת ובקדחת מהתענג; vv. 47, 53, 56, לשמה למשל ולשנינה; vv. 27, 28, 37, ובדלקת וברד; v. 57. Hence MT, which reads וְכָעַס as a verb, is unquestionably to be preferred. Nor can וְחָלְיוֹ be emended to וָחֳלִי (so most), because it would be syntactically unrelated to the verse. If the text is to be changed, וְחָלִי לוֹ proposed by Del. is not too distant graphically. Actually even this emendation is not required. וְחָלְיוֹ constitutes an elliptical clause equivalent to וְחָלִי לוֹ; cf. Gen. 22:24, ופילגשו = ופילגש לו; Nu. 12:6, אם יהיה נביאכם ה' = ; and especially Ps. 115:7, ... רגליהם ידיהם; אם יהיה לכם נביא ה' by the side of אף להם ... אזנים להם in v. 6. Hence the latter half of the v. is to be rendered lit. "he is greatly vexed, and he has illness and anger."

5:17. טוב אשר יפה is not a Graecism καλὸς κἀγαθός (ag. Gr.), for then אשר would not have been used (Bar. Levy). Hoel. calls the phrase "hässlich" and places the pause after טוב, which he renders: "Here is what I have found good." Not only is this, however, poor Hebrew, but the rest of the v. is poorly connected. Del. long ago compared Hos. 12:9, עון אשר חטא. Apparently we have here an idiom heightening the effect, like "good and proper," "dulce et decorum," etc. מספר is an acc. of time, and carries the connotation of paucity, "during the few years, etc."; cf. 2:3; 6:12; Job 16:22; and especially Deut. 33:6.

5:18. A highly characteristic expression of Koheleth's philosophy and style. The enjoyment of life is possible only to the man to whom God grants the power of partaking of its blessings, by spending some of his substance instead of hoarding it all. The verb השׁליט has an Aramaic coloring; cf. Dan. 2:38, 48. (Ps. 119:133, אל תשלט בי כל און, often adduced as a parallel, is not apposite. In the Psalm "sin" rules over man, here man "rules" over his possessions.) Koheleth's use of the verb persists in the Yiddish idiom, which declares that a miser has no שליטה over his possessions, i. e. no power to use them for his own good. Koheleth, using the religious terminology of his day, says that God has not given him this power.

5:19. In this verse, the crux מַעֲנֶה is rendered variously: 1) "distracts or occupies him" (LXX περισπᾷ αὐτὸν, P מענא ליה, V occupet, reading or interpreting the verb as מַעֲנֶהו, from ענה, "to be concerned, preoccupied" [1:13], and עִנְיָן "matter"). Wr. Bar. accordingly render the verse, "For he will not think much on the days of his life, for God occupies him with the joy of his heart." This view is not appropriate to the context. That joy deadens man's sensibility to the brevity of life is, to be sure, a perfectly sound idea, but it does not occur elsewhere in the book. Koheleth regards joy not as a narcotic but as the fulfillment of the will of God. 2) "God agrees with (einstimmt) the joy of his heart" (Ibn E., Leimdörfer). But even this does not fully express Koheleth's thought that it is God's *will*, not merely His *consent*, that man enjoy life (cf. 2:24; 5:18; 9:7). 3) "Reveals himself" (Levy) is far-fetched. 4) Hoel. virtually gives up the text.

Actually, matters are not hopeless. The verb מענה is best derived from the verb ענה, "answer," which possesses the connotation "answer for"; cf. Gen. 41:16, אלהים יענה את שלום פרעה, hence "provide"; cf. Hos. 2:23, 24 את אענה את השמים והם יענו את היצהר האדמה ואת הדגן ואת התירוש ואת היצהר. On the basis of these passages Dr. (BH) emends מענה to ענה in the Kal, but it may be a Hiphil in all these passages that is required for our meaning. Actually all the verbs are identical with the Hiphil (except for אָעֱנֶה). Or our verb here may be a *Rückbildung* from יַעֲנֶה, just as מֵשִׂים (Job 4:20), the Hiphil of שִׂים, is created from יָשִׂים, which appears like the Hiphil of an ע"ו verb. Our passage could then mean "God provides the joy in a man's heart" (so virtually Reutschli). With regard to the Beth of בשמחת, Hebrew may use either an acc. or the Beth of means (cf. פערה פיה, Isa. 5:14, and פערו עלי בפיהם, Job 16:10; תפש, Gen. 39:12; Deut. 21:19, and many other instances), since the object of the act may alternatively be conceived of as the means of performing the act. Preferably the verb should be revocalized, with the Vvs., as מַעֲנֵהוּ and rendered "God provides him (i. e. man) with the joy of his heart."

The difficulty encountered with the verb has been due in large measure to the failure to recognize the structure of vv. 17–19. Thus Ha. and Sieg. delete our verse entirely. The passage exhibits "alternate structure" a, b, a', b', where two statements are made and then each is validated in turn. Thus in Deut. 22:25–27, two decisions are set forth (vv. 25b and 26a) and then a reason for each is given (v. 26b and 27). Ehr. called attention to this same structure in Ps. 33:21–22. Our passage should be interpreted similarly: Man should enjoy his few days on earth (v. 17) because "not long will he remember the days of his life" (19a). Whoever has been granted the means to enjoy the blessings of life (v. 18) should do so, "because it is God who provides man with the joy in his heart" (v. 19b). For the sake of clarity the translation renders the passage in the order 17, 19a, 18, 19b.

The opening clause may also be treated as an instance of

"anticipation" (so Ibn E., Hertz.) — כי לא הרבה יזכר את ימי
חייו; cf. Gen. 1:4; Ecc. 3:21; 6:10. The
rendering would then be, "for let him remember that the days
of his life are not many." On the other hand, הרבה = "much"
can easily carry the connotation "long," so that the word order
may be preserved: "For not long will he remember the days of
his life, i. e. man will not be able to look back upon a long
career on earth."

6:1. Twenty Hebrew mss. add חולָה after רָעָה as in 5:12,
but this is an instance of the scribal tendency to "level" or make
a text uniform, hence MT is to be preferred as original. רַבָּה
may be interpreted as "great, serious" (so Ibn Ezra, Wr. Bar.
Hoel.); cf. 8:6; or, better, as "common, prevalent" (so Vulgate,
AV). Levy's rendering, "it is stronger than man," is unacceptable. In Ex. 23:29, which he compares, the preposition means
"against," not "than."

6:2. כבוד means "honor, position" (Wr. Hoel.) rather than
"abundance, wealth" (Gins. Hertz. Ehr. Levy), since the entire
phrase occurs in II Chr. 1:11 with reference to King Solomon.
איננו חסר לנפשו is not impersonal "there is nothing lacking"
(V, T, Sieg.), but "he lacks nothing" (LXX Wr. Ehr.). לנפשו =
"for himself."

מִכֹּל is partitive; cf. Gen. 6:2, מִכֹּל; Ps. 137:3, מִשִּׁיר. The entire
clause cannot mean "he lacks nothing his soul desires" (so most
commentators), for this directly contradicts his theme, but "he
lacks nothing that he may possibly desire." Note the variation
in tense between the progressive present איננו חסר and the imperfect יתאוה.

איש נכרי is surely not a "foreigner" or even a "man of another
family" (Wr. Sieg. Bar. Hoel.). Koheleth is devoid of strong
nationalistic feeling or of a developed sense of family solidarity.
That a kinsman would inherit the property which a man has failed
to enjoy in his own lifetime would not diminish the tragedy for
Koheleth. The next verse emphatically illustrates this truth.
For Koheleth, the individualist, each man is a stranger to his
fellows, even to members of his own family. There is a distinctly
modern implication here of the essential loneliness of the individual personality.

6:3. אם יוליד איש מאה. Numerous offspring and long life were traditionally regarded as the greatest of blessings (Gen. 24:60; Deut. 11:21; Ps. 127:3, 5; Pr. 28:16). To emend ורב שיהיו ימי־שניו to ורבים יהיו ימי שניו would make the clause redundant after ושנים רבות יחיה. Actually, אם governs the two first clauses until יחיה, while ורב שיהיו introduces a concessive idea, "however many the days of his years may be."

The clause וגם קבורה לא הָיְתָה לו is difficult. The suggested interpretation, "even if the grave did not wait for him, i. e. even if he lived forever" (Kleinert, Gerson, Levy), is ruled out for two reasons. The word for "grave" would be קֶבֶר, and the entire exegesis is far-fetched. The alleged meaning would have been expressed in Hebrew by ראה שחת (Ps. 16:10; 49:10) or ראה מות (Ps. 89:49). קבוּרָה means "proper, dignified burial" (Ehr.). Among the Semites, as among the Greeks, great importance was attached to proper burial; cf. the Taunt Song against the King of Babylon (Isa. 14:19): ואתה השלכת מקברך כנצר נתעב; the curse on Jehoiakim (Jer. 22:19): קבורת חמור יקבר . . . ; and the Gilgamesh epic (*Keilinschriftliche Bibliothek* VI, 265): "He whose body is thrown into the field . . . his spirit rests not in the earth." For this reason, great merit attached to the Jabesh-gileadites for burying Saul and Jonathan's bones (I Sam. 31:11; II Sam. 2:5 ff.).

Against this background our passage is to be understood. The unconventional Wisdom writers are scandalized by the fact that sinners, after successful careers on earth, receive elaborate tribute at their funerals, so that even there justice does not triumph, and the truth remains unspoken; cf. Ecc. 8:10, ובכן והוא לקברות יובל; and Job 21:32 f., מתקו . . . יובל ראיתי רשעים קברים וגו'; לו רגבי נחל. The MT can be rendered only: "If he does not have a proper burial." But would Koheleth regard a joyless existence, even if followed by elaborate funeral rites, as worthwhile? Obviously not. The clause as it stands reduces the sentence to nonsense. Hence the clause is removed by Budde, Vischer and Kuhn to v. 5 and is referred to the still-birth, but it is redundant there. Others delete the troublesome clause entirely, as the work of a Hasid glossator (Hitz., Ha., Jast.).

Actually, all that is required to reveal the irony and power

of the passage is to revocalize לא as לֻא and render "even if he
have an elaborate funeral (on which men lay such great stress)."
In late Hebrew אִלו means "if, even if" (cf. v. 6, ואלו חיה, and
Est. 7:4), and this is the force of לא here. This usage exists not
only in the late Hebrew of Job (16:4), לו יֵשׁ נַפְשְׁכָם, but in the
earlier Hebrew of Jud. 13:23, לו חפץ ה' להמיתנו; and cf. Gen. 50:15
for a related usage — לו ישטמנו יוסף. Probably the confusing of
אם and לו was colloquial and non-literary at the beginning. On
the variant orthography of לו, cf. BDB, 530a; cf. לוא (I Sam.
14:30 a. e.), לא Kethib, לו Qere (II Sam. 18:12; 19:7), and many
instances of erroneous vocalization (e. g. Job 3:16; cf. D. Yellin,
Hiqre Mikra–Iyyob, Jerusalem, 1927, passim).

6:4. This verse and 5a describe the still-born child, who
comes in vain into the world, since he does not see the light of
day and leaves no name behind. The lot of the still-born was
regarded with particular horror, precisely because both avenues
of life, direct and vicarious, were denied to it, since it neither
experienced life nor left any offspring or memory behind; cf.
Job 3:16 and Ps. 58:9. כִּי is adversative = "though." בהבל =
"in vain"; cf. V, *frustra*. שמו, "name = memory"; cf. Ex. 3:15;
Deut. 9:14; I Sam. 24:21, and often.

6:5. נחת does not mean "rest" (Sieg. Budde Hoel.). That
the still-born has more rest than a living human being is obvious
to the point of banality. The idiom נחת ל... מ... means: "There
is greater satisfaction for the one than for the other." Cf. the
Mishnaic phrase נחת רוח, "joy, pleasure," and particularly the
idiomatic usage in נוח לו לאדם שלא נברא משנברא (B. Erubin 13b),
"It is better for man not to have been created than to have been
created" (so Dr. Del. Levy Hertz.). P actually uses the identical
idiom here — ניח להנא. The clause means literally: "There is
greater satisfaction for this one (the still-born) than for the other
(the man who did not enjoy life)." לא ראה ולא ידע = "he had no
knowledge or experience." These connotations of the verb occur
in Isa. 44:9; 53:3; 56:10; Ps. 82:5, and are particularly characteristic of the style of Koheleth, who uses them interchangeably.

6:6. ואלו = simply "if, even if." ראה = "experience, taste";
cf. v. 5. There is great charm in Koheleth's beginning the
sentence with a protasis, and then, instead of an expected

apodosis, ending with a question to which there can be only one answer — in the negative.

6:7. Both in structure and in content, this verse is a conventional *mashal*. Nevertheless, to eliminate v. 7 (McN. Ha.) as a proverb, to delete v. 8 as a gloss (Sieg.) or as two glosses (Ha.), and to drop v. 9 as a gloss (Sieg. McN.) would ruin the context. Bar. recognizes that if these be proverbs, Koheleth may have introduced them himself. Verse 7 makes the true observation that though man strain all his energies in providing for himself, his desires continue to outstrip his accomplishments and he remains unsatisfied. This proverb serves Koheleth as a text for his own conclusion — if this be true, why wear oneself out in acquiring wisdom when it is unaccompanied by the means of enjoying life (v. 8)? Far better, to seize actual pleasure when the opportunity offers (v. 9). גם is adversative, "yet." נפש is the seat of the appetite, hence "stomach" (Isa. 5:14; 29:8; Ps. 107:9; Pr. 16:26), here equivalent to "desire." Cf. the Mishnaic נפש יפה (M. Hullin 4:7), "excellent appetite." P's reading בפיהו is definitely inferior to MT.

6:8. מה-יותר = "what plus, what advantage has the wise man over the fool?" The wise man here is the man who is wise but poor, as the parallel clause indicates. Koheleth always emphasizes the need of joining wisdom and wealth; cf. 7:11 and 9:15 f.

מה לעני יודע להלך נגד החיים is a crux which Ehr. Jast. frankly surrender. The Versions wrestle with the difficulty as well as they can, but they all attest to MT. LXX, literally = "Why does the poor man know to march opposite life?" V, freely, "What (more) has the poor man, unless to march thither where life is?" P: "Why does the poor man know to go to life?" There is no need to assume that P read לָמָּה by dittography from כסיל (ag. Kamenetzky, op. cit., pp. 212 f.). מה means "why" (Ex. 14:15; 17:2 and often). The commentators are not more successful. Gins. renders "What advantage has the poor man over him who knoweth to walk before the living?" The last clause is taken to mean "lead a public life, like a magistrate" (!). No less farfetched is Graetz's interpretation of עני as "ascetic," for which he compares Isa. 58:3, ענה נפש. The views of Ew. and McN. can only be described as homiletic fantasies. Quite aside from the difficulty in meaning, all these views which contrast עני and יודע להלך would require before יודע a Mem which Gins. and Dr. actually supply. Hoel. reads מֵהָעָנִי לַיּוֹדֵעַ לַהֲלֹךְ, which he takes to mean, "What advantage over the poor has the man who knows etc.?" Gal. reads מה לעני ידע להלך וגו', which he renders: "der einsichtige Arme vor dem, der in den (sic) Tag lebt." Aside from the absence of the comparative Mem, there is no evidence for this meaning of the clause.

The simplest view would be to render the second half of the v.: "What advantage has the poor man who knows, etc?" (Wr. Pl.). Classical usage would require the definite article, מה לעני היודע, but its absence may be attributed to Aramaic influence. On the other hand, our identical construction occurs in Arabic: ما لفلان قام. "Why is so-and-so standing?"; in the late Hebrew of Jonah 1:6, מה לך נרדם, "Why are you sleeping?"; and in the Mishnah, מה לזה מביא (Kerithoth 5:2), מה לך מקיף (Middoth 2:2). The older Hebrew construction after מה לפ' is to use not the participle, but the perfect or imperfect (with or without כי); cf. Jud. 18:23, מה-לך כי נזעקת; Isa. 3:15, מלכם תדכאו; מהלך הים כי תנוס, Ps. 114:6. Our passage is therefore to be rendered: "Why should a poor man know how to face life?" This would express a characteristic idea of our author: "What value is there to a poor man's knowing how to live, since he lacks the means for enjoying life?"

להלך נגד החיים is evidently an idiom, the precise meaning of which eludes us today. Hence we cannot tell whether החיים is "life" (Kn. Hitz. Hoel.) or "the living" (Gins. Del. Wr. McN. Bar.). Levy renders similarly — "der das *savoir vivre* versteht." The clause can mean literally either "knows how to meet life, or, face the living."

6:9. The actual enjoyment of life is better than longing for pleasures — "a bird in the hand is worth two in the bush." Yet in the closing formula Koheleth is aware that even joy lacks any absolute value. This limitation on the value of happiness is induced by his recalling the basic ignorance of man, which is the fundamental source of Koheleth's skeptical outlook. Cf. the next section. הלך נפש = "yearning," lit. either "the wandering of desire" (Bar.) or "the yearning of the stomach" (Gal.); cf. נפשי יצאה בדברו (Can. 5:6), "my soul passed out with longing." On this meaning of נפש as the seat of the appetite, cf. Isa. 5:14; 29:8; Ps. 107:9; Pr. 13:25; 27:7, etc.; and see BDB, p. 660b. מראה עינים means here "actual enjoyment"; cf. 11:9, והלך בדרכי לבך ובמראי עיניך. In 5:10, ראות עיניו means "the empty gaze of the eyes (without enjoyment)." Obviously, since ראה means "to experience" (2:1 and *passim*) as well as "to see," both meanings are possible and only the context can determine which is intended. In our verse, the contrast with הלך נפש establishes the significance here.

Section IX — Introductory Note

6:10–12. It is difficult to determine whether this brief passage is an independent unit or the conclusion of the preceding section (5:9 to 6:9). The end of a section can generally be told by Koheleth's reverting to one of his fundamental theses. This characteristic of Koheleth's style is very marked. Thus most sections are concluded by one of three or four basic ideas: a) the weakness and impermanence of man's achievements (I, V, XVI); b) the uncertainty of his fate (XIII, XIV, XV, XVII); c) the impossibility of his attaining to true knowledge and insight into the world (III, IX, X, XI) and consequently; d) the need for man to make joy the goal of his endeavors (II, VIII), a theme which serves also as the conclusion of the book (sec. XVIII).

Our passage might therefore serve as the close of section VIII. It has, however, seemed preferable to regard it as an independent passage both because the preceding passage ends on a characteristic note (6:9) and because v. 10 is not syntactically joined to v. 9. In any event, the two sections are closely linked.

6:10. כבר נקרא שמו = lit. "its name (=essence, nature) has already been called," hence "it has already come into being." Compare the opening lines of the Babylonian Creation epic

Enuma Elish: "When in the heights, heaven was not named, and the earth beneath did not bear a name" (King, *Seven Tablets of Creation*, 1:1; Heidel, *The Babylonian Creation Myth*, ad loc.; and Isa. 40:26, ‏מי ברא אלה . . . לכלם בשם יקרא‏).

The second clause is usually rendered (LXX, V, Bar.), "It is known what man is (or will be) and that he cannot contend with One mightier than he himself." Such a translation, however, does violence to Hebrew style. This idea would have been expressed by ‏ונודע מה הוא האדם‏; cf. the universal use of ‏מה‏ in indirect questions (Gen. 2:19; 37:20; 39:8; Ex. 2:4; Jud. 18:14, ‏דעו מה תעשו‏, etc.). There is no warrant whatever for the interrogative use of ‏אשר‏ here required by this interpretation. After verbs of perception ‏אשר‏ means "that"; cf. Ex. 11:7; Ecc. 8:12. On the other hand, the rendering "it is known that he is man" is syntactically sound, but has no logical and grammatical antecedent for ‏הוא‏. Nor is it at all clear what the words would mean. It is therefore preferable to regard this construction as an example of "anticipation" after a verb of perception. ‏ונודע‏ ‏אשר־הוא אדם ולא יוכל וגו׳‏ is equal to ‏ונודע אשר האדם לא יוכל‏. On this usage, cf. Gen. 1:4 (Ehr. ad loc.); Nu. 32:23, ‏ודעו חטאתכם אשר‏ ‏תמצא אתכם‏, "Know that your sin will overtake you"; Deut. 8:18; Josh. 22:34 (cf. Gordis, *AJSL* [1931], pp. 287 f.). The Kethib ‏שהתקיף‏ is not to be vocalized ‏שָׁהֶתֳּקִיף‏=‏שָׁהוּא תַּקִּיף‏ (Dr. Bar.), or ‏שֶׁהָתַּקִּיף‏ (Wr.), or ‏שֶׁהִתְקִיף‏ (Hertz.), which are all syntactically ruled out. While the Qere here represents the reading of some ancient manuscripts, ‏שֶׁתַּקִּיף‏, the Kethib, represents a conflate of two variants, ‏עם שתקיף ממנו‏ and ‏עם התקיף ממנו‏, both meaning "with the One mightier than he." The reference is obviously to God; cf. Job 9:4, 19, ‏אם לכח אמיץ הנה‏.

On conflation as an early method of dealing with textual variants, see Gordis, BTM, pp. 41 ff., and cf. for example Jer. 2:11, ‏ההמיר‏=‏הֵהָמִיר‏+‏הֲיָמִיר‏; Lam. 5:18 Kethib, ‏על הר ציון שהשמם‏ ‏הֻשַּׁמֵּם‏=‏שָׁמֵם‏+‏שָׁמַם‏.

6:11. ‏כי יש דברים הרבה מרבים הבל‏, lit., "for there are many words that increase vanity." Gal. renders the verse as a conditional sentence: "If many words exist, they increase vanity." ‏דברים‏, not "things" (Pl.), but "words" (LXX, V). Since man is doomed to ignorance, the increase of words is an increase of folly. There is no need to refer the passage to any special intellectual activity such as the discussions of the Sadducees and Pharisees, or to the development of Rabbinic tradition (Del. Wr.). יתר as in v. 8 above=יתרון, "advantage, plus."

6:12. מספר, as in 5:17, emphasizes the brevity of life, lit., "the small number of days," an accusative of time.

עשה = "spend time" in Rabbinic Hebrew (*Gen. R.*, sec. 91, ר' שמעון; עתידין לעשות שם ר"י שנה; *Mid. Shoher Tob* on Ps. 17:14, שעשה במערה). Though it is parallel to the Greek ποιεῖν χρόνον (cf. Acts 15:33) and the Latin *dies facere*, it is not a Graecism (ag. Bar.). This meaning of the verb ʿāsāh probably occurs three times in Ruth 2:19, ואנה עשית, etc. (cf. Ehr. a. o. ad loc.). The clause ויעשם כצל modifies ימי חיי הבלו, "which he spends like a shadow," a classic figure for the brevity and insubstantiality of life. Bar. renders: "for he spends them, etc." This interpretation of the verb is better than the view: "which he shall consider a mere shadow" (T, Ibn E.). LXX read בְּצֵל, which Hertz. accepts, translating "which he spends in the shadow," regarding it as an ironic contrast to תחת השמש. But the MT is substantiated by P. Levy's interpretation, "that he may make them a (protecting) shadow," is unconvincing. The plural ועברו for the verb in P may not go back to וְיַעֲשָׂם but to an inner Syriac error.

אשר = "for, because." The uses of אשר parallel those of כי in earlier Hebrew (cf. Deut. 3:24, אשר מי). On the causal use of אשר, cf. Ecc. 4:9; 8:11. אחריו, which has the meaning "afterwards" (cf. on 9:3), has its usual meaning here, as in 7:14; 10:14 (ag. Levy). Man cannot make peace with the idea that he does not know what happens after he is gone. In *Job* 14:21, Job, too, laments man's lack of knowledge of future events, but for him it is the emotional grief of a father at being unable to share the joys and sorrows of his children. Koheleth's is a purely intellectual regret, perhaps no less poignant on that account.

This verse is deleted as a gloss by Sieg. and as a contraction of four separate glosses by Haupt, while Ehr. eliminates the entire section!

Section X — Introductory Note

7:1–14. This section is a collection of proverbial statements similar to Proverbs in much of its subject matter, in the use of parallelism, both the synonymous (vv. 1, 7, 8) and the antithetic (v. 4), in the employment of contrasts (vv. 2, 3, 5), in the lack of logical connection between the sayings and in the conventional ideas expressed (vv. 3, 4, 5, 7, 8). For these reasons, scholars have tended to excise many of these verses as later additions, either by a single editor (Jastrow), by two (Bar., Podechard, McN.), or by several (Sieg.). There is no agreement on the deletions, Jastrow eliminating vv. 1a, 2c, 3, 5, 6a, 7, 8b, 9, 11, 12; Barton, 1a, 3, 5–9, 11, 12; McNeile, 1a, 4–8, 10–12. Hertz. argues for the genuineness of the entire passage, but is driven to far-fetched interpretation in order to find a unity of theme in the passage. Levy regards vv. 1–6 as the quotation of an ascetic whom Koheleth refutes in the following verses, but the structure of the passage militates against this view.

Actually, we have here a collection of proverbs, containing some original elements of Koheleth's thought, as well as more conventional ideas reflecting his career as a Wisdom teacher. The stamp of his unique style and outlook is unmistakable throughout the section. For v. 2b, cf. 4:2; for v. 6, cf. גם זה הבל; for v. 9a, cf. 5:1 and 8:3 (בהל); for v. 10, cf. 1:9 f. and 6:10a on the monotonous succession of events; for v. 11, cf. 6:8 and 9:16 on Koheleth's attitude towards the uselessness of wisdom without wealth; for v. 13, cf. 1:15 and the phrase הבל ורעות רוח as a description of life as a sorry business; for the style of v. 14 (על דברת, לעמת), cf. 5:15; 3:18; and for its stress on man's ignorance, cf. 6:12.

It is therefore clear that the material is authentically Koheleth's own, or, at least, it has been refracted by his personality. But the nexus is not to be sought in the realm of ideas. We have here a prose heptad, a collection of *seven* utterances, each beginning with *tōbh* (vv. 1, 2, 3, 5, 8, 11 *tōbhāh*, 14 *bᵉyom tōbhāh*). In most instances, each maxim is amplified by related comments, which generally follow, but in one case (v. 13) precede, the

maxim. The notes on the individual verses will indicate how
even the conventional maxims are utilized by Koheleth in his
own special manner. The practice of organizing material on
the basis of similarity of form is common in Rabbinic literature.
Cf. Mishnah *Eduyoth*, chapters 6 to 9, where otherwise unrelated
matters are associated by the rubric העיד; *Yadayim*, ch. 4,
where בו ביום is the formula; and *Pesachim*, ch. 4, where מקום
שנהגו serves similarly as the bond. On the widespread use of the
heptad as a literary form in Biblical and Rabbinic writings, cf.
Gordis, "The Heptad as an Element of Biblical and Rabbinic
Style" (JBL, 1943, vol. 62, pp. 17–26).

Another rhetorical device which occurs several times is
chiasmus. It serves to link the basic theme with the comment
(vv. 3–4, 5–7, perhaps also vv. 16, 17, 19, 20; cf. Ps. 37:16 f. for
a similar use). For details see the Commentary below.

7:1. טוב שם משמן טוב. Both the sentiment expressed and the
paronomasia stamp this stich as a popular proverb. שם means
"good name, reputation"; even when unqualified, cf. Pr. 22:1;
Job 30:8. Levy suggests that the paronomasia depends not
merely on the resemblance of sound between *šēm* and *šemen*,
but also on the idea. An unpleasant odor creates antipathy
(cf. Ex. 5:21, הבאשתם את ריחנו), hence the odor of a good name may
well be compared to the fragrance of fine oil.

The second clause, ויום המות מיום הולדו, need not necessarily
bear a logical connection to the first, the link residing merely in
טוב. Cf. the numerical proverbs (as e. g. Pr. 30:15 ff.), where
there is no logical association among the members. Nonetheless,
Rashi seeks to connect the two stichs by citing Midrashic comparisons. Here, as so often, Rashi's intuition is sound. It is
quite clear that the thought of the second clause is not that of a
popular maxim. It seems rather to be a comment by Koheleth
on the first stich and, in that event, some logical connection would
be expected. Koheleth often quotes a conventional proverb and
adds an unconventional deduction of his own (cf. 4:9 with the
comment 4:10–12, and 5:9 with the comment 5:10).

The bond between the two stichs may be as follows: The
moralists have it that "a good name is better than oil." But a
man's reputation is subject to decline throughout his life, so that

only after he is dead is his "name" secure. It therefore follows
that the day of one's death is better than the day of one's birth.
Thus the popular maxim serves as a text, or pretext, for Koheleth
to voice his conviction that life is meaningless. We may compare
the Rabbinic parable that men would do well to rejoice not when
a ship puts out to sea but when it returns safely to port (Ibn E.,
Sforno). The latter quotes the apposite passage in *Aboth*,
אל תאמן בעצמך עד יום מותך, "Do not trust in thyself until the day
of thy death." Pertinent also is Solon's remark to Croesus that
"no man is to be counted happy until he has closed his life
happily" (Herod. 1, 32).

The relationship of the two stichs may rest on a closer basis.
Perhaps the oil reminded Koheleth of the bathing of an infant
at birth. In Ez. 16:4, to be sure, the description of the process
after birth includes washing the infant in water, rubbing him
down with salt and wrapping him in swaddling clothes, and
nothing is said of oil. However, the common use of oil as an
external application among the Egyptians (Erman, *Life in
Ancient Egypt*, p. 229), the Homeric Greeks and the Hebrews,
its frequent employment for medicinal purposes (Papyrus Ebers,
Pliny XV, 4, 7; XXIII, 3, 4), and, above all, its use after bathing
(Ez. 16:9; Ruth 3:3) make it likely that it was used for the
bathing of the new-born infant as well. In discussing the
procedure with new-born infants, the Talmud (B. Shab. 129b)
reports the practice "of hiding the after-birth in basins of oil."
This widespread use of oil at birth suggests to Koheleth that
if a reputation is better than oil, it follows that the day of death
is preferable to the day of one's birth.

The suffix of הולדו is uncommon, but the deletion of the Vav
creates an impossible text. Even הֻלָּדֶת, suggested by Dr., is
unsatisfactory without an article. That LXX and P do not
express the suffix proves nothing as to the reading before them.

Apparently יום הולדו is to be translated "the day of one's
birth," the impersonal use of the third person suffix occurring
in 8:16, שנה בעיניו איננו ראה, as Wr. points out. In general, Koheleth
has difficulty in expressing the impersonal; cf. v. 5: מאיש שמע
שיר כסילים, "than for one to hear the praise of fools."

7:2. This entire verse may be a conventional proverb,

which Koheleth may have written himself or quoted from others. On the other hand, the first half may represent the accepted doctrine that levity is improper, to which Koheleth adds the reflection that the house of mourning is to be preferred because it reminds man of the transitoriness of life. נתן אל לב, "lay it to heart," corresponds to the classical שים לב אל (Ex. 9:21; I Sam. 25:25; II Sam. 18:3), which occurs with varying constructions; cf. *BDB*, p. 963b.

The lesson to which Koheleth refers is not to practice kindness toward the dead, since each man will need the same kindness from his neighbor (Ra.), nor to strive after a good name (Sforno), but to see that the inevitable end of man is death (Ibn Ezra).

7:3. כעס, "sorrow, vexation" (Wr.), not "anger" (V). That v. 9 uses כעס in the meaning of "anger" is additional proof that these proverbs were assembled from various sources and that therefore the section does not constitute a logical unity (ag. Hertz., Levy). רֹעַ פָּנִים = "sadness" (cf. Gen. 40:7; Neh. 2:2).

יִיטַב לֵב is taken to mean "the heart is made happy" (Hertz.) or "the heart becomes better" (Luther), but the first view creates an inner contradiction which is not resolved by calling it a "paradox": "A sad countenance gladdens the heart." The second is irrelevant to Koheleth's thinking. לב is best taken in the meaning of "understanding," which it possesses in v. 7 below as well as in Jer. 5:21; Hos. 7:11; Pr. 15:32; 19:8; Ecc. 10:3 (cf. BDB, s. v. 3), in spite of the common Biblical idiom of טוב לב meaning joy and gladness (e. g. Est. 1:10; 5:9; Ecc. 9:7; 11:9, etc.).

Bar. compares the Greek proverb "to suffer is to learn" and the doctrine of suffering as a discipline in Job 33:19–23. But since Koheleth does not discern a moral purpose in suffering, Bar. believes that this verse cannot be authentic and he deletes it. However, Koheleth is not urging the moral benefit of suffering. He merely observes that a sad face reflects a wise mind. In spite of Koheleth's praise of joy and his theoretic depreciation of wisdom, he cannot conquer his innate bias against empty frivolity, the mark of a foolish mind.

That stich b refers to the improvement of the mind rather than the attainment of joy is clear from the next verse, which is chiastically linked to ours, and is concerned with the wise. See note following.

7:4. A comment amplifying the previous verse. Its integral relationship is indicated by the chiastic arrangement of the two verses: 3b and 4a deal with the sadness of the wise; 3a and 4b with the levity of the fools.

Abraham Ibn Ezra's own tribulations are reflected in his comment ad loc.: "Even when the wise do not go to the house of mourning, the house of mourning is always within them."

7:5. נערת = "reproof"; cf. Pr. 13:1, where it is parallel to מוסר. מאיש שמע is unusual, but it is to be preferred on the principle of *difficilior lectio* to the suggested מִשְּׁמֹעַ. It is apparently a mode of expressing the impersonal "than for one to hear the praise of fools" (cf. on 7:1).

שיר means not "the boisterous song of the revelers in the house of mirth" (Wr. Bar.), but "praise" (V, *adulatio*; Mid. Rabba ad loc.; Ehr.). It is not necessarily an Aramaism, in spite of the Aramaic שבחא, which means both "song" and "praise." The semantic development is natural in all languages; cf. such Biblical passages as Isa. 42:10 and Ps. 149:1, where *šir* is parallel to *tehillah*, and see further Jer. 20:13; Ps. 106:12; cf. also II Chr. 5:13. Note also the passage in the old Hebrew prayer *Yištabaḥ*, שיר ושבחה הלל וזמרה עז וממשלה. This, in the opinion of Samuel ben Meir, Maimonides and Mordecai, is referred to in the Mishnah (Pes. 10:7), ואומר עליו ברכת השיר, which Samuel ben Meir in his commentary on B. Pes. 118a explicitly defines as "praise": וזו היא ברכת השיר במתניתין כלומר ברכת השבח.

7:6. Koheleth's literary skill is evidenced not merely in the paronomasia of סירים, "thorns" (Isa. 34:13; Hos. 2:8), and סיר, "pot" (Ex. 16:3; Ps. 60:10) but, even more clearly in the excellence of the figure. The senseless talk and empty laughter of fools crackle and sizzle like thorns under a heated pot.

שחק, "laughter." Ehr.'s attractive suggestion that the word means "applause" is unfortunately unattested elsewhere.

וגם זה הבל may refer to the laughter of fools (Ibn Ezra) or to the general theme of the passage as explained in the next verse. Moffatt links the phrase to the next verse and interprets: "This too is vain: for a judge to make a fool of himself by oppression or for life to be ruined by the taking of bribes." It is simpler to refer זה to טוב לשמע גערת חכם (Euringer, Levy). Koheleth warns his readers that even the advice to prefer the reproof of the wise to the praise of fools is to be taken with a grain of salt, for even the wise are not above self-seeking and personal advantage. Culture and character are not synonymous. An educational leader of our day once said to the writer, "I have never believed that the higher education was conducive to the higher morality" (Cyrus Adler). See also note on the following verse.

7:7. עֹשֶׁק usually means "oppression, injustice" (Ewald). Hence the stich is generally rendered: "Oppression turns the wise man into a fool" (JPSV, Hertz.). On this interpretation, however, the second stich does not parallel the first: "A gift destroys the understanding." To create a parallelism, עֹשֶׁק has been emended to עֵשֶׂק = Mishnaic עֵסֶק, "business, affair" (on the orthography, cf. Gen. 26:20), or to עֹשֶׁר, "wealth." It is preferable to follow the suggestion of M. Seidel (*Debir*, vol. 1, Berlin, 1923, p. 34), who interprets עֹשֶׁק as "bribe, gift," hence parallel to מַתָּנָה. He regards עשק as a root of contrasted significance (*aḍḍad*) with two meanings, "rob, despoil" and also "add, grant," and he compares Isa. 38:14, עָשְׁקָה לִּי, which he interprets as "help me, be gracious unto me" (cf. Kimhi ad loc.). The other alternative is to render עֹשֶׁק as "extortion" (Wr. Jast.).

וִיאַבֵּד is masculine, preceding its apparent feminine subject מתנה, a very common usage; cf. Ges.-K., sec. 145, 7, a, and such passages as Isa. 2:7; 9:18; 14:11, etc. אֶת לֵב, without the article, is irregular (Ges.-K., 117c), but not without analogy, especially in late Hebrew, where, under the influence of the Aramaic, the determinate status becomes equivalent to the absolute. On the idiom "destroy understanding," cf. Jer. 4:9, יאבד לב המלך; Hos. 4:11, יקח לב; and Mid. *Gen. Rab.*, sec. 56, סבא סבא אובדת לבך.

מַתָּנָה is derived by the Midrash (on Ecc. 7:17) from the Mishnaic adjective מָתוּן ("moderate, equable," e. g. in *Ab.* 1:2). On this basis Dobsevage long ago suggested for the second stich "And it (i. e. oppression) destroys the calm spirit." Evidently unaware of the older suggestion, Dr. (BH) emends מתנה

to מְחוּנִים. This gives the verse an excellent meaning in itself, but not in our context. The parallelism favors the MT. It is noteworthy that the Vss. also derived מתנה from the root מתן, which they interpreted as "strong, powerful," and treated the *He* as the archaic masculine suffix. Hence LXX: "the heart of his strength." The reading of V, "the vigor of his heart," is an erroneous retroversion of the construct, "the heart of his vigor." For a similar instance in LXX, see Job 10:20, and cf. Driver-Gray, *ICC on Job*, vol. II, p. 65, and Gordis, *JQR*, 1936, vol. 27, pp. 40 f.

There still remains the problem of connection, which Renan abandons by dropping the כִּי in his translation. On the other hand, Del., followed by Gal., suggests that a verse or a half-verse similar to Pr. 16:8 fell out between vv. 6 and 7. Aside from the necessity of making this unsupported assumption, the idea would be much too conventional for Koheleth. Hertz. places v. 7 after vv. 11 and 12, a procedure which does not help matters, besides being without warrant in the Versions. Actually, the reason for v. 11 is expressed in v. 12, which is introduced by כִּי, so that v. 7 is not required for that purpose, nor, indeed, does it bear on the same theme. While vv. 11 and 12 stress the value of wealth and wisdom, when possessed jointly, v. 7 discusses the effect of a bribe on the exercise of unbiased judgment.

Having noted the value of heeding the reproof of the wise, rather than the empty praise of fools, Koheleth is too perspicacious not to know that the motives of the wise are not always lofty and disinterested, hence "but this, too, is vanity" in 7:6.

Once again, an instance of chiasmus occurs in these verses, 5–7. Verse 5a is qualified by 6c and 7 and verse 5b is validated by 6a and b: "It is better to hear the reproof of the wise rather than the praise of fools, which is empty of meaning, like crackling thorns, yet even this is vain, for the wise are often open to corruption."

7:8. Another proverb of the *tōbh* collection. The two stichs are logically connected. The "end of a matter is better than its beginning," since only at its conclusion can it be properly

evaluated. It therefore follows that it is better for a man to be
patient until the end than to be conceited at the beginning of an
undertaking. Cf. the maxim אל יתהלל חגר כמפתח (I Kings 20:11).

It is astonishing that the connection between the two stichs
has not been generally noted (except by Ehr., Levy). This
relationship makes it clear that דבר is not "word" (LXX, P,
V, Eur.), but "thing, matter." LXX may have read the Mem
of מראשיתו with דבר, hence the plural.

אֶרֶךְ is an adjective (Ibn Ezra, who compares הָלַךְ, יָתָר, יֶלֶד;
Wr.), the construct of אָרֵךְ (so BDB), rather than a noun (Hitzig).
וּגְבַהּ is likewise an adjective, "lofty," the construct of גָּבֹהַּ (so
Ew., BDB) or perhaps of גָּבֵהַּ. ארך רוח is not "forbearing"
(Wr.), but "patient" (BDB); cf. קצר רוח, "impatience" (Ex. 6:9;
Nu. 21:4; Mi. 2:7; Job 21:4). גבה רוח, "lofty of spirit, i. e.
"proud"; cf. גבה עינים (Ps. 101:5); גבה לב (Pr. 16:5); and the
Mishnaic רוח גבוהה (Aboth 5:19), "an arrogant spirit."

7:9. This v. and the following expand on the theme of
v. 8 — impatience is foolish and anger is a form of impatience.
בהל is a favorite word of Koheleth (5:1; 8:3). Though the sense
"be dismayed" (e. g. Gen. 45:3; I Sam. 28:21) is early, the
meaning "hasten" is late, occurring only in Proverbs, Esther,
Chronicles and Koheleth. כעס in 7:3 represents "seriousness of
disposition." Here it means "uncontrolled bad temper."

7:10. Another form of impatience with life and its limitations
lies in glorifying the past. As surely as there is nothing new
under the sun (1:9) and therefore no progress in the future, so
there is no decline from the past — life simply remains the same
(הימים שום, Ibn Ezra). Horace's criticism of the *querulus laudator
temporis acti* (*Ars poetica* 173) comes to mind. מה היה, not "Why
is it that, etc.?" (Bar.), but "What has happened?"

מחכמה = lit. "out of wisdom, hence wisely." LXX and P
may have read בחכמה, but this may be a matter of Greek idiom;
thus Targum renders על חוכמתא. More probably it is due to a
failure to understand the force of the Hebrew idiom. The Mem
is a Mem of condition; cf. Hos. 9:11 f., מלדה, מבטן, מהריון, מאדם;
Job 3:11, מרחם; and Aboth 4:9, כל המקיים את התורה מעוני סופו לקיימה
מעושר.

7:11. A characteristic observation of Koheleth. He cannot dismiss the value of wisdom as non-existent, but he is aware that it is honored, and therefore efficacious, only when it is allied with means (so Del. Wr.). Cf. 9:15 f. and the device of having Solomon, who combined both attributes of wealth and wisdom, speak in the opening sections of the book (1:2 to 2:26).

LXX, V and T attest the Masoretic reading עם. P's reading מן is definitely inferior (ag. Lambert, REJ, 1902; Zap.; Hertz. מעם). Cf. Mishnah Aboth 2:2, יפה תלמוד תורה עם דרך ארץ, aptly cited by Del.

יותר is a noun in Koheleth (cf. 6:8, 11), "advantage." ראי שמש, "all who live," a striking phrase for the sun-intoxicated Koheleth; cf. 11:7, ומתוק האור וטוב לעינים לראות את השמש. The expression entered the folk-speech; cf. Mishnah Ned. 3:7, הנודר מרואי החמה אסור אף מסומין, "He who takes a vow to enjoy no benefits from 'those who see the sun' may not enjoy a benefit even from the blind." This is not a Graecism (cf. *Odyssey*, IV, 540), as Ps. 58:9, בל חזו שמש; Ps. 49:20; and Job 3:16 demonstrate. Levy renders the Lamed of לראי as "in the presence of"; cf. Gen. 23:11; 45:1.

P read מן מאני זינא, "than weapons," for עם נחלה. That it mis-read נחלה as חיל (so Bar.) is unlikely. Hertz. is undoubtedly closer to the truth in suggesting that P interpreted the passage after 9:18, טובה חכמה מכלי קרב. P's rendering here may have crept in from the later passage. Hertz. does not notice, however, that P is therefore no longer a witness for a genuine reading מנחלה (or מעם נחלה) which he suggests. See above.

7:12. A difficult verse. LXX read for the opening stich: ὅτι ἐν σκιᾷ αὐτῆς ἡ σοφία ὡς σκιὰ τοῦ ἀργυρίου = כּי בְּצִלָּה הַחָכְמָה בְּצֵל הַכָּסֶף. This equivalence Euringer has not noted fully. Thus it attests to the Beth of the first בְּצֵל. P and V, which make the two phrases a comparison, need not have read two Kaphs כצל ... כצל (ag. BH), as is proved by T, which likewise inter-prets as a comparison, yet reads the MT: ארום היכמא דמסתתר נברא בטלל חוכמתא היכדין מסתתר בטלל כספא. It is obvious that in the face of a difficult text, the Versions seek to interpret as best they can, and no deduction may legitimately be made as to variant readings in their Hebrew manuscripts.

Del., followed by Wr., renders "In the shadow is wisdom,

in the shadow is money," reading בְּצֵל, but this seems difficult. Even less in keeping with the tenor of Koheleth's thought is Galling's reading: כִּי לֹא חָכְמָה כְּצֵל הַכָּסֶף, which he renders: "For wisdom is not like fleeting money."

H. Hirschberg has made the attractive suggestion that the reading should be כִּי בְּטֵלָה חָכְמָה בָּטֵל הַכָּסֶף, "when wisdom ceases, the money ceases," a proposal requiring the change of only one letter, the *Sade* to a *Teth*. Hence there is no need of assuming an Aramaic original for Koheleth (ag. Zimmermann, Ginsberg). But the idea that where there is no wisdom, the money disappears, would have been expressed in some such manner as אם אין חכמה אין כסף; cf. Mishnah Aboth 3:17. On the problems of interpretation raised by this emendation, cf. Gordis, "Koheleth — Hebrew or Aramaic," scheduled to appear shortly in *JBL*.

C. H. Gordon, *Ugaritic Literature* (Rome, 1949), p. 133, finds the phrase *ṣl ksp* in the epic *Baal and Anat* 51:II, 27, which thus offers a parallel for MT, though the meaning is different. See also Chapter 6, note 47.

The two best views of the passage are: 1) to read . . . בְּצֵל בְּצֵל and render: "The protection of wisdom is like the protection of money" (so Ehr., BH, Bar., Levy; cf. Rashi); and 2) "For there is the (double) protection of wisdom and the protection of money" (so virtually Ibn Ezra), which carries on the thought of the preceding verse. The Beth is the *Beth essentiae* (cf. Ges.-K., 119i), and does not appear in translation.

In the second clause, the Masorah puts the pause at דעת, which has a *Zakeph katan*, while LXX, P, V join דעת and חכמה. דעת is taken by P, V, Wr., JPSV, Hertz., as a noun, "yet an advantage of knowledge is that wisdom gives life, etc." But this idea would have been expressed by only one synonym here: יִתְרוֹן דַּעַת (הַחָכְמָה *or*) תְּחַיֶּה בְּעָלֶיהָ, "The advantage of wisdom is that it gives life." Hence it is better to regard דעת as the inf. construct and the Vav as introducing a subordinate clause. Render: "With the advantage of knowing that wisdom preserves the life of those who possess it."

בְּעָלֶיהָ, "its possessors." The suffix refers to חכמה, or somewhat more remotely and therefore less probably to נחלה in v. 11.

7:13. This verse and the following are an admirable epitome of Koheleth's thought — God is all-powerful, man must resign himself to ignorance regarding the meaning and purpose of life. Hence, he must take good and evil in his stride, enjoying the good while he can and remembering it during the days of trouble.

Pl., p. 166, cites some striking Stoic and Epicurean parallels in thought but not in spirit.

לְתַקֵּן, here in the Piel, which is more common in Rabbinic Hebrew than the Kal used in 1:15. LXX reads מֵעֲשֵׂי, in the plural.

7:14. רְאֵה, with an Athnah, indicates that its object is not נַם אֶת זֶה, but the entire clause: נַם אֶת זֶה....הָאֱלֹהִים, "God has set this (the good) against the other (the evil)." ... עַל דִּבְרַת שׁ is a conjunction, "in order that," used only here in Hebrew; the Aramaic occurs in Dan. 2:30; 4:14. In 3:18; 8:2 and Ps. 110:4 עַל דִּבְרַת is a preposition. אַחֲרָיו, "after him," i. e. after his lifetime, in the future; cf. 6:12 (so Hertz.). LXX read or misread הָיָה as חָיָה and misunderstood עַל דִּבְרַת as an absolute noun (so also A and Th.).

V interprets the latter half freely: "for as God has made this, so He has made that, so that man may not find any just complaints against Him (querimonias)." מְאוּמָה is here interpreted from מוּם; cf. Job 31:7, מְאוּם. V here gives a Rabbinic interpretation; cf. Rashi, להרהר אחריו של הקב"ה. So also Burkitt, Odeberg. הָיָה בְטוֹב, "enjoy the good," V, fruere bonis, lit. "be in the good."

Hertz. and Ehr. render עַל דִּבְרַת שׁ as "because," and Levy compares Gen. 12:17, עַל דְּבַר, "because of." The interpretation "in order that" is preferable, not only because of the usage in Daniel, but because of the context here. God sends good and evil into the world in bewildering array, so that man cannot gather from the flux of events the meaning of things.

Section XI — Introductory Note

7:15–25. Koheleth now urges the doctrine of the "golden mean," from a point of view uniquely his own. This characteristic idea of Greek philosophy, μηδὲν ἄγαν (Theognis, 402), the μέσως ἔχειν of Aristotle (Nicomachean Ethics, II, 6, 7), exercised a profound fascination upon many Jewish minds in the Middle

Ages, notably that of Maimonides, who built his entire ethical system upon it (cf. his "Shemoneh Perakim," commentary on Aboth). It was doubtless familiar to Koheleth as part of the intellectual climate of his age; cf. his use of the "four elements" in 1:4 ff. However, he validates it not metaphysically, but in terms of his own experience. Righteousness is no guarantee of happiness or success in life (v. 15; cf. 8:9 ff., especially 8:12a, 14; 9:2), and wisdom is often a source of misery (cf. 1:18). Hence both these goals must not be pursued too zealously (v. 16). On the other hand, he cannot recommend the opposite practices of "wickedness" and "folly" either (v. 17). Koheleth is a realist, not an iconoclast, and he knows that "wickedness," the violation of the accepted canons of society, generally brings its penalties. As for folly, he cannot overcome his prejudice against it, whatever his logic may say to the contrary.

For Koheleth, as for all the Wisdom Teachers, "righteousness" and "wisdom" are synonymous, as are "wickedness" and "folly," except, of course, that Koheleth uses these terms in his own way.

What is therefore best is a moderate course between both extremes (v. 18). A few traditional apothegms are then cited (vv. 19, 20) which apparently emphasize that man cannot hope to attain to perfection. Koheleth then warns against an attitude of superiority toward the failings of others (vv. 21 f.).

It should be noted that the section closes on the theme with which it began: vv. 23 f. emphasize that true Wisdom is beyond man (cf. v. 16) and v. 25 stresses that wickedness and folly lead to destruction (cf. v. 17). For details, see the Commentary on the individual verses.

7:15. This verse may be an illustration of man's ignorance, and therefore connected with the preceding passage. It seems preferable, however, to regard it as the basis for the plea that follows. Since there is no correspondence between virtue and happiness and between vice and misery, man should avoid either extreme.

בצדקו. The Beth may be taken temporally, and rendered "in," "with" (Del., Vischer), or "by means of" (Ibn Ezra, Jastrow). It is best taken adversatively, "in spite of" (Wr.

Del. Hertz. Levy); cf. Deut. 1:32, ובדבר הזה, "in spite of this fact." מאריך = "live long" (sc. יָמִים in 8:13). Perhaps Pr. 28:2 offers an instance of this ellipsis.

For Koheleth, righteousness and wisdom mean seeking happiness in life, which includes obeying the fundamental laws of morality and religion, since without them man cannot normally hope to survive, let alone attain to well-being.

This passage is extremely interesting for an understanding of Koheleth's thought-processes and style. "He who reverences God" will take hold of both "good" and "evil," in moderation, to be sure. The phrase is identical with "the man pleasing to God" (2:26).

7:16. תִּתְחַכַּם = "be overzealous for wisdom." Sieg. compares הִתְנַבָּא, "play the prophet." תִּתְשׁוֹמֵם = תִּתְשׁוֹמֵם, a syncopated Hithpolel of שמם, "destroy," hence "be desolated." The verb usually occurs in metathesis, as in Ps. 143:4 (יִשְׁתּוֹמֵם), where it means "be astonished," the meaning which LXX, V and P erroneously attribute to the verb here.

יותר = "unduly"; cf. 2:15.

It should be noted that the Aramaic *Ahiqar Proverbs of Elephantine* disclose a striking parallel to this verse and the following, unfortunately fragmentary. Papyrus 56, col. II, ll. 5, 6 reads:

אל תהעדי מנך חכמתא ו . . .
אל תסתכל כביר ואל ידעך ח . . .

Cf. E. Sachau, *Aramäische Papyrus und Ostraka* (Leipzig, 1911), p. 172; A. Ungnad, *Aramäische Papyrus aus Elephantine* (Leipzig, 1911); and M. L. Margolis, in *JQR*, vol. 2, 1912, p. 441.

7:17. בלא עתך = "before your time"; cf. Job 22:16, אשר קמטו בלא עת.

7:18. יצא את כלם does not mean "will escape" both (Hertz., Sieg.), or "comes forth of all things well" (Pl.). It is an idiom familiar in Mishnaic Hebrew, יצא ידי חובתו, "do one's duty," originally יצא מידי חובתו, "be released from the power of the obligation." It is often further shortened to יצא; cf. Ber. 2:1, אם כוון לבו יצא, "if he reads with inwardness, he fulfills his obligation"; Pes. 86b, כל מה שיאמר לך בעל הבית עשה חוץ מצא, "Whatever the master of the house asks of you, do, except if he says 'Fulfill your duty (by proxy).' " V, properly, "nihil negligit"; Rashi, ידי שניהם, followed by Del., "both" (Ehr.).

18b is therefore not a pious gloss (ag. Bar. Gr. Sieg. McN.), but, as Hertz. notes, the point and climax of the preceding, without which it would be meaningless.

7:19–20. The connection of these verses with the preceding is not obvious, though some association between them evidently exists. V. 19 may be a quotation of a conventional proverb, extolling wisdom as giving a man the self-assurance he needs. The theme is common in Wisdom teaching (cf. Pr. 21:22; 24:5). The structure of the verse, as well as the reference to "the ten rulers," makes it certain that we have a proverb, original or borrowed, here. Koheleth characteristically negates this praise of Wisdom by citing (v. 20) another accepted principle, that perfect goodness, which is identical for the Wisdom writers with wisdom (cf. vv. 15 f. above), is never attainable to man. On the use of *contrasting quotations*, cf. note on Ecc. 4:5 and 6; Job 12:12a and 13, and Intro. The verse here is virtually a quotation of the passage in Solomon's prayer at the dedication of the Temple (I Ki. 8:46): כי אין אדם אשר לא יחטא.

Levy suggests another plausible approach to the understanding of the context. He regards vv. 16, 17, 19 and 20 as being in a *chiastic arrangement*, v. 19 giving the reason for avoiding undue folly (v. 17), and v. 20 the reason for not displaying undue zeal for righteousness (v. 16). On Koheleth's use of chiasmus (a, b, b', a'), see our notes on 2:24–26 and 4:13–14. For an instance of chiasmus without a formal connection (like כי), cf. 11:3–4. In our passage v. 19 lacks the connective, while v. 20 has it. For an example of alternate structure in Koheleth (a, b, a', b') cf. 5:17–19. Other Biblical instances of chiastic structure occur in Ps. 1:5, 6; Pr. 23:15, 16; Job 20:2, 3; Lam. 2:13. For other examples of alternate structure, see Ex. 29:27; Deut. 22:25–27; Hos. 5:3; Ps. 33:20, 21. On the entire subject, see Gordis, *MHHH*, pp. 151 ff.

We hesitate to accept Levy's view, because of the intervening verse 18, which disturbs the chiasmus. To make the connection clear, it would be necessary to repeat the relevant phrases from vv. 16 and 17 before vv. 20 and 19 respectively.

Whether we regard the passage as contrasting quotations or as a chiastic arrangement, there is obviously no need to delete v. 19 (ag. Dr. Sieg. McN. Ha. Bar.) or v. 20 (Sieg. Haupt, Pod.). The juxtaposition of wisdom and righteousness in these two verses, exactly as in verse 16 above, speaks for the authenticity of our passage.

The root עז is generally used intransitively, "be strong." Hence BDB renders: "Wisdom is strong for the wise." This is forced. The verb requires a transitive meaning here: "gives strength," as V, P recognize; cf. Ps. 68:29; Pr. 8:28, where בְּעָזּוֹ is parallel to בְּאָמְצוֹ. LXX treated תָּעֹז as an abbreviation for תַּעֲזֹר, "help," hence βοηθήσει.

The "ten rulers" do not refer to .the עשרה בטלנין, "ten men of leisure," mentioned in the Mishnah (Meg. 1:3) (ag. Wr. Bar. Tyl.). The phrase is a reference to the δέκα πρῶτοι, who governed Hellenistic cities, including largely Jewish cities such as Tiberias (Josephus, *Vita* 13 and 57), perhaps even Jerusalem (*Ant.*, XX, 8, 11).

7:20. צדיק באָרץ has been "anticipated" from the subordinate clause and =וגו'. כי אדם אין אשר צדיק בארץ ויעשה טוב ונו'. Cf. Gen. 1:4, and Gordis, "A Note on Joshua 22:34," in *AJSL*, 1931, pp. 287 f., for other instances of this usage. Ehr. renders: "For there is no man so very righteous in the land, that, etc."

7:21, 22. This recognition of the imperfect nature of man has a practical corollary — one must avoid a hypercritical attitude toward the failings of others, which, as Koheleth has seen by observation, is a common manifestation of this "over-righteousness." It is both unfair to others and leads only to one's own misery, since one is likely to hear "Hinter der Wand, die eigene Schand."

7:21. ידברו, impersonal, lit. "that men speak"; cf. Gen. 29:9, אשר לא =ונללו. "so that"; cf. Gen. 11:7, אשר לא ישמעו, virtually = פן, "lest." קלל, which usually means "curse," here has its original and less extreme sense of "declare contemptible, revile," from קל, "light"; cf. Akkadian *kalâlu*, Ethiopic II "despise," and the similar Canaanism in the Tel-el Amarna Letters; see F. Bohl, *Die Sprache der Amarnabriefe*, p. 67.

7:22. LXX misread יֵדַע as יָרַע and then paraphrased our text in a conflate of two renderings: "For often he will injure you and many times he will hurt your heart, just as you have injured others," probably due to an Aquilan reading (Montfaucon, Euringer, Wr.).

7:23, 24. Koheleth's conclusion on his lifelong search for Wisdom — it is beyond him. This is a thoroughgoing contradiction to the confident assertion of the Lawgiver that the Divine imperative "is not too difficult nor far off . . . nor in heaven nor beyond the sea" (Deut. 30:11–14). Exactly like the poet in *Job*, ch. 28, Koheleth has sought the fundamental Wisdom (*Hahokmah*, Job 28:12, 20), but he could find only the practical Wisdom (*hokmah*), which advises that "Fear of the Lord is wisdom, and avoiding evil is understanding" (Job 28:28). It is virtually the same conclusion that Koheleth states in v. 25b. See below. But his entire book indicates that he never reconciles himself to these limitations on man's wisdom.

These verses, which stress the unattainability of Wisdom, validate v. 16, exactly as v. 25, which declares that wickedness and folly are madness, justifies v. 17. See note on v. 25.

7:23. נסה governs a direct object. Hence בחכמה would most naturally mean "in wisdom, wisely"; cf. 2:3. But Hebrew frequently interchanges the direct object and the Beth of means; cf. פֹּעֵר בפה (Job 16:10) and פָּעַר פה (Isa. 5:14), שָׁאַל את (Josh. 9:14) and שָׁאַל ב (Jud. 1:1), since the object of the action may be viewed as the means of the action. See note on מַעֲנֶה (5:19) and Ges.-K., sec. 119q. On our verb, cf. Jud. 6:39, אֲנַסֶּה נא רק הפעם בגזה. Our passage may therefore mean: "All this I tested concerning Wisdom." Note the definite art. בְּחָכְמָה and cf. 1:13; Job 28:12, *Hokmah par excellence*, as against practical Wisdom, *hokmah* without the article (Job 28:28).

7:24. For מה שהיה, LXX, followed by P, read מִשֶּׁהָיָה, and P construes וְעָמֹק עָמֹק as a superlative, "the deepest of the deep." MT is preferable. Levy cleverly renders the first stich as equivalent to רחוק מה שהיה רחוק, "Far off is that which was far off," i. e. there is no growth in understanding. The stich is best rendered, "Far off is all that has come into being, i. e. all that exists" (so Rashi, Del.). עמק עמק may be taken as a superlative, "very, very deep" (so most), or "the deep remains deep" (so Gal.).

7:25. For וְלִבִּי read בְּלִבִּי, with 79 mss., Tar., V (cf. 2:3), but not LXX or P. In ולדעת רשע כסל והסכלות הוללות, we have the double accusative after a verb of cognition (so Wr. Levy, Bar.); cf. 1:17 and the paper there cited. The Vss. which did not recognize the construction render variously. LXX: "the folly of the wicked"; T: חובא דשטיא. P: "the wickedness of the fool," רשיעותא דסכלא, for רשע כסל, and adds the copula "and" before הוללות, which Hertz. and others needlessly follow. The use or absence of the article (הסכלות and רשע respectively) in the statement of a general truth is in accordance with Hebrew syntax (Ges.-K., sec. 126; M. H. Segal, *Dikduk Leshon Hamishnah*, sec. 82, 83, 85, 87). The fluctuation in usage occurs in classical Hebrew; cf. Ex. 23:9, וגר ... הגר. It becomes more prevalent in Mishnaic Hebrew, under the influence of Aramaic; cf. the old Wedding Benediction (B. Kethuboth 8a) משמח חתן עם הכלה. On the entire usage of the article in Koheleth, see Gordis, "The Original Language of Qoheleth," in *JQR*, vol. 37, 1, pp. 81–83. Note, too, the absence of the Lamed with בקש after לדעת ולתור. לדעת is the infinitive construct consecutive, and there is no need to read וידעתי; cf. Ecc. 2:3; 3:18; 9:1; Ges.-K., sec. 114, p (so also Levy).

חשבון, familiar in later Hebrew in the meaning "calculation, sum," has the meaning "conclusion, substance of thought," here and in 7:27. In 7:29 and 9:10 (also in II Chr. 26:15) it means "contrivance, device." There is no reason for assuming two distinct nouns, חָשְׁבוֹן and חִשָּׁבוֹן, to account for חִשְּׁבֹנוֹת (against BDB). The noun occurs in two forms, with *dageš lene* and without, the first syllable having either hireq or seghol (חִשָּׁבוֹן or חָשְׁבוֹן). הוֹלֵלוּת need not be revocalized as הוֹלֵלוּת (ag. Kit.) because of 10:13. Abstract nouns with the ōth ending are common; cf. בְּחוּרוֹת by the side of יַלְדוּת, and see 1:17, הֹלֵלוּת וְשִׂכְלוּת. The second half of this verse: "to see that wickedness is foolishness and folly is madness," is declared to be irrelevant to the discussion on wisdom and hence is deleted by Sieg. and Ha., or regarded as meaningless (Hertz.). It has not been noted that the reference to רָשָׁע and סִכְלוּת is completely identical with the verbs תִּרְשַׁע and תְּהִי סָכָל in v. 17. The usage is similar to that of 1:17, where the succeeding verse takes up חכמה and דעת, the two subjects of v. 17. See note there. It is therefore clear that our verse, with vv. 23, 24, represents the conclusion of the section introduced in v. 15, and amplified in vv. 16 and 17. Koheleth repeats that he has made himself familiar with both wisdom (25a) and folly (25b). The extremes of either are sure to lead to unfortunate results. Hence the wise man will avoid both in favor of the "golden mean."

Section XII — Introductory Note

7:26–29. This famous passage in which Koheleth expresses his distrust of women testifies to the attraction they hold over him. Their physical charms ("her hands," v. 26) and their emotional appeal ("her heart," v. 26) are alike dangerous to man, because honor, rare among men, is non-existent among women.

"The man pleasing to God" and "the sinner" are to be understood in Koheleth's spirit (cf. 2:26), as representing him who seeks happiness wisely and him who fails to do so, respectively. Hence, this is not a gloss of the Hasid (ag. McN. Bar.). No less unsatisfactory is Hertz., who finds here a theological disquisition!

That this is only one aspect of Koheleth's attitude toward women is clear from his counsel urging, "behold life with the woman thou lovest" (9:9). The ideal remains before him, no matter how often the reality has brought him disappointment — a clue to the idealistic source from which his cynicism flows. Levy calls attention to both these attitudes in Hesiod, *Works and Days*. On the one hand, "Let no woman becloud your mind with her lascivious loins" (l. 372), but also,

> "When you reach the proper age,
> Bring your consort into your home,
> For no greater blessing can a man attain
> Than an understanding wife." (ll. 693, 700)

The two attitudes are, of course, very common in Wisdom literature. See the references to Proverbs and Ben Sira cited in Gordis, SBWL, pp. 111 ff. Levy unnecessarily assumes that the uncomplimentary opinion on women in v. 28 is a quotation by Koheleth of a standpoint which he rejects.

It is generally overlooked that Koheleth does not have too high a regard for the character of the male sex either, since he finds men only one-tenth of one percent better than the women! Having reached this result, he concludes by saying that the human race itself leaves much to be desired.

Budde, Sieg., McN., Bar., Jastrow regard v. 29 as a general observation concerning the perversion of the originally straight-forward nature of man and eliminate it as a gloss. This is the most natural meaning of the verse, but there is no need to excise it. Koheleth was familiar with the Paradise Story (cf. 12:7, based on Gen. 3:19), and therefore with Gen. 4:20–22, which attributes the arts and sciences to the descendants of Cain. Koheleth may well have regarded "civilization" as a source of moral corruption. Cf. the abundant Greek parallels cited by Plumptre. Hertz. takes this verse to mean that the search for Wisdom is against the will of God, because God wants ἁπλότης, "simplicity," but this attitude is alien to our author.

Rashi and Sforno (also, apparently, Ibn Ezra) relate the verse to the pristine innocence of Adam before the Fall, the pronoun "they" referring to Adam and Eve. It would be tempting to accept Graetz's view (adopted by Zap., Levy) and to associate this verse with the preceding theme of the unworthiness of women, who are full of devices and lack the simple honesty of the menfolk! But it is likelier that the verse refers to mankind as a whole. See note on v. 29 for details.

7:26. As in several other instances, a new section begins with Vav, a characteristic of Koheleth's style.

וּמֹצֵא is vocalized as a Tertiae Yod, as is usual in the Mishnah with this root.

הִיא is difficult. It serves not as a copula (ag. Bar.) but as a means of resuming the subject with emphasis and introducing two instances of *casus pendens* (אשר היא מצודים וחרמים לבה, אסורים

ידיה) with the suffixes of לבה and ידיה referring back to היא. Cf. Gen. 9:3, כל רמש אשר הוא חי, and the other instances cited in Driver, *Hebrew Tenses*, 3rd ed., 1892, sec. 199, obs. So apparently the accents, which link מצודים and וחרמים together (Darga, Tebir). LXX divides differently, lit., "she is prey, and dragnets her heart, fetters to her hands." Similarly, V, P. The Masoretic division is superior.

מְצוֹדִים, pl. of מָצוֹד (Pr. 12:12; Job 19:6), by the side of the feminine מְצוֹדָה (Ecc. 9:12; plural מְצוֹדוֹת, Ez. 19:9), "nets." חֲרָם is a synonym (Mi. 7:2; Hab. 1:15). אֲסוּרִים is the plural of אָסוּר, "band, bond" (Jer. 37:15, sing.; plural, Jud. 15:14).

7:27. אמרה קהלת, an erroneous division of the words אמר הקהלת. On "Koheleth" with the article, cf. 12:8 — evidence of its original character as a common noun. LXX expresses the article here. אחת לאחת, "one added to one," a long process of adding detail to detail. Is it a subtle reference to more than one unfortunate experience with the gentler sex?

חשבון, "conclusion of thought"; see above on v. 25.

7:28. אדם, which is normally common in gender (cf. Gen. 1:27), is here restricted in meaning to "man, male," equivalent to איש, by a widespread linguistic process noted by Ehr. on Gen. 3:1, which we may call "abstraction." When a general term is used in conjunction with a more specific one, the former is restricted in meaning to those elements not included in the latter. Thus, since our passage uses the general term אדם as well as the more specific אשה, the latter abstracts from the former, so that אדם now means "all human beings *except women*, hence, males." Cf. Gen. 3:16, 17 ולאדם . . . אמר האשה ואל. We may adduce such examples of the usage as גוים = "nations (except Israel), hence Gentiles," or the use in Jewish ritual of ישראל by the side of "Kohen" and "Levite" to refer to non-Levitical Israelites only. There is accordingly no need to assume a Graecism (ag. Levy, Palm.). Nor does this usage prove "northern Canaanite" influence, as proposed by Gordon, *Ugaritic Literature* (Rome, 1949) p. 133. The Phoenician usage he adduces from the *Azitawadd Text* II 4:5 with 'dm parallel to 'št probably derives from the same linguistic process. On the alleged "Canaanite" influence in Koheleth, see chap. *VI*, note 47 above.

7:29. If this v. is to be interpreted as referring to women (so Graetz, Zap. Gers.), אדם will again refer to the male sex (see on v. 28). המה, though masculine, would refer to women, a usage which occurs elsewhere; cf. Zc. 5:10; Can. 6:8; Ruth 1:22. The verse would then mean: "God made the menfolk straight, but they (i. e. the women) sought out many devices."

The plural pronoun המה, however, in contradistinction to the singular or collective אדם, militates against this view. Even more telling is the fact that Koheleth can hardly be described as having a high opinion of the menfolk, which would be the implication of v. 29a on this view.

The verse is best taken as a reference to human perversity as a whole, while v. 28 has declared the women to be only a little worse, if possible, than the men. This weakness Koheleth attributes not to God's implanting but to men's propensity to eschew the straight path in favor of machinations. That evil is not God's will, but man's doing, is the general standpoint of Wisdom literature (Job 5:6, 7; Lam. 3:31–42) and of traditional Judaism as a whole; cf. the classic formulation (Ber. 33b; Meg. 25a): הכל בידי שמים חוץ מיראת שמים.

Section XIII — Introductory Note

8:1–9. On the emphasis in Wisdom on loyalty to the king, and such other qualities as unquestioning obedience, sobriety, zeal and hard work, see Pr. 14:35; 16:14; 19:12; 20:2; 22:29; 23:1; Ecc. 10:4; B. S. 9:13; 13:2–20, among others. For the entire subject, see SBWL, pp. 93 f., and for parallels in Oriental Wisdom, cf. Fichtner, *op. cit.*, pp. 15 f.

It is not easy to determine which king is meant in this section, but the advice would be appropriate for those having relations with either the Ptolemaic or the Seleucid rulers, or with their deputies in Palestine. The existence of such relationships between Jewish patrician families and the foreign courts is strikingly demonstrated in the history of the Tobiades; cf., *inter alia*, A. Buechler, *Die Oniaden und die Tobiaden*; E. Schuerer, *Geschichte des juedischen Volkes*. J. Klausner actually attributes our book to Joseph ben Tobia (*Bime Bayyit Sheni*, Tel-Aviv, 1930, pp. 160–75).

The progress of Koheleth's thought is well illustrated here. As a Wisdom teacher, whose pupils were drawn from the upper classes, Koheleth teaches these practical traits, but from the recognition of the shifting winds of favor in the royal court, he rises to a perception which becomes fundamental to his outlook, and to which he gives eloquent expression: the basic ignorance of man regarding life and his own destiny (v. 8). There is, therefore, no ground for eliminating this section in whole or in part, with Haupt and Sieg., who delete it entirely, or with McN., Bar. and Jast., who delete vv. 1, 2b, 5, and 6a.

8:1. כהחכם is an uncontracted form, like כְּהַחֲלֹנוֹת, Ez. 40:25; 47:22; II Chr. 10:7 a. e. (cf. Ges.-K., 352b, note 2). There is no need to emend to כה חכם (ag. V, Sym., A, Ehr., Hertz.).

פשׁר, related to פתר, means "solution, interpretation, hence the true, underlying meaning."

Following Ew. and Hitz., Hertz. takes the second half of the verse as a quotation of a proverb praising wisdom, and suggests reversing the two halves of the verse, in order to give some meaning to the first half. The verse would then begin by praising wisdom, but would then add that truly wise men are few and far between. It would then be linked to the preceding section.

This radical procedure is not necessary. The following note will make the meaning clear, without transposing the text. האיר פנים is used everywhere else of the face of God, as in the Priestly Blessing (Num. 6:25), and in other passages based upon it (Ps. 31:17; 67:2; 80:4, 8, 20; 119:135; Dan. 9:17). "To light up, make the face shine" means "to show oneself gracious toward"; cf. Num. 6:25b and Dan. 9:17. Here the stress is not upon the gracious act, but upon *appearing* gracious toward one's associates in court, whatever may be one's real feelings. A court official cannot display his dislikes or anger at will. His wisdom will impel him to maintain his suavity and poise under all circumstances.

עֹז פָּנָיו is read by LXX (ἀναιδής) as עַז, which Sieg. and BDB accept, but that would necessitate the change to עַז פָּנִים. The change is unnecessary. The suffix in פניו refers back to

אדם (so most comm.) or possibly may be rendered impersonally as "one's boldness"; cf. 7:1, יום הולדו, "the day of one's birth," and note there.

The phrase עַז פָּנִים occurs in Mishnaic Hebrew in the sense "impudent, bold" (Ber. 16b; Shab. 30b; Betz. 25b), a meaning adopted here by Del., Wild. However, as the passage in Aboth 5:20, עז פנים לגיהנם ובשת פנים לגן עדן, "The bold-faced man is for Gehinnom, the shame-faced man for Paradise," indicates, the phrase may refer not only to actions, but also to the outer demeanor. A courtier will avoid the appearance of being over-bold and aggressive. His good sense will lead him to disguise such an expression. Dissembling is important for the politician, then as now!

יְשֻׁנֶּא is vocalized like a Tertiae Yod, though the orthography derives from a Tertiae Aleph root (cf. II Ki. 25:29; Lam. 4:1). Both conjugations virtually coalesce in Mishnaic Hebrew; cf. 7:26 above, וּמוֹצֵא. The root has the nuance of "disguise" in the idiom שָׁנָה טַעַם, I Sam. 21:14; Ps. 34:1, and in I Ki. 14:2. LXX and P misread the verb as יִשָּׂנֵא: "will be hated," thus attesting to the Masoretic spelling. V: "et potentissimus faciem illius commutabit" = וְעֹז פָּנָיו יְשֻׁנֶּא.

The Talmud (B. Taan. 7:2) uses the Tertiae Aleph spelling of the verb homiletically: כל אדם שיש לו עזות פנים מותר לשנאותו, "A man who is impudent may be hated," and cites our verse as proof. This entire passage is imitated, and the orthography and root of ישנא are incidentally attested, in Ben Sira 13:24, לב אנוש ישנא פניו אם לטוב אם לרע. The second half of our verse may be paraphrased as follows: "Wisdom will teach one to be gracious and to hide any undue aggressiveness of demeanor."

8:2. אני is unusual. It has been suggested that it be treated as a dittography from ישנא, or to read את, ostensibly based upon LXX, P, which omit the word entirely (so Eur. Bar.), but את would normally require a determinative noun: את פי המלך שמר (cf. 12:13, את מצותיו שמור). V read אֲנִי פִּי מָלָךְ שְׁמַר. This is the interpretation of J. Sanh. 21b: אני פי מלך מלכי המלכין אשמור שאמר לי בסיני אנכי ה' אלהיך ועל דברת לא יהיה לך אלהים אחרים. Another suggestion has been to add אמרתי (cf. 2:1; 3:17, 18) (Gins., Sieg., Del., Wr., Hertz.), but there is no textual warrant for the loss of an entire word. A third view is to emend אני to בְּנִי (Wildeboer). Aside from the fact that the change from Aleph to Beth is graphically distant, the word בְּנִי, which is very common in Prov., chapters 1 to 9, and in Rabbinic literature (see SBWL, p. 84, n. 9), does not occur in our book except in the Epilogue, which is the addition of an editor. See note on that passage.

The solution lies elsewhere. The MT has a parallel in Rabbinic literature (B. Kid. 44a), where the first person pronoun introduces a statement without a verb: אמר רב נחמן בר יצחק אנא לא אר רב אבין ברבי חייא ולא רב אבין בר כהנא אלא רב אבין סתם, "Rabbi Nahman bar Isaac said: *I report this tradition*, not in the name of R. Abin ben Hiyya or R. Abin bar Kahana, but simply in the name of R. Abin (without a patronymic)." In our passage, אני is accordingly to be rendered "I declare." Other Biblical examples occur in Hos. 12:9 (אפרים) and Jer. 50:7 (ה'), on which see QBROL.

ועל דברת שבועת אלהים. The Vav emphasizes the reason, "and that because of the oath of God." אלהים is either a subjective or an objective genitive. The oath of God may mean the oath that God has sworn to the king (see Hertz. ad loc.), but is better taken to mean "the oath of loyalty sworn to the king in the name of God" (so most comm.). Koheleth is not concerned with proving the legitimacy of the ruler, especially a foreign one, but with indicating his power; cf. v. 3. On the other hand, once a vow has been sworn to the monarch, it should be fulfilled. On Koheleth's view of religious propriety, see 5:3–5.

8:3. תבהל, "hasten" in late Hebrew (cf. Pr. 28:22; 20:21 Qere; Est. 8:14, a. e.), is a popular word with Koheleth (5:1; 7:9). Here it governs תֵּלֵךְ in lieu of a complementary infinitive, as in Ecc. 7:9. For this characteristic Hebrew construction, see I Sam. 2:3; Hos. 1:6; 5:11; Lam. 4:14; and Ges.-K., 120, 2b.

LXX and P add אל תבהל to v. 2, which is unlikely. P, V, and 116 mss. supply a Vav before אל, but this merely is an attempt to soften the transition rather than an authentic reading.

מפניו תלך, "to leave his presence" (cf. Hos. 11:2), means to break with the king. It may possibly mean "to rebel," "to flee the court" (so Wr. Pl.), but a stronger verb would then be expected. Probably it means to "leave one's post" when events seem unfavorable.

Pl. compares Epicurus' counsel that the wise man should at every opportune season (καιρός; cf. LXX on vv. 6, 7) court the favor of the king (Diogenes Laertes X, 1, 121).

עמד ב, "persist in," apparently a late usage, which is paralleled in the Mishnaic לא עמדתי על מדותי, "I never insisted upon retaliation" (B. Meg. 28a; also Kid. 71a).

8:4. For stich a, LXX renders "As the king, having power, speaks," vocalizing כַּאֲשֶׁר דְּבַר הַמֶּלֶךְ שִׁלְטוֹן (or דִּבֶּר), which is, of course, impossible Hebrew. P renders similarly, "As the king speaks, he rules" (שליט). MT is in accordance with Hebrew idiom — lit. "inasmuch as the king's word is power." For the use of a predicate nominative instead of an adjective, cf. Ps. 120:7, אני שלום, "I am peaceful." An interesting parallel occurs in the Egyptian *Instruction of Sehetepibre*, which urges submission to the king, because "the king is Vital Force and his mouth Abundance."

8:5. מצוה here means "the royal command"; for the abs. sing., cf. I Ki. 2:43; for the constr. sing., cf. Isa. 29:13; Jer. 35:18; for the plural, cf. Pr. 10:8; Neh. 10:33.

For ומשפט LXX and 15 mss. read משפט, but in v. 6 LXX renders the Vav. The MT may have the same meaning, the phrase עת ומשפט constituting a hendiadys, as often; cf. Gen. 3:16, עצבונך והרנך; Jer. 29:11, אחרית ותקוה; II Chr. 32:1, הדברים והאמת; Job 10:17, חליפות וצבא; Job 25:2, המשל ופחד; and such passages as Isa. 53:7; Job 5:15; 10:12, where the construction has not been recognized. Hence עת ומשפט means lit. "the time of propriety = the proper time." עת itself may, however, be rendered as "the proper time" (cf. Deut. 11:14; Jer. 5:24; II Ki. 5:26; Ps. 119:126; Ecc. 3:1 ff.), and משפט as "the proper procedure" (cf. Isa. 28:26; also I Ki. 5:8; Isa. 40:14). The phrase would then mean "the proper time and manner of procedure."

לב חכם is taken as a construct by LXX, V, P: "the heart (or mind) of the wise man." In the absence of the article, it seems preferable to regard חכם as an adjective, "a wise heart."

8:6. For רעת האדם רבה עליו, LXX read דַּעַת. רָעַת is definitely to be preferred.

The second half is generally taken to mean "man's punishment is too heavy for him." Actually רעת האדם is man's evil, his inherent weakness, of which Koheleth is acutely conscious.

The clause continues the theme of 5b and 6a. A wise courtier will find an opportunity to execute his designs, because human weakness is widespread, and an opening is sure to appear.

8:7. P and V paraphrase the second half of the verse. For MT מה שיהיה, P and V read מה שהיה, and Jerome in his Commentary specifically declares that he has the latter reading. But MT is definitely superior, as the next verse indicates.

Bar. refers this verse to the unpredictability of the despot's actions, an idea which is certainly in Koheleth's mind. But Koheleth formulates it in general terms, and so it serves as an expression of his underlying conviction of man's ignorance and powerlessness (v. 8); cf. Ibn Ezra, who recognizes the connection of ideas: ואילו היה יודע מתי ימות מה יועילנו כי אין אדם שיש לו יכולת לכלוא את הרוח.

8:8. This verse has been referred to the idea that even the tyrant has no power over death and must succumb to it (Levy, Pl., Jast.). In Talleyrand's words, "even the worst despotism, as in Czarist Russia, is tempered by assassination." But the phrasing is much too general for this specific idea that even the king must die. It is more natural to see here a formulation of Koheleth's recurring theme of man's ignorance, which is suggested by v. 7, in which Koheleth has reminded the would-be royal servant that conditions at court are uncertain and subject to sudden change.

רוח has been rendered "wind" (Hertz., Pl., Bar., JPSV, Moffatt; cf. Pr. 30:4). It is better taken to mean "the spirit of life"; cf. 3:21; 12:7 (T, V, Levy), as the parallelism with the succeeding clause indicates. LXX πνεῦμα, which means both "wind" and "spirit," is undeterminative.

כלא, "shut in, confine"; cf. Nu. 11:28; I Sam. 6:10; and Ps. 88:9, כְּלָא וְלֹא אֵצֵא. From this last passage it is clear that כלא רוח is the opposite of תצא רוחו, "the spirit goes forth, dies," as in Ps. 146:4. No man is able to shut in the spirit of life and prevent the soul from escaping (cf. Rashi). LXX and P render ביום מלחמה for the Masoretic במלחמה, an example of "leveling" due to ביום המות.

משלחת, which occurs in the phrase משלחת מלאכי רעים, "a deputation of evil angels" (Ps. 78:49), has been interpreted variously: 1) "discharge." 2) "furlough" (Bar., Hertz., Del., Moffatt). They call attention to the provisions for furlough in Deut. 20:1 ff., which Judah the Maccabee is reported to have observed (I Macc. 3:56), while Herodotus (4, 84; 7, 38 f.) reports that the Persians and the Hellenistic Greeks were very rigorous in this regard (Herod. 4, 84; 7, 38 f.; I Macc. 3:28; 10:36; Josephus, *Ant.*, 12, 9, 3; 13, 2, 4). 3) "despatching," ἀποστολή (LXX). 4) "escape" (פולטא P, Levy). 5) "weapon" (Ehr., Mid. *Deut. Rabba*, par. 9), but without any real warrant in usage. 6) Or it is emended to מְלָחָשׁ, "amulet" (Kuhn, Gal.). The most appropriate meaning here is "control"; cf. אדום ומואב משלוח ידם ובני עמון משמעתם (Isa. 11:14). This assumes an ellipsis for משלחת יד. For such an elliptic phrase, cf. note on מאריך in 8:12 and כרת in I Sam. 20:16; 22:8; Isa. 57:8. משמעת, which is parallel to משלוח יד, occurs in the *Mesha Inscription*, l. 28, כי כל דיבן משמעת (lit. "for all Dibon was obedience") (cf. G. A. Cooke, *Text-Book of North-Semitic Inscriptions*, Oxford, 1903, p. 14).

With regard to רָשָׁע, Ibn Ezra makes two interesting alternative suggestions: a) that the noun means "activity, movement," comparing Job 34:29, והוא ישקט ומי ירשע; and b) that רָשָׁע is a synonym for "money," שרובו הוא מקובץ מרשע, "because in most cases it is acquired wickedly!"

רָשָׁע is actually emended to עֹשֶׁר by Dr., Renan, Gal., but the change creates a moralistic sentiment (cf. Ps. 49:7 ff.) not characteristic of Koheleth. On the other hand, the MT as it stands is entirely appropriate to Koheleth. He is too honest and clear-eyed a thinker to become a consistent heretic. His observation teaches him that wickedness often leads to disaster, so that even evil-doing cannot guarantee success! The text serves as an excellent link with the next section (8:10 to 9:3), in which Koheleth points out that retribution may operate at times, but is unpredictable. It is this uncertainty which is at the root of Koheleth's tragic view of life.

בעליו, lit. "its master." "The master of evil" is the evildoer; cf. 10:11, בעל הלשון, "master of the tongue, charmer"; Gen. 37:19, בעל החלמות, "master of dreams, dreamer"; II Kings 1:8, בעל שער, "master of hair, hairy man."

8:9. A closing verse, summarizing his observations on royal power given above; note the verb שלט in the section in vv. 4, 8 (twice). ונתון is the inf. abs. consec. (cf. 9:11; Gen. 41:43; Est. 2:3, a. e., particularly common in late Biblical books) and is equal to ונתתי את לבי; cf. Ges.-K., 113,4a.

LXX read אֶת for עֵת. MT is preferable; עֵת is the accus. of time; cf. Jer. 51:33; Ecc. 1:7, מקום שׁ (Del.).

לְרַע לוֹ, lit. "for hurt, for him, hence, for his hurt"; cf. לטוב לנו, Deut. 6:24; לטוב לך, Deut. 10:13, "for good, for thee." There is no need to read לְהָרַע (Kit.) or לָרַע as a verb, on the basis of the renderings of LXX, P, Jerome (Commentary), who are paraphrasing (ag. Hertz.).

Section XIV — Introductory Note

8:10 to 9:3. In this section, which extends to 9:3 and then blends directly into the next, Koheleth deals with the failures of the retributive process. Vv. 11–13 offer the major difficulty, since they assert the conventional idea that punishment will overtake the sinner and the righteous man will ultimately be rewarded. Since these vv. seem to contradict the very next verse (14), many scholars delete them *in toto* (Sieg., Haupt, McN., Bar.) or in part (vv. 12, 13, Eissfeldt, Volz).

Neither procedure commends itself, because of both the larger context of Koheleth's thought and specific difficulties of interpretation. Koheleth does not really believe that evil *always* triumphs (cf. 7:17, 25; 8:8d), or he would not have advised against a life of evil-doing (7:17 ff.). He knows that in many cases society does rise to protect itself against anti-social behavior. Thus in 8:14, he is careful to say "there are *some* righteous (יש צדיקים) who encounter the fate of sinners, etc." Moreover, there is nothing intrinsically out of keeping with Koheleth's standpoint in vv. 11 and 12a. Koheleth recognizes that punishment is sometimes delayed, and men are therefore encouraged to do evil, exactly as in 9:3, where he maintains that men are led to evil-doing by the apparent similarity of fate of the righteous and the sinner.

In addition, these verses bear many earmarks of Koheleth's style:

1) אשר = "because" (cf. vv. 11, 12a, 12e, 13c, 15)
2) רע ... רע לב) מלא לב (cf. 9:3, רע לב)
3) יודע (on the participle, cf. 2:19; 3:21; 6:12; 8:1; 11:5, 6 and *passim*; on the root, cf. 1:17; 3:12, 14)
4) כצל (cf. 6:12)
5) ירא̇י האלהים (cf. 5:6; 7:18)
6) כי גם, "although" (cf. 4:14)

Besides, if vv. 11–13 be deleted, the end of v. 10, גם זה הבל, would be followed immediately by v. 14, יש הבל, which is very harsh.

Finally, the deletion of 12b and 13 creates difficulties of interpretation. Those who excise these verses are forced to render כי גם as "nevertheless" and אשר in 12a as "although": "Although a sinner does evil a hundred times, nevertheless I know" (Bar.). Neither rendering is correct. כי גם is a subordinate conjunction like its equivalent גם כי, which means "although, even if" (Isa. 1:15; Hos. 8:10; 9:16; Ps. 23:4) or "even when" (Pr. 22:6; Lam. 3:8). אשר never means "although," but "because," as in v. 11 (cf. BDB, s. v. 8c and באשר) (so, correctly, Hitz., Wr., Del., who follow Rashi, Ibn Ezra). To render כי גם as "surely also," simply because the meaning "although" does not "suit the context" (McN. Bar.), is an *ad hoc* interpretation with a vengeance. Correct syntax is a prerequisite to the establishment of the context.

The syntax of the passage requires that 12b and 13, which are closely linked, constitute a subordinate clause. Hence vv. 11 and 12a are the principal clause, expressing an idea thoroughly congenial to Koheleth's point of view. It may be added that if vv. 12b and 13 emanated from a Hasid glossator, anxious to negate these unorthodox sentiments, he would not have contented himself with putting his own ideas in a subordinate position, but he would have used some such formula as וידעתי גם אני, "But *I* know" (as in 2:14), or ואולם ידעתי.

The obvious meaning of vv. 12b and 13 need not be explained away, when it is noted that they are introduced by יודע, a verb of cognition, a procedure used by Koheleth at times to introduce a quotation of conventional cast which he does not accept (cf. ראיתי, 2:13 f.; אמרתי, 3:18; 9:16).

The sequence of thought in this section may now be grasped in its entirety. The section is introduced by a reflection which the unconventional Wisdom writers found particularly troubling — not only are the evil-doers often successful in life, but they enjoy the pomp and honor of elaborate obsequies after their demise, when their virtues are extolled! Thus even in death justice is cheated. For Job's lament on this theme, see *Job* 21:32 ff., and cf. Ecc. 6:3 and note. In sum, retribution fails to overtake the sinner before or after his death.

This leads to a consideration of the failure of retribution generally. Koheleth is familiar with the accepted explanations, espoused by Job's friends, that retribution is sure to come (vv. 12b and 13; *Job* passim; cf. especially Job's refutation of the doctrine in 21:20 f.). But Koheleth insists that this delay is itself a cause of sin (vv. 11, 12a) and, besides, good men often suffer an evil fate (v. 14). Hence only the pursuit of happiness is a sensible goal for men (v. 15), since man can never understand God's ways (v. 17). For man's future is hidden from him (9:1), and one fate awaits all men in death (9:2), which comes all too soon (9:3). On the entire passage, see QWL, pp. 135 f. Our view of the passage is basically similar to that of Levy.

Moreover, this section on the delay in retribution is most plausibly linked with v. 10, if the closing clause of v. 10 is referred to the wicked who escape their just deserts even in death. The most natural view of the last phrase is "they acted thus." This requires the adoption of the reading וישתבחו, and the theme of the undeserved eulogies of the sinners emerges; cf. Job 21:32 ff. and Ecc. 6:3, and see below.

8:10. A new section in Koheleth is frequently introduced by Vav (cf. 3:16; 4:4; 7:26; 11:7; 12:1; and cf. the classical Biblical usage of *vayᵉhi* at the beginning of a narrative). ובכן occurs in Est. 4:16, and is a common asseverative introducing medieval Hebrew Piyyutim; cf. ובכן תן פחדך, ובכן לך הכל יכתירו, etc., in the High Holy Day liturgy.

The first half of the verse is manifestly not in order. The Versions offer some help in reconstruction. LXX:

καὶ τότε ἴδον ἀσεβεῖς εἰς τάφους εἰσαχθέντας, καὶ ἐκ τοῦ ἁγιοῦ, καὶ ἐπορεύθησαν καὶ ἐπῃνέθησαν ἐν τῇ πόλει, ὅπε

οὕτως ἐποίησαν = (or וּמְקוֹם קדוש (וּמָקְדוֹש מוּבָאִים וּמִקְדֹּש קבר רשעים ראיתי ובכן
.וְהִלְכוּ וְיִשְׁתַּבְּחוּ בָּעִיר אֲשֶׁר כֵּן עָשׂוּ

V is too periphrastic to yield a Hebrew text, but attests the
reading וישתבחו of LXX and קבורים and מקום קדוש of MT, rendering
כן as "justly" (*quasi justorum operum*), so also Symmachus,
τὰ δίκαια. P, which renders: והידין חזית רשיעא דקבירין ואתין ומן
,אתרא דקודשא אזלו ואתטעיו במדינתא דהכנא עבדו and T, which para-
phrases freely, both render the MT. Aquila read וּבָאוּ מְּקוֹם
קָדוֹש and Sym. also read וְהִלְכוּ. In B. Git. 21b, a variant
אל תקרי "do not read" for the MT occurs: אל תקרי וישתכחו אלא
וישתבחו. This is purely a homiletic device, as the other variant
in the same passage shows: אל תקרי קבורים אלא קבוצים. On this
Rabbinic device, cf. I. D. Bamberger, *Kore Beemet; Nahale
Devash* (1867), p. 69a; B. Epstein, *Mekor Barukh* (Vilna, 1928),
vol. 1, pp. 480–574; BTM, pp. 78 ff.

Hertz. follows Rudolph (*ThLZ*, 1927, p. 226; Burkitt, Kuhn),
and reads קְרֵבִים וּבָאִים; he renders thus: "Further, I saw sinners
coming near and entering, while they (the righteous) must leave
the holy place and be forgotten in the city where they acted
properly." This reading, which has no warrant in MT or in
any of the Vss., gives a highly awkward word order and an
unclear sense. Ehr. reads יְהָלָּלוּ וְיִשְׁתַּבְּחוּ, an attractive emendation,
but the prefixed Mem of וממקום favors a verb of motion like
יהלכו. Feigin conjectures that ובאו is an abbreviation for וּבְנֵי
אָדָם, with the final Vav being a later addition.

Based upon LXX, and requiring no consonantal change, the
best reading would be (so BH, Ehr. Gal.): וּבְכֵן רָאִיתִי רְשָׁעִים
קָבָר מוּבָאִים, "I have seen the wicked brought to their grave
with pomp" (cf. קְבוּרָה in 6:3), and stich d would be impersonal,
referring to the participants in the procession: "and when men
walk from the holy place, they are praised in the city where
they acted thus."

מקום קדוש may refer to the cemetery (cf. Latin *locus religiosus*,
German *heiliger Ort*), for which Hebrew, like all languages, has
many euphemisms, as e. g. בית החיים and בית עולם, which are based
on Ecc. 12:5. The phrase may be a euphemism for מקום טמא,
the place of the dead being regarded as defiling (Feigin). On
the root *kādaš* used as a euphemism for *tāmē'*, Feigin compares

Deut. 22:9. In Lev. 7:6, the phrase מקום קדוש is used of the Temple, and in post-Biblical Hebrew of a synagogue. Cf. J. A. Montgomery (*JBL*, 1924, p. 243), who cites the synagogue inscription at 'Ain Duk, אתרה קדישה. Perhaps funeral eulogies were pronounced in the synagogue, at least for important personages, as is the custom to the present day.

The Masoretic vocalization מְמָקוֹם, with Sheva, is explicitly attested in *Ochla Ve'ochla*, p. 92, but de Rossi ms. 413 reads מְמָקוֹם, and this is required here.

Del., following V, Sym. and Ibn Ezra in the interpretation of the last clause (כֵּן = "justly"), regards the verse as chiastic: "The sinners are buried with dignity . . . while forgotten are those who acted righteously." While this interpretation is theoretically possible (cf. II Ki. 7:9; so Ibn Ezra, Del., Levy), the contrast between רשעים and כן עשו is not sufficiently strong to sustain this interpretation, and Koheleth never uses כן in the sense of "justly." For this contrast, צדיק is the usual term (cf. 3:17; 7:20; 9:2).

8:11. אשר, "because"; cf. Gen. 30:18; 31:49; 34:13, 27; 42:21; Nu. 20:13; I Sam. 2:23; 15:15; 20:42; 25:26; Jer. 16:13; Job 34:27; Dan. 1:10, and elsewhere; cf. BDB, s. v. אשר 8c, p. 83b. The use occurs four (or five) times in our section, thus affording proof of the authenticity of the passage: here and in vv. 12a, 12e (probably), 13, and 15.

פתגם is a Persian loan-word (Old Pers. *patigama*, New Pers. *paigam*, "message") via the Aramaic פתגם, hence the permanent *kameṣ* even in the construct, as in Est. 1:20, "decree, edict." פתגם מעשה הרעה is here an obj. gen. = "judgment upon an evil deed." נַעֲשָׂה would indicate that פתגם is fem., unlike the passage in Est.; hence Albrecht, Hitz. vocalize נַעֲשָׂה, but it may be common in gender (Del., Wr.). מלא לב, "have the heart full, possess the courage"; cf. Est. 7:5; Ecc. 9:3.

LXX and P read מַעֲשֵׂה as עֹשֵׂי = "doers," but this may be purely interpretive and not a variant reading; cf. Rashi ad loc.: שאין הקדוש ברוך הוא ממהר להפרע מן עושי הרע.

8:12. אשר cannot mean "although," for which there is no warrant here or elsewhere; see note on v. 11. Its meaning is "because" (so Rashi, Ibn Ezra). The postponement of punishment is the great incentive to human wrongdoing.

מֵאַת is either a construct, sc. פַּעַם (not פְּעָמִים, ag. BDB), hence "a hundred times"; cf. Gen. 11:10; 21:5; Ex. 38:25; Est. 1:4 (מֵאַת יוֹם); or it may be an archaic absolute (cf. יְרָאַת, דֵּעַת), and modify רָע, which it follows for the sake of emphasis. Note that מאה invariably governs a singular and never occurs without a noun. Hence רע מאת = lit. "a hundred evils." For the inverted word order, cf. Nu. 28:27, פרים בני בקר שנים; idem 29:8, and passim; Gen. 32:15, a. e. This word order is particularly common in the later books; cf. I Chr. 25:5, בנות שלש; II Chr. 29:21, etc. Cf. Ges.-K., sec. 134, 1, c. The Vss. misunderstood the phrase and sought to render it variously.

Eur. equates LXX ἀπὸ τότε with מֵאַת. More probably it was taken as מֵעַת or less likely מֵאַז. A, Sym., Th. ἀπέθανεν equated it with מֵת. V contains a conflate: attamen peccator ex eo quod centies facit malum — the first reading apparently = מַאֲתוֹ from מאת ומאריך, the second attesting the MT. Barton follows McN. in postulating an original reading עָשָׂה רָעָה מְאֹד, "does evil exceedingly," but this is impossible Hebrew. No less outlandish is Hertz.'s proposed emendation וּמֵהַאֲרִיךְ לוֹ, "and because of the patience shown him (by God)." MT is considerably superior.

כי גם = "although" (cf. Ecc. 4:14; 8:16), a usage characteristic of Koheleth, and, like גם כי (Isa. 1:15; Hos. 8:10; 9:16; Ps. 23:4), "even if, although," introducing a subordinate clause.

יודע, a verb of cognition, introduces a restatement of a conventional idea, which Koheleth does not accept, vv. 12b, 13. His own reaction to the doctrine of the ultimate punishment of the sinner is given in vv. 14 and 15 (introduced by ושבחתי). Cf. 2:13–15 for a similar structure: vv. 13, 14a quote a conventional idea, introduced by the verb of cognition ראיתי, while 14b, 15 (introduced by וידעתי and ואמרתי) present Koheleth's reaction. The relative אשר, following יודע, may introduce a direct quotation; cf. I Sam. 15:20; II Sam. 1:4; Ges.-K., 157c. אשר ייראו מלפניו = either "who fear God" or "because they fear God" (cf. note on v. 11). The latter view is preferable because of the parallel of 13b.

ומאריך = an elliptical idiom for ומאריך אף לו, "is long suffering with him" (V, Sym. Th. Mend. Sieg. Levy); cf. note on משלחת (8:8), and such an ellipsis as כרת for כרת ברית (I Sam. 20:16; 22:8, etc.).

8:13. כצל is compared with ולא יאריך ימים (so the accents). Cf. Job 8:9 for the familiar simile. Levy's view, "he will not live his life any longer, as the shadow lengthens in the evening," is far-fetched, the essential element, "in the evening," being unexpressed. LXX reads בְּצֵל, against P, V, which read MT. אשר = "because," as in vv. 11, 15.

8:14. מעשה, "result of action, recompense"; cf. Isa. 32:17, מעשה הצדקה, "product of righteousness"; Hab. 3:17, מעשה זית, "product of the olive tree."

8:15. אשר, "because, for."

הוא refers to the actions described in the preceding infinitives.

ילונו, "accompany," a late use, used only in the Niphal elsewhere in the Bible (cf. Gen. 29:34; Isa. 14:1; 56:3; Est. 9:27, a. e.), and in the Piel in Mishnaic Hebrew (cf. Aboth 6:9, אין מלווין לו לאדם), and less commonly in the Hiphil, ואם הלוהו (Ber. 18a).

8:16. ענין, "business, occupation, activity."

The second half of the v. has a pronominal subject without an antecedent. The clause constitutes an instance of "anticipation," being really a subordinate clause, modifying אדם in v. 17 (כי גם = "although"). It has probably been removed from its logical position, because it cannot be inserted into v. 17, even after אדם, without creating an impossibly awkward structure. The simplest way to render the passage is to translate ראיתי of v. 17 before 16b: "I saw that though man sleep neither by day nor by night, he cannot discover, etc."

The idiom "see sleep" is regarded as unusual by Bar. Hertz., who cite Latin usage (Cicero, *Ad Familiares*, VII, 30; Terence), but it occurs in Mishnaic Hebrew (Tos. Sukkah 4:5, לא היינו רואין שינה), where it is used quite idiomatically, so that its dependence on our passage, though possible, is not likely.

8:17. מעשה האלהים is another instance of "anticipation," having been lifted out of the subordinate clause ... כִּי; cf. Gen. 1:4, וירא אלהים את האור כי טוב = וירא אלהים כי האור טוב. In our passage, however, the "anticipated" noun is recapitulated in the subordinate clause by המעשה.

בשל אשר is a late Hebrew idiom, perhaps a rendering of the Aramaic . . . בדיל ד, "on account of which, for the sake of which, *um dessen willen*" (so Rashi, Ibn Ezra); cf. Jonah 1:7, 12, בשלי, בשלמי, "on account of whom, of me," and Targum Onkelos on Gen. 12:13; 30:27, בדיל, "on account of." The emendation וכל אשר, based on LXX, V, P, may represent a free rendering of the intent of the passage; at all events it is inferior (ag. Levy) to MT.

יעמל לבקש, lit. "will labor hard to find, will search hard."

יאמר לדעת, lit. "believe to learn it, i. e. think he is about to learn it"; cf. II Sam. 21:16; II Chr. 13:8; 32:1. Gal. reads: וגם אם יאמר אחכם לדעת, "Even if one says, 'I am wise to understand.'"

9:1. For ולבור את, LXX and P read וְלִבִּי רָאָה, which is accepted by most moderns (but not by Gal.), but this is a case of leveling an unfamiliar phrase to the ordinary (cf. 1:16), and is not to be preferred, especially since the emended text would read אֶל לִבִּי . . . וְלִבִּי (twice). ולבור is an infinitive construct consecutive equivalent to a finite verb; cf. Ges.-K., 113, 4a. בור is an ע"ו form for the more common geminate; cf. יָגֻד (Gen. 49:19) from גדד and יָרוּן (Pr. 29:6) from רנן.

עֲבָדֵיהֶם, an Aramaic word, retaining the permanent *kames* (cf. note on 8:11), and meaning "work"; cf. מַעְבָּדֵיהֶם, Job 34:25.

אהבה and שנאה are not qualified by a suffix, as in 9:6, hence not "man's love and hate" (ag. Ibn Ezra, Wr.), but "love and hate *par excellence*, i. e. God's love and hate" (so Bar.); cf. Ps. 2:7, חק, "God's law." V, while rendering freely in a moralistic vein, has caught the force of the passage: "Nevertheless, man does not know whether he be worthy of love or hate"; so Rashi. Gal. arrives at the same sense for the passage as do we, but his emended text is linguistically inferior to MT.

LXX adds the first three words from v. 2 and then renders הכל לפניהם הבל באשר לכל. P adopts this reading, but has a conflate, reading הכל in v. 2 again: כל דקדמוהי הבלא כלא איך דלכל. It is possible that הבל fell out at the end of v. 1 by haplography, and v. 2 is to begin with באשר (so Bar. BH). Ehr., who also adopts this reading, interprets, "Everything that has happened

in the past is vanity, without effect on their future" (cf. 1:11;
2:7, 9, and לְפָנִים, "past") (so Kuhn, Allgeier, Ode. Hertz.). But
this idea is irrelevant here. Koheleth's theme is not that vanity
awaits men, but that the future is uncertain. So V: *omnia in
futurum servantur incerta.* This thought is far better expressed
by the MT הכל לפניהם, "everything is before them, i. e. anything
may happen to them." Levy renders: "everything is in God's
power" (the plural suffix referring to God; cf. Gen. 24:51; Josh.
10:12), but this is not likely. The suffix refers to "the righteous
and wise" — their course is no guarantee of happiness.

9:2. See note on v. 1. On the basis of LXX and perhaps V
(but not P), some read here: באשר לכל מקרה אחד. While this is
possible, the more natural word order would have been באשר
לכל מקרה אחד; cf. 3:19, ומקרה אחד להם. LXX reads באשר for
כאשר in 8:16 as well. Moreover, the context of v. 1 (on which
see above), as well as that of our v., loses by the change. הכל
כאשר לכל, "Everything is like everything else, one fate awaits
all men," is an excellent statement of the theme which the
rendering of the verse elaborates. Far from being "artificial and
unhebraic" (Hertz.), the idiom is paralleled by other *idem per
idem* constructions, through which Hebrew expresses the idea
of indefiniteness, as e. g..Ex. 3:14, אהיה אשר אהיה, "I am whatever
I am"; Ex. 4:13, שלח נא ביד תשלח, "Send whomever Thou wouldst
send," or the late Hebrew אונקלוס תרגם מה שתרגם, "Onkelos translated whatever he translated." Hence our phrase means literally, "anything may happen to anyone."

LXX, P, V insert וְלָרַע after לטוב, which may indeed have
fallen out, but which is more probably an example of tacit correction by the translator. Död., Schmidt, Bick., Sieg., Levy,
Bar. drop לטוב instead, but neither procedure is absolutely
necessary. The absence of ולרע in the Hebrew may rest on
rhythmic grounds — לטוב ולטהור is longer than ולטמא — in order
to balance the next stich, in which לאשר איננו זבח is longer than
ולזבח. In the closing stich the phrase כאשר שבועה ירא is longer
than its contrast הנשבע, because it comes at the end of the
passage, where there is a well-attested tendency to lengthen the
final phrase. Cf. the closing stichs of Pss. 8, 20, 63, 67, 84 *inter
alia*, and see MHHH, pp. 144 ff. While the order in each pair

has the virtuous precede the sinner, this is reversed in the case of the last pair, to end on a favorable note, בכי טוב, as in 3:8.

Monotony is avoided in this long series by having the first three pairs governed by the Lamed after מקרה, while the last two pairs employ the coordinate construction of the double Kaph, which is often used to compare two objects; cf. Isa. 24:2. This construction requires כנשבע for the Masoretic הנשבע.

On שבועה ירא, cf. the Mishnaic idiom ירא חטא, "fears, hence avoids sin" (Del.).

Koheleth has little use for sacrifices; cf. 4:17. So, too, though for different reasons, the Essenes opposed animal sacrifices (Josephus, *Ant.*, XVIII, 1, 5). The avoidance even of true oaths was a mark of piety; cf. Zc. 5:3. The Essenes refused to swear under any circumstances (Josephus, *Ant.*, XV, 10, 4; *War*, II, 8, 6). Rabbinic law reduced the occasions for oaths very drastically, treating the legal obligation to swear as a kind of punishment, as it was felt by the people to be. As is well known, the evidence of witnesses was never "buttressed" by oaths in Talmudic law, a procedure that avoided the perjury with which our modern age reeks, and which incidentally attested to a high standard of truth-telling.

9:3. LXX agrees with MT in reading נעשה as a perfect, "has taken place," but the difference in meaning from the participle is very slight.

הוללות (cf. 1:17; 2:12; 7:25; הוללות, 10:13) means "madness," a word which Koheleth uses to describe unbridled and un-principled conduct, which results from the conviction that life is meaningless and that there is no moral law operating in the world.

For ואחריו LXX and P read ואחריהם, which is obviously an effort to bring the suffix into harmony with the plural subject. Like the emendation ואחריתם (Sym., BH), it is unnecessary. The suffix Vav is a petrified ending (as in יַחְדָּו), the word meaning "afterwards" (so Ehr. Levy). On this usage, cf. our note on 3:22.

The last phrase, in Wildeboer's fine words, constitutes "a consciously fragmentary clause — and then off to the dead — which breaks off like life itself." It seems likely that these words express the *thought* of men who yield to madness: "for they know that afterwards they are off to the dead!" For other examples of quotations that present the unspoken thought and attitude of the subject, cf. Job 31:3–4, 14–15, and QBROL, in *HUCA*, 1949, pp. 181–86.

Section XV — Introductory Note

9:4–12. Koheleth's two basic themes — the inevitability of death and the supreme duty of man to derive the most from life — now attain to passionate expression in a section which is virtually the culmination of the preceding. Beginning in ordinary prose (vv. 4 f.), he goes over to rhythmic prose (v. 6), which then rises to rhythmic verse (vv. 7–9). Beyond this climax, the passage becomes rhythmic prose once more (vv. 9b–11), and then ends as it began, in normal prose (v. 12).

The verse form here is 4:4:

לֵךְ אֱכֹל בְּשִׂמְחָה לַחְמֶ֫ךָ ‖ וּשֲׁתֵה בְלֶב־טוֹב יֵינֶ֫ךָ

כִּי כְבָר רָצָה הָאֱלֹהִים אֶת־מַעֲשֶׂ֫יךָ

בְּכָל־עֵת יִהְיוּ בְגָדֶ֫יךָ לְבָנִים ‖ וְשֶׁמֶן עַל־רֹאשְׁךָ אַל־יֶחְסָר

רְאֵה חַיִּים עִם־אִשָּׁה אֲשֶׁר־אָהַ֫בְתָּ ‖ כָּל־יְמֵי חַיֵּי הֶבְלֶ֫ךָ

On the double beat on אל יחסר and הבלך, cf. MHHH, pp. 140 f.

In v. 9, the verse ends with the first הבלך, after which the passage becomes prose (see above). This shift within the same verse occurs in Egyptian literature, as in the "Hymn of the Victories of Thutmosis III" (c. 1470 B. C. E.), where the introduction in exalted prose is followed by ten strophes written in strictly regular form, ending in a non-rhythmic conclusion. The last two lines of the tenth strophe are directly linked to the prose; the entire passage is thus given by A. Erman, *The Literature of the Ancient Egyptians* (New York, 1927), p. 257:

"I cause them to behold thy majesty as thy twain brethren,
  Whose hands I have joined for thee in victory,
and thy two sisters have I put behind thee as a protection,
while the arms of my majesty are lifted and dispel what is evil."

In the famous "Victory Stele of Merneptah" (c. 1230 B.C.E.), the bulk is in non-rhythmic form except for the close, containing the famous reference to Israel, which exhibits the rhythm and parallelism characteristic of ancient Near Eastern poetry (cf. op. cit., pp. 274–78).

The Bible contains many examples of poetic fragments imbedded in prose narratives (e. g. Gen. 21:7; Jud. 15:16), but a more direct parallel to our passage is afforded by Jacob's address to Laban (Gen. 31:36–42), which begins in prose (vv. 36b, 37), then becomes verse principally in the 4:4 rhythm (vv. 38, 39, 40), and then reverts to prose (vv. 41 f.).

The theme of this passage, *carpe diem*, bulks large in the literature of the world, and such figures as Lucretius, Horace and Herrick come to mind. More germane to our passage than the parallels adduced from Greek, Latin and modern authors is the striking section in the *Gilgamesh Epic*, Old Babylonian Version, Meissner fragment (Tablet X, column iii, lines 6–14):

> Thou, O Gilgamesh, let thy belly be full;
> Day and night be thou merry;
> Make every day (a day of) rejoicing.
> Day and night do thou dance and play.
> Let thy raiment be clean;
> Thy head be washed, (and) thy self be bathed in water.
> Cherish the little one holding thy hand,
> (And) let the wife rejoice in thy bosom.
> This is the lot of mankind.

(Translation of A. Heidel, *The Gilgamesh Epic and O. T. Parallels*, Chicago, 1946, p. 70; text published by Meissner in *Mitteilungen der vorderasiatischen Gesellschaft*, VII, 1902, Heft 1, pp. 14 f.)

From Egypt comes the "Song of the Harpist," dated by Erman toward the end of the Middle Kingdom (circa the 18th century B. C. E.):

> "Follow thy desire, so long as thou livest. Put myrrh on thy head, clothe thee in fine linen, and anoint thee with the genuine marvels of the god.
> "Increase yet more the delights that thou hast, and let not thine heart grow faint. Follow thy desire and do good

to thyself (?). Do what thou requirest (?) upon earth, and vex not thy heart — until that day of lamentation cometh upon thee" (tr. by A. M. Blackman, in A. Erman, op. cit., p. 133.)

It is obvious (ag. Bar.) that there can be no question of borrowing in so universally human a context, unless there were some unusual feature in common, or at least the same sequence of details. None of these factors obtains here. The Babylonian poet speaks of the joy of children, which is lacking in Koheleth, while the Egyptian poet lacks the reference to the love of woman found in the Hebrew sage. Virtually the only feature in common is the emphasis upon clean clothes (and even the fine oil mentioned is missing in the Babylonian poem). In addition, the long interval of time separating these poems from Koheleth rules out the possibility of borrowing, though it is quite conceivable that the theme was a conventionally popular one throughout the Orient. Nor is there need to assume Greek influence.

9:4. כי is here used as an emphatic particle, to introduce the section, a usage common elsewhere in Biblical Hebrew, as e. g. Nu. 23:23; Isa. 15:1; Amos 3:7; Pr. 30:2; Job 5:2; 28:1 (cf. *JAOS*, vol. 63, 1943, p. 176).

מי אשר is taken as an interrogative by LXX and as a rhetorical question by V (*nemo*), but not by P, which correctly recognizes it as a relative equivalent to the more classical כל אשר; cf. Ex. 32:33; II Sam. 20:11; Ecc. 5:9; and see *BDB*, p. 567a, bottom.

The Kethib יְבָחַר is inferior to the Qere יְחֻבַּר, which is attested by all the Vss., though the pausal accent on the word (Zakeph katan) would seem to follow the Kethib (see Levy ad loc.).

בטחון, "hope, the possibility of an improvement even in the most wretched lot." In II Ki. 18:19; Isa. 36:4, the word means "trust, security." In later Hebrew the sense of the word in our passage was further broadened to mean "faith in God, especially under adversity."

לְכָלב contains the Lamed emphaticus, like the Arabic *la*, Akkadian *lu*; cf. Isa. 32:1b (*ūl'sārīm*); Ps. 32:6 (*l[e]šeteph*); II Chr.

7:21 (*lekhol*), a. e. It is therefore left unexpressed by the Vss., which treat כלב as the subject. הוא is the copula; cf. Deut. 4:39. On the variation in the use or absence of the article character-istic of the book, cf. OLQ, pp. 81 ff. Recognition of the usage obviates the need for Ehr.'s complicated interpretation.

It is interesting that Ibn Ezra regards this verse (and v. 11) as a citation of the common opinion of men. As a matter of fact, the second half of verse 4 bears the stamp of a popular proverb (cf. Pl.). If it be so regarded, v. 5 would be Koheleth's comment, justifying the popular view, but on very modest grounds characteristically his own. On this type of quotation and ironic comment, see *QWL*, pp. 132 ff.; *QBROL*, pp. 198–207, and notes on 7:1 ff. It makes little difference here, however, whether v. 4 is a statement of the accepted view or Koheleth's own.

The dog was despised in the East (I Sam. 24:14; II Sam. 3:8; 16:9), while the lion was the royal animal (Gen. 49:9).

Levy and Allgeier accept the Kethib יְבָחַר, the former render-ing "Who is preferred? All the living have hope!" But the assumed use of אל כל החיים is unhebraic.

9:5. Consciousness on any terms is preferable to non-existence, and knowledge, however limited and melancholy in content, is better than ignorance. Here speaks Koheleth, the lover of life and the devotee of wisdom; cf. Sec. XVI.

There is more than an assonance in זכר and שכר. The dead lack the one reward conceivably open to them, that of being remembered. The following verse reminds us that the dead can no longer participate in the activities of the living world (cf. Ps. 88:11; 115:17; Job 14:21 f.). This idea is reproduced and opposed in *Wisdom of Solomon* 2:4 in a passage which is a polemic against Koheleth's views (2:1–9). The assonance here of *zēkher* and *sākhār*, like that of *šēm* and *šemen* in 7:1 and *sīr* in 7:6 (meaning "thorn" and "pot"), would be lost in Aramaic. This fact constitutes part of the evidence for the originality of the Hebrew text; cf. QHA.

9:7. On the contents and the poetic meter, see the Intr. Note.

The language of stich c is highly significant for understand-

ing Koheleth's use of religious terminology. He who has enjoyed the delights of life has thereby (כבר, "already") won the
favor of God. The verb רצה, with God as subject, is used of the
accepting of offerings on the altar (Deut. 33:11; II Sam. 24:23;
Amos 5:22, and often).

9:8. White robes were a sign of joy, as was fragrant oil;
cf. the Egyptian and Babylonian parallels in the Intr. Note,
and such passages as II Sam. 12:20; Ps. 23:5; 45:8; Pr. 27:9;
and Horace, *Satires*, II, 61, *Festos albatus celebret*. Hence the
righteous are pictured as arrayed in white garments in the world
to come (Rev. 3:4, 5; 7:9; B. Shab. 114a).

9:9. On the use of both verse and prose in the same sentence,
see the Intr. Note. LXX (cod. Alex.) and T omit כל ימי הבלך,
but this phrase is attested by LXX (cod. B and others), V, and,
remarkably enough, by P, which omits the entire clause אשר
נתן לך . . . הבלך, an error of homoioteleuton, which could not
have happened unless the eye of the translator, or scribe, had
leaped from the first הבלך to the second! (so also Hertz.). While
many modern commentators omit the latter phrase (Eur. Sieg.
McN. Ehr. Bar. Hertz. Gal.), it is worth noting that the phrase
is not an exact repetition of the former, but a shorter form. Thus
it gives a haunting effect, like the Kinah rhythm, and is to be
retained (so Hitz. Luz. Levy).

For הוא in our Occidental texts, the Oriental read היא Kethib,
הוא Qere. This Kethib would refer to the woman, but the
masculine is preferable, referring to the enjoyment of life as a
whole.

אשה occurs without the article. On Koheleth's irregular use
of the article, see OLQ, pp. 81 ff. It is, however, quite likely
that אשה with the article omitted means "woman," and not
"wife." Koheleth was almost surely a bachelor, and was certainly no apologist for the marriage institution. In its refutation
of Koheleth's ideas, *Wisdom of Solomon* (2:9) apparently did
not refer the "woman" to the one taken in marriage:

> Leave we everywhere the tokens of our joy,
> For this is our lot and our portion is this.
>
> (tr. Goodrick, *Book of Wisdom*, p. 108)

9:10. A memorable plea for partaking actively in all the joyful experiences open to man.

As against the usual Masoretic accentuation, which places a Tiphha at בכחך, Kittel cites some mss. which place the secondary pause at לעשות, thus linking בכחך עשה, which is undoubtedly required by the context (so also LXX). חשבון, "contrivance, mental activity, thought" (LXX λογισμός, V *ratio*, P מחשבתא); cf. on 7:29. In origin, the noun is an infinitive, as is מחשבה. Its paralleling מעשה indicates that it does not mean "reckoning, judgment (of God)."

Koheleth generally espouses the old Hebrew (and Semitic) view of the after-life as a shadowy, gloomy existence lacking in interest and activity. This old view was maintained by the Wisdom writers, even though they were familiar with the newer views of life after death and the final judgment of the wicked and the righteous, which had begun to make headway among the people. This conservatism in Wisdom is in harmony with its upper-class origin and orientation. See *SBWL*, pp. 101 ff. Heidel (*Gilgamesh Epic and O. T. Parallels*, pp. 183 ff.), who recognizes the old view among the Babylonians, argues that the Hebrews never believed in a shadowy, all-inclusive after-life, but he overlooks our explicit passage, among others, and his evidence from other Biblical sources is unconvincing.

תמצא ידך, "be able" (cf. I Sam. 10:7, עשה לך אשר תמצא ידך), not = "afford" as in Lev. 25:28; 12:8 (ag. Ehr. Jast.). Hence בכחך has its usual meaning here, "strength," not "wealth," as in Pr. 5:10; Job 6:22.

9:11. שבתי וראה, "I saw again" (ag. Ibn Ezra).

חן is attested by all the Vss. (so also Ehr. Jast.). Many modern scholars read הון, as parallel to עשר (Jast.). But the MT implies that men of knowledge often lack the "grace" required to win the favor of their fellows upon which success depends (so T, which adds, somewhat too narrowly, למשכח רחמין בעיני מלכא). Koheleth's realistic observation runs counter to the conventional Wisdom doctrine in Pr. 13:15, "good sense wins favor."

By polarization עֵת, "time," and פֶּגַע, "encounter, occurrence," develop negative connotations, "evil time, hour of doom" (cf. 9:12a; Ps. 81:16; B. Sheb. 15b, שיר של פגעים), though the nouns do occur with the qualifying adjective רע (cf. 9:12b; I Ki. 5:18; Ber. 16b, פגע רע).

תחת השמש is an instance of "anticipation," the phrase being drawn from the subordinate to the main clause,=שבתי וראה כי תחת השמש לא לקלים המרוץ.

The three nouns חכמים, נבנים, ידעים are in the same sequence as חכמה, בינה, דעת in Isa. 11:2 (Del.), but the prophetic conception of these virtues is very different from that of Wisdom.

This and the following verse mark either the end of the preceding section, as we prefer to regard it, or the beginning of the next (Hertz.). In either event, they serve to link the sections together.

9:12. כי גם may mean "for indeed" (Hertz., Bar.), and the main clause would then end with בפח (so the accents). But in view of the double use of כדנים . . . כהם which is apparently correlative, and the fact that the comparison with the fishes and the birds would more naturally stress the suddenness of their capture rather than their lack of foreknowledge of the event, it seems best to interpret כי גם as "although" (cf. on 8:12, 16), and to place the pause at עת. עתו, "hour of doom"; cf. the preceding verse and Ps. 81:16.

For MT כָּהֵם (II Sam. 24:3 = I Chr. 21:3; II Chr. 9:11) P read or interpreted כה (הכנא). The Mem may then be read (Pod. Ode. Hertz.) with the participle as מְיֻקָּשִׁים, "entrapped." However, the Mem of the old Kal passive (or Pual, which it resembles in form) is frequently dropped; cf. אֻכָּל (Ex. 3:2); יֻלַּד (Jud. 13:8); לֻקַּח (II Ki. 2:10); זֹרָה (Isa. 30:24); and Ges.-K., sec. 52, end. Hence there is no need to emend the MT (cf. Ibn Ezra, Bar.).

In מצודה רעה, the adjective is dropped by BH, but obviously the net (cf. מָצוֹד, Pr. 12:12; Job 19:6; Ecc. 7:26; מְצוֹדָה, Ez. 19:9; מְצוּדָה, Ez. 12:13; 17:20; Ps. 66:11) is evil from the standpoint of its victims, which Koheleth has here adopted.

This passage seems to have been the basis of R. Akiba's great saying in Aboth 3:25, הכל נתון בערבון ומצודה פרושה על כל החיים, "Everything is given in pledge, and a net is spread over all the living."

Section XVI — Introductory Note

9:13 to **10:1.** As an instance of the low repute in which
wisdom is held when unaccompanied by wealth or power (cf.
7:11), Koheleth narrates the incident of a city saved by the
sagacity of a poor man whose very name is forgotten (vv. 14 ff.).
Countless efforts have been made to identify the incident, but
to no avail. Thus Hitzig identifies the city with Dora, which
was besieged unsuccessfully by Antiochus the Great in 218
B. C. E. (Polybius, V, 66), but no incident is reported about a
"poor man." Wr. adduces the deliverance of Abel-Beth-Maacah
by a "wise woman" (II Sam. 20:15 ff.). Even less likely are
the suggestions which would refer the passage to such incidents
in history as Themistocles' treatment by the Athenians (Ewald)
or the well-known feat of Archimedes at the siege of Syracuse
(Friedlaender).

Levy has wisely remarked that had the incident remained
in history, there would be no point to Koheleth's complaint that
the wisdom of the poor is forgotten! Most probably Koheleth
is inventing a *typical* case (or generalizing) in order to illustrate
his point, rather than invoking a specific historical incident.
This is a well attested literary usage, which occurs also in 4:13 ff.
Thus in the Egyptian *The Admonitions of a Prophet* (or *Sage*)
(Erman, *op. cit.*, p. 108), the varied poems and counsels contain
a section beginning: "There was once a man that was old and
stood in the presence of death, etc." In the *Instruction for King
Merikere*, the advice to the young ruler-to-be is largely in the
form of admonitions, but we find this incident: "There rose up
one, a ruler in the city, and his heart was oppressed by reason
of the Delta" (Erman, p. 80). The same usage occurs in the
Cynic-Stoic diatribe. The fragmentary character of both
Egyptian documents makes it impossible to be certain whether
these are actual events or imaginary illustrations, but the similar
usage in the Greek diatribes points to the latter alternative.

In the closing portion of this section, vv. 9:16 to 10:1, Sieg.
McN. Bar. Jast. delete 9:17 and 10:1 as Hokmah glosses, but
unnecessarily. In the first instance, Koheleth was a teacher of
Wisdom, and so would naturally cite the literature or formulate

its ideas himself (see Introduction). Aside from this general consideration, a careful study of the passage indicates its authenticity. V. 16, which is obviously Koheleth's, being the conclusion of the incident (vv. 14 f.), is couched in the form of contrasting proverbs, the first declaring, "Wisdom is better than strength," followed by the observation, "The wisdom of the poor man is despised, and his words go unheeded." Were the following verses the work of a conventional Hokmah glossator, they would glorify wisdom. Instead, we have two proverbs extolling wisdom (vv. 17, 18a), but they are followed at once by two utterances which declare that a single fool can undo the fruits of a great deal of wisdom (9:18b; 10:1) — and it is these that have the last word! On this use of contrasting proverbs in which the latter expresses the author's standpoint, see 4:5 f.; Job 12:12 f.; 32:7 f.; and *QWL*, pp. 137–40; *QBROL*, pp. 207–10. In no other way could Koheleth express his "prejudice" in favor of Wisdom from which he could not "free" himself, conscious though he was of its tragic limitations.

If 9:16a is authentic, so is v. 18a, which is almost identical with it in form as well as idea. See n. on 9:17 on the method of introducing quotations.

חוטא, "sinner," in v. 18 bears a nuance which it develops in Wisdom literature, as equivalent to "fool," a perfectly logical extension of its basic meaning of "one who misses the mark" (cf. Pr. 14:21; 19:2).

9:13. חכמה, which is attested by all the Vss., is in apposition with זה, literally, "as wisdom, as an example of Wisdom." To delete it (Jast.) vitiates the meaning of the entire passage.

גדולה, "subjectively great, significant"; cf. this late use in Jonah 4:1; Est. 10:3, גדול ליהודים, "great in the eyes of the Jews." It is equivalent in earlier Hebrew to גדול ... בעיני עבדי פרעה (Ex. 11:3) or גדול לפני אדניו (II Ki. 5:1) (Wright).

9:14. Most modern commentators emend מצודים to מצורים and compare Deut. 20:20; Isa. 29:3 (BH, Fried., Del.), basing themselves on the Vss. (LXX χάρακας, "palisades," V *munitiones*, P קלקומא); not T, which interprets as "nets." This is an erroneous deduction from the Vss. Actually no plural of מצור occurs in the Bible, though there is a noun מצורה which does occur in the plural (Isa. 29:3; II Chr. 11:11; 12:4; 21:3). Moreover, there is no need to emend the text. Our noun is the plural of the masc. מָצוֹד; cf. Job 19:6, וּמְצוּדוֹ עָלַי הִקִּיף, where the verb "surround" indicates a siege, not a net (ag. BDB). Cf. also forms like מְצָד (I Chr. 12:8) and the fem. מְצוֹדָה (Isa. 29:7), which occurs more frequently as מְצוּדָה (Ps. 31:3). Its meaning is "siegeworks," which took the form of a citadel, constructed outside the city walls, for the purpose of raining missiles into the city and upon its defenders. Cf. *dayek* and *solelah*. Ehr. points out that the German *Bollwerk*, "defense," originally meant "siegeworks." On both types of plural for מצוד, cf. מבשלות (Ez. 46:23) and מבשלים (46:24); זְכֻרִים (Job 13:12) and זְכֻרוֹת (Est. 6:1); מְכוֹנִים (Ps. 104:5) and מְכוֹנוֹת (I Ki. 7:27, and *passim*).

9:15. ומצא is impersonal, sc. הַמּוֹצֵא; cf. וַיֹּאמֶר לְיוֹסֵף, Gen. 48:1; וַיֻּגַּד לְיַעֲקֹב, Gen. 48:2.

There is no need to add a Vav before חכם (ag. Hertz.); the asyndeton is emphatic: lit. "a poor man, but wise." LXX and V, which insert a copula, are striving for a "smooth" translation. P reproduces MT.

ומלט is later Hebrew for the classical וימלט, "and he saved." Hertz. follows McN. Volz and Kuhn in rendering "he *could have saved* the city." This is ruled out by the rest of the verse, "and no one remembered the poor man," which would be meaningless if no saving act had actually taken place. זכר means "remember, make mention of," not "think of," which would be expressed by חשב. Moreover, there is no evidence for the assumed use of the perfect here for a pluperfect. Hertz. cites Ges.-K., sec. 106, 4, but none of the examples there quoted are parallel. The perfect in this sense is used *only in conditional sentences*: a) in the protasis (Job 23:10; Ruth 1:12, כִּי אָמַרְתִּי); b) in the apodosis, where the protasis is introduced by לוּלֵי or לוּלֵא (Gen. 31:42; 43:10; Jud. 14:18; Ps. 94:17) or לוּ (Jud. 13:23; I Sam. 13:13, where לָא is to be read for לֹא; II Ki. 13:19, where לוֹ הִכִּיתָ is to be read for לְהַכּוֹת); or c) in virtual conditional sentences, after כִּמְעַט ("If . . ., this would almost have happened"; Gen. 26:10; Ps. 73:2; 94:17; 119:87) or after כִּי עַתָּה (Job 3:13, where לֹא is perhaps to be read in v. 10). Nor is it true that there is no other way, as Hertz. maintains, to express

the suggested idea. Biblical Hebrew could well say ויהי לאל
ידו למלט את העיר for "He could have saved the city"; as e. g.
Gen. 31:29, יש לאל ידי לעשות וגו׳.

9:16. The literal renderings of P and LXX are conscious
of the contradiction between the first stich and the rest of the
verse. V recognizes the problem and interpolates *quo modo*,
"how," before stich b. Ibn Ezra, followed by Ehr., supplies a
concessive אם, "although," before stich b, but Ruth 2:9, which
Ibn Ezra adduces, is not even remotely parallel. On the entire
context, see Intr. Note.

9:17. While the quotations in the previous verse are introduced by אמרתי, there is no external sign of the quotation here
or in the verses following. On these two methods of introducing
quotations, cf. Ex. 18:3 as against 18:4; Job 12:12 f. as against
32:7 f.; the discussion in *QBROL*, pp. 207–10. בנחת, which has the
disjunctive accent, Tiphha, is to be construed with דברי and
rendered "the words of the wise spoken quietly" (cf. בשובה
ונחת, "quietness," Isa. 30:15), thus constituting a contrast with
זעקת (Ibn Ezra, Wr.). For this reason the interpretation of the
phrase as "heard with pleasure" (Rashi) is unacceptable. LXX
translates "rulers" in the plural, perhaps to parallel "wise men"
in the first clause. Apparently mistaking the figure in "ruler
over fools," it renders כסילים abstractly as "follies," like other
abstract nouns that appear as plural in form.

מושל בכסילים is not a Greek idiom; cf. II Sam. 23:3, משל באדם;
cf. נבור בבהמה, Pr. 30:30; מלך על כל בני שחץ, Job 41:26 (so Bar.).
Gal. reads: ובזעקה משלי כסילים, "but the parables of fools (are
heard) with shouting," but this interesting emendation is not
essential.

9:18. חוטא in this context is equivalent to "fool"; see Intr.
Note. While LXX, V, T render the MT, P reads the word as
חַטָּא, which is preferred by Sieg., Del., BH, but the contrasting
use of abstract and concrete nouns is common; cf. 10:6, סָכָל and
עֲשִׁירִים.

קרב is an Aramaism, used only in late Hebrew (Ps. 55:22;
68:31; 78:9; 144:1. In II Sam. 17:11 read בְּקִרְבָּם).
There may be a word play here: Wisdom is described as

"good" and then folly as more powerful than much "good" (Hertz.).

10:1. This difficult verse proved a stumbling block to the Vss. LXX: "Dying flies befoul the dressing (σκευασίαν) of the oil of a relish. Costly (is) a little of wisdom above the glory of great folly." P: "As flies that are dead befoul a vessel of perfumed oil, weightier than wisdom and a multitude of praise (ומן סונאת תושבחתא) is light folly." V: "Dying flies destroy the sweetness of oil. More precious than wisdom and glory is a little folly in time" (*parva et ad tempus stultitia*). T, very periphrastically: "The evil inclination which dwells at the gates of the heart (cf. Gen. 4:7) is like a fly, and causes death in the world, because the wise man befouls himself at the time that he sins and he destroys the good name which before had resembled good oil (cf. 7:1) which is perfumed with spices, and how proper and more weighty (יאי ויקיר) than the wisdom of the wise (read חוכמת חכימין for חוכמתא חכימין) and the riches of the rich is a man whose folly is slight and light (זעיר וקליל)."

McN., who is followed by Bar., suggests that the original text, which can be reconstructed from LXX, read: יקר מעט מחכמה מכבוד סכלות רב. It was then transformed by P into יקר מחכמה ומכבוד רב סכלות מעט. V then omitted רב, MT dropped the Vav! This alleged original reading, which glorifies Wisdom, was antithetic to the first half of the verse. Hence the "Rabbinic revisers" in P, V and MT present a text in harmony with the first half. Here, contrary to the usual assumption that the "unorthodox" sentiments of Koheleth were "corrected" by conventional (Hokmah) glossators, we are asked to assume the opposite — that a proverb extolling wisdom was, by a complicated process, transformed into an aphorism denying its power!

The entire theory is based on a failure to evaluate the evidence of the ancient Vss. properly. The passage affords an excellent insight into the methods of the ancient translators. In dealing with difficult passages they fell back upon several devices, a few of which are here illustrated: a) contracting a difficult passage, as e. g. V on stich a. b) embodying two interpretations of a doubtful passage in a conflate: מכבוד P, "multitude" and "praise"; LXX, "glory" and "great" (folly); מעט T, "slight" and "light"; V, "little" and "at the right time." c) paraphrasing widely; cf. Targum. d) varying the construction; thus LXX regards מעט as modifying מחכמה.

In addition, the texts of the Vss. have themselves undergone inner errors, because of the difficulty and incomprehensibility of the passage. Thus scholars (e. g. Gal.) delete יַבִּיעַ as a dittography of יבאיש, and point to its absence in LXX. But LXX does read a noun σκευασία — "dressing" — and P (which often follows LXX) reads מאנא — "vessel." The explanation lies in an inner Greek error — the word should be σκεῦος, "vessel"; cf. LXX for כלי, Gen. 27:3; Jer. 22:28. P still had the correct reading in the Greek text before it. LXX either interpreted יביע as a noun meaning vessel, "that which flows," or misread יביע as גְּבִיעַ. Similarly, in T's rendering of יקר by יאי ויקיר, the first word seems to be an erroneous dittography of the second. V seems to have read מעט as מעת, "at the time," or to have interpreted it temporally, like כִּמְעַט (cf. Ps. 2:12; 81:15; Job 32:22, "quickly"). Difficult as the passage is, the MT, which lies at the basis of all the aberrations of the Vss., is superior to them.

זבובי מות need not be emended to זְבוּב יָמוּת (Luz. Gr. Fried. Del. Gal.), in spite of the singular verb which follows (cf. Gen. 27:29; Ex. 31:14; Lev. 17:14; Isa. 2:18; Joel 1:20; Pr. 3:18; Job 12:7; and see Ges.-K., sec. 145, 4 and 5). Koheleth's use of agreement is often irregular; cf. 1:10, 16; 2:7. The phrase is to be taken to mean not "death-dealing flies" (Ges. Del. Wr. Wild. Sieg.) on the basis of כלי מות, "deadly weapons" (Ps. 7:14), or "dead flies" (P, Hitz. Now. Bar.), which would have been expressed simply as זבובים מתים, but as "dying flies," lit. "flies about to die," which float about in the precious oil, a common sight in the East. Cf. such examples of the epexegetical genitive as בֶּן הַכּוֹת, Deut. 25:2, "man worthy of flogging"; I Sam. 20:31, בֶּן מָוֶת, "a man destined to die"; אנשי מות, II Sam. 19:29. The comparison, as Levy points out, is as apt as it would be familiar. Dying flies have little power to accomplish anything, yet they can destroy the oil; so fools, impotent to achieve any good, can yet destroy what has been created by dint of wisdom. This view of the passage is taken by Jerome (*muscae morientes*), Rashi (קרובים למות), and Levy.

The singular verb יבאיש after the plural זבובי may have been induced by the singular מות.

יביע is generally regarded as a Hiphil of נבע, "flows," hence "sucks up, absorbs," or of בעע, בוע (cf. Ar. بَعَّ), "effervesces, creates a scum" (cf. אֲבַעְבֻּעֹת); on the *Primae Nun* analogy, cf. יַנִּיח from נוח. If taken as a verb, it would be an instance of verbal asyndeton (Rashi Del. Wr. Hertz.). The context, however, requires a noun, as LXX and P recognize, to mean a "container." Perhaps the horn in which oil was carried was called יַבִּיעַ, "the flowing vessel." On nouns with preformative Yod, cf. יְבוּל, יְקוּם, and proper nouns like יעקב, יצחק, etc.

There is no need to emend רוקח to רָקַח (with LXX and the free reading of P and V), in spite of יֵין הָרְקַח (Can. 8:2). יקר is an Aramaism, "heavier," "weightier" (Rashi, Del.); cf. יקירה (Dan. 2:11). It occurs in another figurative sense, "grievous," in Ps. 116:15, where it also comes at the beginning of the clause, with the subject at the very end: יקר בעיני ה' המותה לחסידיו, "Grievous in the eyes of the Lord is the death of His loved ones." מחכמה מכבוד is lit. "more than wisdom in abundance." On this meaning of כבוד, cf. Isa. 10:3, where the noun means "wealth," and especially Isa. 5:13, where it means "multitude." So rendered, the phrase is a contrast to סכלות מעט, an advantage lacking in Levy's rendering, "than wisdom and wealth," and in that of Hertz., "than wisdom and honor."

The general theme is illustrated by 9:18b. The verse is to be rendered: "As dying flies befoul the container of perfumer's oil, so a little folly outweighs a wealth of wisdom."

Section XVII — Introductory Note

10:2 to 11:6. That the maxims in this section are appropriate to the work of a teacher of Wisdom is clear. Even an unconventional Hakam like Koheleth, whose career was the teaching of upper-class youth (see Intro.), would warn his charges against foolishness (vv. 2 f.), as well as against faint-heartedness and haste in the face of changing currents at court (v. 4), a theme on which he has subtly commented already in 8:5b. This fluctuation in fortune suggests to Koheleth the observation, particularly sad to a conservative, that an unstable society may give importance to upstarts and fools, while the rich and the well-born (the contrast is instructive) may lose their positions (vv. 5–7). He then warns against seeking to trap one's neighbor, since the evil may well recoil upon one's own head (vv. 8 f.).

The following verses are obscure. Apparently they urge the need to prepare beforetimes for any undertaking (10 f.). Koheleth then stresses the gift of skillful and concise speech (vv. 12–14a), the need of which is justified by one of his two fundamental premises: man cannot really know the future (v. 14b, c).

Another reflection on the fruitless exertions of the fool (v. 15) is succeeded by some observations on the character of good and evil rulers (vv. 16 f.). Following another proverb on laziness (v. 18), Koheleth emphasizes the importance of money (v. 19), to which he has referred elsewhere (7:11; 9:14 ff.), and the dangers involved in cursing the powers that be (v. 20), a theme he has also treated before (8:2, 4, 5). Both ideas are thoroughly congenial to the upper-class milieu in which Koheleth functioned. He differs from the conventional teachers of Wisdom in that he validates his opinion not by means of high-sounding phrases, but on the ground of prudence.

He then advises the merchant to scatter his possessions in various undertakings, since the future is both unsafe and uncertain (11:1 f.), and mere waiting for a favorable opportunity is foolish (vv. 3 f.). Koheleth is, however, always more than merely the teacher of practical Wisdom. The practical uncertainties of life recall the great mystery of existence, of which Koheleth never loses sight (vv. 5–6). It serves as the coda here, as in many sections of the book.

Del. a long time ago lamented: "How much time, thought and paper have been wasted, in order to connect this verse-group with the preceding!" (p. 366). Since his day, new attempts, like those of Levy and Hertz., cannot be described as successful. The former sees in the passage a warning against the fool who is too patient (10:2–11) and the fool who is too loud (12–20)!

The latter sees in the passage changes on the theme of the relativity of all mundane affairs. See our comments on the succeeding verses. That the connection is introduced by the exegete and is not in the text is obvious from the wide discrepancy in views.

The variety of subject matter and the lack of logical organization in this section are normal in Oriental Wisdom literature, as the Hebrew *Book of Proverbs* and the Egyptian *Maxims of Amenemope* demonstrate.

Some critics reject many of these verses as the work of the Hokmah glossator. Bar. thus deletes 12 out of 24 verses: 10:2, 3, 8–14a, 15, 18, 19. Ehr. actually doubts whether there is any authentic material from 10:8 to the end of the book! But this procedure rests upon a failure to grasp the full complexity of Koheleth's role; he was not merely an unconventional sage, but also, and principally, a Hakam, a professional teacher of Wisdom (cf. 12:9). Koheleth might quite properly create or reproduce maxims reflecting the accepted procedure for achieving worldly success and well-being. Several of these themes (vv. 4, 19, 20), as has been noted, he has himself discussed elsewhere. Other ideas he justifies from his own unique standpoint (10:14b, c; 11:2, 5). These passages are closely linked to the preceding, vv. 12–14a; 11:1, 2a, 3, 4, 6, and thus attest to their authenticity. His melancholy observations on the social and political order (5–7, 16 f.) are thoroughly in keeping with his point of view. Nor is there any good ground for rejecting the remaining passages which scorn the fool (vv. 2, 3, 12, 13, 14a, 15), oppose plotting (vv. 8, 9), and warn against laziness and inefficiency (vv. 10, 11, 18).

10:2. לב is "understanding, mind"; cf. Pr. 8:5 a. e., and the next verse. לימינו, "at his right," is figurative for "to his aid, support," just as "to his left" means "to his injury." This is in accordance with a widespread folk belief, doubtless based on the skill of the average right hand as against the awkwardness of the left. Cf. the German *recht*, English *right*, which both mean "correct, just," as well as Greek σκαιός, "awkward," ἀριστερός, "clumsy, ominous," Latin *sinistra*, French *gauche*, "awkward." The "right hand" of God is a saving instrument; Ex. 15:6, 12;

Isa. 41:10; Ps. 20:7; 21:9; 48:11. Cf. the name "Benjamin." In B. Shab. 63a a homiletic interpretation of Pr. 3:16 uses the denominative Hiphil verbs מיימינים and משמאילים in the sense of "study the Torah properly" and "improperly" respectively (see Rashi ad loc.); the Pual מיומן, "strongest, the right" (Hul. 91a). In our passage, the words do not have a moral connotation (ag. Del. Reuss, Now.), but a practical one. A fool, as the next verse suggests, relies on his own understanding and gets into trouble.

10:3. The Kethib כְּשֶׁהַסָּכָל and the Qere כְּשֶׂכָל are equally acceptable, since Koheleth fluctuates in the use of the article; cf. *OLQ*, pp. 81 ff. The Kethib may be preferable, as Pod. suggests, on euphonic grounds, as it separates the two sibilants.

LXX is the only possible witness among the ancient Versions to the use or absence of the article, since Aramaic and Syriac use the determinative status even for undeterminative nouns, while Latin has no article (ag. Hertz.). LXX reads the Qere here, thus bearing testimony to its existence as a variant in the text, since it is not to be assumed that the Kethib-Qere apparatus of the Masoretes was already in existence at so early a date. Cf. *BTM*, pp. 61 f. גם בדרך, "even on the road," doing nothing even when he is not engaged in some undertaking. ואמר is rendered "thinks" (by LXX, P, V), hence "He thinks that everyone is a fool" (V, Midrash ad loc., Levy). P vocalized סָכָל, "The fool is wise in his own eyes, and thus joins conceit to folly!" On the other hand, the first half of the verse would rather imply: "He announces to all that he himself is a fool" (so Tar. freely, Rashi, Ibn Ezra, Hertz.). Hence וְאָמַר is probably to be vocalized וְאָמַר (so LXX, P, V, T).

10:4. רוח, "anger"; cf. 7:9; Pr. 16:32; and Jud. 8:3, אז רפתה רוחם. The advice is identical with that in 8:3. מקום, "post, official position"; cf. I Ki. 20:24, likewise a late passage.

מרפא, which occurs also in the spelling מרפה in one passage (Jer. 8:15), may represent a confusion of the two related roots רפא, "heal," and רפה, "sink, relax," especially since ל"א and ל"י verbs tended to coalesce in later Hebrew, under Aramaic influence. Thus the noun means: 1) "healing, cure" (II Chr. 21:18; 36:16; Pr. 4:22; 6:15; 29:1); 2) "well-being" (Pr. 13:17; Jer.

14:19 par. to טוב); and 3) also "relaxation of spirit, calmness," particularly in Wisdom; cf. Pr. 12:18b, לשון חכמים מרפא, contrast stich a; 14:30, לב מרפא, "equable spirit," opp. קנאה; 15:4, מרפא לשון, "soothing tongue" (Toy). In our passage it means "calmness, composure" (so Hertz.). The theme is identical with 8:3; Pr. 16:14.

תַּנַּח and יַנִּיחַ are metaplastic forms of the Hiphil of נוח. תַּנַּח = "abandon" (Jer. 14:9; Ps. 119:121). יַנִּיחַ = "allay." On the semantic development, cf. the English "allay" from Old English alaien, allegen, "lay down, put down," which now means "assuage." Hence there is no need to revocalize as יַנִּיחַ (ag. Wild.), to derive the required sense.

Levy regards this verse as a quotation, citing the counsel of the "fool" who urges the stubborn retention of one's post even when the king is angry. But it is not likely that Koheleth would oppose this procedure. He advises it himself in 8:3. Hertz. comes to the opposite conclusion! He follows Luther and joins verse 4 to the preceding. While the fool quickly betrays his folly, a wise man will not be stampeded into panic by untoward developments at court. The absence of a connecting link in the passage does not militate against this view, as this is characteristic of Koheleth; cf. 11:3, 4. There is, however, too wide a gap in thought between the two verses to make this proposed contrast plausible. On the absence of connection among the proverbs of this group, see Intr. Note.

10:5. In כשגגה, the Kaph is not to be rendered "like, as," but "indeed." On this asseverative Kaph, which occurs also in Ugaritic and in such Biblical passages as Nu. 11:1; Isa. (Kethib) 10:13; 29:2c; Hos. 4:4c; 5:10; Obad. 1:11e; Ps. 119:9b; 122:3; Pr. 16:27b; Job 3:5c; Lam. 1:20; and Neh. 7:2, see *JAOS*, 63, 1943, pp. 176 ff. The entire clause is meaningless if the Kaph is regarded as comparative. When it is recognized as asseverative, its force is clear: the fluctuations in the structure of society which Koheleth laments as an evil (vv. 6, 7) are errors chargeable to the whims or prejudices of the ruler. There may be an ironic overtone in Koheleth's using שגגה for "error"; the word properly means "unwitting sin."

Here Hertz. finds a contrast to verse 4: There are times

when wisdom, however useful, does not avail. But this has to be read into the text. The effort to create continuity here must be pronounced more ingenious than convincing.

10:6. For סָכָל, "folly," LXX and V render "fool (i. e. סָכָל)," which is parallel to ועשירים, but the use of the abstract for the concrete is well attested (cf., inter alia, 9:18), and the MT is to be preferred on the principle of *difficilior lectio*.

The contrast of "fool" and "rich" is characteristic of Wisdom literature, which is generally opposed to social change. For examples in Hebrew Wisdom, see *SBWL*, esp. pp. 113 ff. In the Egyptian *Admonitions of a Prophet* (end of Old Kingdom), First Poem, the author laments: "Nay, but poor men now possess fine things, He who once made for himself no sandals, now possesseth riches" (Erman, *op. cit.*, p. 95).

Even more apposite for the contrast in our verse are the following lines from the Second Poem of the same composition (Erman, pp. 100 f.): "Behold a thing hath been done that hath not happened aforetimes. It is come to this that the king hath been taken away by *poor men.*

"Behold it is come to this that the land is despoiled of the kingship by a few *senseless people.*" (Italics ours)

בַּמְּרוֹמִים רַבִּים, "in the great heights." There is no need to revocalize as בִּמְרוֹמִים, because of the irregular use of the article throughout the book, as well as the fluctuating usage of Mishnaic Hebrew; cf. המערכה גדולה (Tamid 2:4). There is Biblical warrant for these variations in such passages as הגפן נכריה (Jer. 2:21), הגוים רבים (Ez. 39:27), etc.; cf. M. H. Segal, *Dikduk*, sec. 85; *OLQ*, pp. 81 ff. Verses 6 and 7 are not in chiastic, but in alternate parallelism, 6a being parallel to 7a and 6b to 7b (ag. Hertz.).

10:8. The theme of verses 8 f. is common in popular apothegms; cf. Ps. 7:16; 9:16; Pr. 26:27; Ben Sira 23:26. It is not strange that it is paralleled in Egyptian literature (cf. Humbert, pp. 53, 121). Hertz. interprets these verses here in involved fashion to mean that all things are relative, and that positive acts may lead to negative consequences. But the simple meaning is thoroughly appropriate to Koheleth's role as a Wisdom teacher, who enjoins care and circumspection in all the affairs of life.

גומץ is an Aramaism, "pit," occurring in the Targum of Pr. 22:14; 23:27 for שוחה and of 26:27 for שחת.

10:9. יעצב, from עצב, "be sad," develops the meaning "be (physically) hurt," as the root צער, "grieve," develops the sense "be ill, suffer" (physically) in Rabbinic Hebrew; המצטער פטור מן הסוכה (B. Sukkah 26a). On this use of עצב, cf. Gen. 3:16 f., עצב and עצבון. The verb occurs, we believe, in another Biblical passage, Zc. 11:16, where הַנִּצָּבָה is a defective spelling for הַנֶּעֱצָבָה, "the injured one"; cf. *RBRH*, pp. 189 f.

יסכן is also late Hebrew, a denominative from סכנה, "danger" (Ibn Ezra).

10:10. In this crux, the Masorah notes the Oriental reading לו for לא, which P reproduces and perhaps LXX (if αὐτῷ fell out after αὐτός). The Vss. render variously, but do not always make sense themselves! V, reading לא (לו) פנים for לא לְפָנִים, and P, וחללים for וחילים, are not helpful. See the full discussion in Ginsburg, ad loc.; however, he does not recognize that LXX and P follow the Oriental reading here. Similarly, R. Ammi's Haggadic interpretation of this verse in Taanith 7b does not disregard the negative, as H. Malter, *The Treatise Taanit of the B. T.* (Phila., 1928, p. 49, n. 115), believes, but is based also on the Madinhae text לו. For other evidence of Oriental readings in the Babylonian Talmud, which have been overlooked, cf. *BTM*, p. 77.

The same divergence, both with regard to the general sense of the verse and to the detailed exegesis, is apparent in the medieval and modern commentators. The following meanings have been suggested, among others: 1) "Wisdom is more powerful even than iron weapons"; cf. 9:18 (Rashi). 2) "Wisdom is better than labor" (Ibn Ezra). 3) "When the iron has not been whetted, more strength is needed" (so variously Luther, AV, Bar.). 4) "In resisting tyranny with inadequate means, the rebel succeeds only in strengthening the army of the tyrant" (Gins.). 5) "It is wise to use one's talents at the right time" (Hitz. Wild., Levy). 6) Reading for the last clause הַכְשִׁרוֹן וְיִתְרוֹן חָכְמָה, Hertz. renders: "When the iron becomes dull, and no one has sharpened the edge, and one must use all one's

strength, is there then any profit or advantage to wisdom?"
The proposed reading, however, is unhebraic. It would necessarily have been something like הַכִּשְׁרוֹן וְיִתְרוֹן לַחָכְמָה, and besides,
the use of כשרון in this sense is doubtful; cf. on 5:10. 7) Reading
וְהוּא לֹא קִלְקְלוֹ, "he did not sharpen it," and ואין יתרון וכשרון חכמה,
"there is no profit or gain to wisdom" (Gal.), but this is linguistically dubious. 8) Render: "Can the iron become blunt,
if no one ruined the edge?", on the basis of the common Mishnaic
qilqel, "ruin" (H. Hirschberg). This interpretation, however,
is not in harmony with the context and requires other deletions
and transpositions in the text, as Hirschberg recognizes.

The suggested view here is advanced very tentatively:
קָהָה, Piel, is intransitive (cf. וְכִהֲתָה כָל־רוּחַ, Ez. 21:12), perhaps
because the verb may contain an attenuated vowel, and is
equivalent to the Pual קֻהָה; cf. מֻדָּד, Job 7:4, and S. Pinsker,
Mabo' Lannikkud Ha'ashuri, p. 153; Rabinowitz-Obronin, *Job*
(Tel-Aviv, 1916), p. 19.

ברזל = lit. "iron, tool of iron, axe"; cf. Deut. 27:5; Josh. 8:31;
Pr. 27:17; Isa. 10:34.

והוא = "a man, someone"; cf. the identical use in Job 13:28.
It may occur also in Job 8:16, where הוא introduces a new subject,
the righteous (vv. 16–19), as against the wicked described above
(vv. 12–15).

פנים is generally given the meaning "edge," on the slender
basis of Ez. 21:21 and the use of פי חרב for "edge of a sword."
It may perhaps be rendered with Gins. = לפנים, "beforehand"
(cf. V, *ut prius*).

קלקל, a quadriliteral from קלל, "polish" (Ez. 1:7; Dan.
10:6), hence "sharpen."

וחילים יגבר, "then he must exert his strength"; the Vav introduces the apodosis after אם. On this usage, cf. the next verse;
Ex. 19:5; 23:22; and *BDB*, p. 254b. On the idiom, cf. גברו חיל
(Job 21:7), "grow in strength"; here the Piel gives the clause
transitive force: "he must increase his force." ויתרון הכשיר חכמה
is emended by some to ויתרון חכמה הכשיר, "the advantage of
wisdom lies in preparing" (BH), or to ויתרון הַכָּשֵׁר חָכְמָה, "the
advantage of the skillful one is wisdom" (BH). In view of the
difficulties that still remain, it is best to retain the MT, and

render, against the accents which link the first two words: "It is an advantage to prepare one's skill in advance."

On כשר, cf. the frequent Rabbinic use of the verb in the sense "make fit," "prepare," as e. g. in Mid. Gen. Rab., sec. 56, the slaughtering knife is called *ma'akeleth* לפי שמכשרת את האוכלין, "because it readies the food for eating," and especially with regard to Levitical impurity, B. Hul. 35b, וכי הדם מכשיר, "does the blood render it fit for ritual impurity?" חכמה is here used as "technical skill"; cf. its use for the pursuits of the architect (Ex. 28:3; 31:3; 35:10; 36:8), the weaver (Ex. 35:25), the metal refiner (Jer. 10:9), and the sailor (Ez. 27:8; Ps. 107:27).

The entire verse is to be rendered: "If an axe is blunt, and a man does not sharpen it beforehand, then he must exert all his strength to wield it, but it is an advantage to prepare one's skill in advance." The theme is the virtue of being prepared for any given task — a typical maxim of prudence, of which there are many in this section. See Intr. Note and the following verses.

10:11. בלא לחש means lit. "without a charm," i. e. "before it is charmed"; cf. Job 15:32, בלא יומו, "before his day." This may mean either that the charm is used to make the snake bite or to ward off the biting (Ra. Bar.). In either event, once the snake has bitten, the charmer's art is useless. There is no use locking the stable after the horse is stolen. The verse thus offers another illustration of the importance of being prepared beforehand, and thus is linked with the preceding, even though there is no connecting word. On this characteristic of Koheleth's style in proverbs, cf. 7:4a, 8b; 11:4. Ibn Ezra and the Vulgate refer the verse to the slanderer; cf. the denominative verb *lašan*, Ps. 101:5; Pr. 30:10.

On the Vav of ויתרון, introducing the apodosis, cf. on 10:10.

10:12. תבלענו, fem. sing. after the feminine plural verb תשיגהו כמים בלהות; cf. Job 27:20, שפתות.

10:14. מה שיהיה is read as מה שָׁהָיָה by LXX, V, P, Sym.; it is accepted by Eur. Nonetheless, MT is to be preferred on several grounds. First, we should have expected, linguistically, that Koheleth, who writes late Hebrew, would, in referring to past events, use not the imperfect לא יֵדַע, which he uses exclusively to refer to the future (8:5, 5; 9:12), but the participle, which is his favorite tense for referring to general truths (6:8; 8:1, 7; 9:1; 11:5, 6). Second, it is not true that man does not know the past, to some extent at least. Third, the burden of Koheleth's complaint is the lack of knowledge of the future, so that the emphasis is not misplaced. Fourth, our verse is almost identical with 8:7, where the Versions reproduce the MT, with both halves referring exclusively to the future. Koheleth is saying that man does not know the events of tomorrow which represent the culmination of his own efforts, nor is there a comrade to tell him what happens after he is gone. From a more personal and emotional basis, the same theme is stressed in Job 14:21, "His children may grow great, but he will not know it, or decline, and he will be unaware of it."

There is, accordingly, no reason for accepting the reading of LXX, or for assuming, as does Levy, that the words . . . לא ידע מאחריו are a quotation of the fool's meaningless chatter.

10:15. The feminine verb after the subject עמל, which is elsewhere always masculine, would imply that the noun is common in gender. Ibn Ezra calls attention to כבוד, which is always masculine, except in Gen. 49:6. Cf. also המון, feminine only in Job 31:34 and Ecc. 5:9 (cf. ad loc.). The singular suffix on the verb is distributive, especially since both the singular suffix and the plural in הכסילים are here used generically; cf. Deut. 21:10; 28:48; Hos. 4:8; Zc. 14:12; Ps. 5:10 for the distributive use, and for this generic use, Isa. 5:23, וצדקת צדיקים יסירו ממנו, and Ges.-K., sec. 145, 5, note.

As is to be expected, the Vss. "level" the difficulties, LXX translating the verse entirely in the singular, V and P entirely in the plural. Ehr. (so also Budde, Hertz.) reads עֲמַל הַכְּסִיל מָתַי יְיַגְּעֶנּוּ, "When will the fool's labor (in idle chatter) tire him?"

The second half of the verse bears the unmistakable sign of an idiom, the precise sense of which now eludes us, like the similar phrase in 4:13, אשר לא ידע להזהר עוד. The words "Who does not know how to go to the city" seem to imply extreme stupidity, like the English colloquialism, "He does not know enough to come in out of the rain." Gr. thinks of the Essenes who avoided cities (Josephus, *Ant.*, XVIII, 1, 5). Levy refers to the Talmudic tale of the traveler who asked a lad, "By which way can we get to the city?" (Erub. 53b). Wild. interprets it to mean that asking a fool for directions is wasted effort. The difficulties of stich b are not solved by Ehr.'s view that עיר means "angel" (Dan. 4:10, 14, 20), or by Hertz., who separates the two halves of the verse and assigns them to separate sections. Cf. on verse 16.

An interesting parallel to our passage not hitherto noted may be adduced. In Babylonia, "the reproach 'they had no king' and 'knew not a city' had been used against the invaders with the plain implication that they were barbarians" (Gadd, in *Myth and Ritual*, ed. S. H. Hooke, p. 44). The resemblance to our verse and to the following, which refers to an unworthy king, is striking. It suggests that Koheleth may here be describing various types of "uncivilized behavior."

Our passage seems to say that the fool grows tired even when, knowing nothing, he accomplishes nothing.

10:16. For ארץ, LXX, followed by P, renders עיר, but this is unquestionably an error induced by v. 15b, an instance of "leveling" on the part of the translators.

Drinking in the morning was opposed as a sign of dissolute-ness. Cf. Isa. 5:11; Acts 2:15; and classical sources like Cicero, *Philippic* II, 41, *Ab hora tertia bibebatur, ludebatur, vomebatur*, "From the third hour, i. e. nine o'clock, they would drink, gamble and vomit up their food (to be able to gorge themselves anew)"; Juvenal, *Satires*, i, 49 f.; Catullus, *Carmen*, 47, 11, 5 f.

נער, "youth, child, even infant" (Ex. 2:6; I Sam. 1:24), by a natural extension of meaning, develops the connotation "inexperienced, foolish," as in Pr. 1:4, where it is parallel to פתאים, "fools." On a parallel semantic development of פתי, "fool," and فتى, "youth," and רובה in both meanings, see "Note on Job 26:3," in *Jewish Forum*, October, 1945, p. 1.

Hertz. adds 15b as a second stich here, thus creating a tristich in verse 16 as in verse 17. He renders:

> "Woe to thee, O land whose king is a child,
> And does not yet know how to go to the city,
> And whose princes feast in the morning."

אִי as an interjection does not occur elsewhere in Biblical Hebrew except above in 4:10. אִי כָבוֹד in I Sam. 4:21 may originally have been a theophorous name (cf. אִיזבל), but it is regarded by the Biblical writer as the negative particle, hence "inglorious" (נלה כבוד מישראל). The interjection is common in Rabbinic Hebrew, and need not be emended to אוֹי (ag. Ehr.); cf. B. Taanith 7a, אי חכמה; B. Rosh Hashanah 19a, אי שמים, a. e.

Levy (pp. 32, 126) regards vv. 16–19 as a satiric poem written against the five-year-old Ptolemy V Epiphanes, a literary genre characteristic of the mockery-loving Alexandrians, and thus concludes that Koheleth left Palestine and settled in Egypt. Since there is no reference to the revolt against Ptolemy's regent Agathocles, the book must have been ended before 203 B. C. E. This is a considerable structure to raise on a few proverbial utterances, and the context does not gain in unity from this gratuitous assumption. On the so-called Greek elements and the date of Koheleth, see Intro.

10:17. אַשְׁרֵיךְ, instead of אַשְׁרַיִךְ, is a petrified form used as an interjection, derived from the common form אַשְׁרֵי (Ges.-K., sec. 91b).

For בן חורים, Winckler (*Alt-Orientalische Forschungen*, II, 1898, p. 147), followed by Zap. and Hertz., reads בן בחורים, "a young man," as a contrast to נער. But see our note on נער above. Besides, there is no abstract noun בחורים meaning "youth"; Nu. 11:28, משרת משה מבחריו, usually cited as an example of this assumed word, is, however, highly doubtful, and probably means "of his chosen ones" or "of his young men" (so LXX, V, Samaritan Pentateuch, which read בחיריו). The abstract noun is בחורות, and is used in Koheleth only (11:9; 12:1). Were this Koheleth's intent, he would naturally have used, as indeed H. Hirschberg proposes, שמלכך בחור as a contrast to מלכך נער, a word common in Biblical and post-Biblical Hebrew (cf. Isa. 62:5; I Sam. 9:2; and below in 11:9). The MT is to be retained, both because it is attested by all the Vss., and because it is in harmony with the social background of the book. The phrase בן חורים means lit. "the son of nobles, nobly born." The late Hebrew חורים, frequent in Neh. (cf. 2:16; Jer. 27:20; I Ki. 21:8, 11) and meaning "nobles," is derived from the Semitic root חרר, Arabic حر, "Be or be set free," Syriac אחב, "set free," late Hebrew בן חורין, "free man." Ehr.'s rendering, "A free-man, not dependent upon his advisor," does not commend itself. A worthy king, in Koheleth's opinion, is one who is born to his position, not "a slave who becomes a king which the earth cannot bear," according to Pr. 30:21 f. The upper-class viewpoint of these passages is clear, but they represent a true understanding of human nature nevertheless. בגבורה, lit. "in (or for) strength," is generally taken to mean "for replenishing their vigor." F. Zimmermann has argued that the word is a mistranslation of the Syriac בחוסנא, "in moderation." But this translation-hypothesis is generally untenable, and unnecessary here. Cf. Chapter VII above and notes 12 and 22. If the meaning "self-control" be required here, it would easily develop from "strength"; cf. Pr. 16:32, איזהו גבור הכובש, and ומשל ברוחו מלכד עיר Aboth 4:1, את יצרו. Cf. JQR, vol. 35, 1945, p. 26; OLQ, pp. 73 f.; and "Koheleth — Hebrew or Aramaic," in JBL. P interprets the sense as בכשירותא = "properly."

בשתי = "for drunkenness"; cf. שְׁתִיָּה, Est. 1:8, and בְּכִי and בְּכִיָה. LXX "and not to be ashamed" = בֹּשֶׁת, if it is not rendering freely; cf. for example V ad luxuriam!

10:18. Wild., followed by Hertz. in the effort to establish continuity of context, regards the house as a figure for the state! This is far-fetched.

For the hapax legomenon בעצלתים some read either בְּעַצְלָת (cf. Pr. 31:27) or בעצלות ידים (BH). The dual form may have been induced by ידים in the second stich (Ibn Ezra). On the other hand, it is more likely that the dual is to be construed as an intensive; cf. the common use of דלתים ובריח (I Sam. 23:7; Jer. 49:31); cf. also Deut. 3:5; Isa. 45:1; Job 38:8, 10; and such forms as the proper names כושן רשעתים (Jud. 3:8, 10) and מרתים (Jer. 50:21) and perhaps צהרים (Del. Wr. Bar. BDB). The use of the plural of an abstract noun in LXX and V testifies to the dual of MT.

מְקָרֶה, "beam-work, ceiling," has various forms in Biblical and Rabbinic Hebrew: קוֹרָה (Gen. 19:8); תִּקְרָה (B. Metz. 117a), whence the denominative verb קָרָה (Ps. 104:3, a. e.). שפלות ידים, lit. "lowering of the hands," is a vivid phrase for "slackness, inactivity." The word שפלות is then used in the same sense; cf. B. Sotah 48a and the Aramaic Targum on Jer. 49:24 and P here. דלף = "flow." The noun דֶּלֶף is used of the drip of rain (Pr. 19:13; 27:15).

10:19. לשחוק, "for laughter, i. e. for pleasure." Levy attributes a sexual connotation to the word here, "licentiousness." While the cognate root צחק is so interpreted in Rabbinic literature, this usage is exclusively homiletic; cf. Midrash Gen. Rabbah 53:11, where Gen. 21:9 is interpreted אין מצחק אלא גלוי עריות, but even in the Midrash this view is followed by others which refer the verb to idolatry and murder.

עשים לחם is a late idiom for "make a feast"; cf. Ez. 4:15. The plural is impersonal.

חיים is rendered "the living" by the Vss. The verb שמח has either a personal object (e. g. Isa. 56:7; Jer. 20:15) or לב (Pr. 15:30; 27:9, etc.). However, the noun may be the plural of חַיָּה, "soul," like נֶפֶשׁ, which means the seat of animal appetite (cf. Job 38:39), and thus may be rendered "the soul" (cf. Ps. 143:3; Job 33:18, 20, 22, 28; 36:14; Ez. 7:13).

Aside from the general fluctuation in the use of the article in Koheleth, to which attention has been called, the use of the article here with *keseph*, after its absence with *sehok, lehem* and *yayin*, gives the noun emphasis: "but it is money that provides it all!"

יענה is a stumbling block to the Vss. LXX ἐπακούσεται, "hear" (on ἐπακούω as an equivalent for ענה, cf. Gen. 30:33; Hos. 2:23). This is corrected by Schleusner according to the Complutensian Bible to ὑπακούσεται, "answer, obey, submit." V *et pecuniae obediunt omnia*. Both renderings are derived from ענה, "submit" (cf. Ex. 10:3; Isa. 53:7; Ps. 119:107). P gives a conflate, וכספא ממסך ומענא, which expresses a truth all its own: "Money crushes and tortures them in everything." T יסהיד עליהון, from ענה, "testify." The meaning of יענה here is "provides," lit. "answers for," as in 5:19 and Gen. 41:16; Hos. 2:23 f. See note on 5:19.

10:20. במדעך is emended to בְּמַצָּעֲךָ, "your couch," by Perles in order to make it parallel to בחדרי משכבך (so Ehr.). On the other hand, M. Seidel (in the Hebrew journal *Debir*, vol. 1,

Berlin, 1923, p. 33) suggests that מדע itself means "study chamber," and cites Targum on Ps. 68:13, מלכותא עם חיליהון אטלטלו מן פלטריהון וחכימיא אטלטלו מן מדעיהון. L. Koehler, *Lexicon*, s. v., interprets it to mean "bed-room" on the basis of the sexual connotation of *yada'*.

The best view of the noun is to render it "in your mind, thought" (so Vss., most comm.). Levy points out the thought-sequence: "A *king* is not to be cursed even in *thought*; while a *rich man* whose power is less (and whose spies are less ubiquitous) not in the privacy of *one's bed-chamber*."

The accepted view "mind" is not mere hyperbole like the "hundred" in 6:3 or the "two thousand" in 6:6! What is in a man's mind may emerge in sleep (cf. the next stich), or may otherwise be blurted out in an unguarded moment, as experience taught long before Freud's *Psychopathology of Everyday Life* supplied a theoretical explanation. Hence the accepted rendering is to be preferred. On the theme, cf. the proverb אזנים לכותל, *Lev. Rab.*, ch. 32; *Koheleth R.* ad loc.; *Midrash Tillim*, ch. 7; and the French proverb "les murailles ont des oreilles," the German "die Wände haben Ohren," etc.

On the Qere כנפים as against the Kethib הכנפים, cf. the variations in the use of the article — הקול and דבר. Hertz. finds it "incomprehensible" that the Qere deletes the article in the Kethib; the answer is that the Qere is not a correction, but a variant reading. See *BTM*, pp. 15–39. On בעל הכנפים, cf. Dan. 8:6, 20, בעל הקרנים.

11:1. This famous passage was traditionally referred to the practice of charity (T, Rashi, Gins. Kn. Wr. Ehr.), like Goethe's lines in the *West-östlicher Diwan*, which may be based on our passage: "Was willst du untersuchen, Wohin die Milde fliesst? Ins Wasser wirf deine Kuchen — Wer weiss, wer sie geniesst?"

In favor of this view an Arabic proverb is adduced from Diaz' *Merkwürdigkeiten von Asien*. The proverb is the culmination of a story about Mohammed ben Hassan, who daily threw loaves into the water and thus saved the life of the adopted son of the Caliph, Mutawakkal, who had been shipwrecked. Mohammed saw in it the proof of a proverb he had learned as a boy, "Do good, cast thy bread upon the waters, and one day thou shalt be rewarded." But Barton recognizes that the proverb may be an echo of this verse in Koheleth. It therefore follows that the saying attests to the *traditional* interpretation of our verse, and not necessarily to its authentic meaning. What is more, this reference to liberality is not in keeping with Koheleth's general outlook, nor is it relevant to the realistic tone of the section in which it occurs.

Hence, most modern comm. regard it as advice with regard to commerce (Mich. Död. Mend., Del. Wr.): "Send your goods overseas," where the profits are likely to be large, while the next verse urges diversifying one's undertakings to reduce the attendant risks. This is, by all odds, the most likely view of the passage.

Hertz., after a lengthy discussion, renders כי in v. 1 f. as "though," and interprets the passage as underscoring the uncertainty of life: "Cast your bread upon the waters (a total loss), yet you may find it; carefully divide and husband your possessions, yet evil may come and destroy them." Even less likely is Levy: "Send your capital overseas — out of Alexandria."

11:2. The use of consecutive numbers as a literary device is common in Biblical literature, and has many Semitic analogies. Often the ascending series is followed by a list equal to the larger number, as e. g. "three" and "four" in Pr. 30:15, 18, 21, 29, "six" and "seven" in Pr. 6:16. At other times, as in our passage, no such enumeration follows, and the numbers are used to indicate "several." Cf. "three" and "four" in Amos 1:3, 6, 9, 11, 13; 2:4, etc., and "seven" and "eight" in Mi. 5:4.

The v. does not refer to spreading one's charities, but to avoiding "putting all one's eggs into one basket." The reason is clear: one cannot tell "what will be evil upon the earth," or where disaster will strike.

11:3, 4. LXX and P follow the Masoretic division after נשם, but V attaches נשם to the following. Rhythmically, the first view is preferable, since in Hebrew metrics the shorter stich normally follows after the longer (except at the end of a poem or section; cf. *MHHH*, pp. 142 ff.).

יהוא is an anomalous form, for which 4 mss. read הוא. MT may perhaps intend יְהוּא or יְהֱוֶה, "will be" (so BH). The Vss.

naturally translate "will be." The late Hebrew form would be יְהָא. The form may be a conflate of שָׁם הוּא (cf. Job 3:19 in another sense) and שָׁם יִהְיֶה. On conflates as a Masoretic device for preserving variants, cf. *BTM*, pp. 40 ff.

The intent of the verse has been conceived variously: 1) Man's weakness and his inability to change the laws of nature (Del. Hertz.). V. 4 is then taken to mean that there is no value in practising magical arts with the clouds or the winds (McN. Bar.). But their reference to Hos. 4:12, עַמִּי בְּעֵצוֹ יִשְׁאָל, is irrelevant, for there the tree (or the rod) is the instrument, not the object, of magical intervention. 2) As a protest against cowards, who put off any activity because conditions will surely change of themselves by-and-by (Levy).

It has not been noted that vv. 3 and 4 stand in a chiastic relation to each other, 3a and 4b both being concerned with the clouds and rain, while 3b and 4a refer to the effects of the wind. The latter is mentioned in 4a and implied in 3b, which deals with a tree falling. For other examples of chiasmus, see Hos. 2:21 f.; 8:14b–c; Pr. 1:5; 23:15 f.; Job 20:3 f.; Lam. 2:13; and cf. *JThS*, vol. 1934, pp. 163 f., and *MHHH*, pp. 152 ff. The meaning is now clear: As in vv. 5 and 6, Koheleth is here urging the importance of energetic labor for success. Hence, there is no use for the farmer to postpone his labor, waiting for the propitious rains or the favorable winds. The processes of nature follow the laws of their being, without needing the help of man or being responsive to his desires. To make the connection clear, we have added to v. 4 the words: "Therefore, on with your work!"

שמר, "watches, waits for"; cf. I Sam. 19:11; Ps. 130:5; Job 24:15.

11:5. Koheleth here calls attention to the greatest miracle of all, the origin of life, which remains a mystery, and is therefore symbolic of the mystery of the world, of which he is always conscious. The genesis of man in the womb was a source of wonder to the ancient Hebrews; cf. Ps. 139:13–16; Job 10:11 f.; II Macc. 7:22; and Koheleth R. 5:10.

For כאשר, LXX and P (but not V, T) read באשר, "since, inasmuch as," but the MT is vouched for by the correlative

כבה, "just as . . . so." רוח, lit. "breath," is the symbol and sign
of life, and hence may be rendered "the spirit of life"; cf. 3:21
and Gen. 6:17; 7:15; Ez. 37:5, and *passim*. See note on 8:8.

The sheva under the first Beth in בְּבֶטֶן makes the noun a construct, so that it is generally rendered lit. "the belly of a pregnant
woman" (so LXX, V, and P, which has evidently suffered contraction in this passage). On this use of מלאה, cf. Yeb. 16:1,
יצתה מלאה, the Latin *plena* (Ovid, *Metam.* x. 465), and in a related
sense Ruth 1:21. On the other hand, Ibn Ezra suggests that
מלאה may be an adjective modifying בטן, which is feminine, and
for the vocalization he compares לְאִישׁ הֶעָשִׁיר, II Sam. 12:4. We
may add יום הששי, Gen. 1:31; cf. also I Sam. 25:10; Jer. 46:49, a. e.
The use of a determinative adjective with an undeterminative
noun is exceedingly common in Mishnaic Hebrew; cf. מים הרעים
(Aboth 1:11); נפש היפה (Hul. 4:7); and see Segal, *Dikduk*, sec.
86, 1, 2. Hence the phrase means "the pregnant stomach."

כעצמים, though so read by LXX, V, P, must be read as
בעצמים (so Tar. Ehr. BH, Levy, Pod. Zap.). If two distinct
comparisons were being introduced in the verse, such as the
wind or spirit *and* the organs of a foetus (so Hertz.), a copula
would have been required, such as וכעצמים, and even then the
text would be unsatisfactory, since the two comparisons are by
no means parallel.

The plural of עצם is used to denote the entire organism; cf.
Isa. 66:14; Ps. 6:3; Pr. 3:8; 14:30, the singular in Pr. 15:30;
16:24; and *BDB*, s. v., sec. d. Here it denotes "the embryo."

11:6. Because of the proximity of this verse to the preceding
and the use of זרע, the Talmud (B. Yeb. 62b), the Midrash and
Gr. refer it to the begetting of children in one's early and one's
later years. The reference to birth in v. 5, however, is purely
for purposes of comparison; the essential meaning of the passage (cf. n. on vv. 3, 4) is a warning against indolence. This is
a popular theme of the Wisdom teachers, which Koheleth
validates in terms of the unpredictability of the future. Hence
it is best interpreted literally as urging diligence in one's work.

Against Sieg.'s observation that it does not matter whether
one sows in the morning or in the evening, Levy cites the second
part of the *Works and Days* of Hesiod, who advises when to sow

and build. Koheleth may be using this widespread superstition to urge steady and unremitting attention to the tasks in hand, if one is to attain success. Or the reference to "morning" and "evening" may be metaphorical, meaning "all the time."

כשר, "be proper, succeed," a late Hebrew word; cf. 10:10; Est. 8:5.

כאחד, which was not understood by LXX, is an Aramaism (=כַּחֲדָה, Dan. 2:35; כחדא, Targum on Gen. 13:6) occurring in late Hebrew and meaning "together, altogether" (Isa. 65:25; Ezra 2:64; 3:9; 6:20; Neh. 7:66; II Chr. 5:13). Here it is used to denote "equally, lit. like one another"; cf. P, איך חד.

Section XVIII — Introductory Note

11:7 to 12:8. As Koheleth approaches the climax of his thought, the passion of his feelings converts his prose into rhythmic beats. As in Biblical and Semitic verse generally, no single meter is used exclusively. The section begins with two-beat stichs (vv. 7, 8), then goes over into three beats (vv. 9, 10). Beginning with 12:1, the Kinah rhythm becomes more pronounced, the melancholy echo-effect being achieved by having the opening stich longer than the following, either through more beats per stich (4:3 and 3:2) or through more syllables within the same number of beats. On these principles of Hebrew metrics, cf. *MHHH* passim, especially pp. 141–46.

Recognizing that the meter cannot always be determined with certainty, we submit the following summary of the facts:

$$11:7 - 2:2:2$$
$$11:8 - 2:2:2: \parallel 2:2:2^1$$
$$11:9 - 3:3:3:3:3:3^2$$

[1] The opening stichs a and d have more syllables than the succeeding stichs.

[2] *Bīmei bᵉḥūrōtekhā*, in spite of its length, receives one beat, because it corresponds in idea to *beyaldutekha*; cf. for example Ps. 114:1, where *me'am lo'ez*, being parallel to *mimmiṣráyim*, receives only one beat; and see also Nu. 23:7; Isa. 1:4; Mi. 6:7; and *MHHH*, p. 141. *Ubhmarei 'einekhā* probably receives three beats. If not, we have a 3:2 rhythm in the center of this verse.

11:10 — 3:3:3
12:1 — 4:3 ‖ 3:3[3]
12:2 — 3:3:3[4]
12:3 — 3:3 ‖ 3:3[5]
12:4 — 3:3:3:3
12:5 — 3:2 ‖ 2:2:2 ‖ 4:3
12:6 — 4:3:3:3
12:7 — 4:4
12:8 — 2:2:2

Obviously, arguments for deletion and emendation based on metric considerations (as in Hertz.) are unacceptable, particularly in a passage exhibiting such marked variations in structure.

In this passage, 11:9e, 10c and 12:1a have often been deleted as a Hasid's glosses (so Bar.), a procedure based upon an erroneous exegesis and failure to penetrate to the spirit and style of Koheleth. See Intro. and notes on these individual verses, as well as Intr. Note on 12:1 ff.

11:7. On the Vav as introducing a new theme in Koheleth, see 3:16; 4:4; 7:26; 8:10; 12:1. On the idea, cf. Euripides, *Iphigenia in Aulis*, l. 1219: ἡδὺ γὰρ τὸ φῶς. There is no real likelihood of borrowing, merely a coincidence in the work of two great writers. We may also compare the *Gilgamesh Epic*, Tablet X, col. 1, line 13: "Let my eyes see the sun, that I may be sated with light." For stich b, P reads ויתיר לחזי שמשא, an interpolation from 7:11, inserted after the original rendering fell out.

11:8. את ימי החשך is an instance of "anticipation," hence to be rendered: "let him remember that the days of darkness will be many." ימי החשך cannot mean "old age" (ag. Ehr.), for there is no warrant that they will be many! חשך is an epithet for "death"; cf. 6:4; I Sam. 2:9; Job 10:21; 17:13; 18:18; Ps. 88:13;

---

[3] Stich b may contain four beats rather than three, a view which gives the verse a 4:4 ‖ 3:3 pattern instead. On the other hand, if *bīmei beḥūrōtekhā* here were to receive one beat, as in 11:9 (cf. note 2 above), the verse would have a 3:3 ‖ 3:3 meter.

[4] The first stich has more syllables.

[5] *Bayyom* introduces the theme by anacrusis, which is outside the rhythm-pattern; cf. Ps. 1:1, *'ašrei ha'iš*.

Pr. 20:20. כל שבא הבל, "everything that follows is worthless, nothingness"; cf. הבאות, Isa. 41:22; מכאן ולהבא (B. Sanh. 27a), "from the present to the future"; and the common phrase לעתיד לבוא.

As far as the individual is concerned, death ends all. The basic concern of Wisdom with the happiness of the individual is not qualified in Koheleth by identification either with one's people or with posterity (cf. 1:11; 4:16; 9:15) or with one's family (cf. 2:18 ff., 21; 7:26 ff.). The final clause is not a moralizing phrase, "when a man understands that the days of darkness are coming, all the pleasures of life will become worthless in his eyes" (Ibn Ezra), but, on the contrary, a justification for seeking enjoyment in this world.

11:9. While the Beth of בילדותך and בימי may be construed as introducing the object of שמח (cf. II Sam. 13:28; Est. 1:10, השמח בחלקו; כטוב לב המלך ביין, Aboth 4:1; so Ehr.), it is better taken temporally: "in the time of your youth" (so most comm.).

בחרות here and in 12:1, "youth"; cf. נעורים (Isa. 54:6, a. e.) and נעורות (Jer. 32:30).

והלך בדרכי לבך ובמראי עיניך. The heart and the eyes are the organs of desire against which the conventional moralists warned: "That ye may not go after your eyes and after your hearts, after which ye are wont to go astray" (Num. 15:39). For Koheleth, the enjoyment of life becomes the highest dictate of life. See Intro. The Egyptian *Instruction of Ptah-hotep* (2870–2675 B. C. E.) counsels: "Follow thy heart so long as thou livest" (Erman, op. cit., p. 58).

The Kethib וּבְמַרְאֵי is a plural, for which cf. Dan. 1:15; Can. 2:14 ("face, appearance"). In the abstract sense of "sight," "desire," it does not occur elsewhere. Hence the singular in the Qere is generally preferred. The plural may have been induced by the proximity of the plural בדרכי; cf. the form מוֹבָא (II Sam. 3:25, Qere; Ez. 43:11), an assonance with מוֹצָא. See B. M. Lewin, זווג מלים בתנ״ך, many of whose instances, however, must be used with caution.

On מראה עינים as "sight (and enjoying) of the eyes," cf. Ecc. 6:9 and ראה בטוב in 2:1 and elsewhere.

The Vav of ודע has been generally taken as adversative,

"but know," thus introducing a warning note against the perils of pleasure (so most recently Hertz.). Most modern commentators have regarded the clause as the gloss of a Hasid (McN. Bar. Budde Volz). Actually, the Vav is consecutive (so LXX, V, P, Gr. Levy), and it introduces the heart of Koheleth's viewpoint, "and know that for all these God will bring you to judgment, i. e. for all the joys which He has extended to you and which it is His will that you enjoy." The authenticity of the clause is today increasingly being recognized (Zap. Pod. Levy, Gr. Ode., Kuhn, Hertz.), on varying and not always convincing grounds.

For this use of a religious vocabulary to express an unconventional viewpoint, which is characteristic of Koheleth, see Intro. and notes on such passages as 2:26; 5:18, 19; 7:18; 9:7. It is, however, not limited to Koheleth; see Pr. 23:19; Ben Sira 14:11; and such Talmudic utterances as P. Kiddushin, end; B. Erubin 54a; B. Nedarim 10a, and parallels, cited in the Intro.

That this stylistic usage may have led pious readers astray into regarding these passages as moralistic, and thus helped to win a place for the book in the canon, is very possible, but it is not likely that Koheleth chose this mode of expression with this purpose in mind, as Levy suggests. The entire conception of a canon of the Hagiographa, by the side of the Torah and the Prophets, was still in process of crystallization when Koheleth lived, and he could not have expected that his contemporary reflections would ever be admitted to the company of ancient and hallowed works. Cf. the Prologue to the Greek version of Ben Sira (132 B. C. E.), which speaks of "the Law, the Prophets and the others who followed after them," and again "the other books of our fathers" and "the rest of the books." This reference to the Hagiographa, written by Ben Sira's grandson nearly a century after Koheleth, demonstrates that the concept was still very fluid.

On the structure of this passage as a whole, it may be noted that Koheleth states his theme (that the enjoyment of life is imperative) three times: in 11:7–8a, b, again in 11:9a, b, c, d, and finally in 11:10:a, b. Each time he assigns a reason, the first time because life is fleeting (11:8c, d) and the second time because that is the will of God (11:9e), while the third time he restates *both* reasons, in 11:10c and 12:1a. The unity and integrity of this passage is thus unassailable when correctly interpreted.

11:10. כעס, "vexation, madness"; cf. 1:18; 2:23; 7:3; also 5:16 and Ps. 6:8; 10:14. רעה, lit. "evil event," here, "grief, sorrow"; cf. Jer. 44:17; Ps. 90:15; Pr. 22:3; 27:12, and often. והשחרות proved a stumbling block to the Vss. It is rendered homiletically 1) as "folly" (LXX ἄνοια) or "ignorance" (P ולא ידעתא), a meaning arrived at by equating "youth" and "folly"; and as 2) "desire" (V *voluptas*), doubtless by a similar identification (cf. שחר, "seek"). Its meaning here is undoubtedly 3) "youth," though the etymology is unclear. It may be derived from the idea of "dawn" (Ibn Ezra), or more probably, from youth's being the period of dark hair (Tar. יומי דאוכמות שער) as against שיבה, "old age, white hair" (T, Rashi, Wild. Del. BDB, Bar.). Cf. also the metathesized cognate *šariḥ*, "youth," in Arabic.

כי הילדות והשחרות הבל, the closing stich, has been deleted by many modern commentators as a Hasid's gloss, directly contradicting the hedonistic tenor of the passage. This view rests upon a faulty exegesis — הבל here has its original meaning "breath, vapor." The word occurs in its concrete sense in Mishnaic Hebrew (Shab. 119b): הבל תינוקות של בית רבן, "the breath of school children"; הבל של תנור, "vapors of the oven" (Koheleth R. 1:2). This literal meaning actually occurs in the Bible, though rarely, as e. g. Ps. 144:4, אדם להבל דמה, "Man is compared to a breath." Usually, it is used figuratively to denote the insubstantial and worthless (Ps. 62:10; II Ki. 17:15 and often), the superlative being expressed by הבל הבלים. Yet it may be used with equal aptness to describe the brevity of life, as in Job 7:16: מאסתי לא לעלם אחיה חדל ממני כי הבל ימי, "I despise my existence; *I shall not live forever*; cease from me, my life is but a breath." Hence our stich is to be rendered: "For childhood and youth are a fleeting breath." The same nuance is present in Ecc. 6:12; 9:9. On the thought-sequence of the passage 11:7 to 12:1, see note on v. 9.

Special Introductory Note

12:1 ff. Chapter 12 contains the moving "Allegory of Old Age," as practically all commentators have recognized from the Talmud to our day. While its general intent as a description of the progressive debility and decay of old age is clear, there is no agreement as to details. Actually, no view is free from difficulties. Several of the lines do not seem to be allegorical, but are most naturally to be taken as literal descriptions of the state of the old man: vv. 2 (doubtful), 4c, d, 5. In addition, some stichs are highly obscure (4c, d, 5c, d, e).

The principal views taken of the passage are as follows:

1. Each phrase describes the waning of strength in a specific organ of the body (Talmud, B. Shab. 152a; Midrash; Ibn Ezra). In support of this usage, the Talmud, loc. cit., quotes Rabbi Joshua ben Hananiah's description of his own failing powers: טור תלג סחרוני גלידין כלבוהי לא נבחין טחנוהי לא טחנין, "The mountain is snow, it is surrounded by ice, the dogs do not bark, and the grinders do not grind." The Talmudic passage deals with figures, like snow and ice, which symbolize old age, and the absence of "barkers" and "grinders" therefore suggests the weakness of the voice and of the teeth. It lends support to this interpretation of 12:3, but not of the other verses. While this allegorical interpretation seems plausible, or at least possible, in some verses (see notes below for details), it is far-fetched in others, and the poetic power of the section is gravely weakened, if there is need of a glossary for identifying each phrase.

2. The blotting out of life is described as an advancing storm, against which the inmates of the house are filled with terror, and try fruitlessly to take cover (Gins., Umbreit, Pl.). Aside from the grave difficulties involved in reading a reference to a storm into many lines (3c, d, 4c, 5c, d, 6), there is actually no mention of the storm. גשם in v. 2 is mentioned in passing and means a "rain."

3. The approach of death is pictured as the fall of night (Mich. Del.) or as 4. "the seven days of death," the wintry weather

preceding the Palestinian spring (Wetz. Wr. Hertz.). However, large parts of vv. 3, 4, 5 and 6 are inappropriate to
either theory.

5. In view of the disadvantages of these approaches, another
   view may be suggested: the decay of vitality is pictured
   under the guise of the ruin of a wealthy estate, when the
   guardians of the entrance grow faint, the slave women
   grinding at the mill become few, the ladies of the household
   no longer appear at the lattices (vv. 3, 4), and the wells
   are suffered to fall into disrepair (v. 6). Only vv. 1, 2 and
   5 are difficult to explain in terms of this metaphor, but see
   below.

6. Most plausibly, old age is pictured here without one line
   of thought being maintained throughout, perhaps because
   allegory was an unfamiliar stylistic form for Koheleth, as
   Gal. suggests (p. 89). In some instances, organs of the body
   may be intended by an allegorical reference; in others, general
   metaphors of dissolution are used. In still others, the words
   are to be understood literally (so essentially McN. Bar.
   Gal.). In support of this view, we may recall the Biblical
   practice of citing more than one metaphor to illustrate a
   point, without any *mark of transition*; cf. Ps. 23 (vv. 1–4 —
   the shepherd, vv. 5–6 — the host); Ps. 48 (v. 7 — a woman in
   travail, v. 8 — a storm, reading with Ehr. כְּרוּחַ); perhaps
   Ps. 127 (vv. 4, 5a — a battle, v. 5b — a case before judgment); Ps. 133 (v. 2 — oil, v. 3 — dew).

As has been noted above, some features (like 5a, b, 7) are
best taken literally and not figuratively. In most cases, the
deterioration of the estate seems to set the basic pattern (vv. 3,
4 and 6; see No. 5 above), but many of the figures serve simul-
taneously to picture the decay of the bodily organs (vv. 3, 4a).
As a symbol of approaching death, the picture of darkness is
invoked (v. 2), or the ruin of the well, the source of water,
symbol of life (v. 6).

Under other circumstances, the reader's inability to grasp
the poem's precise intent at so many points, coupled with the
author's failure to carry his metaphor through consistently,

would have doomed the passage. It is a tribute to its greatness and vividness that nevertheless it casts a powerful spell upon the reader as a masterly "Allegory of Old Age."

12:1. The MT, בוראיך, is attested to by all the Vss., which render "Creator." That they translate in the singular is no evidence of the spelling without Yod, since they follow their own usage. The Yod is deleted by Baer on the basis of a few mss. (so Eur.), but this is unnecessary. The form with Yod, generally explained as a plural of majesty, is used with reference to God in Isa. 54:5, כִּי בֹעֲלַיִךְ עֹשַׂיִךְ; Ps. 149:2, עֹשָׂיו; Job 35:10, עֹשָׂי; cf. also Midrash Gen. Rab., ch. 10, קוניהם. This usage may be not "the plural of majesty," but rather the suffix added to a ל"י form (בעליך in Isa. 54:5 would be in the plural because of the assonance with עֹשַׂיִך; cf. note on 11:9). The vocalization of Koheleth frequently follows the Mishnaic usage of treating ל"א verbs as ל"י; cf. וּמוֹצָא, 7:26; חוֹטָא, 9:18; hence our form here may be בורא on ל"י analogy with suffix.

Many modern comm. delete the first stich, because of the erroneous view that it is a moralizing gloss. Others emend בוראיך to בְּרוּאֶיךָ, "well-being" (Ehr.), or בְּאֵרְךָ, "your well," or בּוֹרְךָ, "your pit" (Schmidt, Gr. Levy Gal.), and see in it a metaphoric reference to one's wife or to death (so Gal.). For such metaphoric uses, cf. Pr. 5:15, שתה מים מבורך ונחלים מתוך בארך; 5:18; also Isa. 51:1; Can. 4:12, 15; B. Taanith 9a. Aside from the fact that there is no witness to such a reading, the meaning is not suitable here. For Koheleth, sexual experience represents only one segment of experience, not the whole purpose of life, which is what we should expect here at the climax and conclusion of his work. Moreover, it is doubtful whether the phrase "*remember* your well" would of itself suggest the theme of love in our context. On the other hand, Koheleth's conception of God's will for man is superbly expressed by MT: "Remember what God wishes of you, the enjoyment of life!" The verb "remember" is particularly appropriate in solemn adjuration, couched in characteristically religious form: cf. Ex. 20:8; Deut. 25:17; 32:7; Isa. 44:21; Mi. 6:5; Job 4:7.

עַד אשר לא, a pleonastic phrase, "until, not before"; cf. עַד לֹא, Pr. 8:26, and the common Mishnaic idiom עַד — שלא (e. g. B.

Ber. 3:5). ימי הרעה, "evil days," a reference to old age, in which there is no pleasure.

The striking homiletic use of this verse by R. Akiba to point up the saying of Akabya ben Mahalalel in Aboth 3:1 deserves to be cited: "Consider three things and you will not come into the power of sin: Know whence you came (באךן = "your source"), whither you are going (בורך = "your grave"), and before Whom you are destined to give an accounting (בוראיך = "your Creator"). It is cited in the Midrash ad loc. and in Lev. Rab., chap. 18, from P. Sotah II, 2.

12:2. In interpreting this and the following verses, the following views discussed in the Introductory Note to 12:1 will be taken into account: A) each phrase refers to an organ of the body; B) a storm; C) the decay of an estate; D) the eclectic view, which, in addition to literal elements, includes features drawn from A and C.

A. The sun refers to the light of the face (Tar.) or forehead (Tal. Rashi). "The light" is the eyes (Tar.) or the nose (Tal. Rashi). "The moon" is the cheeks (Tar.) or the soul (Tal. Rashi). "The stars" are the eyeballs (Tar.) or the cheeks (Tal. Rashi). "The clouds after the rains" are the darkening of the light after weeping (Tar. Tal. Rashi).

B. The darkening skies at the time of the storm.

D. To be taken literally — "For the old man the world grows dark, and even after a rain, it is not the sun but the clouds that appear" (Ibn E., Jastrow).

והאור cannot have a specific meaning, in view of the explicit mention of sun, moon and stars, nor can it be deleted without destroying the 3:3:3 rhythm. This consideration militates against the emendation השמש המאירה (ag. Gal.). The stich והאור והירח והכוכבים is best taken with P, as a hendiadys: "and the light *of* the moon and the stars." Kamenetzky's view that P's reading is a late correction rests on a failure to realize that P is interpreting MT, not emending it. For examples of hendiadys, cf. Gen. 3:16, עצבונך והרנך, "the pain of thy conceiving"; I Sam. 15:23, ואון ותרפים, "the sin of teraphim"; Isa. 53:8, מעצר וממשפט, "because of the suppression of justice"; Jer. 29:11, אחרית ותקוה, "future of hope"; Job 10:17, חליפות וצבא, "changes of service";

ibid. 10:12, חיים וחסד, "a life of free grace"; ibid. 25:2, המשל ופחד, "the dominion of fear"; II Chr. 32:1, הדברים והאמת, "words of truth"; Ecc. 8:6, 7 (perhaps), עת ומשפט, "a time of propriety, the proper time." On the juxtaposition of אור and ירח, cf. Isa. 13:10; Jer. 31:34; Ez. 32:7. On the use of the double Vav meaning "both . . . and," hence והאור והירח והכוכבים, "and the light both of the moon and the stars," cf. Com. on 2:12 and the examples adduced there, and see BDB, p. 253a.

12:3. זוע, "tremble." התעות, "become bent, crooked." הטחנות, "grinding women," slaves to whom this back-breaking toil was assigned; cf. Ex. 11:5. בטלו, an Aramaism (cf. G. A. Cooke, *NSI*, p. 335, and Jastrow, s. v.) used in Mishnaic Hebrew meaning a) "cease to be," בטל דבר בטלה אהבה (Aboth 5:16), "when the object ceases to exist, love ceases"; b) "cease from labor, be idle"; אם בטלת מן התורה, "If you are idle and desist from the Torah" (Aboth 4:10). The Biblical roots חדל and שבת parallel these two meanings.

הראות, the ladies of the household, who were enjoined from mingling with the men, according to Oriental custom, and therefore were wont to peer through the lattice-work of the mansion.

ארבות, is used elsewhere of openings in the roof, such as sluices in the heavens, through which the rain pours (Gen. 7:11; II Ki. 7:2, 19; Mal. 3:11), of openings through which smoke is emitted (Hos. 13:3), and of openings in dovecotes (Isa. 60:8). Here it refers to openings in the side of the building, either "windows" or "the opening panels of sliding doors" (B. Yoma 76a, כמה ארובות יש בדלת, "how many panels are there in a door?"). מעטו is intransitive in the Piel here.

A. "The watchmen of the house" refers to the knees (Tar.), "the ribs" (Tal. Rashi), the legs (Pl.), the arms (Del. Hertz.), or the hands (Ha. Levy). "The strong men" are the arms (Tar. Pl.) or the thighs (Tal. Rashi Ibn E., Hitz. Del. Wr. Hertz.). "The grinding women" are the teeth (Tar. Tal. Rashi and modern comm.). "The peering ladies" are the eyes (Tar. Tal. Rashi and modern comm.).

B. The strongest spirits quail before the storm and all activity ceases.

C. As the estate declines, the guardians at the gate grow old and feeble, the slave-women few and idle, and the high-born ladies no longer peer through the lattice-work.

D. The naturalness of the metaphors used to refer to the limbs of the body, the teeth and the eyes is obvious; cf. the similar Talmudic passage (B. Shab. 152a) cited on 12:1. Note, too, the agreement on many of the details here among the various interpreters. The scene depicted here seems that of an estate falling into ruin.

12:4. The passive form in MT וְסֻגְּרוּ (so P) is preferable to the active form וְסָגְרוּ in LXX. דְלָתַיִם, dual, referring to the double gates at the entrance to the estate. בַּשּׁוּק, construed as a noun by LXX, V, P, is the infinitive construct. The second half of the verse, which apparently abandons the metaphor, is extremely difficult. ויקום לקול הצפור has been emended to וְיִקְּמַל קוֹל, "the voice of the bird decays" (deJong, Wild. Zap. Levy), or to וְיִדֹּם קוֹל (Pod. Volz), but, as Hertz. observes, MT is at least equally good, being supported not only by the Vss., but also by the contrast between ויקום and וישחו. Equally striking, though not too helpful, is the possible similarity between צפור and בנות השיר, "daughters of song," which may well be an epithet for "birds"; cf. 10:20, עוף and בעל כנפים, and בת היענה (Lev. 11:16), and רְנָנִים for "ostrich" (Job 39:13).

The first half of the verse is interpreted variously:

A. "The doors" are the feet (Tar.) or the bodily apertures (Tal. Rashi) or the lips (Ibn Ezra, Hitz. Vaih. Wr. Sieg. Bar., who compares Mi. 7:5; Ps. 141:3). It is best taken to refer to deafness (so Hertz. Levy): "The old man cannot hear the noise of the market-place" (Ehr.). The mill is the appetite (Tar.) or the digestive function (Tal. Levy, Ra. Ibn E. Ha.) or the voice (Hertz.).

B. At the approach of the storm, all openings are closed.

C. A picture of the progressive decline of life and activity on the estate.

D. The detailed equivalences of A are not convincing. The first half is best taken as a continuation of the picture of the decay of the mansion in v. 3.

ויקום לקול הצפור, "he rises at the sound of the bird, i. e. the old man is easily wakened" (Tar. Tal. Rashi, Wr. Wild. Ha.), or: "he is reduced to the sound of a bird, i. e. his voice becomes high-pitched" (Ew. Hitzig Ehr. Pl. Hertz.).

בנות השיר, "the throat" (Ibn E.) or "the tones" (Ges.-K. Kn. Bar. Hertz.); cf. the Mishnaic בת קול, "echo."

"All the daughters of song are brought low" is taken to mean "he becomes deaf" (V, Kn. Ehr. Levy) or "he loses the capacity to sing" (Kn.), or "his voice becomes weak" (Grotius, Hitz. Hertz.), or "he loses his zest for singers"; cf. II Sam. 19:36, אם אשמע עוד בקול שרים ושרות (Del. Wr. Wild. McN. Ha. Tal. Rashi).

12:5. The first two stichs are taken literally by all interpreters (except Tar.) to mean that the old man fears a height and finds terrors in a walk, because of his shortness of breath and the stiffness of his limbs (Rashi and all).

While the Vss. all read a plural for יראו (LXX alone reading יראו from ראה), the entire context is in the singular, and the final Vav is best deleted as a dittography (BH). חתחתים, a quadriliteral from חתת, "fear, be terrified."

Stichs c, d, and e are obviously figurative, but the meaning is far from clear. The Vss., however, all attest to MT. LXX renders וינאץ by ἀνθήσει, "will bloom." On διασκεδάννυμι, "be scattered," for ותפר, cf. Theod. on Job 5:12; Jer. 33:20, 21; Pr. 15:22; Isa. 24:19 and LXX on Gen. 17:14; Lev. 26:15; Deut. 31:16; Jud. 2:1, etc.; this meaning P has translated in ותבדר קפר, the first of its two conflate renderings. Kamenetzky has completely failed to grasp P's rendering of stichs c, d, and e: ונבע עלוהי שהרא ונפרע שרדא ונסגא קמצא ותתבדר קפר ותבטלי בישנותא. He renders: "Sleeplessness will blossom for him like the locust — and the poor cease (to live?)". Actually P has conflate readings for both stichs c and e. Stich c, וינאץ השקד, is rendered 1) "for sleeplessness will blossom for him" and 2) "the bitter almond-tree will be destroyed." Stich d is translated "the locust will grow great" (i. e. heavy = ויסתבל). Stich e, ותפר האביונה, is rendered: 1) "the caperberry will be scattered" (so LXX); and 2) "the olive will be destroyed" (= MT). For this Syriac noun, cf. the Aramaic בישני (Peah 7:1), "a species of olive," probably chosen as an etymological equivalent for אביונה.

וינאץ השקד, "the almond will blossom," is best taken to refer to the white hair of the old man (Rashi, Kn. Ew. Bar.). Though the almond is pink at the base when it blooms in January, it becomes white at the tip within a month (cf. Post, in J. Hastings, *Dictionary of the Bible*, vol. 1, p. 67a). The Aleph is a plene orthography; cf. קאם, Hos. 10:14; ראשים, Pr. 13:23 (so Del., Ges.-K., BDB, Bar.).

Because of the Aleph in וינאץ, DeJong, Wild. render "he will despise the almond (i. e. refuse to eat)." This free rendering of the verb may underlie the Talmudic interpretation: "the head of the spinal column will be broken from leanness like the almond."

Levy (pp. 134–36) has recourse to Freudian categories of the relation of dreams, wit and the unconscious, and to Eisler's studies of Oriental word-mysticism (*Himmelszelt und Weltenmantel*, II, pp. 702 f.; *Kuba-Kybele*). He sees here a verbal metaphor, שקד, "almond," recalling the verb שקד, "be watchful," as in Jer. 1:11 f. (cf. Amos 8:2, קיץ and קץ), and reading וינאץ הַשָּׁקֵד, he renders: "he despises wakefulness: i. e. he dozes off." The implication is that for the old man the sexual passion is so weak that he falls into slumber instead!

ויסתבל החגב, "the grasshopper will become a burden, be dragged along," from סבל, "bear a load" (cf. Gen. 49:15, לסבל; מְסֻבָּלִים, Ps. 144:14). This is referred to the back of the pelvic cavity (the Arabic cognate حجبة is the point of the hip-bone) and is taken to indicate stiffness of the joints (Del. Now. Wild.) or as a metaphor for the bent figure of the old man (so Zöckler) or to indicate that the smallest object is a burden (Pl. Wr.). T renders: "the ankles will swell up"; the Talmud (B. Shab. 152a), החגב אלו העגבות, sees here an allusion to the *membrum virile* (so Rashi, Ibn E. Gr. Levy and Luz.). The latter sees a wordplay on חגב and עגב, "make love"; cf. Ez. 23:11; 33:32. Hence "sexual satisfaction (or, the privy parts) becomes a burden."

האביונה, "caperberry," so called because of its supposed power to stimulate sexual desire, from אבה, "wish, desire" (Maas. 4:6;

Ra., Ibn E., and G. F. Moore, in *JBL*, X, pp. 55 ff.). וְתָפֵר, the Hiphil of פרר, is always transitive elsewhere, "destroy, annul, make void"; cf. II Sam. 15:34; Ezra 4:5, and frequently. Here it requires an intransitive meaning, "be useless" (Del. Wild.). Hence it is emended by some to the Hophal וְתֻפַר, "is made ineffectual" (BDB), but note that מָעַטוּ in v. 3 is also intransitive here. On the basis of the parallelism, some emend to וְתִפְרַח (Perles) or וְתִפְרָה (cf. Isa. 11:1), which would be graphically even closer (BH). Aquila derives the word from פרה (cf. G. F. Moore, in *JBL*, ibid., p. 60) and renders: "the caperberry blooms." Targum's rendering is ותתמנע מן משכנא (read משכבא), "you will cease from sexual intercourse."

Because of the manifold difficulties in interpretation, Hertz., followed by Gal., discards the allegorical view of stichs c, d and e and takes them literally to be a description of spring: "the almond will bloom, the grasshopper will be laden with food and the caperberry will blossom. A new spring will come, but the old man will not be there to enjoy it, because he will have gone to his eternal home." In spite of its attractiveness, this view does not commend itself: 1) the symbols of spring are far from clear and certainly not the most characteristic signs of the season. Contrast Can. 2:11 ff. 2) the *basic idea* that the old man will not witness the spring is *unexpressed*. 3) כִּי *can* mean "but," but this is not the natural meaning here.

That the first half of this verse has a sexual connotation seems clear from the following considerations: 1) The failing of sexual powers is an outstanding feature of old age, and is not expressed elsewhere in the passage. 2) It is precisely this feature that would be expressed in veiled and figurative form; cf. the idiom האדע בין טוב לרע in Barzillai's words to David (II Sam. 19:36), and see "The Significance of the Paradise Myth," AJSL, vol. 52 (1936), pp. 86–94. 3) This implication is clear in אביונה, "the berry of desire." 4) Koheleth is conscious of the importance of this aspect of life (cf. 9:9), and he certainly does not overlook its physical aspects.

Hence stichs d and e are to be understood as follows: The grasshopper becomes a burden (either as a figure for the *membrum virile* or by a play between חגב and ענב) and the caperberry is useless to stimulate desire (leaving the Masoretic vocalization unchanged, or reading וְתֻפַר; see above). In stich c, the reading וְיָנֵאץ, "he will despise the almond," is not likely, since in both stichs, d and e, the noun following is the subject and not the object of the verb. Since the proposed sexual interpretation of stich c is forced, it is best taken as referring to the white hair of old age: "The almond will blossom."

The second half of the verse, unlike the first, is crystal-clear.

בֵּית עלמו, "the eternal home," is the grave. On the widespread usage of this phrase, cf. Tobit 3:6, τόπος αἰώνιος, the Talmud (B. Sanh. 19a), בֵּית עלמין, and the Qoran (41:28), dār-ul-ḥuldi, the Latin phrase domus aeterna, the Palmyrene (Lidzbarski, Handbuch, p. 235, 1898, etc.) and the Punic (cf. J. A. Wilson, in JNES, 1944, p. 208).

הסופדים, "hired mourners"; cf. Jer. 22:18; 34:5; and מקוננות, Jer. 9:16. This element of the conventional last rites of the Semitic world is singled out here with ironic intent — a man's life has drawn to a close, irrevocably and finally, after a long period of decline, yet the tragedy constitutes merely one more professional routine for the hired mourners — the vanity of life is climaxed by the vanity of death!

12:6. For the first verb, LXX, V, P express "is destroyed," which many equate with יִנָּתֵק (BH, Ges. BDB, Eur. Ehr.). The Kethib ירחק, "be distant," is unsatisfactory. The Qere יֵרָתֵק may be a privative Niphal from רָתוֹק, "chain" (I Ki. 6:21, Qere; Ez. 7:23; רְתֻקָה, Isa. 40:19), hence "be severed." Cf. יִזְמֵר, Isa. 5:6, "be pruned, have the twigs (זְמוֹרָה) removed," and see Ges.-K., sec. 67, note IV.

וְתָרֻץ is ע"ו analogy for ע"ע (cf. יְרוּץ, Isa. 42:4; יָרוּן, Pr. 29:6), hence from רעע, "be smashed." גֻּלָּה, "bowl"; cf. Zc. 4:2, 3, a. e. מַבּוּע, "fountain"; cf. Isa. 35:7; 49:10.

The advent of death is pictured metaphorically in this verse. According to most commentators (Del. Sieg. Pl. Wr. Bar.), two figures are employed: a lamp (stichs a and b), and a fountain (stichs c and d). A golden lamp, held by a silver cord, is shattered when the cord is severed and the light goes out. The image may be based on Zc. 4:2, 3 (Pl. Wr. Del. Sieg. McN. Wild. Bar.). The second figure pictures the breaking of the pitcher at the well, when the wheel by which it is usually raised is shattered.

While the change of metaphor is possible, it remains harsh. Levy, following Ibn Ezra, argues convincingly that there is only one figure here, that of a well, worked by a cord tied to a wheel. One end of the cord has a pitcher, the other a metal ball (גְּלָּה; cf. I Ki. 7:41 f.) as a counterweight. When the cord is torn, ball, pitcher and wheel all fall to the bottom and are broken.

Detailed identifications have been proposed as follows: "The silver cord" is the tongue (Tar.) or the spine (Rashi, Ha. Levy) or the soul (Del.). "The golden bowl" is the marrow (Tar. Ha.) or the *membrum virile* (Rashi) or the head (Del. Levy). "The pitcher" is the gall (Tar.) or the stomach (Rashi) or the heart (Levy), and "the wheel" is the body (Tar.) or the eyeball (Rashi, Levy).

These equivalents do not commend themselves, not only because they are far from conclusive, as the variations indicate, but because they make the passage exceedingly prosaic. Moreover, since the verse follows the reference to "the eternal home" (v. 5), it must describe death generally, rather than refer to specific details. Levy is led to reverse 6 and 5b because of his interpretation — an unnecessary procedure. Water is the symbol of life; cf., inter alia, Jer. 2:13; Ps. 36:9; the destruction of the well is a moving metaphor describing the advent of death.

The unforgettable picture of old age here given is utilized by the Syriac Apocalypse of Baruch to describe the decay of the world: "The youth of the world is past and the strength of creation is already exhausted and the advent of the times is very short, yea and they have passed by. The pitcher is near the cistern, the ship to port, and the course of the journey to the city, and life to its consummation" (II Baruch 85:10).

12:7. The verse reflects Koheleth's familiarity with the Torah, being obviously based on Gen. 2:7 and 3:19. The parallel structure of the entire passage makes it impossible to assume that stich b is an interpolation, while the deletion of the entire verse (so Sieg.) would deprive the poem of an impressive close. Nor is it necessary or possible to see in it the quotation of the elegy of the mourners, who repeat conventional ideas (so Levy). Note the intervening verse 6 between the reference to the mourners and our verse.

The Allegory, which began with a call "Remember thy Creator," closes with the return of man's spirit to God, "Who gave it." This is not in contradiction to 3:21, which expresses Koheleth's skepticism about the doctrine that there is a difference between the fate of the beast, the spirit of which goes "downward," and that of man, whose soul goes "upward." This verse affirms what Koheleth does not deny, that life comes from God. Before the mystery of death, only the language of religion proves adequate (cf. Bar. and Hertz. ad loc.). But Koheleth does not conceive of God as Comforter or Redeemer (Hertz.).

וְיָשֹׁב, the jussive instead of the indicative יָשׁוּב, is anomalous.

12:8. אמר הקוהלת may be the insertion of the editor, whose Epilogue follows. The phrase in 7:27 is to be corrected accordingly. On the use of the article, see note on 1:1.

Section XIX — Introductory Note

12:9 ff. It has been noted since Döderlein that the last six verses of the book are not from Koheleth's own hand, since they speak of him in the third person, while throughout the book Koheleth refers to himself in the first person. So, too, the use of בני (v. 12) characteristic of Wisdom, as in Proverbs, *passim* (cf. SBWL, p. 84, n. 9), does not occur in Koheleth proper. Hence the contradiction between the sentiments expressed in vv. 13 f. and the rest of the book needs no explanation, and the various efforts to harmonize them are uncalled for.

Nonetheless, the importance of this Epilogue has not been adequately noted. We have here a prime source of information on Koheleth's life and work emanating from his own time, probably from a contemporary who knew him personally. Note the resemblances in vocabulary, reflecting the same period and environment: תקן, חפץ, הזהר, מעשה, נעלם, יותר, as well as the new words אזן, דרבן, and the conventional use of מצוה and יראת אלהים.

The Epilogue may be, as Hertz. has noted, an apology and

defense of the book against such criticisms as *Wisdom of Solomon*, chap. 2, contains. We learn from it that Koheleth was a *hakam*, a teacher of Wisdom (v. 9a, b). He did not content himself with the professional activity which was limited to the scions of the upper classes, but sought to teach *the people*, העם, by his literary work, collecting (חקר, lit. "search out") proverbs, and by composing (תקן) original contributions to this literature (v. 9b) — welcome testimony to both the original and the quoted material in his book. There is no reason for seeing a reference here to the book of Proverbs (ag. Hitz. Wild. Bar.). Finally, Koheleth is praised — perhaps not without some degree of criticism — for seeking attractive words in which to set down the truth (v. 11).

That the editor, who was fascinated by the book, as is clear from v. 9, did not endorse Koheleth's standpoint *in toto* may be implied in 10a.

In v. 11 he pays tribute to the stimulation ("goads") afforded by the writings of the "Wise" and the firm support ("fixed nails") that they give to human life. With a breadth of view particularly striking in a conventional believer, and, for that matter, rare anywhere, he declares that even these ideas, which might challenge an unquestioning faith, are nevertheless derived from a Divine source (v. 11c). This tolerance lies at the basis of the process that led to the canonization of the Hebrew Scriptures, so that works of conflicting viewpoints, as for instance Haggai vs. Zechariah, Ruth vs. Ezra-Nehemiah, Jonah vs. Nahum and Obadiah, could be and were included in the canon of Holy Writ. Cf. on the subject M. L. Margolis, *The Hebrew Scripture in the Making* (Phila., 1922).

In v. 12 he voices his doubts about the value of many books, especially those similar to Koheleth, while in vv. 13 f. he affirms his own faith in God and loyalty to His Commandments, coupled with his conviction that retribution does operate in the world.

It is possible that these concluding verses are not a unit (so Bar. Ehr. Hertz.), vv. 8 ff. emanating from one editor, vv. 11 f. from another, and vv. 13 f. from a third. Gal. assigns vv. 9–11 to a pupil of Koheleth, and vv. 12–14 to a Wisdom teacher. Jastrow finds eleven distinct interpolations! However, there is no contradiction within this section, and the progression of thought in the passage is thoroughly satisfactory. Besides, this assumption complicates the time-factor required for the composition of the book, its redaction and supplementation, its popular acceptance and its canonization. All this must have taken place in the interval between the third century B. C. E., when Greek ideas begin to permeate Palestinian Jewry, and the composition of Ben Sira (c. 190 B. C. E.), who borrows phrases from the book (see Intro.). Hence the entire Epilogue is best regarded as a unit. Hertz. recognizes that the various verses are not in conflict with each other.

The editor, like every reader, has selected those aspects of Koheleth which were most congenial to him. While he has not done full justice to the temper and world-view of Koheleth, the ideas he stresses — the fear of God and obedience to His commandments — are part of Koheleth's outlook, granted his right to define his terms.

Krochmal's view, adopted by Gr., that the three closing verses served originally as the colophon for the entire Biblical canon and dated from the Council of Jabneh (90 C. E.), rests, in large measure at least, upon the Rabbinic interpretation of v. 12: כל המכניס לתוך ביתו יותר מכ״ד ספרים מהומה הוא מכניס בביתו (Mid. Koh. Rabba ad loc.), but this homily, which derives from the assonance of מהמה and מהומה, has no warrant in the Biblical text. It is ruled out, too, by external evidence of date. While v. 13 could conceivably serve as a conclusion to the canon of Scripture as a whole, v. 14 seems specifically directed against Koheleth's doubts about retribution, to which he has given so much attention (cf. 8:9 to 9:3).

12:9. The LXX erroneously treats the three clauses as coordinate, by inserting καί before עוד. The Masorah puts a *zakeph gadol* on the word ויתר, in order to separate it from the following: "Moreover, etc."; so LXX περισσόν. The construction ויתר... ש עוד, however, while not precisely paralleled elsewhere, is similar to the Mishnaic .... ש and יותר ממה ש... יותר מש (so Rashi); cf. יותר ממה שהעגל רוצה לינק הפרה רוצה להיניק (Pes. 112a), "More than the calf wishes to suck, the cow wishes to suckle"; יותר משהאיש רוצה לישא האשה רוצה להנשא (B. Yeb. 113a), "More than a man wishes to marry, a woman wishes to be married." Here, the construction introduces a subordinate clause: lit. "more than (or, besides the fact that) Koheleth was a sage, he also taught the people knowledge." The point of the contrast has hitherto escaped notice. Koheleth was not merely a professional Wisdom teacher whose activity was limited to the scions of the rich; through his writings he taught Wisdom to the *people*. LXX ἄνθρωπον for העם may be an aural error of אדם for העם.

The precise character of Koheleth's literary activity is indicated in the three verbs following:

The difficult אזן is rendered variously by the Vss: 1) as אזן by LXX, which also read תקן as a noun, "order"; and 2) as "heard" (P, T); 3) as "narrated," by V, which doubtless treated the verb as causative: "he made men hear" (similarly Ibn Ezra); and 4) as "he listened to the people" (Levy). Most modern scholars derive it from Arabic وزن "weigh," Hebrew מאזנים, "scales," hence "test, prove" (BDB, Bar., Hertz.). Perhaps the verb means "measure out, scan" (so Ibn Ezra, Ges.-Buhl), and is an allusion to the formulation of proverbs in rhythm and parallelism.

חקר, "search out," occurs in the Piel only here, the vocalization being due to the assonance with the nearby Piel verbs. It refers to the collecting of proverbial material written by others. תקן, which occurs elsewhere in Koheleth (1:15; 7:13), does not mean here "arrange, set in order" (ag. BDB), but "compose, fashion," an allusion to the original writing of the author; cf. the description of King David in Ben Sira 47:9, נגינות שיר לפני מזבח וקול המזמור נבלים תיקן, "Melodies of song before the altar, and the sound of the song on the harp, did he fashion."

12:10. דברי חפץ, "attractive words, lit. words of delight"; cf. 12:1. Koheleth had sought to set forth his ideas in elegant form. Though there may be a veiled criticism in this compliment, as though to say that Koheleth had strained unduly after literary effect, it is not necessary to render stich b with Ehr. as a contrast: "But what should rightly be written are words of truth." The editor does not react as negatively to Koheleth as this interpretation would imply; cf. vv. 9 and 11. וְכָתוּב, though vouched for by LXX, is difficult. MT can be rendered only: "What was (or is) written properly are words of truth" (so Levy), or "that which was written uprightly, even words of truth" (JPSV). Hence the word is to be vocalized as וְכָתַב (so 5 mss., BH), or, better, as an infinitive, וְכָתוֹב, either as an inf. consecutive (="and he wrote") or as the object of בקש, "and (he sought) to write honestly, words of truth." יֹשֶׁר is an adv. acc., "honestly."

12:11. דרבנות, "goads," from the Arabic root *dariba*, "train" (cf. I Sam. 13:21), so called because it served as a guide to the cattle, as the other term מלמד הבקר (Jud. 3:31; cf. M. Kelim 9:6; J. Sanh. X, 28a) indicates. משמרות נטועים, "well-fixed nails," is taken by Ehr. as a contrast: "The words of the wise, i. e. the Apocryphal literature, may be goads, but it is the accepted collections that are like firmly planted nails, though the former too are divinely inspired." However, the asyndetonic relation of the last stich in the verse makes it virtually certain that it is not in contrast to stich b; consequently stich b must be parallel to stich a. That מַשְׂמֵר (cf. Isa. 41:7; I Chr. 22:3; II Chr. 3:9 with Samekh) is a synonym for דרבן and not a contrast is clear from Maimonides, *Commentary on the Mishnah, Kelim* 9:6 (מלמד הוא כלי עץ ובסופו גם כן מסמר של ברזל).

בעלי אספות, a hapax legomenon, the precise meaning of which would shed valuable light on the intellectual life of the time. אֲסֻפּוֹת is a noun like חֲנֻכָּה, אֲחֻזָּה, "estate"; cf. Barth, *Nominalbildung*, sec. 95a. Levy interprets "like nails fixed that keep the herds together," and compares Isa. 52:12, מְאַסִּפְכֶם, which, Duhm suggests, is a term for the shepherd at the rear of the herd. The phrase has been taken to mean either a) "masters of assemblies or councils of scholars" (B. Sanh. 12a; J. Sanh. X, 28a; Num. R. 14; Tar.; Ges.-Thes., BDB, Del. Sieg.), or b) "lords (or members) of collections," a reference to the wise utterances themselves (Hitz. Now. Del. Wr. McN. Bar. Ode. Hertz.). While the latter view has a difficulty in בעלי, it is to be preferred to the first because of the parallelism with דברי חכמים. In a more poetic passage, the word דברי might have been regarded as understood before בעלי אספות, "the words of the masters of assemblies" (cf. V *quae per magistrorum consilium*; so Ibn Ezra), but this is not likely here. Ehr.'s clever emendation of בַּעֲלֵי to בָּעֱלִי, "pestle" (Pr. 27:22), is unconvincing, as is the V rendering of the word, *in altum* — "upwards."

P's rendering of בעלי אספות as מרי אסכפתא, "masters of the threshold," derives the word from סַף. It is noteworthy that Ibn Janaḥ renders it similarly, "like nails planted in the threshold," and he compares Neh. 12:25; I Chr. 26:15, בֵּית הָאֲסֻפִּים, which he renders "watchmen of the threshold." נתנו מרעה אחד, "given from the same shepherd." This is not a reference to Solomon (ag. Del. McN.), since the editor does not speak of Solomon as the author, but to God, Who is often described by this epithet (Gen. 49:24; Isa. 40:11; Ps. 23:1; 80:2; 95:7). The figure may have been chosen because of the agricultural term דרבן. The clause sets forth a claim for the inspired character even of the books of Wisdom, which so often parted company with the accepted religious ideas of the time. (See Ibn Ezra ad loc.) Gal. reads וּנְתָנָם רֹעֶה חַדִּים, "which the shepherd made sharp." The phrase, it must be admitted, is obscure. P renders it twice, the second time through a conflate in v. 14: דמן אומנא חד אתיהב לכלנש, "from one master was it given to all men."

12:12. ויתר מהמה, "More than these matters, furthermore" (so V, *hic amplius*, JPSV, Hertz. Cf. על כל אלה, 11:9). This indefinite meaning of the pronoun is preferable to relating the pronoun to the writings referred to above (Ehr. Bar.) which are alone regarded as inspired.

הזהר, "take heed, be warned"; cf. 4:13. עשות ספרים הרבה, "the composing of many books." אין קץ is a predicate nominative: "has no end," or a predicate adjective: "is without end, is endless."

The rendering which links הזהר and עשות, "Be careful about making many books without end," for which השמרו לכם עלות בהר (Ex. 19:12) is cited (Ibn Ezra, Ibn Janaḥ), creates a tautology and disrupts the parallelism. The Vss. follow the Masorah in placing the pause at הזהר.

להג, "study"; cf. Arabic *lahija*, "apply oneself assiduously." יגעת בשר, "is a weariness of the flesh, destroys one's strength." The writer warns against too many books and excessive study. There is nothing in the passage to suggest a reference to the canon (ag. Ehr.), and the second stich militates against it. Cf. Intr. Note.

12:13. סוף, a late Hebrew and Aramaic word (Ecc. 3:11;

II Chr. 20:16, and often in the Mishnah), "the conclusion of the matter."

זה כל האדם, a pregnant idiom, characteristically Hebrew, for "this is the whole duty of man"; cf. Ps. 110:3, עמך נדבות, "thy people are freely offering themselves"; Ps. 109:4, אני תפלה, "I am at prayer"; Ps. 120:7, אני שלום, "I am seeking peace"; Isa. 28:12, זאת המנוחה הניחו לעיף, "This is the secret of rest — give rest to the weary"; Job 8:9, כי תמול אנחנו, lit. "we are yesterday, our life is as brief as yesterday"; Job 5:25; idem 29:15, עינים הייתי לעור, as against the phrase in Nu. 10:31, והיית לנו לעינים; cf. Ges.-K., sec. 141, I e: "Dass jedoch die Sprache auch die kühnsten Verbindungen nicht scheut, um die unbedingte Zusammengehörigkeit des Subjekts und des Prädikatsbegriffes recht nachdrücklich zu betonen." There is no reason for assuming an Aramaic original; cf. OLQ, pp. 74 f., and QHA.

This verse lies at the basis of Ben Sira 43:27, עוד כאלה לא נוסף וקץ דבר הוא הכל, but this citation or reminiscence in the later writer hardly proves that v. 13 was the end of our book (ag. Bar.).

הכל נשמע is rendered a) "hear all!" (LXX; P, reading שְׁמַע); b) "let us hear everything" (V audiamus, Wild. Ha. AV, Pl.); c) "everything is understood" (Levy); or d) "everything has been heard" (Ibn Ezra Gins. Del. Wr. McN. JPSV).

12:14. Gal. reads האדם instead of מעשה, but this is graphically distant. The absence of the article in מעשה after את is paralleled in many passages of early Hebrew (cf. Ex. 21:28, את איש; I Sam. 24:5, את כנף; II Sam. 4:11, את איש צדיק; 5:24, את קול צעדה; 18:18, את מצבת; Ez. 16:32, את זרים). This erratic use of the article becomes more pronounced under the influence of Aramaic, where the determinative status, which contains the article, loses its meaning and becomes virtually equivalent to the absolute. On the subject, cf. OLQ, pp. 81–83; Ges.-K., sec. 117, 126; M. H. Segal, Dikduk Leshon Hamishnah, pp. 53–56; and such passages as Ecc. 9:9; 10:20; Ps. 146:9; Ps. 148:9, 10. This is no evidence of translation from the Aramaic.

נעלם, "hidden thing," is generalized by V, errata = "sins."

In order to conclude on a positive note, the Masorah ordains the repetition of v. 13 after the last verse at public readings of the book, as is the case in Isaiah, The Twelve (Minor Prophets), and Lamentations (סימן יתק"ק).

NOTES TO CHAPTERS I TO XVI

NOTES ON CHAPTER I

[1] A. B. Ehrlich, *Die Psalmen* (Berlin, 1905), p. vi.

[2] Cf. the brief but suggestive work, all too generally overlooked, of M. L. Margolis, *The Hebrew Scriptures in the Making* (Philadelphia, 1922), chaps. IV and V, especially pp. 78 f.

[3] Cf. G. R. Driver-J. C. Miles, *The Assyrian Laws* (Oxford, 1935); J. M. P. Smith, *Origin and History of Hebrew Law* (Chicago, 1931).

[4] On the extent of Hebrew Wisdom, cf. Rankin, op. cit., pp. 1 f.; Fichtner, op. cit., pp. 7–13; and the discussion in *SBWL*, note 2.

[5] Cf. Judges 9:7 ff.; I Sam. 24:13; II Sam. 14:14; II Kings 14:9.

[6] Cf., for example, Tobit 4:13 ff.; 12:6 ff.; 14:9 ff.

[7] The most important documents are listed in Fichtner, op. cit., pp. 3–5. The principal texts are accessible in H. Gressmann, *Altorientalische Texte zum A. T.* (2nd ed., Berlin-Leipzig, 1926), pp. 25–29, 33–46, translated by Herman Ranke; and in A. Erman, *The Literature of the Ancient Egyptians*, translated by A. M. Blackman (New York, 1927), pp. 54–131. On the relationship of Egyptian and Hebrew Wisdom, see P. Humbert, *Recherches sur les sources Egyptiennes de la Littérature sapientiale d'Israël* (Neuchâtel, 1929), who assumes Israelite borrowing throughout rather than parallel development. A superb edition in English of the literature is now available in J. B. Pritchard, *Ancient Near Eastern Texts Relating to the O. T.* (Princeton, 1950).

[8] Erman, op. cit., p. 54.

[9] Cf. Erman, op. cit., pp. 188 ff.

[10] Erman, p. 75; Fichtner, p. 3.

[11] On the extensive literature since the publication of the text by W. A. Budge in 1923, see, *inter alia*, Fichtner, op. cit., p. 4, n. 3; Barton, *Archaeology and the Bible*, 7th ed. (Philadelphia, 1937), pp. 511 ff.; L. Finkelstein, *The Pharisees* (Philadelphia, 1938), vol. 1, pp. 203 ff.; vol. 2, p. 678.

[12] So H. O. Lange, in *Kgl. Danske Vidensk Selskab. Hist. fil. Med. XI*, 2 (1925); W. O. E. Oesterley, in *ZATW*, 1927, p. 23; R. O. Kevin, in *JSOR*, 1930, pp. 115 ff.

[13] Cf., for example, the Commentary of W. O. E. Oesterley, *The Book of Proverbs* (Philadelphia, 1929), esp. pp. XLVI ff. and LIV.

[14] Cf. Pr. 30:21 f.; Job 19:15 f.; 30:1 f.; Ecc. 10:6 f.; and *SBWL*, pp. 113 ff., for the light that this characteristic sheds on the class orientation of Wisdom.

[15] Cf. Gressmann, op. cit., pp. 28 f.

[16] Cf. Ecc. 9:9 ff., and see Commentary below for details.

[17] Cf. the remarks of Fichtner, p. 6.

[18] Cf. B. Meissner, *Babylonien und Assyrien*, II, pp. 424 ff.; Ebeling, "Reste Akkadischer Weisheitsliteratur," in *Meissner Festschrift*, 1928, vol. I, pp. 21 ff.

[19] Cf. Ebeling, in Gressmann, op. cit., pp. 201 f.

[20] Cf. B. Meissner, op. cit., p. 430; Th. Noeldeke, *Untersuchungen zum Ahikar-Roman* (1913); A. E. Cowley, *Aramaic Papyri of the Fifth Cent. B. C. E.* (Oxford, 1923).

[21] It is older than the new Assyrian and the new Babylonian copies in which the poem has reached us; cf. Fichtner, op. cit., p. 6; Ebeling, op. cit., p. 273.

[22] Cf. section *XI*, 7 ff., with Ecc. 1:11; 4:16; 9:15; section *XII*, 5 f., with Pr. 30:2 f.; Ecc. 3:11, and Ecc. *passim*.

[23] Ebeling, op. cit., pp. 287 ff.

[24] This usage, so crucial for the understanding of Wisdom literature in general and Koheleth in particular, has not been adequately recognized heretofore. See "Quotations as a Literary Usage in Biblical, Rabbinic and Oriental Literature," in *HUCA*, vol. 22 (1949), esp. pp. 198–207, and see below, ch. XII.

NOTES ON CHAPTER II

[1] Hosea 8:12, reading with the Kethib רבו and revocalizing the noun תורתי as a plural (note the closing verb) to read: אֶכְתָּוב־לוֹ רִבּוֹ תּוֹרָתִי כְּמוֹ־זָר נֶחְשָׁבוּ.

[2] On the complex question of the literary history of the Pentateuch, far from settled today, see, *inter alia*, R. H. Pfeiffer, *Introduction to the O. T.* (New York, 1941); W. F. Albright, *From the Stone Age to Christianity*; and Y. Kaufman's massive work, *Toledot Ha'emunah Hayyisre'elit* (Jerusalem, 1937–), 7 volumes published thus far. For a brief survey of the three strands of Biblical cultural development, cf. R. Gordis, "The Bible as a Cultural Monument," in L. Finkelstein, ed., *The Jews, Their History, Culture, and Religion* (New York, 1949), vol. 1, pp. 457–96.

[3] On the stages of development in Hebrew prophecy, cf. the last-named paper, pp. 469–82, and the literature there cited.

[4] Cf., for example, the Book of the Covenant (Ex., chaps. 21 to 23) and the Holiness Code (Lev., chaps. 18–21), and, in the Book of Leviticus, the laws of sacrifice (chaps. 1 to 5; note particularly 5:20–26), of leprosy (chaps. 13 to 14), and of ritual impurity (ch. 15), etc.

[5] Cf. Jer. 12:1 ff.; 31:28 ff.; Ez. 18:1 ff.

[6] Cf. M. Shab. 18:3; Rosh Hashanah 2:5; and B. Erub. 45a.

[7] Cf. *ḥīdāh*, "riddle, mysterious saying," and *māshāl*, "proverb," terms applied both to the song played on the *kinnor* (Ps. 49:5; 78:2) and to the teaching of the sages (Pr. 1:6).

[8] Or "five thousand" with LXX.

⁹ Cf. W. F. Albright, "The Canaanite Origin of Israelite Musical Guilds," as yet unpublished.

¹⁰ Cf. Arabic *mathala* II "represent, use a verse as a proverb," Akkadian *mašâlu*, Ethiopian *masala*, Aramaic *methal*, "be like," Syriac *methal*, "compare."

¹¹ In its first meaning, *sophia* is applied to Hephaestus, the god of fire and the arts, to Athena, to Daedalus, the craftsman and artist, and to the Telchines, a primitive tribe who are represented under three aspects: 1) as cultivators of the soil and ministers of the gods; 2) as sorcerers and envious demons, who had the power to bring on hail, rain, and snow, and to destroy animals and plants; and 3) as artists working in brass and iron. (Gen. 4:20–22 offers a suggestive parallel.) *Sophia* is used of such crafts as carpentry, driving a chariot, medicine and surgery. It is used preëminently of singing, music and poetry (*Homeric Hymn to Mercury*, lines 483, 511; Pindar, *Odes*, 1, 187; Xenophon, *Anabasis*, 1, 2, 8). On the usage of all three terms here discussed, cf. Liddell-Scott, *Greek Lexicon*, s. v.

¹² Pindar, *Odes*, 1, 15; Euripides, *Iphigenia in Tauris*, 1238; Plato, *Laws*, 696c. See Liddell-Scott, op. cit., s. v.

¹³ Pindar, I, 5, 36; Aeschylus, *Fragmenta*, 320; cf. Liddell-Scott, op. cit., s. v.

¹⁴ Cf., *inter alia*, Xenophon, *Memorabilia*, 1, 6, 13; Thucydides, 3, 38; Plato, *Protagoras*, 313c.

¹⁵ For a detailed presentation of the evidence of these parallels with Greece, cf. *SBWL*, pp. 84 ff.

¹⁶ Cf. on Solomon as "wise" I Ki. 5:10–14; as the hero of many marriages, idem 11:1 ff. See also R. Gordis, "A Wedding Song for Solomon," in *JBL*, 1944, vol. 63, pp. 263–70, for an ancient wedding song celebrating one of his nuptial adventures.

¹⁷ Cf. the old Talmudic tradition in B. Keth. 16b: כיצד מרקדין לפני הכלה בית שמאי אומרים כלה כמות שהיא בית הלל אומרים כלה נאה וחסודה, "How is one to dance before (i. e. praise) the bride? The Shammaites declare: 'By praising her for the qualities she actually possesses.' The Hillelites say: 'By praising every bride as beautiful and gracious.' " The East-European Jewish custom of having a *badḥan* or humorous rhymster at weddings has counterparts among many peoples.

¹⁸ Cf. Margolis, op. cit., p. 80. Pfeiffer, *Intro. to O. T.* (New York, 1941), who regards the championing of the Levites against the priests as the chief purpose of the Chronicles (pp. 794 ff.), notes that for the historian the musical guilds are the most important of the Levites (pp. 797 f.). The low opinion of the historical credibility of the Chronicler, which prevailed in the recent past, is increasingly felt to be unjustified. Cf. F. von Rad, *Das Geschichtsbild der chronistischen Werke* (Stuttgart, 1930); M. Noth, *Ueberlieferungs-geschichtliche Studien* (Halle, 1943); W. F. Albright, *From the Stone Age to Christianity* (Baltimore, 1940), p. 208; *idem*, in *Alexander Marx Jubilee Volumes* (English volume), pp. 61 ff.; and the writer, *ibidem*, pp. 369 ff. Cf. also n. 9 above.

[19] On Solomon's commercial and diplomatic relations, cf. I Ki. 9:11 ff., 24–28; 10:26–29.

[20] Budge assigns the latter work, the most important of all for Hebrew Wisdom, to the 18th dynasty, Erman-Lange to the 21st or 22nd dynasty (c. 1st millennium), Griffiths to the 21st to 26th dynasty.

[21] Besides, several expressions imply an early concept of God, with strong anthropomorphic overtones. The description of oil (אשר בי יכבדו אלהים ואנשים, v. 9) and of wine (המשמח אלהים ואנשים, v. 13) reflects antique religious practices and attitudes (cf. Moore, *ICC, Judges*, p. 274).

[22] The clause ולא ישא אלהים נפש is meaningless. It has been rendered: 1) "And God does not take away life" (Dr.), 2) "God does not respect any person" (JPSV), 3) "God will not take away the life of him that thinketh thoughts," reading חֹשֵׁב for וְחָשַׁב (Ew. Wel. Dr.). The correct reading has been preserved in LXX (ed. Lagarde), which seems to have been the text of Theodotion (Field): καὶ οὐκ ἐλπίζει ἐπ' αὐτῷ ψυχή, "and no one hopes for it." This presupposes אֲלֵיהֶם for אֱלֹהִים. H. P. Smith, *ICC on Samuel*, p. 337, is on the right track, but the reading אֵלָיו that he suggests is graphically too distant from the MT אלהים, and besides the antecedent מים is plural. The clause is impersonal: ולא ישא (הנושא) אליהם (אל המים) נפש. On the idiom נשא נפש אל, "yearn for, desire," cf. Deut. 24:15; Hos. 4:8; Ps. 24:4; 25:1; 86:4; 143:8; Pr. 19:18.

[23] Cf. the most recent commentaries on *Proverbs* of Oesterley (1929), Gemser (1937), Torczyner (Tur-Sinai; 1947), and Greenstone (1950).

[24] Nothing can be hazarded regarding the date or character of such books as *Ben La'anah* and *Ben Tagla*, which are mentioned in Rabbinic literature together with *Ben Sira* (J. Sanh. X, 28a; Mid. Koheleth Rabba on 12:12).

NOTES ON CHAPTER III

[1] Zc. 4:10.

[2] Cf. Josephus, *Antiquities*, XI, 7, 1; XII, 4,6.

[3] Cf. E. Bickermann, *Der Gott der Makkabäer* (Berlin, 1937), and now R. H. Pfeiffer, *History of New Testament Times* (New York, 1949), for the background of the period.

[4] Cf. Neh. 8:1–8; 9:1–4; 10:1 ff.

[5] For the enormous literature on Tannaitic and pre-Tannaitic Judaism, we may cite I. H. Weiss, *Dor Dor Vedorshav* (Vienna, 1871–91); R. T. Herford, *Pharisaism* (London, 1912); idem, *The Pharisees* (London, 1924); G. F. Moore, *Judaism* (Cambridge, 1927), 3 vols.; Ch. Tschernowitz, *Toledoth Hahalakhah*, 4 vols. (New York, 1934–50); L. Finkelstein, *The Pharisees* (Phila., 1938), 2 vols.; idem, *Haperushim ve-Anshe Kenesset Hagedolah* (New York, 1950).

[6] On the Apocalyptic literature, cf. R. H. Charles, *Apocrypha and Pseudepigrapha of the Old Testament*, 2 vols. (Oxford, 1913); R. H. Pfeiffer,

op. cit., pp. 74 ff.; and H. H. Rowley, *The Relevance of Apocalyptic* (London, 1944).

⁷ Not Wisdom *par excellence* (*Hahokmah*), hence no definite article — *hokmah*.

⁸ Cf. ch. XI below.

⁹ See below, ch. XII, and the literature there cited.

¹⁰ On the Tobiades, cf. A. Buechler, *Die Tobiaden und die Oniaden* (Vienna, 1899); E. Schuerer, *Geschichte des juedischen Volkes im Zeitalter Jesu Christi*, 3rd and 4th ed. (Leipzig, 1901–11), vol. 1, pp. 195 f.; S. Zeitlin, "The Tobias Family and the Hasmoneans," in *PAAJR*, vol. IV, 1933, pp. 169–223; L. Finkelstein, *The Pharisees*, vol. 2, pp. 580–87. It is interesting to recall that J. Klausner suggested long ago that Joseph ben Tobias was the author of *Koheleth*; see his book, *Bimei Bayyit Sheni* (Tel-Aviv, 1930), pp. 160–75, in which the paper is reprinted.

¹¹ Cf. Isa. 5:8 ff.; Micah 3:3; Jer. 34:8 ff. for the prophetic protest against the same process in the First Temple days, and Lev., ch. 25, for Biblical legislation designed to halt, or, at least, interfere with, the trend.

¹² For the evidence in detail, cf. Gordis, "The Social Background of Wisdom Literature," in *HUCA*, 1944, pp. 77–116. The views of L. Finkelstein on the class origins of the Wisdom books are summarized and analyzed there in note 8. The book of Koheleth is ascribed by him to a plebeian cynic (pp. 235 ff.). Finkelstein discounts as imaginative Koheleth's picture of himself as a rich man (ch. 2), and stresses his preoccupation with social justice. He attributes the passages extolling diligence and wealth (4:5; 7:11; 10:18; 11:9) to a glossator. But if all references to the enjoyment of life as a goal are regarded as unauthentic, a much larger number of passages must be excised. It may be added that social injustice does not bulk so large in Koheleth's consciousness as the unattainability of true wisdom and the vanity of labor. Only one passage, 4:1 ff., deals with social oppression, while the latter themes run through the book. The orientation of Koheleth seems definitely "upper-class," as the evidence indicates.

¹³ Cf. his *Israel's Wisdom Literature*, p. 178, in his discussion of the rise of the idea of an after-life.

¹⁴ Plato, *Protagoras* 1, pp. 317 ff. (Loeb Classics, New York, 1924, Plato, vol. IV, p. 124).

¹⁵ *Cambridge Ancient History* (New York, 1927), vol. V, pp. 24, 377.

¹⁶ Ben Sira 51:25b, "Acquire Wisdom for yourselves without money," is a poetical statement of the idea that wisdom is easily attained. Cf. the following verse, "She is nigh unto them that seek her," and the well-known passage, Isa. 55:1 f., upon which Ben Sira undoubtedly bases himself.

¹⁷ Cf. E. Zeller, *Pre-Socratic Philosophy* (London, 1881), vol. 2, pp. 394–516. G. Grote's classic rehabilitation of the sophist movement is to be found in his *A History of Greece* (London, 1851, and often reprinted), ch. 67. A lively recent account is to be found in W. Durant, *The Life of Greece* (New York, 1939), pp. 358–66. A critical evaluation is to be found in W. T. Stace, *A Critical History of Greek Philosophy* (London, 1928), pp. 106–26.

¹⁸ "My son = my pupil," though references to the instruction of parents are common. So C. H. Toy, *ICC on Proverbs* (New York, 1902), pp. 8, 12. Professor Louis Ginzberg has pointed out that *beni* was the accepted form of address of a master to his disciple in Tannaitic and early Amoraic times; cf., for example, B. Sanh. 11a, שב בני שב, and L. Ginzberg, *Commentary on the Jerusalem Talmud* (New York, 1940), vol. 1, pp. 238, 300. It is noteworthy that Koheleth does not use the term, probably because the book was not a *vademecum* for youth, but rather a personal notebook. See below, ch. XIII. The term "my son" does occur in the Epilogue (12:12), constituting additional evidence that it emanates from another hand, that of a conventional Wisdom teacher. In 8:2, the emendation of *'ani* into *beni* is unnecessary. See Commentary ad loc.

¹⁹ Cf., *inter alia*, Pr. 5:7 ff.; 6:24 ff.; 7:5 ff.; 23:27 f.; Ben Sira 26:5 ff., 19; and see SBWL, pp. 111 ff.

²⁰ Toy, op. cit., p. 31, notes "the absence of characteristic national traits," and says, "If for the name JHVH we substitute 'God,' there is not a sentence or a paragraph in the Proverbs which would not be as suitable for any other people as for Israel." Hermann Gunkel, in *Religion in Geschichte und Gegenwart*, believes that "the Hebrew Proverb literature was in its beginning altogether secular . . . . The religious motive was introduced later."

²¹ On the origin of the proper names in *Job*, cf. Driver-Gray, *ICC on Job* (New York, 1921), vol. I, pp. 37 ff.; G. Hoelscher, *Das Buch Hiob* (Tuebingen, 1937), p. 2. The locales from which the names are drawn are Edom and Arabia.

²² Cf. Proverbs of Amenemope (Col. XXV, l. 496), "The strength of Ra is to him that is on the road," as an instance of a popular saying.

²³ Thus, taking chapter 16 at random, we find JHVH used ten times, of which at least four are in stock phrases (vv. 5, 6, 7?, 20). On divine Names in Wisdom, see Fichtner, pp. 103 ff.; Rankin, p. 39, note; and Cassuto, cited in note 24 below.

²⁴ JHVH and *'adōnai* occur in the poetry of Job a) in 12:9, which is either an interpolation or, more probably, a reminiscence of Isa. 41:20c, a stock phrase; b) in 28:28, in what is again a typical phrase of the Wisdom schools (the entire chapter is almost certainly an independent poem); and c) in 38:1; 40:1, in the superscriptions. In *Koheleth* even the Temple is called *bet 'elōhim*, not *bet JHVH* (4:17). Cf. also U. Cassuto, *Torat Hateudot Vesidduram shel Siphrei Hatorah* (Jerusalem, 1942), p. 28: "The *minim*, that is to say, the Sadducees, scions of the aristocracy exposed to the influence of the international Wisdom of the time, and especially to 'Greek wisdom,' which, like the international Wisdom, was accustomed to call the Deity by its general name, tended to see in this practice a mark of progress as against the national tradition which held fast to the 'personal' name JHVH." Cf. also pp. 21, 23 ff.

²⁵ Cf. Hoelscher's correct conclusion, op. cit., p. 7, that the author of *Job* was a Palestinian who had travelled widely, hence his familiarity with

Egyptian flora and fauna, the Sinai desert, and the hail, ice, and snow of the north, probably the Lebanon region.

²⁶ Pr. 2:16 ff.; 5:9, 15; 7:5 ff.; 22:14; 23:27; 30:20; B. S. 9:1 ff.; 19:2 f.; 23:16; 25:2; 36:30.

²⁷ *Peninim* occurs four times in Proverbs (3:15; 8:11; 20:15; 31:10), once in *Job* (28:18), and only once more in the entire O. T. (Lam. 4:7).

²⁸ Cf. Pr. 17:1.

²⁹ Pr. 23:1 f., 20 f., 29 ff.; 30:8–10; Ecc. 7:16 f.; B. S. 18:30 ff.

³⁰ Cf., *inter alia*, Pr. 3:28; 22:22.

³¹ For details, see *SBWL*, pp. 93 ff.; and cf. Pr. 6:1–5; 11:13; 17:13; 22:26 f.; 20:16 = 27:13.

³² Cf. Pr. 10:2, 16, 22; 11:28; 12:22.

³³ Cf. M. Lohr, *Sozialismus und Individualismus im A. T.* (Giessen, 1906); W. O. E. Oesterley and T. H. Robinson, *Hebrew Religion* (New York, 1930), pp. 219 f., 251 ff.; Rankin, op. cit., pp. 53–98.

³⁴ Cf. the classical passages Jer. 31:26 ff.; Ez. 18:1 ff.

³⁵ Cf. Oesterley and Robinson, op. cit., p. 223; Rankin, op. cit., pp. 124–197.

³⁶ Cf. B. S. 10:11. Particularly interesting is 7:17. Ben Sira declares: "Humble thy pride greatly, for the expectation of man is worms." His grandson and Greek translator gives it a Pharisaic interpretation: "Humble thy soul greatly, for the punishment of the ungodly is fire and worms." On the denial of an after-life in Wisdom, cf. also Job 14:11 ff.; Ecc. 3:20 f.; 9:10, 12.

³⁷ G. F. Moore, *History of Religions* (New York, 1913), vol. I, p. 286.

³⁸ Cf. Am. 5:18 ff.; Isa. 2:12; Jer. 4:23.

³⁹ Isa. 2:2; Mi. 4:1; Hos. 3:5; Jer. 23:20; 30:24; 48:47; 49:39; Ez. 38:8, 16.

⁴⁰ Cf. B. S. 15:11, 16; 21:11; 37:3; and L. Finkelstein, *The Pharisees*, pp. 202, 250–54; and *SBWL*, pp. 107 ff.

⁴¹ Op. cit., pp. 108 f., for the evidence.

⁴² See note 36 above.

⁴³ See op. cit., p. 110, for the evidence, based on Ecc. 4:17 to 5:3; 9:2; and Pr. 3:9; 15:8; 21:3, 7. Particularly noteworthy is the divorce of ritual from morality in the incidental reference in Pr. 7:14; see also Pr. 17:1.

⁴⁴ Cf. B. S. 26:29; 27:2; Pr. 12:11; 27:23; 28:19; Ecc. 5:8.

⁴⁵ For the evidence of social conservatism in *Job*, cf. *SBWL*, pp. 113 ff.

⁴⁶ This was true of *Proverbs*, *Job* and *Ben Sira* and particularly of *Ecclesiastes*. The Rabbinic sources are given op. cit., n. 85. On the canonicity of *Ecclesiastes*, see the chapter below.

NOTES ON CHAPTER IV

¹ Its oldest source is in the title, verse 1 of ch. 1.

² Midrash *Shir Hashirim Rabba* 1:1, sec. 10: רבי יונתן אומר שיר השירים כתב תחילה ואחר כך משלי ואח״כ קוהלת ומייתי ליה רבי יונתן מדרך ארץ כשאדם נער אומר

דברי זמר הנדיל אומר דברי משלות הזקין אומר דברי הבלים ר' ינאי חמוי דרבי אמי אמר
הכל מודים שקוהלת בסוף אמרה.

³ *Shir Hashirim Rabba* 1:1, sec. 10: רבי חייא רבה אמר משלי כתב תחלה ואח"כ
שיר השירים ואחר כך קוהלת.

⁴ *Shir Hashirim Rabba* 1:1, sec. 10: תני רבי חייא רבה רק לעת זקנת שלמה שרתה
עליו רוח הקודש ואמר ג' ספרים משלי וקוהלת ושיר השירים.

⁵ *B. Bathra* 14b: סידרן של כתובים רות וספר תהלים ואיוב ומשלי קוהלת שיר השירים
וקינות ודניאל ומגלת אסתר עזרא ודברי הימים.

⁶ *Ibid.*: ומי כתבן . . . . חזקיה וסיעתו כתבו ישעיה משלי שיר השירים וקוהלת.

⁷ עתק *Kal* = "move, advance" (Job 14:18); *Hiphil* = "move" (Gen. 12:8; 26:22), "remove" (Job 32:15), hence "copy" in Pr. 25:1, which is rendered by LXX ἐξεγράψαντο; V, transtulerant. On the basis of the root meaning, "remove," the verb העתיקו is homiletically interpreted in Rabbinic literature as 1) "removed," hence, "suppressed" — העתיקו מלמד שגנוזים היו (Yalkut Shimeoni, Proverbs, sec. 961). 2) "set aside," hence "interpreted" — דבר אחר אין העתיקו אלא פירשו (ibid.; cf. also *Aboth de R. Nathan*, ed. Schechter, Version B, ch. 1). 3) On the basis of עתיק, "old, advanced in years," the verb is rendered "they considered with deliberation" — ולא העתיקו אלא שהמתינו (*Aboth de R. Nathan*, loc. cit.).

⁸ Cf. the standard commentaries on Isa. 6:1; Jer. 1:1; Hos. 1:1; Mi. 1:1; and on the titles of the Psalms.

⁹ Hence, the effort of Jastrow to equate *Koheleth* with *Shelomoh* and the *gematria* proposed by Zimmermann, according to which the Aramaic כנש"ה is numerically equivalent to שלמה at 375, are unacceptable. See Commentary on 1:1 for details.

¹⁰ Thus, in addition to the *Wisdom of Solomon* and the *Psalms of Solomon*, works are attributed to Adam and Eve, Enoch, Noah, the Patriarchs of the Twelve Tribes, Moses, Isaiah, Manasseh, Jeremiah and Baruch. Cf. the opening words of the Book of Enoch: "The words of the blessing of Enoch" (1:1). In *The Testaments of the Twelve Patriarchs* we read "The copy of the Testament of Reuben" (1:1), "the copy of the words of Simon," etc. The *Assumption of Moses* opens with the words (1:1) "The Testament of Moses," etc., and *The Apocalypse of Baruch* with "How the Lord came to Baruch son of Neriah" (1:1). So, too, IV Ezra. It is noteworthy that the Apocryphal *Wisdom of Solomon*, which is, in part at least, a refutation of *Koheleth*, does not claim to be the work of Solomon. The growth of the tradition of its Solomonic authorship may be traced from the oldest mention circa 200 C. E. in the *Muratorian Canon* (p. 11a, 1.8), which speaks of it as simply *Sapientia*, but adds the words: *ab amicis Solomonis in honorem ipsius scripta*. The Church Fathers Clement, Tertullian and Cyprian already refer to it as the *Wisdom of Solomon*. The Latin Version calls it *Liber Sapientiae*. Holmes' assumption (R. H. Charles, *Apocrypha and Pseudepigrapha of the O. T.*, vol. 1, p. 519) that Jerome, recognizing that Solomon was not its author, was responsible for dropping Solomon from the title in the Latin Version, is not convincing, since Jerome explicitly indicates that he did not alter the extant translation. On the entire subject, see R. H. Charles, *Apocrypha*

and Pseudepigrapha of the O. T. (Oxford, 1913), and the introductions to the various books; C. C. Torrey, *The Apocryphal Literature* (New Haven, 1945); R. H. Pfeiffer, *History of New Testament Times With an Introduction to the Apocrypha* (New York, 1949); S. Zeitlin, "Jewish Apocryphal Literature," in JQR, vol. 40, 1950, pp. 223–250.

[11] Cf. *Midrash Koheleth Rabba* 3:11: אילו אחר אמר את הכל עשה יפה בעתו
הייתי אומר זה שלא אכל פרוסה מימיו הוא אומר את הכל עשה יפה בעתו אלא שלמה ...
לפי שכתוב בו (מלכים א' ה') ויהי לחם שלמה ליום אחד שלשים כור סלת וגו' לזה נאה לומר
את הכל עשה יפה בעתו ד"א אילו אחר אמר הבל הבלים אמר קוהלת הייתי אומר זה שלא
קנה ב' פרוטות מימיו הוא פירת בממונו של עולם ואומר הבל הבלים אלא זה שלמה שכתוב
בו ויתן המלך את הכסף בירושלים כאבנים וגו' .... לזה נאה לומר הבל הבלים.

[12] Cf. Com. ad loc.

[13] Cf. 2:7, where the verb is plural (*hāyū*); cf. also 1:16; 2:9, and see Com. ad loc.

[14] The controversy is recorded in the *Mishnah, Eduy.* 5:3; *Tos. Yad.* 2:14. In M. *Yad.* 3:5 the full discussion followed by the decision in its favor is cited: שיר השירים וקהלת מטמאין את הידים ר' יהודה אומר שיר השירים מטמאין את הידים וקהלת
מחלוקת ר' יוסי אומר קהלת אינו מטמא את הידים ושיר השירים מחלוקת ר' שמעון אומר מקולי
בית שמאי ומחומרי בית הלל אמר רבי שמעון בן עזאי מקובל אני מפי שבעים ושנים זקנים ביום
שהושיבו את רבי אלעזר בן עזריה בישיבה ששיר השירים וקהלת מטמאין את הידים אמר רבי
עקיבא חס ושלום לא נחלק אדם מישראל על שיר השירים .... ואם נחלקו לא נחלקו אלא
על קהלת אמר ר' יוחנן בן יהושע בן חמיו של ר' עקיבא כדברי בן עזאי כך נחלקו וכן נמרו.

[15] On the canonization of the Wisdom books, see F. Buhl, *Canon and Text of the O. T.* (Edinburgh, 1892), pp. 3–32; H. E. Ryle, *Canon of the O. T.*, 2nd. ed. (London, 1909); as well as the suggestive treatments of Max L. Margolis, *The Hebrew Scriptures in the Making* (Phila., 1922), pp. 83–96, and S. Zeitlin, "An Historical Study of the Canonization of the Hebrew Scriptures," in *Proceedings of the American Academy for Jewish Research*, vol. III, 1932, pp. 121–58. See also Pfeiffer, *Introduction*, pp. 50-70. On the canonicity of Koheleth, see L. Ginzberg, *Legends of the Jews* (Phila., 1928), vol. 6, p. 301, n. 93.

It is generally agreed that the Hebrew canon was fixed even before the historic session of the academy at Jamnia in 90 C. E. At these sessions (referred to in Talmudic literature as *bō bayōm* ("that very day"), the status of various Biblical books was discussed purely as an academic question, prior to the official ratification by the scholars of what was generally accepted (cf. Buhl, op. cit., pp. 25–27; Margolis, op. cit., p. 88). Many of the sources cited below use the phrase בקשו לגנוז, which has sometimes been taken to mean "sought to declare uncanonical." As S. Zeitlin has demonstrated, the phrase means "sought to store away from public reading, so as not to be studied and interpreted in the academies" (op. cit., pp. 124 ff.). The Talmudic phrase for "uncanonical" is אינו מטמא את הידים, "does not defile the hands."

[16] Cf. *Shab.* 30a, b: שדבריו סותרין זה את זה.

[17] Cf. *Aboth de R. Nathan*, ch. 1, both versions (pp. 2, 3, ed. Schechter): מפני שהם (היו אומרים) משלות ואינן מן הכתובים.

[18] מפני שהיא חכמתו של שלמה (*Tos. Yad.* 2:14, ed. Zuckermandl, p. 683; *Meg.* 7a).

[19] מפני שמצאו בו דברים הטמים לצד מינות (*Pesikta de Rab Kahana*, piska 8, p. 61a (ed. Buber); *Lev. Rab.* 28:1; *Koheleth R.* 3:1; Jerome, *Commentary on Ecc.* 12:13.

[20] מכאן ואילך "henceforth," *Tos. Yad.* 2:13; *B. Shab.* 100b.

[21] In 1:3 Koheleth doubts the value of toil. The Midrash asks, "Does Solomon doubt the value of laboring in the Torah? By no means; when he says, 'What value is there in all his labor,' he means *man's* labor, which is of no use, not labor *in the Torah*!" (*Pesikta de Rab Kahana*, piska 8, 61a, b, and parallels).

Ecc. 3:21 expresses skepticism as to the survival of the soul of man. The Midrash refers the verse to the different destinies awaiting the righteous and the wicked in the afterworld (*Mid. Koheleth Rabba* ad loc.):
מטרונא אחת שאלה לר' יוסי בר חלפתא מה'ד ומי יודע רוח בני האדם העולה היא למעלה
אמר לה אלו נשמותיהם של צדיקים שהן נתונות באוצר .... אמרה ליה ומה'ד ורוח הבהמה
הירדת היא למטה לארץ אמר לה אלו הן נשמותיהן של רשעים שהן יורדות לניהנם למטה וגו'.
Note the LXX: καὶ τίς οἶδεν τὸ πνεῦμα υἱῶν τοῦ ἀνθρώπου εἰ ἀναβαίνει αὐτὸ εἰς ἄνω; καὶ πνεῦμα τοῦ κτήνους εἰ καταβαίνει αὐτὸ κάτω εἰς τὴν γῆν; In this latter passage, the Targum, like the LXX, renders literally.

P. Churgin, *Targum Kethubim* (New York, 1945), p. 165, plausibly suggests that the Targum is a composite of many versions, and that the rendering of this particular verse emanates from a literalistic Aramaic translation, rather than from a homiletic one.

[22] See Ch. XI below, and the Commentary passim.

[23] This is explicit in the tradition cited above in note 1, which assumes that Solomon wrote the book in his youth, because it deals with love. That it was widely regarded as a love song is clear from the emphatic statement in *B. Sanh.* 101a: הקורא פסוק של שיר השירים ועושה אותו כמין זמר והקורא פסוק בבית משתאות מביא רעה לעולם. The reading in *Tos. Sanh.* 12:10 may be the more original: ר' עקיבא אומר המנענע קולו בשיר השירים בבית המשתאות ועושה אותו כמין זמר אין לו חלק לעוה'ב, "He who chants the Song of Songs in a banquet hall and treats it as a secular song has no share in the world to come." R. Akiba's panegyric of the book: שכל כתובים קודש ושיר השירים קודש קדשים, "All the books of Scripture are holy, but the *Song of Songs* is the holy of holies" (*M. Yad.* 3:5), is a passionate defense of its sanctity against what must have been strong doubts that refused to be suppressed.

NOTES ON CHAPTER V

[1] See below, ch. XII.

[2] So Hertzberg, p. 22.

[3] So Hertzberg, p. 23.

[4] On the various dates proposed for *Job*, cf. R. H. Pfeiffer, *inter alia, Introduction to the Old Testament*, pp. 675–79; also R. Gordis, "A New

Introduction to the Book of Job," in *Menorah Journal* (vol. 37, 1949), pp. 329–358. *Job* is probably to be dated before the 3rd century B. C. E.

⁵ In *OLZ*, 1921, pp. 11–15; cf. Hertzberg, op. cit., p. 23.

⁶ The use of a similar phrase in II Chr. 1:11 and Ecc. 5:18; 6:2 is thoroughly explicable in view of the fact that both were Second Temple writers. The comparison of life to "a shadow" in I Chr. 29:15 and Ecc. 6:12; 8:13 represents one of the commonest metaphors in literature; cf. Job 8:9.

⁷ Cf. Wright, *Ecc.*, pp. 41 ff.; Barton, *ICC*, pp. 53 ff.; Hertzberg, pp. 23 f. Frequently the parallels rest upon a doubtful exegesis of the passages in *Ben Sira*.

⁸ For which Ecc. 3:20–21 and Ben Sira 40:11; Ecc. 1:4 and B. S. 14:18 (Hebrew) have been compared.

⁹ Treated in Ecc. 9:9 ff. and B. S. 14:11 f.; Ecc. 11:10 and Ben Sira 30:23.

¹⁰ Cf. Ecc. 3:11 and Ben Sira 39:16; Ecc. 3:14; 8:17 and Ben Sira 18:6.

¹¹ This familiar idea is treated in Ecc. 10:8; Ben Sira 27:26; and, *inter alia*, in Ps. 7:16; Pr. 26:27.

¹² Cf. Ecc. 8:12; Ben Sira 1:13; and the Bible *passim*.

¹³ Ecc. 5:1b. Ben Sira 7:14 is much closer to Mat. 6:7, "And in praying, use not vain repetitions," than to Koheleth.

¹⁴ Treated in Ecc. 9:16; Ben Sira 13:22c.

¹⁵ Cf. Ecc. 5:2, 6; Ben Sira 34:7; and such Talmudic formulations as אי אפשר לחלום בלי דברים בטלים (B. Ber. 55a), "A dream is impossible without meaningless elements in it," and דברי חלומות לא מעלין ולא מורידין (B. Sanh. 30a), "Dreams are of no practical efficacy."

¹⁶ This theme is discussed in Ecc. 5:3; Ben Sira 18:22; and Deut. 23:22 ff.

¹⁷ Cf. Ecc. 5:11b with Ben Sira 34:1 (Hebrew); Ecc. 7:8b with Ben Sira 5:11b (Heb.); Ecc. 10:2–3, 12–13 with Ben Sira 21:25–26; Ecc. 1:18 with Ben Sira 21:12; Ecc. 7:6 with Ben Sira 21:20. These and similar "parallels" are given by Grimme, p. 30; McNeile, p. 38; Holmes, p. 525.

¹⁸ So most scholars, as, e. g., Tyler, Wright, Toy, art. "Ecclesiasticus," in *Encyclopaedia Britannica*; E. Kautzsch, *Apokryphen*, I, pp. 234 ff.; Box and Oesterley, in R. H. Charles, *Apocrypha and Pseudepigrapha of the Old Testament*, vol. 1, p. 293. Pfeiffer, *History of New Testament Times* (New York, 1949), p. 401, n. 20, is almost alone today in believing that Koheleth was written after Ben Sira.

¹⁹ Cf. the discussion of both passages in our commentary on 3:15. Levy (pp. 27 ff.) has demonstrated that the usual rendering of the stich in Ben Sira as "For God is the avenger of the persecuted," which is obviously not the meaning in *Koheleth*, is incorrect for Ben Sira as well, who uses the phrase virtually in Koheleth's sense.

²⁰ The Syriac reads: "Take heed to thyself in the time of thy youth."

²¹ Recognized by Hertzberg, p. 23.

²² Cf. *Midrash Koheleth Rabba* ad loc., where, in addition to interpretations which refer the verse to agriculture and to the study of the Torah, the text reads: רבי יהושע אומר נשאת אשה בילדותך ומתה תשא בזקנותך היו לך בנים בילדותך יהיו

לך בנים בזקנותך . . . . . רבי נתן פתר קרייא באשה אם לקחת אשה בנערותך לקח
בזקנותך וגו'.

²³ Cf. these examples:

אדם אחד מאלף מצאתי 7:28 *Ecc.*	אנשי שלומך יהיו רבים ובעל 6:5 *B. S.*
	סודך אחד מאלף
אם טוב ואם רע 12:14 *Ecc.*	אם לטוב אם לרע 13:24 *B. S.*
שומר מצוה לא ידע דבר רע 8:5 *Ecc.*	אשר תדע שומר מצוה 37:12 *B. S.*
ויתר שהיה קהלת חכם עוד למד 12:9 *Ecc.*	ויש חכם לעמו יחכם פרי דעתו 37:23 *B. S.*
דעת את העם	בנויתם
סוף דבר 12:13 *Ecc.*	קץ דבר 43:27 *B. S.*

²⁴ Cf. Com. ad loc.

²⁵ Cf. the testimony of the *Ethiopic Enoch* (104:10): "I know this secret, that many sinners will change and distort the words of truth, hold evil discourses and lie, devise great deceptions and write books on their discourses." The frequent Talmudic discussions on the books of the Sadducees and the *Minim* need only be recalled. The latter is a general term for "heretics" and included not only aberrations from normative Judaism, but various schools of skepticism and disbelief. Greek literature, with its unsettling effect on traditional Jewish attitudes, also was available in Palestine in the Mishnaic period (and probably earlier), as is clear from a careful analysis of the Mishnah, Yad. 4:4; cf. Gordis, " 'Homeric' Books in Palestine," in *JQR*, vol. 38, 1948, pp. 359–68. The considerable impact of Greek culture on Palestinian Jewry and on normative Judaism, which has been generally underestimated, is surveyed in S. Lieberman's highly significant studies, *Greek in Jewish Palestine* (New York, 1942) and *Hellenism in Jewish Palestine* (New York, 1950).

²⁶ Galling doubts that *Wisdom of Solomon* is a polemic against Koheleth.

NOTES ON CHAPTER VI

¹ On the spirit and scope of Koheleth, see chaps. X and XIV below. On the date, see ch. VIII below.

² That the text contains Greek words and idioms was maintained by van der Palm, Zirkel, Graetz, Tyler, Plumptre, Siegfried and Wildeboer. The view is denied by Delitzsch, Renan, Menzel, Nowack, McNeile, Zapletal and Barton.

³ The evidence may be summarized as follows: A) Several of these alleged Graecisms occur in Semitic inscriptions. Thus תחת השמש (1:3 and often) is not a rendering of ὑφ' ἡλίῳ. It occurs in the Phoenician inscriptions of Tabnit and Eshmunazar. ראי השמש (7:11) is not a foreign phrase. B) Several are not Greek, but Persian words: פרדסים (2:5) and פתגם (8:11). C) Other locutions can be validated in Biblical usage: תור (1:13); מקרה (2:14 a. e.); הלך נפש (6:9); מענה (5:19); טוב אשר יפה (5:17); עשות טוב (3:12); או יותר (2:15); אדם (7:28). D) Others have their analogues in Mishnaic Hebrew: the difficult

הילד השני (4:15); יצא את כלם (7:18); מלאה (11:5). E) In several instances where extant parallels are lacking, the phrase is perfectly idiomatic, even inevitable, in Hebrew, as e. g. יום טובה (7:14); מה שהיה (1:9; 3:15; 6:10).

The one instance which Barton concedes to be a Graecism, ויעשם (6:12) (=χρόνον ποιεῖν, "spend time"), is a common Mishnaic usage. Cf. Mid. Gen. R., sec. 91: בישרם שעתידין לעשות שם ר"י שנה, "He announced to them that they were destined to spend 210 years there"; idem, sec. 22:4: לא עשה הבל בעולם יותר מנ' יום, "Abel did not spend more than fifty days in the world"; Mid. Tehillim on Ps. 17:14: ר' שמעון שעשה במערה, etc. In spite of the absence at present of early Hebrew parallels, the idiom may be indigenously Hebrew. Or it may have entered Hebrew from the spoken Greek of the streets. In any event, its use does not betoken any literary influence from the Greek. So, too, שנה בעיניו איננו ראה (8:16), which Hertzberg assumes to be foreign, occurs in an old Rabbinic source in Tosefta Sukkah 4:5, לא היינו רואין שינה, which is obviously not a direct reminiscence of our verse. On the entire subject, see the convenient summation in Barton, pp. 32–34, and the briefer treatment in Hertz., p. 47, and the detailed discussion on each of these passages in our Commentary. See also ch. VII, note 29.

4 Cf. O. Pfleiderer, Die Philosophie des Heraklit (Berlin, 1886), pp. 255 ff.

5 Cf. M. Friedlaender, Griechische Philosophie im A. T. (Berlin, 1904), to which E. Sellin replied in Spuren griechischer Philosophie im A. T. (Leipzig, 1905).

6 For the direct application of Aristotle's idea to Jewish ethics, cf. Maimonides, Commentary on the Mishnah Abot, Shemoneh Perakim, ed. by J. I. Gorfinkle (New York, 1912), and cf. D. Rosin, Die Ethik des Maimonides (Breslau, 1876).

7 Cf. Hertzberg, p. 49, and the literature there cited.

8 Proposed by Tyler, Ecclesiastes (p. 11), and followed by Plumptre, Siegfried, and Haupt. Cf. Barton's refutation, pp. 34 ff.

9 This doctrine, first enunciated by the Ionic philosopher Anaximander (cf. W. T. Stace, A Critical History of Greek Philosophy, London, 1928, p. 25), influenced Rabbinic thought; cf. הקב"ה היה בונה עולמות ומחריבן ובונה עולמות ומחריבן עד שברא את אלו אמר דין הניין לי (Mid. Gen. R., sec. 9; Koheleth R. 3:11), "God kept on creating worlds and destroying them, until He created this one, whereupon He said, 'This pleases me.'"

10 Cf. 3:11; 6:12; 7:14; 11:5; and see ch. XIV below.

11 This suggestion was advanced by P. Kleinert, Theologische Studien und Kritiken (1909), and by Allgeier in his commentary (1925), p. 11. It is defended by L. Levy, Das Buch Qoheleth (Leipzig, 1912), pp. 11 ff., with important modifications. He believes that Koheleth found these ideas already incorporated in the popular Wisdom literature of 3rd century Palestine. Cf. also R. Bultmann, Der Stil der paulinischen Predigt und die kynisch-stoische Diatribe (Göttingen, 1910), and see Hertzberg, op. cit., p. 48.

12 On the use of quotations, see the chapter below, and our study, "Quotations As a Literary Usage in Biblical, Rabbinic and Oriental Literature,"

in *HUCA*, 1949, pp. 157–218. The repetition of phrases, and the use of incidents, real or imaginary, as illustrations are frequent in Egyptian Wisdom writings. See our Intr. Note on 4:13 ff. and 9:14 ff.

¹³ Thus Levy (pp. 14 ff.) regards הבל as equivalent to τῦφος, "illusion"; רעות רוח as eq. to κενὴ δόξα, "empty notion." Not only are these terms not parallel in meaning, but each of them has an authentic Semitic semantic development. Cf. Com. on 1:2 and 1:14. With regard to Levy's equating עינן with the Greek πρᾶγμα, Hertz. (p. 48, n.) also calls attention to the fact that LXX never renders עינן by the common Greek πρᾶγμα, but always by the rarer circumstantial word περισπασμός, "distracting business." It may be added that הבל is always rendered by LXX as ματαιότης. It should be self-evident that even when similar meanings develop in two words in different languages, this does not suffice of itself to prove borrowing, but merely parallel semantic development.

¹⁴ Fragment no. 189, ed. Diels, *apud Levy*, p. 18.

¹⁵ Against Levy, who assumes a direct contact, for which no evidence is available, especially since the words of Aristippus have been completely lost! Levy's discussion (pp. 18 ff.) merely demonstrates that similar temperaments, reacting to similar issues, may well arrive at parallel attitudes.

¹⁶ For Koheleth's spiritual development, see ch. X below. An adumbration of the theme of man's inability to know the future is to be found perhaps in Job's lament that man cannot participate in the joys and sorrows of his own children (Job 14:21 f.), although even here the emotional aspect is more pronounced than the intellectual.

¹⁷ *Apud Diogenes Laertes*, II, 99; cf. Th. Gomperz, *Die Lebensauffassung der griechischen Philosophen*, p. 148.

¹⁸ Gomperz, op. cit., pp. 213 f.

¹⁹ Cf. especially Tyler, op. cit., pp. 18 ff.

²⁰ Cf. "Social Background of Wisdom Literature," in *HUCA*, 1944, pp. 102–105.

²¹ Published by B. Meissner, in *Mitteilungen der vorderasiatischen Gesellschaft*, 1902, Heft I, and cited by Barton, op. cit., p. 39.

²² Cf. E. Caird, *Lectures in the Evolution of Religion*, vol. I, chaps. 7, 10, 13, 14.

²³ Cf. E. J. Dillon, *Skeptics of the O. T.* (London, 1895).

²⁴ So A. Bertholet, *Kulturgeschichte Israels* (1919), p. 223. Cf. also D. S. Margoliouth, in *The Expositor*, 1911, p. 463: "Ecclesiastes is one of several attempts at introducing Greek philosophy to Hebrew readers."

²⁵ Op. cit., p. 43.

²⁶ Cf., for example, Levy, pp. 16 ff.

²⁷ Cf., for example, Gen. 8:22; Jer. 5:22; Ps. 104; Job, chaps. 38 to 41, and often.

²⁸ Cf., for example, Job 14:5; Isa. 29:16; 45:9; Jer. 18:6; Ps. 139; Pr. 16:4, 9, etc.

²⁹ The ageless problem of free will vs. determinism was one of the issues between the Pharisees and the Sadducees. Cf. L. Finkelstein, *The Pharisees*

(Phila., 1938). For the bearing of this controversy on the social standpoint of Wisdom, cf. *SBWL*, pp. 107–109.

30 הכל בידי שמים חוץ מיראת שמים (Ber. 33b; Meg. 25a).

31 הכל צפוי והרשות נתונה (Ab. 3:15).

32 Cf., for example, Ex. 33:20, 23; Isa. 6:5; Hos. 11:9; Ps. 115:16. The unique separateness of God is the fundamental connotation of the term *kadosh* in the theology of Isaiah. The Maimonidean doctrine of "negative attributes" thus represents an intellectual formulation and extension of an indigenous Hebrew outlook. Cf. the anonymous "Hymn of Glory" in the liturgy for a poetic statement of this approach.

33 Isa. 45:18. The attitude of Rabbinic Judaism, which is reflected in the elaborate system of benedictions for physical pleasures, needs no validation. Other Rabbinic utterances on the enjoyment of life will be adduced below.

34 Op. cit., p. 34.

35 Actually this Greek influence is considerably less extensive in the view of G. Hoelscher, *Geschichte der israelitischen und juedischen Religion* (Giessen, 1922), p. 161: "Any deeper spiritual influence on the part of Greece in the 3rd or 2nd century B. C. upon the educated upper classes in the Oriental cities, let alone upon the masses of the people, can hardly be considered." On this view, the argument in the text above is even stronger. Hertzberg, on the other hand, declares that the East during the Hellenistic age was steeped in Greek philosophy. Rankin, op. cit., p. 141, adopts an intermediate position. Similarly, J. Klausner, *Mi-Yeshu ad Paulus* (Tel-Aviv, 1940), vol. 2, p. 156, emphasizes the Greek influence in the general atmosphere rather than in the schools. This position we believe closest to the truth.

36 Cf. the sensible judgment of Budde *apud* Kautzsch, 3rd ed., who saw in Koheleth only "Funken, die von allen Schulen hier und da aufzufliegen scheinen."

37 Cf. Hertzberg, p. 50. Ideas parallel in Koheleth with Theognis were pointed out by P. Kleinert, *Theologische Studien und Kritiken* (1909), p. 516, and by H. Ranston, *Ecclesiastes and the Early Greek Wisdom Literature* (London, 1925); *idem, O. T. Wisdom Books and Their Teaching* (London, 1930). They are on a par with the striking similarities existing between Koheleth and Marcus Aurelius; cf. Podechard, pp. 87 ff.

38 Cf. chap. XII below.

39 Originated by Empedocles of Agrigentum (495–435 B. C. E.), but the idea quickly became the property of many schools. He himself was an eclectic, and the idea of the "roots of all" may be older than his formulation. Cf. Stace, op. cit., pp. 81 ff.

40 Especially by P. Humbert, *Recherches sur les sources Egyptiennes de la Littérature sapientiale d'Israël* (Neuchâtel, 1929), chap. IV, pp. 107 ff.

41 See chap. I.

42 See our Commentary on the important passages 4:13 and 9:14 ff., where Egyptian Wisdom indicates the use of typical incidents cited or invented to prove a point. Cf. also Humbert, p. 117. See the Commentary also on 2:12; 8:4; 9:9; 10:6; 11:9 for valuable light from Egyptian Wisdom.

[43] There is no reason for accepting Humbert's view that "Koheleth's doubts about life and his 'disabused *carpe diem*' are not Hebrew" (op. cit., p. 110). Similarly with the idea that the enjoyment of life is "the gift of God." That the king is called "God" in 4:2 (Humbert, p. 119) is not true, and what is more, the usage can be validated for Jewish thought; cf. the Midrashic interpretations of Ex. 21:6; 22:7. On the use of white garments in 9:8, cf. Est. 8:15. On the prohibition against cursing the king (10:20), Humbert cites the Insinger Papyrus; he overlooks Ex. 22:27.

[44] Thus Humbert argues that the description of building operations in 2:4 ff. is too elaborate for Palestine (p. 114) and that a hierarchy of officials (referred to in 5:7) must also be Egyptian (p. 117). Contrasts in society were far from unknown in Palestine (ag. Humbert, p. 121); cf. *inter alia* I Sam. 2:4–8; Isa. 3:1–5; Micah 7:6 and indeed the Psalms and the Prophets *passim*. The idiom *bēt 'ōlām*, which occurs in Ecc. 12:5 and in the Greek text of Tobit 3:6, is not an Egyptian borrowing (idem, p. 123); it occurs in Palmyrene. Cf. Com. ad loc.

[45] Humbert, p. 124.

[46] Cf. 11:4; 12:2; 4:17 ff.

[47] It was doubtless to be expected that, with the discovery of Ugaritic and the strong activity in this field, the effort would be made to give Koheleth a Ugaritic provenance. This has now been done by C. H. Gordon, *Ugaritic Literature* (Rome, 1949), p. 133, who, on the basis of several linguistic features, to be discussed below, declares: "I cannot help feeling that the Northern character of *Ecclesiastes* should be stressed, rather than its reputed 'very late' and 'Greek' character. It is basically not a philosophic treatise of Greece, and whatever Greek elements there may be in it must have come through Phoenician channels." Gordon is correct in minimizing Greek influence in Koheleth, but his theory of Ugaritic (or north-Canaanite) influence is on a par with the search in earlier days for Greek, Babylonian or Egyptian sources for our book. All told, Gordon finds three usages in Ugaritic parallel to Koheleth (4:2; 7:12, 28). The first and third are thoroughly explicable on the basis of Hebrew usage, though the Canaanite analogies he adduces are interesting. The second (*Baal and Anat*, 51:II, 27), which Gordon, op. cit., p. 29, reads *ṣl ksp*, "the shadow of silver," is a remarkable parallel to Ecc. 7:12, particularly welcome because the authenticity of the latter passage has been attacked. However, even if Gordon's reading be correct (disputed by H. L. Ginsberg, in *JAOS*, 1950, vol. 70, p. 159), the meaning differs in the two passages. Cf. the Com. on these three passages for details.

NOTES ON CHAPTER VII

[1] Cf. his *Commentary* on *Song of Songs and Ecclesiastes* (Edinburgh, 1877), pp. 190–200.

[2] As e. g. 1) *'āthāh*, "come," Deut. 33:2; Mi. 4:8; Jer. 3:22; and often in *Deutero-Isaiah* and *Job*; or 2) the accusative Lamed, as e. g. after *'āhabh* (Lev.

19:18, 34; II Sam. 3:30) or *hārag* (II Sam. 3:30, etc.) (cf. BDB, *Lexicon*, p. 512a, 32).

This influence was not restricted to vocabulary. The recognition of the direct and early impact of Aramaic on the inflection of Hebrew was one of the most significant contributions of M. L. Margolis to the field of Semitic linguistics. Cf. his important paper, "The Feminine Ending T in Hebrew," in *AJSL*, vol. 12, 1896, pp. 3–35, his chart on Hebrew phonetics prepared for the Hebrew University in Jerusalem, and see the evaluation by E. A. Speiser in the forthcoming *Max Leopold Margolis Memorial Volume*.

³ Cf. Hos. 12:2, *rā'āh*, parallel to *rādaph*. See Commentary on 1:14 below.

⁴ Thus the common Mishnaic word *nᵉkhāsīm*, "possessions," which occurs only in Ecc. (5:18; 6:2) and II Chr. (1:11, 12), occurs once more in Josh. 22:8; *'Ašiāh*, "reservoir," not to be found in the Bible at all, occurs only in the Hebrew text of *Ben Sira* (50:3) and in the *Mesha Inscription* (l. 9) in the form *'ašuaḥ*. W. F. Albright discovered the "late" Hebrew verb *kibbēl*, "receive, accept" (Job 2:10; Est. 9:27), in a Tel-el-Amarna letter of the 14th century B. C. E. Cf. *BASOR*, no. 89, 1943, pp. 29 ff., and see our remarks, "Studies in the Relationship of Biblical and Rabbinic Hebrew," in the *Louis Ginzberg Jubilee Volume I*, pp. 174 ff.

⁵ The evidence, first assembled by Delitzsch in his *Kommentar zu Koheleth*, was republished in English with supplementary material by Wright, op. cit., pp. 488–500; cf. also Barton, pp. 52 f.; and it is referred to in all the commentaries. There is, naturally, room for divergent views on some details.

⁶ פרדס 2:5; פתגם 8:11. On their etymology, see Com. ad loc.

⁷ Cf. הֶבֶל construct (1:2); כבר (1:10 and *passim*); מדינה (2:8; 5:7); שבח (4:2); עינין (1:13 and *passim*); תקן (1:15; 7:13); שיר (7:5; see Com. ad loc.); תקיף (6:10); על דברת (3:18; 7:14); פשר (8:1); שלטון (8:4, 8); עֶבְדֵּיהֶם (9:1); קרב (9:18); נומץ (10:8); סכן (10:9); בן חורים (10:17); מדע (10:20); בטל (12:3). On these examples, some of which occur elsewhere in late Biblical passages, see the Commentary for details.

⁸ For כל־עמת (5:15), cf. לעמת (Lev. 3:9) and מלעמת (I Ki. 7:20); for נכסים (5:18; 6:2), cf. Josh. 22:8; on חשבון (7:25, 27; 9:10), cf. the same noun as an ancient place-name (Num. 21:26 ff., a. e.); for משלחת (8:8), cf. Ps. 78:49; for דרבנות (12:11), cf. I Sam. 13:21; for אי ("woe") (4:10; 10:16), cf. the folk-etymology of *Ichabod* in I Sam. 4:21, and cf. B. Taan. 7:12, אי חכם, and elsewhere. For the conjunction ש (instead of אשר) in 2:22; 3:18, cf. Jud. 5:7; 7:12; 8:26; Ps. 144:15; 146:5; Job 19:29 (?); Can. 1:6; restored by Albright also in Num. 24:3, 15. On the root כשר (2:21; 4:4; 5:10, etc.), cf. Est. 8:5. נכסים, חשבון, כשר and ש are exceedingly common in Rabbinic Hebrew.

⁹ Such are abstract nouns ending in *ōn* as יתרון, חשבון, כשרון, שלטון, or in *ūth* as רעות (1:14), שכלות (1:17), סכלות (2:3), הוללות (10:13), שפלות (10:18). The confusion of ל"א and ל"י forms is not always conclusive for the author, since it often inheres in the vocalization (חוֹטֵא 2:26; 8:12; 9:18; וּמוֹצֵא 7:26), but cf. the orthography of feminine יָצָא (10:5) and of יָשְׁנָא (8:1). On the other hand, classical Biblical forms like הריון, פדיון and דמות may indicate that these forms were indigenous also to Hebrew, especially since the form exists also in Arabic.

¹⁰ Vav consecutive occurs only 3 times (1:17; 4:1, 7). The participle, used virtually as a present tense, is very common (1:4–8; 2:14; 3:20 f.; 4:5; 6:12; 8:12, 14, 16; 9:5; 10:3) with the pronouns as subject (1:5, 7; 7:26). אני occurs to the complete exclusion of אנכי. See Barton, p. 53.

¹¹ Cf. Gesenius-Kautzsch, *Hebräische Grammatik* (28th ed.), sec. 126; M. H. Segal, *Dikduk Leshon Hamishnah* (Tel-Aviv, 1936), pp. 53–56, esp. sec. 82, 83, 85, 87; and our discussion in *JQR*, vol. 37, 1946, pp. 81–83.

¹² First tentatively suggested by F. C. Burkitt ("Is Ecclesiastes a Translation?", in *JThS*, 1921, vol. 22, pp. 23 ff.), it was energetically maintained by F. Zimmermann in "The Aramaic Provenance of Koheleth," in *JQR*, vol. 36, 1945, pp. 17 ff., and reiterated by him in "The Question of Hebrew in Qohelet," in *JQR*, vol. 40, 1949. He is supported by C. C. Torrey, "The Question of the Original Language of Qohelet," in *JQR*, vol. 39, 1948, pp. 151 ff. Our refutation of the translation-hypothesis (see the following notes) is to be found in "The Original Language of Qoheleth," in *JQR*, vol. 37, 1946, pp. 67–84, and in "The Translation Theory of Qohelet Re-examined," in *JQR*, vol. 40, 1949, pp. 103–16. The interested reader is referred to all these papers for details. Suffice it here that Torrey is constrained to admit, "I find myself generally in agreement with Gordis in the details of his criticism" (p. 152), and though he calls for additional evidence to support the theory, none is forthcoming in either his own or Zimmermann's second and even longer paper. Nor are we able to regard as convincing the argumentation of H. L. Ginsberg, *Studies in Koheleth* (New York, 1950), that "Koheleth wrote in Aramaic" (pp. 16–40), a detailed analysis of which is presented in our paper, "Qoheleth — Hebrew or Aramaic," scheduled to appear in *JBL* in June, 1952.

¹³ Thus בן חורים in 10:17 by the side of the Mishnaic form בן חורין, which shows the stronger Aramaic influence.

¹⁴ Thus חֵפֶץ in 3:1, 17; 5:7; 8:6, regarded by Zimmermann (op. cit., p. 19) and Torrey (op. cit., pp. 154 f.) as a "retroversion" of the Aramaic צְבוּ, "thing," which "genuine Hebrew does not know" (Torrey, *ibid.*), actually represents a common semantic development; cf. Arabic شَيْء "thing," from شاء "desire." What is more, the noun חֵפֶץ does occur in Biblical Hebrew and in the Mishnah, and its meaning in Koheleth is intermediate between these two stages.

The semantics of the Hebrew root *ḥāfēṣ* has three stages: 1) classical Hebrew, "wish, desire"; 2) *ḥēfeṣ*, "object of will, hence affair, matter"; and 3) finally, Mishnaic *ḥēfeṣ*, "object of desire, hence thing." Actually, in *Koheleth* the word does not mean "thing," but still retains its volitional nuance, and means "phenomenon, pursuit, activity, affair," very similar in meaning to the later Hebrew עֵסֶק, as it is clear from the context in each of the passages where חֵפֶץ occurs.

Moreover, this meaning of *ḥēfeṣ*, "activity, affair," does occur elsewhere in late Biblical Hebrew; cf. Isa. 58:3, 13, and probably also in Pr. 31:13.

¹⁵ This is the case with passages like 1:5; 7:5; 6:2; 7:20; 10:17; 5:17 and 12:13 (pp. 71–74); 7:29 (p. 76); 5:16a (p. 76); 11:1; 12:1; 5:5 (p. 78); and 7:10

(p. 79), which Zimmermann regards as his best evidence. The page numbers in parentheses in this and the two following notes refer to the discussion of these passages in the paper "The Original Language of Qoheleth," cited above in note 12.

¹⁶ See the discussion on 5:6 (p. 75); 5:16b (pp. 76 f.); 7:12 (p. 77); 9:1–2 (pp. 77 f.); 4:16, 17 (p. 79); 5:8 (p. 80).

¹⁷ This is the case in 11:1 (p. 78); 2:16 (p. 80).

¹⁸ Thus Abraham Ibn Ezra suggests that Job is a translation from the Arabic (cf. his commentary on Job 2:11). Carlyle says: "Biblical critics seem agreed that our own book of Job was written in that (i. e. Arab) region of the world. One feels indeed as if it were not Hebrew; such a noble universality different from noble patriotism or sectarianism reigns in it" (*Heroes and Hero Worship*, in the chapter "The Hero as Prophet"). Carlyle's motive is scarcely to be regarded as objective. R. H. Pfeiffer, *Introduction to the Old Testament*, New York, 1941, pp. 670, 678–83, assumes an "Edomite" original for Job. Torrey has been a persistent advocate of the translation-hypothesis for the Hebrew portions of *Daniel*, the book of *Esther*, and the Gospels. Cf. our brief discussion of his views in *JQR*, 1949, vol. 39, pp. 103 f., and notes 3–8.

¹⁹ Poetic authors might consciously seek to archaize in the classic style, though even here telltale signs of late style would appear, as in Ps. 116 and 139.

²⁰ Thus עֲבָדֵיהֶם, not עֲבָדֵיהוֹן (9:1), בֶּן חוֹרִים (10:17), not the Aramaic בֶּן חוֹרִין.

²¹ Cf. notes 8, 9, 10 and 14 above.

²² Cf. the examples proposed by H. L. Ginsberg, op. cit., who argues his case with an assurance that this writer cannot share. At times, the arguments previously advanced against the translation-hypothesis are ignored outright or their implication is overlooked and dismissed without justification. In other instances, alternative explanations of the facts are confidently brushed aside. For a detailed discussion, see the literature cited in note 12.

²³ For other stylistic considerations of moment, see the forthcoming paper in *JBL* cited in note 12.

²⁴ Ginsberg, op. cit., p. 40 ff., dates it in the 3rd century.

²⁵ Cf. ch. V above for the evidence.

²⁶ Cf. ch. VI above and note 2.

²⁷ Cf. the detailed refutation of alleged Graecisms in McNeile, op. cit., pp. 30–43, and Barton, pp. 32 f.

²⁸ For details, see ch. VI, note 3.

²⁹ פַּרְדֵּס, like παράδεισος, is derived from the Persian *pairi-daēza*. For Greek and Latin words in Rabbinic Hebrew, see S. Krauss, *Griechische und Lateinische Lehnwörter im Talmud, Midrasch und Targum* (Berlin, 1898–99); S. Lieberman, *Greek in Jewish Palestine* (New York, 1942). Greek words occur in the Bible in Dan. 3:5 and perhaps in 3:4. Cf. J. A. Montgomery, in *ICC on Daniel* (New York, 1927), pp. 22 f. On the other hand, אַפִּרְיוֹן in Can. 3:9 is not necessarily the Greek φορεῖον. There are strong grounds for assuming that the song in which it occurs goes back to the 10th century B. C. E. and that the word is derived from the Sanskrit *paryanka*, being one of several

borrowings from India in this period, like *qōph* and *tukki* (I Ki. 10:22). Cf. "A Wedding Song for Solomon," in *JBL*, 1944, vol. 63, pp. 263 ff.; and see *BDB*, s. v.

³⁰ On the alleged Egyptian provenance of the book, cf. Humbert, *Recherches*, pp. 107 ff.; P. Kleinert, *Theologische Studien und Kritiken*, 1909; Levy, op. cit., p. 32; these arguments are effectively answered by Hertzberg, op. cit., pp. 19–22.

NOTES ON CHAPTER VIII

¹ Cf., for example, Isa. 40:25; 42:8; 43:11; and esp. 44:6–20, 24; 45:5–7, 20; 46:5 f.; 51:9 f.

² Cf. Ecc. 3:20 f.; 9:10, 12; Job 14:11 ff.; and see *SBWL*, pp. 102 ff., for a fuller evaluation of this trait in Wisdom literature.

³ Cf. the chapter above on Greek cultural influences. On recent discoveries concerning Greek commercial penetration in the East, see W. F. Albright, *The Archaeology of Palestine* (Middlesex, 1947), p. 143.

⁴ Cf. Humbert, op. cit.; Fichtner, pp. 21 f.

⁵ Cf. Ecc. 8:2 ff.; 10:16 f.

⁶ For a brief recent survey of the checkered political history of Palestine, see now R. H. Pfeiffer, *History of N. T. Times* (New York, 1949), pp. 8–9, and the standard histories of Graetz, Schuerer, Oesterley and Robinson, Olmstead, etc.

⁷ Cf. the chapter below for details, and note the discussion of the significant semantic development of the noun *ḥēfeṣ*, where Koheleth stands midway between the classic Biblical and the Mishnaic usage (*JQR*, 1949, vol. 39, pp. 108 ff.).

⁸ This latter identification is ruled out, together with Graetz's entire theory of a Herodian date for the book, by the data which establish the absolute *terminus non post quem* as the date of *Ben Sira*, 190 B. C. E. (see below in the text).

⁹ Op. cit., pp. 61 f.

¹⁰ Cf. Polybius, V, 66.

¹¹ On the difficult phrase *hayyeledh haššeni* (lit., "the second lad"), see the Commentary ad loc.

¹² Levy (p. 31) finds in *melekh gādhōl* a reference to Antiochus the Great, on the ground that the phrase is a translation of βασιλεὺς μέγας. But this title, which is a continuation of the old Assyrian *šarru rabû* (cf. Isa. 36:4, המלך הגדול, and Hos. 5:13; 10:6, reading מלכי רב for מלך ירב), could apply to any occupant of the throne, even the Egyptian Ptolemy III being described by the same title. Cf. Bouché-Leclerq, *Histoire des Lagides*, vol. 1, p. 296, n. 3.

¹³ To escape the difficulty, Hertz. follows McNeile, Volz and Kuhn in rendering *umillaṭ* as "he *could have* saved the city." But this is syntactically and exegetically impossible (see Com. on 9:15). Moreover, it is unnecessary in view of the evidence presented above in the text.

¹⁴ Cf. especially the "*ṭōbh* collection" in 7:1–19; 4:9, 13; 6:9; and see Com. ad loc. For this frequent usage in Wisdom apothegms, cf. Ps. 112:5; Pr. 12:9; 15:16 f.; 16:8, 19,32; 17:1; 19:1; 21:9, 19; 25:24; 27:10; 28:6. K. Galling recognizes this usage in his commentary, p. 48; cf. also *ZATW*, 1932, p. 287.

¹⁵ A. Erman, *The Literature of the Ancient Egyptians*, p. 108.

¹⁶ Erman, op. cit., p. 80.

¹⁷ Cf. Bultmann, op. cit., p. 50. See also above, ch. VI.

¹⁸ Hence a Persian date (Del. Cheyne) is unacceptable.

¹⁹ Hitzig, Noeldeke, Kuenen, Tyler, Kleinert, Levy and Hertzberg set the date of Koheleth at 200 B. C. E., but this date does not allow sufficient time for Ben Sira's utilization of the text in 190 B. C. E. The same consideration rules out absolutely the proposed dates of 125 B. C. E. (Renan), 100 (Leimdörfer, König, Haupt), or the age of Herod, 37–4 B. C. E. (Graetz, Gerson).

²⁰ Against D. S. Margoliouth, in *Expositor*, 1911, p. 409, and Humbert, *Recherches*, p. 113.

²¹ Cf. Hertzberg, p. 19.

²² Against Kleinert, p. 500, and against Levy (p. 32), who believes that he was born in Palestine, but emigrated to Alexandria, where he wrote chaps. 8–12.

²³ Cf. Hertzberg, p. 22.

NOTES ON CHAPTER IX

¹ Cf. B. Shab. 30b.

² For a conspectus of the older history of the interpretation, cf. C. D. Ginsburg, *Coheleth* (London, 1861), pp. 27–223; and for the more modern period, cf. Barton, op. cit., pp. 18–31, as well as the other standard commentaries.

³ Cf. Midrash *Koheleth Rabba* 2:25: כל אכילה ושתיה שנאמר במגילה הזאת בתורה ובמעשים טובים הכתוב מדבר.

⁴ Cf. ch. XV.

⁵ So among the Church Fathers, Gregory of Nyasa and Gregory the Great. Cf. also D. Leimdörfer's *Die Lösung des Qoheletsrätsels durch den Philosophen Baruch ibn Baruch*. This 16th century thinker saw the book as a debate between "illusion" (=*Koheleth*) and the "divine Reason" (=son of David). Herder and Eichhorn regarded the book as a record of debates.

⁶ Cf. B. Shab. 63a; Yeb. 11b; and frequently: אין מקרא יוצא מידי פשוטו.

⁷ The literature on these Scrolls is already tremendous. *BASOR* and *BA* are prime sources, and discussions have appeared in *JBL*, *JNES*, *JQR* and elsewhere since 1949.

⁸ According to Barton (p. 45), the Hasid added 2:26; 3:17; 7:18b, 26b, 29; 8:2b, 3a, 5, 6a, 11–13; 11:9b; 12:1a, 13, 14. McNeile attributes also 3:14b; 5:1–7 to the same hand. The Hokmah glossator, Barton holds, is responsible for 5:3, 7a; 7:1a, 3, 5–9, 11, 12, 19; 8:1; 9:17–18; 10:1–3, 8, 14a, 15, 18, 19. To

these McNeile, Siegfried and Haupt would add 4:9–12. Podechard posits two Epilogists, one a pupil of Koheleth, who wrote 12:9–12; 1:2; 7:27 f. and 12:8. The second, a Hasid, is the author of 12:13 f.; 2:26a, b; 3:17; 7:26b; 8:5–8, 11–13; 11:9c. Podechard admits that Koheleth himself may have added these last passages at a later time. Finally, a Hakham glossator added the poetical *meshalim* 4:5, 9–12; 5:2, 6a; 6:7; 7:1–12, 18–22; 8:1, 2a, 3, 4; 9:17 f.; 10:1–4, 10–14a, 15–20; 11:1–4, 6. Other glossators added 4:17 to 5:6 and 12:2–6. Galling finds considerably fewer additions: 3:17; 8:5, 12b, 13a; 11:9c, these being made "in the spirit of right belief"; also 3:15; 4:17d; 5:6c, 19; 7:4, 25c; 9:3c, 5c, d, 9b, 18b; 10:14b. In 3:21 and 9:1 he finds Masoretic corrections made on dogmatic grounds.

The Commentary on each passage indicates the specific grounds for rejecting this approach. The authentic stamp of Koheleth's outlook is clear in most of these alleged "Hasid" passages (2:26; 3:14b; 5:1–7; 7:18b, 26b, 29; 8:2b, 3a, 5–8, 11, 12a, 13b; 11:9c; 12:1a) and, above all, in 1:2; 12:8, which express the theme of the book. As for several others (3:17; 8:12b, 13), Koheleth is citing conventional doctrine.

Similarly, as to the passages attributed to the Hokmah glossator, largely because of the *mashal* form in which they are cast (Barton, Podechard, p. 46), most of them are thoroughly congenial to Koheleth's standpoint (5:3, 7a; 6:7; 7:1a, 3, 5–9, 11, 12, 27 f., 18–22; 8:1–4; 10:1–4, 8–14a, 15–20; 11:1–4, 6), or are quoted as a text for his own commentary (4:5 f., 9–12; 7:1a, 19; 9:17–18). On the existence of *mashal* collections in Koheleth, particularly the *tōbh* series in ch. 7, and the miscellany in ch. 10, see the Commentary. The passages 4:17 to 5:6 and 12:2–6 are among the most characteristic for Koheleth's outlook. That the Epilogue (12:9–14) does not emanate from Koheleth is clear from the third person employed and from other evidence.

⁹ Cf. on this extra-canonical literature, in addition to R. H. Charles' standard work, *Apocrypha and Pseudepigrapha of the O. T.* (Oxford, 1913), the stimulating treatment of C. C. Torrey, *The Apocryphal Literature* (New Haven, 1945), and the indispensable work of R. H. Pfeiffer, *History of N. T. Times With an Introduction to the Apocrypha* (New York, 1949); cf. also S. Zeitlin, "Jewish Apocryphal Literature," in *JQR*, vol. 40, 1950, pp. 223–50.

¹⁰ Even the originals of works like *Esdras* and *Baruch*, in which "no sectarian eccentricity is to be discovered" (G. F. Moore, *Judaism*, vol. 2, p. 344), met the same fate, and only accident preserved the Hebrew of *Ben Sira* in part. *Wisdom of Solomon* may have been ruled out automatically because it was composed in Greek.

¹¹ Pfeiffer, op. cit., p. 401, note 20, is virtually alone in maintaining that Ben Sira precedes Koheleth.

¹² On the relationship of Ben Sira and Koheleth, see ch. V.

¹³ On the date of Koheleth, see ch. VIII. Several decades after the death of Alexander the Great (323 B. C. E.) must have been required for Greek ideas to penetrate into Palestine. Ben Sira is dated at about 190 B. C. E., on the basis of the Preface to the Greek translation, prepared by his grandson, who came to Egypt in the 38th year of Ptolemy VII Euergetes, hence 132

B. C. E., the reference to Simon the High Priest, and other factors. Cf. Smend (pp. XIV ff.), and Pfeiffer, op. cit., pp. 364 ff.

[14] The unity of the book, maintained only by Genung and Cornill in the 19th century, is today recognized from somewhat varying points of view by an increasing number of scholars. Cf. L. Levy, *Das Buch Qoheleth* (Leipzig, 1912), esp. pp. 61 ff.; W. Hertzberg, *Der Prediger* (Leipzig, 1932), and see his vigorous words, pp. 18 f.; D. B. MacDonald, *The Hebrew Literary Genius* (Princeton, 1933); idem, *The Hebrew Philosophical Genius* (Princeton, 1936). Most recent are Kurt Galling in *Die Fünf Megillot*, in the Eissfeldt *Handbuch zum Alten Testament* series (Tübingen, 1940), who distinguishes thirty-seven proverbs in the book, taken over, modified or opposed by the author, so that no rearrangements and a minimum of excisions are required; and J. J. Weber, *Le Livre de Job-L'Ecclésiaste* (Paris, 1947), who sees the book as a unity with diverse thoughts at various times, except for the first three and the last six verses, which he attributes to a pupil of the author.

[15] Cf. Intr. Note on 9:9 ff. in the Commentary. We do not agree with Hertzberg, who finds 3 Epilogists (vv. 9–11; v. 12; vv. 13 f.).

[16] Note the reference to *Koheleth ben David*, the oldest source we possess for the theory of the Solomonic authorship of Koheleth. The author, even when adopting the guise of Solomon, does not call himself "ben David."

[17] On the other hand, they may well go back to the author. Barton (p. 44) argues that in 1:2 and 12:8 the words *'āmar Kōhelet* interrupt the rhythm. This contention is difficult to follow; the phrase occurs in verses which are in two-beat rhythm, so that it may be maintained that it is essential to the rhythm (2:2:2:2) in 1:2 and 12:8 as well as in 7:27.

[18] For a brief summary of our view as to how these passages are to be understood, see note 8 above.

[19] Cf. Commentary ad loc.

[20] Cf. above, ch. I, and the literature there cited.

[21] Cf. below, ch. XI.

[22] Cf. ch. XII and the literature cited in note 1.

NOTES ON CHAPTER X

[1] On Klausner's theory, see below, note 16.

[2] The purpose of the Solomonic device is clearly recognized by the *Midrash Koheleth Rabbah* 3:11: "If someone else had said, 'He has made everything proper in its time' (3:11), I should say, 'This fellow who never ate a crust of bread in his life says so!' but Solomon, 'whose bread daily was thirty kor of fine flour' (I Kings 5:2), may properly say so. Another view, If any one else had said, 'Vanity of vanities,' I should say, 'This fellow, who never owned two cents, presumes to despise all the wealth of the world!' "

[3] The editor has already accepted the Solomonic authorship. There is no reason for assuming that this editor is identical with the Epilogist of 12:13 f. (ag. Hertz.). The Epilogist of 12:9 obviously knew Koheleth as a *hakam*,

not as King Solomon. Hertzberg (p. 29) is correct in rejecting the view that "king" is intended as a technical term for head of a school, as suggested by Haupt (*Qoheleth oder Weltschmerz*, p. IV), who regarded him as a Sadducean physician, and by Humbert (op. cit.), who found it an example of Egyptian influence. This usage, which incidentally can be validated from Rabbinic literature, as e. g. מאן מלכי רבנן, "Who are called 'kings'? The Rabbis" (Git. 62a; Ber. 64a), is entirely irrelevant here.

⁴ Cf. ch. IV, above, and Com. ad loc.

⁵ Cf. the glorification of the rustic life in Greek and Latin literature in the *Idylls* of Theocritus, Bion, and Moschus, the *Letters* of Cicero, and the *Bucolics* and *Eclogues* of Vergil.

⁶ So also Hertzberg, pp. 21 ff., and most commentators.

⁷ See ch. VIII, above.

⁸ Note the use of the third person in referring to Koheleth, instead of the first person that he himself uses throughout the book. The contradiction between the views of vv. 13 f. and the rest of the book, and also the possible criticism of Koheleth in v. 10a, indicate that these lines emanate from a contemporary of more conventional cast than Koheleth, and may also hint at opposition to the book in some circles. These conclusions are not affected even if it be assumed that several Epilogists were at work instead of one. For details, cf. Intr. Note on 12:9 ff.

⁹ For the resemblances in vocabulary, see Intr. Note referred to above, and note the use of *bᵉnî* (v. 12), a technical term of Wisdom literature common in *Proverbs*.

¹⁰ On the upper-class origin of Wisdom, see above, ch. III.

¹¹ A passage like 4:1 ff., intense as it is, is virtually alone. Laments on governmental corruption (5:7) are at least as frequent among the upper classes, who have dealings with the state and pay the bulk of the taxes, as among the poor. The references to "the wisdom of the poor being despised" (9:16; cf. also 7:11) are a proverbial utterance rather than a purely personal reaction.

¹² Cf. *supra*, ch. V.

¹³ Cf. 6:2; and see also 2:18, 21; 4:8; 5:10.

¹⁴ Cf. 4:8–12; 5:13.

¹⁵ Cf. 11:9; 12:1a and 9:10. Unlike Marcus Aurelius, his "Catalogue of the Seasons" (3:1 ff.) makes no reference to raising children. When Job laments his ignorance of the future, he stresses his inability to share the joys and sorrows of his offspring (14:21 f.). Koheleth's frequent reference to man's ignorance of the future (as e. g. 3:22; 6:12) has no such personal aspect.

¹⁶ Efforts to identify Koheleth with a specific individual have been made, but cannot be said to carry conviction. J. Klausner declared Hyrcanus ben Joseph the Tobiade to be the author (*Habayyit Hasheni Bigedullato*, Jerusalem, 1930, pp. 160–175), a view which he first presented 20 years earlier. He based his opinion principally on the description of the palace that Hyrcanus built at Arak-el-Emir, to which he withdrew after Palestine came into the possession of the Seleucids (cf. Josephus, *Antiquities*, 12, 4, 11, and the literature cited

in *SBWL*, p. 81, n. 6). This fortress he regards as identical with Koheleth's enterprise described in 2:4–10. Notwithstanding Klausner's confidence in this theory, the spirit of the passage in Koheleth, particularly 2:10, is poles apart from that of a royal favorite fallen from grace and seeking refuge in the wilderness. So, too, the nationalistic spirit that Klausner attributes to Hyrcanus is entirely absent in Koheleth.

On the other hand, Levy, op. cit., pp. 39 ff., finds a "zwingende Notwendigkeit" (p. 43) to identify the author of Koheleth either with Zadok or Boethus who, according to *Aboth de Rabbi Nathan*, ch. 5, were the founders and heads of the heretical sects of the Sadducees and the Boethusians. Even if this rabbinic tradition be taken at face value, and Zadok and Boethus be not regarded as eponyms for these sects, as is the view of most scholars, the scant information available about them makes any theory as to their authorship of *Koheleth* an instance of *obscura per obscuriora*. Koheleth is not a Sadducean work, for the sect did not emerge until later, in the reign of John Hyrcanus (135–104 B. C. E.). It may, however, be described as proto-Sadducean, reflecting the class orientation of Wisdom as a whole (cf. *SBWL*, esp. p. 77 and note 2). Hence the argument as to its canonization (cf. *ibid.*, p. 117, n. 85, and Barton, op. cit., p. 65).

[17] Cf., *inter alia*, R. H. Charles, *Apocrypha and Pseudepigrapha* (Oxford, 1913), vol. II, pp. 163–624; R. H. Pfeiffer, *History of New Testament Times* (New York, 1949), pp. 74–90; H. H. Rowley, *The Relevance of Apocalyptic* (London, 1944).

[18] It is the merit of J. W. Gaspar, *Social Ideas in the Wisdom Literature of the O. T.* (Washington, 1947), to have stressed this aspect of Wisdom, even to the extent of underestimating its pragmatic character; cf. *JBL*, vol. 78, 1949, pp. 186–91.

[19] Cf., *inter alia*, Fichtner, op. cit., pp. 75 ff., on the limitations of the eudaemonistic motive for morality, and *ibid.*, pp. 81 ff., for the identification of Hokmah with Torah. Cf. also G. F. Moore, *Judaism* (Cambridge, 1927), vol. 1, pp. 38, 263 ff.

[20] Cf. Rosh Hashanah 16b; Suk. 27b: חייב אדם להקביל פני רבו ברגל.

NOTES ON CHAPTER XI

[1] *Kommentar zu Psalmen* (Berlin, 1905), Preface, p. VI.

[2] On the variety and higher unity of the Bible, cf. Gordis, "The Bible as a Cultural Monument," in L. Finkelstein, ed., *The Jews, Their History, Culture, and Religion* (New York, 1949), vol. 1, pp. 457 ff.; esp. pp. 487 ff.

[3] On the discussions regarding the canonicity of *Ezekiel, Proverbs, Ecclesiastes, Song of Songs, Job*, cf. *SBWL*, and the references in the concluding note there.

[4] B. Erub. 13b and parallels: אלו ואלו דברי אלהים חיים.

[5] Cf. chap. VII above.

⁶ Cf. the excellent treatment of the conjunction by S. R. Driver in the *Oxford Lexicon*, s. v.

⁷ Cf. the classic study of S. R. Driver, *Hebrew Tenses* (3rd edition, Oxford, 1892), which has not been outmoded by the comparative Semitic study of a related theme by his son, G. R. Driver, *Problems of the Hebrew Verbal System* (Edinburgh, 1936).

⁸ Cf. his work *The Philosophy of Spinoza* (Cambridge, 1934) and the brief summation of his approach in his Horace M. Kallen Lecture, *Spinoza and Religion* (New York, 1950), from which the quotations in our text above are taken.

⁹ Cf. op. cit., pp. 5 f., 16, for these references.

¹⁰ Thus with regard to immortality, Wolfson remarks (p. 24): "But, while Spinoza's assertion of individual immortality is not inconsistent with his philosophy, it does not necessarily follow from it. It is a gratuitous principle; it is an expression of faith rather than of reason . . . And so, while his conception of immortality betrays no logical inconsistency of thought, it betrays an inconsistency of mood. As is not the case in his speculations about God, the soul, or the revealed law, he is here willing to accept more than the mere use of a term; he is willing to accept a certain belief."

¹¹ Cf. the illuminating comment of Calvin Thomas in his edition of *Goethe's Faust* (Boston, 1906), pp. 248 f., who cites the identical use of the phrase *ein guter Mensch* elsewhere in Goethe's writings.

¹² Cf. B. Ned. 10a: כל המצער עצמו מן היין נקרא חוטא and *ibid.*: ומה זה שלא ציער עצמו אלא מן היין נקרא חוטא המצער עצמו מכל דבר על אחת כמה וכמה.

¹³ Cf. B. Ned. 9b.

¹⁴ Cf. B. Ned. 10a: אמר אביי שמעון שמעון הצדיק ור' שמעון ור' אלעזר הקפר כולן שיטה אחת הן דנזיר חוטא הוי. Abaye said, "Simon the Just, R. Simon and Eleazar Hakappar are all agreed that the Nazir is a sinner." The explanation given in Pseudo-Rashi ad loc., דנזיר חוטא משום דנדר, "the Nazir is a sinner because he pronounced a vow," reflects the ascetic tendencies of the Middle Ages, which could no longer understand the life-affirming attitude of the Talmud. This view is obviously not borne out by the language of the Talmudic quotations.

¹⁵ It is the merit of Graetz and Levy to have first called attention to Rabbinic parallels in usage.

¹⁶ Cf. the *Kal*, "miss," Job 5:24; Pr. 8:36; 19:2; perhaps also Pr. 20:2; Hab. 2:10; and see BDB, s. v. 1, p. 306b; the *Piel*, "bear the loss," Gen. 31:39; the *Hiphil*, "miss the mark" (Jud. 20:16).

¹⁷ Cf. Arabic خطى I "commit an error," II "cause to miss the mark," IV "miss the way"; Ethiopic *hata'a*, "fail to find or have," sometimes, "sin."

¹⁸ See the references in n. 16.

¹⁹ On this meaning for *ḥāṭa'*, cf. Gen. 43:9; Deut. 24:4; Isa. 29:21; Ecc. 5:5; Lam. 3:39; 4:6 (note the identical use of *'avōn*). On this same meaning for *'āšam*, cf. Lev. 4:3, 13, 22; Jer. 2:3; Ps. 34:22 f.; Pr. 30:10; Isa. 24:6; Hos. 5:15; 10:2; 14:1; Joel 1:18; Zc. 11:5. On *'avōn* in this sense, cf. Gen. 4:13; Lev. 26:41; I Sam. 28:10; Isa. 5:18; 40:2; and see BDB, s. v. p. 731a, b.

²⁰ This meaning, rather than that of "miss, lose," may inhere in *ḥōtē'* *naphšō* (Pr. 20:2; Hab. 2:10); cf. the analogous use of *ḥōmēs naphšō* in Pr. 8:36.

²¹ Note the contrast here with חכמה in stich a, and compare 7:17, where *rāšā'* and *sākhāl* are parallel.

²² Cf. 3:17; 7:15; 8:10, 13, 14; 9:2.

²³ Cf. 3:16; 7:25; 8:8.

²⁴ Cf. 3:16; 7:15, 16, 20; 8:14; 9:2.

²⁵ Cf., for example, Gen. 20:11; 42:18; Ex. 1:17, 21; 18:21; Deut. 25:18; Job 6:14; Neh. 5:9, 15; 7:2, where this sense is clear from the context. In I Sam. 23:3; Ps. 55:20; 66:16; Job 1:8, 9; 2:3, the phrase undoubtedly has the same meaning, but the passage is general and gives no clue to the specific force of the idiom. On the other hand, in the idiom *yārē'* (*yir'at*) *JHVH*, where the national name of the Deity is used, it refers either to the literal fear of the power of God (Ex. 9:20) or to the worship of the God of Israel (Josh. 22:25; 24:14; I Sam. 12:14, 24; I Ki. 18:3, 12; II Ki. 4:1; 17:25 ff.; Jonah 1:9; Mal. 3:16; Ps. 15:4; 22:24; 25:12; 34:10; 112:1; 115:11, 13, etc.). At times, particularly in the Prophets, it bears a moral sense like *yārē 'elōhīm* (cf. Isa. 11:3; 33:6; Jer. 5:24; 26:19; Ps. 34:12; II Chr. 19:9). In *Proverbs*, the phrase is roughly equivalent to the modern concept of "religion and morality" as the will of God (see 1:29; 2:5; 8:13; 9:10; 10:27; 14:26 f.; 15:16, 33; 16:6; 19:23; 22:4; 23:17; cf. also *Job* 15:4; 28:28).

²⁶ In 5:6; 7:18; 8:12; 12:13.

NOTES ON CHAPTER XII

¹ A systematic study of the subject was first presented by the writer in "Quotations in Wisdom Literature," in *JQR*, 1939, vol. 30, pp. 123–147. Further researches on a much wider basis led to a more comprehensive paper, "Quotations as a Literary Usage in Biblical, Rabbinic and Oriental Literature," in *HUCA*, 1949, vol. 22, pp. 157 ff. Examples cited in this study, which, incidentally, do not exhaust the material, are drawn from the Bible (Gen. Ex. Deut. Sam. Isa. Jer. Hos. Ps. Pr. Job Ecc.), the Mishnah (Kethuboth, Aboth) and the Babylonian Talmud (tractates Shabbath, Erubin, Taanith, Kethuboth, Kiddushin, Baba Kamma and Baba Metzia), as well as the Egyptian *Admonitions of a Prophet*, the Sumerian epics *Gilgamesh, Enkidu and the Nether World* and *Gilgamesh and the Land of the Living*, and the Babylonian *Complaint on the Injustice of the World*. Only the conclusions pertinent to *Koheleth* are cited here. Levy and Galling have independently recognized the existence of quotations in our book. The same approach with regard to two of the Biblical examples cited in our text (Can. 1:7 f. and Job 22:4 f.) was proposed by N. H. Tur-Sinai (Harry Torczyner) in his paper on the Song of Songs now reprinted in *Halashon Vehasefer*, vol. II (Jerusalem, 5711), pp. 365 f.

² These types, briefly outlined in *JBL*, 1949, vol. 68, p. XVII, are: a. direct quotations of the speech by the subject. b. the development of dialogue. c. direct quotations of the thoughts of the subject. d. citation of prayers.

e. quotations embodying the previous standpoint or thought of the speaker.
f. citation of the hypothetical speech or thought that might or should have
occurred to the subject. g. the use of proverbial quotations to buttress an
argument without comment. h. the use of proverbial quotations as a text
or comment. i. the use of contrasting proverbs. j. quotations used in argumentation.

³ On Koheleth see below. On this usage in *Job*, fundamental for the
understanding of *Job*, chaps. 12, 21, and 42, cf. Gordis, op. cit., pp. 192 ff.,
209 ff.

⁴ Cf. Rashi ad loc. Another instance occurs in Baba Kamma 56a; cf.
QBROL, pp. 194 ff.

⁵ Cf. *QBROL*, pp. 196 ff. Biblical examples of this usage occur in Ex. 23:8;
Deut. 16:19; Ps. 34:12 ff.; Job 2:4 f.; 17:5. Talmudic instances of this usage
are Aboth 4:4, which cites Ben Sira 7:17; Aboth 4:24, which quotes Pr. 24:17 f.;
and B. Keth. 22b, which quotes Pr. 4:24, without any external mark of a
quotation.

⁶ Cambridge, 1931, p. 6.

⁷ Op. cit., pp. 34–43.

⁸ Op. cit., p. 59.

⁹ A. Erman, *The Literature of the Ancient Egyptians* (New York, 1927),
p. 102. He is at a loss to explain the quotation, and asks, "But what is it
doing here?"

¹⁰ Cf. "The Heptad As An Element of Biblical and Rabbinic Style," in
JBL, 1943, vol. 62, pp. 17–26, especially pp. 20 ff.

¹¹ Levy takes the entire verse as a quotation of an ascetic, but is unable
to explain why, if Koheleth is opposed to its theme, he quotes it at all. Levy
overlooks the fact that Koheleth's counsel of joy as the highest good flows from
a profoundly tragic conception of life. Cf. The *Wisdom of Ecclesiastes*, pp. 8–27;
Hertzberg remarks aptly (p. 120), "*Die Grundgestimmtheit macht hier den
fundamentalen Unterschied.*"

¹² While Siegfried, McNeile and Haupt eliminate these verses as glosses,
Barton justly remarks, "It is an open question whether Koheleth himself may
not have introduced them" (op. cit., p. 110). Hertzberg and Levy see no
quotations here at all, but retain the passage as authentic. The closing formula, however, suits a cited aphorism better.

¹³ On the reading לֹא תְבוֹאֵהוּ for לֹא תְבוֹאָה, see Com. ad loc.

¹⁴ On the considerations that militate against regarding vv. 11–13 as
a gloss, and the difficulties encountered by the commentators, see Com.
ad loc.

¹⁵ See E. Ebeling, *Altorientalische Texte zum A. T.*, 2nd ed. (Berlin-
Leipzig, 1926), pp. 287–292, for a German version of the text and annotations,
as well as a brief bibliography.

¹⁶ Prof. Samuel N. Kramer, in a communication to this author.

¹⁷ Cf. Rolfe Humphries' review of Elliott Coleman's *Twenty-seven Night
Sonnets* (Milan, 1949) in *The Nation* (Oct. 1, 1949), p. 332.
He quotes two examples:

and

> Earth has not anything to show more fair
> Than April lights in the smoked-out railroad yards.

> What is so rare as a day in June?
>   It better
> Not get much rarer, I should think;
>   the pause
> At sunrise or at sunset, mainly the latter,
> Is more than I can fill.

In each quotation, the first line is a citation from a familiar poem, the remainder the comment of the author.

[18] On this usage in Job 12:12 f., cf. *QBROL*, pp. 209 f.; and Driver-Gray ad loc.

[19] For the conventional view, cf., among other passages, Pr. 6:6–11; 10:4; 12:24, 27; 13:4; 19:24; 24:33. Koheleth's attitude is expressed in 2:18 ff.; 4:4 ff.; 5:12 ff.; 6:1 ff.

[20] For other, less satisfactory, resolutions of the contradiction, see Com. ad loc.

NOTES ON CHAPTER XIII

[1] For details of Koheleth's stylistic usages, see Levy, pp. 57 ff.

[2] These are 4:17 to 5:6; 5:7; 7:9–10, 13 f., 16–22; 8:2 ff.; 9:7–10; 10:4, 16 f., 20; 11:1–6; 11:9 to 12:2. Cf. Hertzberg, p. 31.

[3] Ag. Volz.

[4] Throughout the "autobiographical" Section II (1:12 to 2:26), but also in III (3:10–15); IV (3:16–22; 4:1–3); V (4:4–8); VIII (5:17); XIII (8:2, 9); XIV (8:10–17; 9:1); XV (9:11); XVI (9:13, 16); XVII (10:5, 7).

[5] Cf. Pr. 7:1 ff.; Ps. 73. See R. Kittel, *Geschichte* (1927), vol. III, 2, pp. 716 f.

[6] Cf. Pr. 1:8, 10, 15; 2:1; 3:1, 11, 21; 4:10, 20; 5:1, 20; 6:1, 3, 20; 7:1; 19:27; 23:15, 19, 26; 24:13, 21; 27:11. On the Rabbinic use of the term, see B. Sanh. 11a, שב בני שב, and cf. the discussion in L. Ginzberg, *Commentary on the Jerusalem Talmud* (New York, 1940), vol. 1, pp. 238, 300.

[7] That it is used in 12:12 is additional proof that the Epilogue is from another hand. The same reason militates against emending אני in 8:2 to בני. See Com. ad loc.

[8] Cf. our study "The Heptad As An Element of Biblical and Rabbinic Style," in *JBL*, 1943, vol. 62, pp. 17–26, for Biblical and Rabbinic evidence on the rhetorical use of seven units and on the linking of material by the same opening word or phrase.

[9] See Intr. Note on both sections.

[10] Cf. Hos. 2:21 f.; 8:14; Ps. 1:5 f.; 37:16 f.; Pr. 23:15 f.; Job 20:2 f.; Lam. 2:13, a. e., and see our remarks in "Al Mibneh Hashirah Ha'ibrit

Hakedumah," in *Sefer Hashanah Lihude Amerikah 5693* (1944), pp. 136–59, esp. pp. 151 ff.

[11] In the passage 11:3, 4, stich a = 3a, "rain," b = 3b, "the wind," c = 4a, "the wind," d = 4b, "rain." For the bearing of this observation on the authenticity of the passage, see the Commentary. Another possible example of chiasmus is the passage 7:16–20; v. 16 ("the righteous") is a, v. 17 (wisdom) is b, v. 19 (wisdom) is c, and v. 20 ("the righteous") is d. V. 18 is the general conclusion, occurring rather unusually in the center. Cf. also 7:5–7, in which 5a = a, 5b = b, 6a, b = c, and 6c, 7 = d. See Com. for details.

[12] Cf. Hos. 5:3; Ps. 33:20 f. for poetic instances of this use.

[13] Cf. Ex. 29:27; Deut. 22:25–27; and see Ehrlich ad loc.

[14] Cf. the passage 2:24–26 in which v. 24a = a, 24b = b, 25 = c, 26 = d. Similarly, in 4:13 f., v. 13a = a, v. 13b = b, 14a = c, 14b = d. This usage is particularly helpful in understanding 5:17–19, where v. 17 = a, v. 18 = b, v. 19a = c, the reason for a, and 19b = d, the reason for b. It is significant that in all these instances, stichs *c* and *d* are both introduced by *ki*, "because." Cf. Com. ad loc. See also Levy, p. 58.

[15] These *Sedarim* are given by C. D. Ginsburg, *The Massorah* (London, 1883, vol. 2, p. 333b) as 1:1; 3:13; 7:1; 9:7. Baer-Delitzsch in their edition *Quinque Volumina* (1886, p. 94) list the second *Seder* as 3:14 instead, for which the former criticizes them in his *Introd. to the Massoretico-Critical Edition of the Hebrew Bible* (London, 1897), pp. 20 f. In addition to the four *Sedarim*, the Masorah divides Koheleth into smaller "open" and "closed" sections (*pethū-hōth, sethūmōth*). As given by Baer-Delitzsch, they are 1:11; 3:8, 13, 22; 4:17; 6:12; 9:6, 10; 11:8; 12:8 (all "closed") and 2:26 ("open"). As Ginsburg (*Introd.*, p. 19) points out, the Masorah is not careful with regard to these divisions, and no list has survived. It may be added that they are of little exegetical value.

[16] Except at the end of chaps. 2, 3, 5, and 6. The division breaks the continuity of thought most markedly at the end of chaps. 4, 8, 9, and 11. It ignores many other changes of theme, on which see below.

[17] Hertzberg, op. cit., pp. 13 f., divides the book into 12 principal sections, all of which (except I, VII, XI, and XII) have subdivisions of their own, so that he finds nearly 30 sections in the book.

[18] Sections IX, 6:12; X, 7:14; XIII, 8:9; XIV, 9:1–3.

[19] Sections I, 1:11; XVII, 11:5–6.

[20] Sections II, 2:26; XVIII, 11:7 to 12:8.

[21] Sections III, 3:13–15; VIII, 6:9; XV, 9:4–12.

[22] Section IV, 4:3.

[23] Cf. the results of M. Thilo's studies (*Der Prediger Salomo*, Bonn, 1923). To a lesser degree, Levy and Hertzberg are forced into the same difficulty by their effort to find logical continuity in the proverb-collections in chaps. 7 and 10. Hertzberg is incorrect in his statement that "es ist *niemals* eine Sammlung von Weisheitslehren wie in Prv." (p. 14, italics ours).

[24] We are unable to accept the conclusion of H. L. Ginsberg, *Studies in Koheleth* (New York, 1950), that the book's theme is how man should use

his wealth. Koheleth's thought encompasses this topic, to be sure, but it is much too varied to be limited to this subject alone.

²⁵ On this concept of "organic thinking" in Rabbinic Judaism, cf. M. Kadushin, *The Theology of Seder Eliahu* (New York, 1932), esp. pp. 17–32; *idem, Organic Thinking* (New York, 1938), esp. pp. 3–16; I. Heinemann, *Darkei Ha'aggadah* (Jerusalem, 1950), pp. 8 ff.

²⁶ Like the older views of Zapletal (1904), Grimme (1896), Sievers (1901) and Haupt (1905), Hertzberg's contention that Koheleth is written in meter is unconvincing. He himself is constrained to say that Koheleth is an "irregular combination of two-beat and three-beat stichs. It happens that one of these will prevail at times, but the normal is the combination (*Zusammenstellung*) of both" (p. 10). But a verse which is a mixture of two meters is not rhythmical. He also maintains that in 64 passages, אשר must be changed to the "original" ש to create the "meter." In addition, he concedes that many verses are "prosaic" (p. 11). Even with all these changes and exceptions, the reader will often find Hertzberg's scansion forced and unconvincing. Cf. Barton's reasoned critique of the older metrical theories (pp. 50 f.), and Levy's analysis of Zapletal's deletions of passages which are crucial to the book, because of his metrical theory (Levy, pp. 63 f.).

²⁷ This was recognized by Bishop Lowth, *Lectures on the Sacred Poetry of the Hebrews*, Lecture XXIV; Ewald in *Dichter des Alten Bundes*; Delitzsch, Renan, Driver in Kittel's *Biblia Hebraica*; Briggs, Genung, Barton, Levy.

²⁸ Cf. 1:18; 2:13, 14a; 4:5, 6, 12; 5:2; 7:1 ff., 19; 8:1; 9:17, 18; 10:2, 8, 18, 19, 20; 11:4.

²⁹ Thus in Section XV (9:4–12), vv. 4, 5, are prose, v. 6, rhythmic prose, vv. 7–9, verse, and vv. 10–12, again rhythmic prose. Similarly, in Section XIII (8:1–9), v. 1 is a proverb in rhythm, and v. 8 is in rhythmic prose, the intervening and succeeding passages being in ordinary prose. So, too, the Catalogue of the Seasons (3:1–8), which is in rhythm, is followed by a prose discussion (vv. 9 ff.).

³⁰ Thus the "Hymn of Victory" of Thutmose III (c. 1470 B. C. E.) goes over from verse to prose *in the same sentence* (cf. the text in Erman, op. cit., p. 257), as is the case in Ecc. 9:8 f.

NOTES ON CHAPTER XIV

¹ Walter Kaufmann, *Existentialism from Dostoevsky to Sartre* (New York, 1956), p. 11.

² *Columbia Encyclopedia* (3rd ed.; New York, 1963), p. 687b.

³ Kaufmann, *op. cit.*, p. 12.

⁴ *Ibid.*

⁵ For an analysis of conventional and unconventional Wisdom in Israel and the ancient Orient, see chaps. I-III in this volume.

⁶ See R. Gordis, *The Book of God and Man—A Study of Job* (Chicago, 1965), esp. chaps. VII-XI.

[7] Ecc. 1:2 ; 12:8.

[8] Ecc. 3:14f.; 6:10ff.; 8:7f., 17; 9:1, 11ff.; 10:14; 11:5.

[9] Ecc. 3:10–11.

[10] See Commentary *ad loc.*, pp. 221f.

[11] Ecc. 5:17–19. See Commentary on the structure and exegesis of this passage. Cf. also Ecc. 2:24ff.; 3:12-13, 22; 6:9; 8:15; 9:7ff.; 11:7–12:8.

[12] Gordis, *op. cit.*, pp. 118, 120.

[13] Cf. Gordis, *op. cit.*, chap. XIV.

[14] Moses Maimonides, *Guide to the Perplexed*, trans. M. Friedlander (New York, 1928), pp. 272, 273.

[15] *Ibid.*, p. 273; see also pp. 275, 276.

[16] *Ibid.*, chap. XXV, p. 309.

[17] Ben Zion Bokser, *The Legacy of Maimonides* (New York, 1950), p. 37.

[18] Julius J. Marke, *The Holmes Reader* (New York, 1955), p. 110. Holmes is, of course, citing Ecc. 9:10.

[19] Harvey Cox, *The Secular City* (New York, 1965), pp. 257, 258.

NOTES ON CHAPTER XV

[1] That is the meaning of Ps. 14:1 = 53:2: "The fool saith in his heart, 'There is no God.'" Cf. Job 22:12–14. Cf. Levy, op. cit., p. 23 on the *"felsenfeste Gottesgewissheit im Judentum."*

[2] Cf. Renan's observation: "Malheur à qui ne se contradit pas au moins une fois par jour. La vue claire d'une vérité ne l'empêche pas de voir tout de suite après la vérité contraire avec la même clarté."

[3] Cf. chap. IV.

[4] Cf. such Rabbinic authorities as Isaac Tirna, *Sefer Minhagim* (Warsaw, 1882), *Comments on Sukkot*, p. 21b: לי נראה טעם לפי שסוכות זמן שמחתנו וספר קוהלת משבח השמחה, "The reason seems to me to be that Sukkot is the season of our rejoicing and the book of Koheleth praises joy"; *Magen Abraham, Hilkhot Pesah*, sec. 490, par. 8, ובסוכות .... קוהלת שהם ימי השמחה, "And on Sukkot, Koheleth is read, because they are days of joy"; *Lebush, Hilkhot Lulav*, 663: סוכות הוא זמן שמחתנו וספר קוהלת משבח ומזרז את הבריות שישמחו בחלקם, "Succot is the season of our rejoicing and the book of Koheleth praises and encourages men to rejoice in their portion."

[5] On Sukkot as "the season of joy," cf. Deut. 16:13 ff. and the traditional descriptive phrase in the liturgy, *zeman simḥathenu*.

NOTES ON CHAPTER XVI

[1] In addition to the independent editions of Baer-Delitzsch (1886) and C. D. Ginsburg (London, 1st ed., 1894; 2nd ed., 1926), Driver edited *Koheleth* in the second edition of R. Kittel's *Biblia Hebraica* (Leipzig, 1913) and Horst in the fourth (1935).

² They are 4:8, 17; 5:8, 10; 6:10; 7:22; 9:4; 10:3, 20; 11:9 and 12:6.

³ Cf. Gordis, *The Biblical Text in the Making* (Phila., 1937), pp. 7–54, for the function of the Kethib-Qere in the Masorah. For the individual passages, consult the Index *ibid.* and the present Commentary ad loc.

⁴ In 10:20.

⁵ In 9:4 and 12:6.

⁶ In 4:8, 17; 5:8, 10; 7:22; 10:3; 11:9. In several of these (4:8, 17) the Qere is the simpler, but not necessarily the original, reading.

⁷ In 6:10. On conflation as a Masoretic device, cf. op. cit., pp. 41 ff., 49.

⁸ Cf. op. cit., Index, p. 215. In 7:2, the Madinhae reads המשתה Kethib; משתה Qere, the latter agreeing with the Ma'arbae text; in 12:12 the Madinhae Kethib is מהמה; Qere מהם, the former agreeing with the Ma'arbae. Only in 9:9, where the Ma'arbae text reads הוא, the Madinhae text reads היא as the Kethib, הוא as the Qere. This Kethib seems to have been read by Peshitta, Vulgate and Targum, which refer the pronoun to "the woman."

⁹ In *Der Masorah-Text des Koheleth* (Leipzig, 1890).

¹⁰ *Ibid.*, pp. 1–44.

¹¹ Rabbinic quotations of the Bible have been collected by V. Aptowitzer, *Das Schriftwort in der rabbinischen Literatur* (Vienna, 1908–15). Barton (p. 17) cites as "interesting" the plene spelling of לתקן (Ecc. 1:15) in the Mishnah and Talmud, but this is the normal orthography in unvocalized Hebrew texts and hence no variant at all. In Ecc. 4:17 (Kethib רגליך; Qere רגלך), the Talmudic derivation in J. Ber. 4d; J. Meg. 71c goes back to the plural of the Kethib, though the passage is cited in our Talmud editions according to the Qere. In the same verse, the reading באשר for כאשר may be a printer's variation in J. Ber. 4d, the likelihood of which Euringer recognizes, but Barton overlooks. In *Sifre* (ed. Friedmann), 60a, the Kethib of 5:8 (היא) is apparently cited. Generally, as in Ecc. 12:6, the Qere is quoted (B. Shab. 151b; Semakhot 44a).

¹² Cf., on the *'al tiqrē* formula, Gordis, op. cit., pp. 78 ff.; and *Enzyklopedia Talmudit* (Jerusalem, 1949), s. v., vol. 2, pp. 1 f.

¹³ Cf. H. B. Swete, *Introduction to O. T. in Greek* (Cambridge, 1914), still the standard treatment of the subject; H. St. John Thackeray, *The Septuagint and Jewish Worship* (London, 1923); and the more recent, briefer, survey in R. H. Pfeiffer, *Introduction to O. T.* (New York, 1941), pp. 104–119. On the Ancient Versions of Koheleth generally, see S. Euringer, op. cit.; Barton, pp. 9–17; Hertzberg, pp. 4 ff.; and the most recent treatment of the Versions in B. J. Roberts, *The O. T. Text and Versions* (Cardiff, 1951), pp. 101–278.

¹⁴ Cf. H. B. Swete, op. cit., pp. 31–42; E. Burkitt, *Fragments of the Book of Kings* (Cambridge, 1897); M. Friedmann, *Onkelos und Akylas* (Vienna, 1896).

¹⁵ Many factors explain these variations. In a not inconsiderable number of passages, LXX preserves older readings, though this was not suspected then either by Jewish or by Christian scholars. Thus Jerome speaks of the Hebrew text as *Hebraica veritas*. In addition, the variations were due to a) errors in comprehension by the Greek translators; b) the incorporation

of rabbinic exegesis into the version; and c) dogmatic changes and additions by the early Christian church.

[16] Since את, which is untranslated when used as the accusative particle, has the meaning of "with" when used prepositionally, Aquila renders it by the Greek preposition meaning "with." Obviously, Gen. 1:1 could not be translated: "In the beginning, God created *with* the heaven and *with* the earth," and Aquila's Jewish readers would understand that fact. The presence of the Greek equivalent of the Hebrew particle would, however, tell the Greek-speaking Jew in the Diaspora what the Palestinian Jew knew, i. e. that the nouns "heaven" and "earth" were preceded in the Hebrew text by את. This was particularly important for Rabbinic Judaism, since R. Akiba and other members of his school were wont to derive legal and Haggadic interpretations from particles like *'eth, 'akh, gam* and *raq*. Cf. B. Pes. 22b, and parallels, for R. Akiba's interpretation of *'eth* even in the verse, "The Lord thy God shalt thou fear" (Deut. 10:20); and see J. Ber. IX, 14b for the formulation: אכין ורקין מיעוטין אתין וגמין ריבויין "the *'akh* and the *raq* imply limitations, the *'eth* and the *gam* extensions, of the Biblical statement." Swete (op. cit., p. 41), who speaks of the "absurdity" of Aquila's version and of its acceptance as due to "prejudice," fails completely to recognize this very practical motivation for the preparation and use of this literalistic translation in the circles of normative Judaism, which were by no means limited to Palestine and Babylonia.

[17] Cf. his *Geschichte der Juden*, vol. IX, p. 437, and his *Koheleth* (Leipzig, 1871), pp. 173–79.

[18] These have been collected by Montfaucon (1713) and by Field (1875).

[19] In the *Sitzungsberichte der preussischen Akademie der Wissenschaften zu Berlin* (1892), I, pp. 3–16; cf. also E. Klostermann, *De Libri Coheleth Versione Alexandrina* (Kiel, 1892), pp. 37 f.

[20] Cf. his *Introduction to Ecclesiastes*, pp. 115–34. He discusses all the "Aquilan" characteristics in the LXX of *Ecclesiastes*. For a brief summary, cf. Barton, p. 9.

[21] So Podechard, op. cit., p. 207; Hertzberg, op. cit., p. 5.

[22] This is basically the view of Graetz, McNeile and Barton.

[23] He informs us that the Jews called this second edition "accurate throughout" (Opera V, pp. 32, 624; *Com. in Ezechiel*, Migne ed., 25, 39).

[24] The Sahidic translation was published by Ciasca, *Sanctorum Bibliorum Fragmenta Copto-Sahidica Musei Borgiani* (1880), vol. II, pp. 195–254.

[25] The patristic writings are the principal source for this version. The readings from this source were collected by P. Sabatier, *Bibliorum Sanctorum Latinae Versiones Antiquae* (Rheims, 1743).

[26] Cf., *inter alia*, Ch. Heller, *Untersuchungen über die Pešita* (Berlin, 1911), and his Hebrew edition of the *Pešita on Genesis* (Berlin, 1928). His basic thesis, the Version's strong dependence on Rabbinic tradition, has been vigorously opposed. On the Syriac and Latin Versions, see now Pfeiffer, op. cit., pp. 119–26; and Roberts' work cited above in note 13.

²⁷ In *ZATW*, vol. 24 (1904), pp. 181–239, and reprinted separately.

²⁸ The antiquity of written Targumim to the Hagiographa is attested by the reference to Rabban Gamaliel's holding a Targum to Job in his hand (Shab. 116a) and by the Mishnah Shab. 16:1: כל כתבי הקודש מצילין אותן מפני הדליקה אף על פי שכתובין בכל לשון. On the other hand, these Targumim are not quoted even in late Midrashim (P. Churgin, *Targum Kethubim*, New York, 1945, p. 14). On the basis of Greek words used and parallels with other Targumim, Churgin concludes that the Targum was written in Palestine and completed before the Arab conquest of the country in 636 C. E. (op. cit., p. 188).

²⁹ Thus the common phrase "under the sun" is rendered by the Targum "in this world." Verse 2:17 is given as "I hate every *evil* life." In general, the Targum follows the Midrash, the temper of which is well illustrated in the generalization (Midrash *Koheleth Rabba* 2:25): כל אכילה ושתייה שנאמר במגילה הזאת בתורה ובמעשים טובים הכתוב מדבר "Wherever 'eating and drinking' are mentioned in this Scroll, the text is referring to Torah and good deeds."

³⁰ On the method of the Targum, cf. S. D. Luzzatto's classic work *Oheb Ger* (Vienna, 1830). Though he is concerned with Onkelos, the principles enunciated there apply *mutatis mutandis* to all the Targumim, and in large measure to all the ancient Versions. The Prophetic Targum has been studied by P. Churgin, *Targum Jonathan to the Prophets* (New Haven, 1927). The *Targum to Ecclesiastes* is treated by the same scholar in his valuable Hebrew work *Targum Kethubim* (New York, 1945), pp. 167–82, cited above.

³¹ See e. g. our Com. on 1:17; 8:10.

³² Cf. Swete, op. cit., pp. 14 f. Jonah Ibn Janah (985–1040) mentions a commentary by Saadiah on Ecclesiastes, but no mss. have survived. Cf. H. Malter, *Saadia Gaon* (Phila., 1921), pp. 324 f. The work published by D. Fränkel, *Koheleth im Perush Rabbenu Saadia Gaon* (Husiatyn, 1903), is not by the Gaon but is based on the work of the Karaite Solomon ben Yeroham.

³³ This is the judgment of nearly all modern students. Cf. e. g. Barton, p. 18; Hertzberg, p. 3. On the theory of an Aramaic original for Koheleth, see above, chap. VII.

³⁴ On the beginnings of Masoretic activity before 70 C. E. cf. Gordis, op. cit., *BTM* (1937), pp. 45–48. This early date for the rise of the Masorah is supported by considerable data in the Talmud and Mishnah generally overlooked, which we hope to collate and interpret in the near future. The error scholars have made is confusing the activity, which was early, with the designation "Masorah," which was late. It may be added that the newly discovered Dead Sea Scrolls, if authentically pre-Christian in date, would lend additional support for this position, though the evidence is extensive even without them. Cf. the writer's remarks in *JNES*, vol. 9 (1950), pp. 45 f., and in *JBL*, vol. 69, 1950, p. x.

³⁵ See Com. on 3:21 and 9:1.

INDEX OF ABBREVIATIONS

Dan. = Daniel
Del. = Delitzsch
Deut. = Deuteronomy
Deut. Rabba = Midrash Deuteronomy Rabba
Dill. = Dillmann
Död. = Döderlein
Dr. = S. R. Driver

Ecc. = Ecclesiastes
ed. = edition, edited by
Eduy. = the tractate Eduyoth
Ehr. = Ehrlich
eq. = equal to, equals
Erub. = the tractate Erubin
esp. = especially
Est. = Esther
Eur. = Euringer
Ew. = Ewald
Ex. = Exodus
Ez. = Ezekiel

f., ff. = following (i. e. and the following verse [verses] or page [pages])
fem. = feminine
Fried. = Friedmann

Gal. = Galling
Gen. = Genesis
Gen. R. = Midrash Genesis Rabba
Gers. = Gerson
Ges. = Gesenius
Ges.-Buhl = W. Gesenius, Hebraeisches und aramaeisches Handwoerterbuch, ed. F. Buhl
Ges.-K. = Gesenius-Kautzsch, *Hebräische Grammatik*
Ges.-Thes. = Wilhelm Gesenius, Thesaurus philologicus criticus linguae Hebraeae et Chaldaeae Veteris Testamenti (Leipzig, 1829–58)
Giese. = Giesebrecht
Gins. = Ginsburg
Git. = the tractate Gittin
Gr. = Graetz

Ha. = Haupt
Hab. = Habakkuk
Hag. = the tractate Hagigah
Heb. = Hebrew
Herod. = Herodotus
Hertz. = Hertzberg
Hitz. = Hitzig
Hoel. = Hoelscher
Hos. = Hosea
Houb. = Houbigant
HUCA = Hebrew Union College Annual
Hul. = the tractate Hullin

I Chr. = I Chronicles
II Chr. = II Chronicles
I Ki. = I Kings
II Ki. = II Kings
I Sam. = I Samuel
II Sam. = II Samuel
Ibn E. = Abraham Ibn Ezra
ICC = International Critical Commentary
inf. = infinitive
Intr. Note = Introductory Note (preceding verse commentary)
Intro. = Introduction
Intro. sec. = Introductory section
Isa. = Isaiah

J. = Jerusalem (Palestinian) Talmud
JAOS = Journal of the American Oriental Society
Jast. = Jastrow
J. Ber. = the Jerusalem Talmud, tractate Berachoth
JBL = Journal of Biblical Literature
J. Kidd. = the Jerusalem Talmud, tractate Kiddushin
JNES = Journal of Near Eastern Studies
Josh. = Joshua
JPSV = Jewish Publication Society Version (of the Bible)
JQR = Jewish Quarterly Review

JRAS = Journal of the Royal Asiatic Society
J. Sanh. = the Jerusalem Talmud, tractate Sanhedrin
JSOR = Journal of the Society for Oriental Research
JThS = Journal of Theological Studies (Oxford)
Jud. = Judges

Ker. = the tractate Kerithoth
Keth. = the tractate Kethuboth
Kirk. = Kirkpatrick
Kit. = Kittel
Kn. = Knobel
Koheleth R. = Midrash Koheleth Rabba

l. = line
Lam. = Lamentations
Lev. = Leviticus
Lev. Rab. = Midrash Leviticus Rabba
Levy = Ludwig Levy
lit. = literally
ll. = lines
loc. cit. = loco citato (in the above-cited place or passage)
Luz. = Luzzatto
LXX = the Septuagint

M. = the Mishnah
Maas. - the tractate Maaseroth
Mal. = Malachi
masc. - masculine
Mat. = Matthew
McN. = McNeile
Meg. = the tractate Megillah
Mend. = Mendelssohn
Metam. = Metamorphoses
MHHH = R. Gordis, "Al Mibneh Hashirah Ha'ibrit Hakedumah," in *Sefer Hashanah Lihude Amerikah 5693* (New York, 1944)
M. Hullin = Mishnah, tractate Hullin

Mi. = Micah
Mich. = Michaelis
Mid. = Midrash
Midrash Ex. R. = Midrash Exodus Rabba
Midrash Gen. Rab. = Midrash Genesis Rabba
Midrash Koh. Rabba = Midrash Koheleth Rabba
M. Pes. = the Mishnah, tractate Pesachim
M. Shab. = the Mishnah, tractate Shabbath
mss. = manuscripts
MT = the Masoretic Text

n. = note
Ned. = the tractate Nedarim
Neh. = Nehemiah
Noel. = Noeldeke
Now. = Nowack
NSI = G. A. Cooke, *A Text-Book of North-Semitic Inscriptions*
N. T. = the New Testament
Nu. = Numbers
Num. R. = Midrash Numbers Rabba

Obad. = Obadiah
obj. gen. = objective genitive
obs. = observation
Ode. = Odeberg
OLQ = R. Gordis, "The Original Language of Qoheleth"
Olsh. = Olshausen
OLZ = Orientalische Literaturzeitung
op. cit. = opere citato (in the above-cited work)
opp. = opposite
O. T. = the Old Testament

p. = page
P = Peshitta
P. = the Palestinian (Jerusalem) Talmud
PAAJR = Proceedings of the American Academy of Jewish Research

Palm. = Palmyrene
par. = parallel
part. = participle
per. = person
Pers. = Persian
Pes. = the tractate Pesachim
pl. = plural
Pl. = Plumptre
Pod. = Podechard
pp. = pages
Pr. = Proverbs
Ps. = Psalm
Pss. = Psalms

QBROL = R. Gordis, "Quotations As a Literary Usage in Biblical, Rabbinic and Oriental Literature"
QHA = R. Gordis, "Qoheleth — Hebrew or Aramaic"
QWL = R. Gordis, "Quotations in Wisdom Literature"

R. = Rabbi
Ra. = Rashi
RB = Revue Biblique
RBRH = R. Gordis, "Studies in the Relationship of Biblical and Rabbinic Hebrew"
Re. = Renan
REJ = Revue des Etudes Juives
Rev. = Revelation
RHPR = Revue de l'Histoire et de la Philosophie des Religions
Rosen. = Rosenmüller

SAB = Sitzungsberichte der Preussischen Akademie . . . Berlin
Sanh. = the tractate Sanhedrin
SBWL = R. Gordis, "The Social Background of Wisdom Literature"
sc. = scilicet
sec. = section
Shab. = the tractate Shabbath

Sheb. = the tractate Shebuoth
Shek. = the tractate Shekalim
Sieg. = Siegfried
sing. = singular
Suk. = the tractate Sukkah
s. v. = sub voce (sub verbo)
Sym. = Symmachus

T = the Aramaic Targum
Tal. = the Talmud
Tar. = the Targum
Th., Theod. = Theodotion
ThLZ = Theologische Literaturzeitung
Tos. = Tosefta
tr. = translated by, translation
trans. = translation
Tyl. = Tyler

v. = verse
V = Vulgate
Vaih. = Vaihinger
vol. = volume
vols. = volumes
vv. = verses
Vvs. = the Versions

Wel. = Wellhausen
Wetz. = Wetzstein
Wild. = Wildeboer
Wr. = Wright

Yad. = the tractate Yadayim
Yeb. = the tractate Yebamoth

Zap. = Zapletal
ZATW = Zeitschrift für die Alttestamentliche Wissenschaft
Zc. = Zechariah
Zeph. = Zephaniah
Zöck. = Zöckler

‖ = parallel to
= equal to, equals

BIBLIOGRAPHY

A. TEXTS AND VERSIONS

I. *The Hebrew Text*
> S. BAER and FR. DELITZSCH, Quinque Volumina (Leipzig, 1886)
>
> C. D. GINSBURG, Masoretic Bible (London, 1st ed., 1894; 2nd ed., 1926)
>
> R. KITTEL, Biblia Hebraica, 4th ed. (Stuttgart, 1937), edited by A. Alt and O. E. Eissfeldt (Masoretic notes by P. Kahle; *Koheleth* edited by F. Horst)

II. *The Septuagint*
> H. B. SWETE, The Old Testament in Greek (Cambridge, 1887–94)
>
> A. RAHLFS, Septuaginta, 2 vols. (Stuttgart, 1935)

III. *Aquila, Symmachus, Theodotion*
> F. FIELD, Origenis Hexaplorum quae Supersunt (Oxford, 1875)

IV. *The Vulgate*
> R. STIER and K. G. W. THEILE, Polyglotten-Bibel, 4th ed. (Bielefeld-Leipzig, 1875)

V. *The Peshitta*
> Kethabe Kadishe, ed. S. LEE (London, 1823)

VI. *Targum*
> Mikraoth Gedoloth, Pentateuch and Megilloth (Vilna, 1912, and often reprinted)

B. SOURCES

The Old Testament

The Apocrypha and Pseudepigrapha (ed. Charles, Oxford, 1913)

The New Testament — Authorized Version

Josephus, Works (Loeb Classics)

Mekilta de-Rabbi Ishmael, ed. J. Z. Lauterbach (Philadelphia, 1933)

Sifre de be Rab, ed. M. Friedmann (Vienna, 1864)

The Mishnah (Vilna ed.), frequently reprinted

Tosefta, ed. M. S. Zuckermandl, 2nd ed. (Jerusalem, 1938)

Aboth de Rabbi Nathan, ed. S. Schechter, 2nd printing (New York, 1945)

Babylonian Talmud (Vilna, 1928), frequently reprinted

Jerusalem Talmud (Krotoschin, 1866)

Midrash Rabba on the Torah and the Megilloth (Vilna ed.), 1938, and frequently reprinted

Pesikta de Rab Kahana, ed. S. Buber, 2nd ed. (Vilna, 1925)

Midrash Tehillim, ed. S. Buber (Vilna, 1891)

C. COMMENTARIES

Rashi (d. 1105), Abraham ibn Ezra (d. 1167), David Kimhi (d. 1235), Obadiah Sforno (d. 1550), F. Hitzig (1847), C. D. Ginsburg (1861), H. Graetz (1871), Th. Tyler (1874), Fr. Delitzsch (1875), E. H. Plumptre (1881), E. Renan (1882), W. Nowack (1883), C. H. H. Wright (1883), G. Bickell (1884), C. Siegfried (1898), G. Wildeboer (1898), A. H. McNeile (1904), P. Haupt (1905), G. A. Barton (1909), V. Zapletal (1911), E. Podechard (1912), L. Levy (1912), A. B. Ehrlich (1914), M. Jastrow (1919), P. Volz (1922), K. Budde (1923), M. Thilo (1923), A. Allgeier (1925), G. Kuhn (1926), W. Vischer (1926), H. Odeberg (1929), B. Gemser (1931), H. W. Hertzberg (1932), K. Galling (1940), J. J. Weber (1947), I. Bettan (1950).

D. STUDIES IN ECCLESIASTES AND WISDOM LITERATURE

BURKITT, F. C., "Is Ecclesiastes a Translation?", in *JThS*, 1921, vol. 22

CHEYNE, T. K., Job and Solomon (New York, 1887)

CHURGIN, P., Targum Kethubim (New York, 1945)

DHORME, P., "L'Ecclésiaste ou Job," in *RB*, vol. 20, 1923

———, Le Livre de Job (Paris, 1926)

DILLMANN, C. F. A., "Über die griechische Übersetzung des Qoheleth," in SAB, vol. 1 (1892) (also his commentaries on the text of the Bible, and his editions of the texts of the Bible and Apocrypha)

DILLON, E. J., Skeptics of the O. T. (London, 1895)

DRIVER, S. R., and GRAY, G. B., ICC on *Job*, 2 vols. (New York, 1921)

EBELING, E., "Reste akkadischer Weisheitsliteratur," in Bruno Meissner Festschrift (vol. I, 1928)

EURINGER, S., Der Masorah-Text des Koheleth (Leipzig, 1890)

FERNÁNDEZ, A., "Es Eclesiastes una versión?", in *Biblica*, vol. 3, 1922

FICHTNER, J., Die altorientalische Weisheitsliteratur in ihrer israelitisch-juedischen Auspraegung (Giessen, 1933)

FRÄNKEL, D., Koheleth im Perush Rabbenu Saadia Gaon (Husiatyn, 1903)

FRIEDLAENDER, M., Griechische Philosophie im A.T. (Berlin, 1904)

GALLING, K., "Kohelet-Studien," in *ZATW*, vol. 48, 1932

GASPAR, J. W., Social Ideas in the Wisdom Literature of the O. T. (Washington, 1947)

GERSON, ADOLF, Der Chacham Kohelet als Philosoph und Politiker (Frankfort on Main, 1905)

GINSBERG, H. L., Studies in Koheleth (New York, 1950)

GOODRICK, A. T. S., The Book of Wisdom (London, 1917)

GORDIS, R., "Ecclesiastes 1:17 — Its Text and Interpretation," in *JBL*, vol. 56, 1937

———, "Mabo Lesafruth HaHokmah," in Sefer Hashanah Lihude Amerikah (1942)

———, "The Heptad As An Element of Biblical and Rabbinic Style," in *JBL*, vol. 62, 1943

———, "Social Background of Wisdom Literature," in *HUCA*, vol. 18, 1944

———, The Wisdom of Ecclesiastes (New York, 1945)

———, "The Original Language of Qoheleth," in *JQR*, vol. 37, 1946

———, "Quotations As a Literary Usage in Biblical, Rabbinic and Oriental Literature," in *HUCA*, vol. 22, 1949

———, "The Translation-Theory of Qohelet Re-examined," in *JQR*, vol. 40, 1949

———, "All Men's Book — A New Introduction to the Book of Job," in Menorah Journal, vol. 37, 1949

———, "Koheleth — Hebrew or Aramaic," in *JBL* (scheduled for publication in June, 1952)

GREENSTONE, J. H., The Book of Proverbs (Philadelphia, 1950)

HOELSCHER, G., Das Buch Hiob (Tuebingen, 1937)

HUMBERT, P., Recherches sur les sources Egyptiennes de la Littérature sapientiale d'Israël (Neuchâtel, 1929)

JOUON, P., "Notes philologiques sur le texte hébreu de l'Eccl.", in *Biblica*, vol. 11, 1930

KAMENETZKY, A. S., "Die P'šita zu Qoheleth," in *ZATW*, vol. 24, 1904 (and separately)

KLOSTERMANN, E., De Libri Coheleth Versione Alexandrina (Kiel, 1892)

KÖNIG, EDUARD, Einleitung in das Alte Testament (Bonn, 1893)

LEIMDÖRFER, DAVID, Die Lösung des Qoheletsrätsels durch den Philosophen Baruch ibn Baruch

————, Der "Prediger Salomonis" in historischer Beleuchtung (Hamburg, 1892)

MACDONALD, D. B., The Hebrew Philosophical Genius (Princeton, 1936)

MENDELSSOHN, MOSES, Bible commentary on Ecclesiastes (Berlin, 1789)

NOELDEKE, TH., Untersuchungen zum Ahikar-Roman (Berlin, 1913)

OESTERLEY, W. O. E., The Book of Proverbs (Phila., 1929)

PEDERSEN, J., "Scepticisme israélite," in *RHPR*, 1930

RANKIN, O. S., Israel's Wisdom Literature (London, 1936)

RANSTON, H., Ecclesiastes and the Early Greek Wisdom Literature (London, 1925)

————, The O. T. Wisdom Books and Their Teaching (London, 1930)

TORREY, C. C., "The Question of the Original Language of Qohelet," in *JQR*, vol. 39, 1948

TOY, C. H., ICC on *Proverbs* (New York, 1902)

TUR-SINAI, N. H. (HARRY TORCZYNER), "Koheleth," in *Halashon Vehasefer*, vol. II (Jerusalem, 1950)

————, Mishlei Shelomoh (Tel-Aviv, 1947)

WETZSTEIN, J. G., Biblischer Commentar über die poetischen Bücher des Alten Testaments (Leipzig, 1875)

ZIMMERMANN, F., "The Aramaic Provenance of Qohelet," in *JQR*, vol. 36, 1945

————, "The Question of Hebrew in Qohelet," in *JQR*, vol. 40, 1949

ZÖCKLER, OTTO, Die Apokryphen des Alten Testaments (Munich, 1891)

ZÖCKLER, OTTO, and STRACK, H. L., ed., Kurzgefasster Kommentar zu den Heiligen Schriften des Alten und Neuen Testaments (9 vols., Nördlingen and Munich, 1887–1905)

E. GENERAL BIBLIOGRAPHY

ALBRIGHT, W. F., The Archaeology of Palestine (Middlesex, 1947)

————, From the Stone Age to Christianity (Baltimore, 1940)

————, "The List of Levitical Cities," in Alexander Marx Jubilee Volumes (New York, 1950)

————, "The Canaanite Origin of Israelite Musical Guilds" (unpublished)

APTOWITZER, V., Das Schriftwort in der rabbinischen Literatur (Vienna, 1908–15)

ARISTOTLE, Nicomachean Ethics (often reprinted)

BAMBERGER, I. D., Kore Beemet (Frankfort, 1871)

BARTH, J., Die Nominalbildung in den semitischen Sprachen (Leipzig, 1889)

BARTON, G. A., Archaeology and the Bible, 7th ed. (Phila., 1937)

BERLIN, M., and ZEVIN, S. J. (ed.), Enzyklopedia Talmudit, 2 vols. (Jerusalem, 1947–   )

BERNFELD, SIMON, Mabo Sifruthi-Histori Lekithebe Hakodesh (4 vols., Berlin and Tel-Aviv, 1923–29)

————, Die jüdische Literatur (Berlin, 1921)

————, Torah, Nebiim Ukethubim. Die Heilige Schrift (Frankfort on Main, 1919)

BERTHOLET, A., A History of Hebrew Civilization (New York, 1926)

BICKERMANN, E., Der Gott der Makkabäer (Berlin, 1937)

BLAU, L., Einleitung in die heilige Schrift (Budapest, 1894)

BOHL, F., Die Sprache der Amarnabriefe (Leipzig, 1909)

BOUCHÉ-LECLERQ, A., Histoire des Lagides, 4 vols. (Paris, 1903–7)

BROWN, F., DRIVER, S. R., and BRIGGS, C. A., A Hebrew and English Lexicon to the O. T. (New York, 1907)

BUECHLER, A., Die Tobiaden und die Oniaden (Vienna, 1899)

BUHL, F., Canon and Text of the O. T. (Edinburgh, 1892)

BULTMANN, R., Der Stil der paulinischen Predigt und die kynisch-stoische Diatribe (Göttingen, 1910)

BURKITT, E., Fragments of the Book of Kings (Cambridge, 1897)

CAIRD, E., Lectures in The Evolution of Religion, 2 vols. (Glasgow, 3rd ed., 1899)

CARLYLE, T., Heroes and Hero Worship (frequently reprinted)

CASPARI, C. P., and MUELLER, A., Arabische Grammatik (4th ed., Halle, 1876)

CASSUTO, U., Torat Hateudot Vesidduram shel Siphrei Hatorah (Jerusalem, 1942)

————, Meadam Ad Noah (Jerusalem, 1944)

CHARLES, R. H., Apocrypha and Pseudepigrapha of the O. T., 2 vols. (Oxford, 1913)

CHURGIN, P., Targum Jonathan to the Prophets (New Haven, 1927)

COOKE, G. A., A Text-Book of North-Semitic Inscriptions (Oxford, 1903)

COWLEY, A. E., Aramaic Papyri of the Fifth Century B. C. (Oxford, 1923)

DELITZSCH, FR., Schreib- und Lesefehler im A. T. (Berlin-Leipzig, 1920)

DIRINGER, D., The Alphabet (London, 1948)

DÖDERLEIN, J. C., Bible commentary and Bible edition (the latter with J. H. MEISNER)

DRIVER, G. R., Problems of the Hebrew Verbal System (Edinburgh, 1936)

DRIVER, G. R., and MILES, J. C., The Assyrian Laws (Oxford, 1943)

DRIVER, S. R., Hebrew Tenses (3rd ed., Oxford, 1892)

————, ICC on Deuteronomy (New York, 1916)

DURANT, W., The Life of Greece (New York, 1939)

EHRLICH, A. B.; Die Psalmen (Berlin, 1905)

EPSTEIN, B., Mekor Barukh, 3 vols. (Vilna, 1928)

ERMAN, A., The Literature of the Ancient Egyptians (translated by A. M. BLACKMAN; New York, 1927)

EWALD, HEINRICH, Bible commentary on the Hagiographa, and his works on the Hebrew language, history, and antiquities

FINKELSTEIN, L., The Pharisees, 2 vols. (Phila., 1938)

————, Haperushim ve-Anshe Kenesset Hagedolah (New York, 1950)

FRENSDORFF, S., ed., Das Buch Ochla Ve'ochla (Hanover, 1864)

FRIEDMANN, M., Onkelos und Akylas (Vienna, 1896)

GEIGER, ABRAHAM, various works on Bible and Biblical exegesis

GESENIUS, W., Hebräische Grammatik, 28th ed., ed. E. Kautzsch (Leipzig, 1889)

GESENIUS, W., Hebraeischcs und aramaeisches Handwoerter-
buch, 17th ed., ed. F. Buhl (Leipzig, 1921)
——, Thesaurus philologicus criticus linguae Hebraeae et
Chaldaeae Veteris Testamenti (Leipzig, 1829–58)
GIESEBRECHT, FRIEDRICH, Bible commentaries, and works on
the Hebrew language, religion, and prophets
GINSBURG, C. D., The Massorah (4 vols., London, 1880–1905)
——, Introduction to the Massoretico-Critical Edition of the
Hebrew Bible (London, 1897)
GINZBERG, L., Commentary on the Jerusalem Talmud, 3 vols.
(New York, 1940)
——, The Legends of the Jews (7 vols., Phila., 1909–38)
GORDIS, R., "A Note on Conditional Sentences in Hebrew," in
JBL, vol. 49, 1930
——, "A Note on Joshua 22:34," in AJSL, vol. 47, 1931
——, "Studies in Hebrew Roots of Contrasted Meanings,"
in JQR, vol. 27, 1936
——, The Biblical Text in the Making (Phila., 1937)
——, "A Note on Yad," in JBL, vol. 62, 1943
——, "The Asseverative Kaph in Hebrew and Ugaritic," in
JAOS, vol. 63, 1943
——, "A Wedding Song for Solomon," in JBL, vol. 63,
1944
——, "Al Mibneh Hashirah Ha'ibrit Hakedumah," in Sefer
Hashanah Lihude Amerikah 5693 (New York, 1944)
——, "Studies in the Relationship of Biblical and Rabbinic
Hebrew," in Louis Ginzberg Jubilee Volumes (New York,
1945)
——, "'Homeric' Books in Palestine," in JQR, vol. 38, 1948
——, "The Bible as a Cultural Monument," in The Jews, Their
History, Culture, and Religion, ed. L. Finkelstein, vol. 1
(New York, 1949)
——, "Primitive Democracy in Ancient Israel — The Biblical
Edah," in Alexander Marx Jubilee Volumes, 1950 (English
section)
GORDON, C. H., Ugaritic Grammar (Rome, 1940)
——, Ugaritic Literature (Rome, 1949)
GRAETZ, H., Geschichte der Juden (Leipzig, 1905–09)
GRESSMANN, H., Altorientalische Texte zum A. T. (2nd ed.,
Berlin-Leipzig, 1926)

GRIMME, HUBERT, Grundzüge der hebräischen Akzent- und
    Vokallehre (Freiburg, 1896)
GROTE, G., A History of Greece (London, 1851)
GROTIUS, HUGO, Bible commentary
HASTINGS, J., ed., Dictionary of the Bible, 5 vols. (New York,
    1899–1902)
HEIDEL, A., The Gilgamesh Epic and O.T. Parallels (Chicago,
    1946)
HELLER, CH., Untersuchungen über die Pešita (Berlin, 1911)
————, Pešita on Genesis (Berlin, 1928)
HOELSCHER, G., Geschichte der israelitischen und juedischen
    Religion (Giessen, 1922)
HOOKE, S. H., Myth and Ritual (London, 1933)
HOUBIGANT, C. F., Notae Criticae in universos Veteris Testa-
    menti Libros (2 vols., Frankfort on Main, 1777)
KAUFMAN, Y., Toledot Ha'emunah Hayyisreelit, 7 vols. (Tel-
    Aviv, 1937–   )
KENNEDY, J., An Aid to the Textual Amendment of the O. T.
    (Edinburgh, 1928)
KIRKPATRICK, A. F., Bible Commentary
KLAUSNER, J., Habayyit Hasheni Bigedullato (Jerusalem, 1930)
————, Yeshu Hanotzri (Jerusalem, 1922)
————, Mi-Yeshu ad Paulus, 2 vols. (Tel-Aviv, 1940)
KLEINERT, P., Theologische Studien und Kritiken (1909)
KNOBEL, AUGUST, Bible Commentary
KOEHLER, L., and BAUMGARTNER, W., Lexicon in Veteris Testa-
    menti Libros (Leiden, 1948–   )
KÖNIG, EDUARD, Die Originalität des neulich entdeckten Hebrä-
    ischen Sirachtextes (Freiburg in B., 1899)
————, Historisch-Comparative Syntax der Hebräischen Sprache
    (Leipzig, 1897)
KRAUSS, S., Griechische und Lateinische Lehnwörter im Talmud,
    Midrasch und Targum (Berlin, 1898–99)
LIDDELL, H. G., and SCOTT, R., A Greek-English Lexicon (New
    York, 1883)
LIDZBARSKI, M., Alt-semitische Texte (Giessen, 1907)
LIEBERMAN, S., Greek in Jewish Palestine (New York, 1942)
————, Hellenism in Jewish Palestine (New York, 1950)
LOHR, M., Sozialismus und Individualismus im A. T. (Giessen,
    1906)

LUZZATTO, S. D., Oheb Ger (Vienna, 1830)

MACDONALD, D. B., The Hebrew Literary Genius (Princeton, 1933)

MAIMONIDES, Commentary on the Mishnah Abot, Shemonah Perakim, ed. J. I. Gorfinkle (New York, 1912)

MALTER, H., The Treatise Taanit of the Babylonian Talmud (Phila., 1928)

MARGOLIS, M. L., The Hebrew Scriptures in the Making (Phila., 1922)

MICHAELIS, J. D., commentaries on and editions of the Bible, and works on Biblical exegesis

MOFFATT, JAMES, Bible translation (New York, 1935)

MOORE, G. F., History of Religions, 2 vols. (New York, 1913)
———, Judaism in the First Centuries of the Christian Era, 3 vols. (Cambridge, 1927)

NOTH, M., Ueberlieferungsgeschichtliche Studien (Halle, 1943)

OESTERLEY, W. O. E., and ROBINSON, T. H., Hebrew Religion (New York, 1930)

PFEIFFER, R. H., Introduction to the O. T. (New York, 1941)
———, History of New Testament Times With an Introduction to the Apocrypha (New York, 1949)

PINSKER, S., Mabo Lannikkud Ha'ashuri (Vienna, 1863)

PLATO, Dialogues (Loeb Classics, 1924)

REUSS, EDUARD, Die Geschichte der Heiligen Schriften Alten Testaments (2nd ed.; Brunswick, 1890) (also his Bible commentary and translation)

ROSENMÜLLER, E. F. K., Biblia Hebraica (Leipzig, 1834)
———, Handbuch der biblischen Alterthumskunde (5 vols., Leipzig, 1923–28)

ROSIN, D., Die Ethik des Maimonides (Breslau, 1876)

ROWLEY, H. H., The Relevance of Apocalyptic (London, 1944)

RYLE, H. E., Canon of the O. T. (2nd ed., London, 1909)

SACHAU, E., Aramäische Papyrus und Ostraka (Leipzig, 1911)

SCHUERER, E., Geschichte des juedischen Volkes im Zeitalter Jesu Christi, 3rd and 4th ed. (Leipzig, 1901–11)

SEGAL, M. H., Dikduk Leshon Hamishnah (Tel-Aviv, 1936)

SEIDEL, M., "Heker Millim," in Debir, vol. 1 (Berlin, 1923)

SELLIN, E., Spuren griechischer Philosophie im A. T. (Leipzig, 1905)

SIEVERS, EDUARD, Metrische Studien (Leipzig, 1901 ff.)

SLOUSCHZ, N., Otzar Hakethobhoth Haphinikioth (Tel-Aviv, 1942)

SMEND, RUDOLF, Die Weisheit des Jesus Sirach (Berlin, 1906)

SMITH, H. P., ICC on Samuel (New York, 1899)

SMITH, J. M. P., Origin and History of Hebrew Law (Chicago, 1931)

STACE, W. T., A Critical History of Greek Philosophy (London, 1928)

SUKENIK, E. L., Megillot Genuzot (Jerusalem, 1948)

SWETE, H. B., Introduction to the O. T. in Greek (Cambridge, 1914)

TAYLOR, ARCHER, The Proverb (Cambridge, 1931)

THACKERAY, H. ST. JOHN, The Septuagint and Jewish Worship (London, 1923)

THOMAS, CALVIN, ed., Goethe's Faust, 2 vols. (Boston, 1906)

TORREY, C. C., The Apocryphal Literature (New Haven, 1945)

TSCHERNOWITZ, CH., Toledoth Hahalakhah, 4 vols. (New York, 1934–50)

TUR-SINAI, N. H. (HARRY TORCZYNER), Halashon Vehasefer, 2 vols. (Jerusalem, 1948 and 1950)

UMBREIT, F. W. C., Bible commentary

UNGNAD, A., Aramäische Papyrus aus Elephantine (Leipzig, 1911)

VON RAD, F., Das Geschichtsbild der chronistischen Werke (Stuttgart, 1930)

WEISS, I. H., Dor Dor Vedorshav, 5 vols. (Vienna, 1871–91)

WINCKLER, H., Alt-Orientalische Forschungen (Leipzig, 1893–1905)

WOLFSON, H. A., The Philosophy of Spinoza (Cambridge, 1934)

———, Spinoza and Religion (New York, 1950)

YELLIN, D., Hiqre Mikra — Iyyob (Jerusalem, 1927)

ZEITLIN, S., "The Tobias Family and the Hasmoneans," in PAAJR, vol. 4, 1933

———, "An Historical Study of the Canonization of the Hebrew Scriptures," in PAAJR, vol. 3, 1932

———, "Jewish Apocryphal Literature," in JQR, vol. 40, 1950

ZELLER, E., Pre-Socratic Philosophy (London, 1881)

ADDITIONAL NOTES ON THE TEXT OF
KOHELETH

1:1 (p. 203). In addition to the Biblical names similar in form to קהלת, cf. also the names of contemporary Arab chiefs, as, e. g., the Nabatean חרתת (=Ḥāretat), 'Οβοδας, etc. Cf. J. T. Milik, in *Revue Biblique*, 1952, vol. 59, p. 591. These parallels, incidentally, strengthen the view of a third-century Palestinian (not Syrian) provenance for the book.

1:3 (p. 205). For an analysis of the various uses of the vocable *'āmāl* frequently used in *Koheleth*, see Supplementary note D, "On the Meaning of *'āmāl* in Koheleth" below (p. 418).

2:3 (p. 216). Par. 4, line 1, should read: The LXX rendering of סִכְלוּת as "joy" is either a free, etc.

2:5 (p. 217). The plural in *īm* of פרדס occurs rarely in Rabbinic Hebrew (cf. B. Pes. 56a, variants in the editions), while the *ōth* ending is increasingly common. Thus in this respect, also Koheleth's language reflects a stage earlier than that of Mishnaic Hebrew, as in the case of *ḥēfeṣ* (see p. 364, n. 94).

2:8 (p. 218). שִׁדָּה occurs in the Tel el-Amarna letter of Amenophis III to Milkiel, governor of Gezer, published by G. Dossin in *Revue Asiatique*, vol. 31, 1934, pp. 125–136. The king asks for forty young women, expressed by the Sumerian ideogram *sal UMUN*, which has as one of its Akkadian equivalents "concubine." The Canaanite gloss is *šādi-tum* (cf. Fossey, in *Revue des Etudes Sémitiques*, 1933, pp. 87 ff.; J. T. Milik, in *Revue Biblique*, 1952, vol. 59, p. 590). Jerome still transliterates our Hebrew phrase as *sadda, saddoth*.

3:11 (p. 231 f.). To the long list of emendations proposed for the crux הָעֹלָם may be added הֶעָמָל (H. L. Ginsberg), which he renders here as "exertion," a curious *volte-face* in view of his insistence that *'āmāl* means only "wealth" (see Supplementary Note D). The emendation produces a strange and unintelligible text: "He has placed exertion in their hearts." Moreover, he leaves unexplained how the familiar *'āmāl* was corrupted into the difficult *'ōlam*.

As we have pointed out, the only meaning of the noun *'ōlam* attested to in any period of the language is "world." We have accordingly rendered the passage, "He has also placed the love of the world in men's hearts." The idea of "love" is implicit in the use of "heart," which is the seat of desire in Biblical psychology. This extended use may also be supported by, and in turn help to explain, the clause וְהוֹלֵלוֹת בִּלְבָבָם in 9:3. On הוֹלֵלוֹת, which is typical of Koheleth's style (2:2, 12; 7:7, 25; 9:3; 10:13), and which means "madness, mad revelry, wickedness," see Comm. p. 213. The clause in 9:3 may therefore be rendered "the love of wickedness is in their hearts."

3:17 (p. 234). The use of Lamed and עַל in parallel phrases is anomalous, in spite of the frequent interchange of עַל and אֶל in Biblical and Rabbinic Hebrew. In Punic, also, the prepositions are used interchangeably (cf. *CIS*, 167, 7, כסף על אחד equal to לאחד; *ibid.* 8, על בני equal to לבני; Lidzbarski, 36, 11,

עַל חַיֵּי equals לְחַיֵּי) (Dahood, *op. cit.*, p. 26). The use of two different but synonymous prepositions in parallel phrases in the same verse is, however, Biblically attested, cf. Isa. 66:10: שמחו את־ירושלם וגילו בה.

4:1 (p. 238 f.). וְאֵין לָהֶם מְנַחֵם is rendered in our translation (p. 158) with virtually all commentators as "with none to comfort them." The proposed emendation of the second מְנַחֵם to מוֹשִׁיעַ (Gr.) or to מַצִּיל (Oort), in order to avoid the repetition, is properly rejected on stylistic grounds (pp. 238 f.). However, the emendations also reflect the feeling that "comforter" is not entirely suitable here.

The root *nāḥam* possesses several distinct senses, not always properly recognized and classified in the Lexica. The basic significance of the root seems to be "to change one's mind." From this meaning are derived a) its most frequent usage, "to comfort," lit. "cause the mourner to change (his state of mind)," as e. g., in Gen. 37:35; 38:12; II Sam. 13:39; Nah. 3:7; Zc. 10:2; Job 16:2; Lam. 1:2, 9, 17, 21; and b) "to rue, regret one's actions" (Gen. 6:6, 7; Ex. 13:17; Num. 23:19; Jer. 20:16; Job 2:14; Zc. 8:14; Ps. 106:45).

In addition, the root *nāḥam* possesses two additional meanings: c) "to pity, be sorry for," probably a metaplastic form for *rāḥam* (Deut. 32:36 = Ps. 135:14; Jud. 21:6, 15; Jer. 15:6; Ps. 90:13, to which Hos. 11:8 נִחוּמָי=רַחֲמָי is to be added). Lastly, there is the meaning, d) "avenge," probably a metaplastic form for *nāqam*, to which it is parallel in Isa. 1:24; also in Gen. 27:42; Isa. 57:6; Ezek. 5:13. This last meaning is the one most appropriate to our passage, where *meʾnaḥem* is virtually equivalent to *gōʾēl* "blood avenger, kinsman, protector." Our clause is therefore to be rendered both times, "with none to avenge them, to defend them."

5:5 (p. 248). Both here and in 7:16, 17 לָמָּה, which is often taken as equivalent to פֶּן, "lest," is better understood as "why" (so AV, SRV, and our translation). The use of a question instead of a statement at the end of a discussion is a charming characteristic of Koheleth's style, adding a touch of liveliness and informality to the text. For additional instances of this use of an interrogative clause as a climax, cf. 2:16; 3:22; 5:15; 6:6, 12; 10:14.

5:8 (p. 250). On the idealization of agriculture as a characteristic of the Wisdom school, reflecting its social orientation, see Pr. 27:23–27, and cf. SBWL.

6:11 (p. 263 f.). Koheleth's question, "Who knows what is good for man in life during the brief days of his vain existence which he spends like a shadow," seems a direct rejoinder to Micah's classic asseveration (6:8), "He has told you, O man, what is good, and what the Lord your God requires of you, to do justice, to love mercy, and to walk humbly with your God." No more striking confrontation of the divergent outlooks of the prophet and of the Biblical Wisdom teacher is conceivable than these two passages.

7:1 (p. 267 f.). In the Commentary it is suggested that the two stichs of the verse are closely related. Man's good name becomes secure only at the time of his death, while oil is employed at the time of the birth of an infant. Though no actual proof was adduced, the assumption for the use of oil at birth was made on the basis of the frequent use of oil for bathing and for medicinal purposes. This inference may now be regarded as a fact, in view of evidence available for the Middle East. The practice is widespread of having infants, shortly after birth, rubbed with oil and salt, among the Christian Arabs of Syria, the Moslem Arabs of Jerusalem and the Bedouins of Arabia Petrae (see J. Morgenstern, *Rites of Birth, Marriage, Death and Kindred Occasions Among the Semites*, Cincinnati, 1966, pp. 7–9, 15, and the sources there cited).

7:17 (p. 277). Cf. also Job 15:32, בְּלֹא יוֹמוֹ תִּמָּלֵא, and the Aramaic Ahikar papyrus, line 102: וּתֵהֵךְ [בֶּן]לָא בְּיוֹמֵיךְ (E. Sachau, *Aramäische Papyrus und Ostraka*, Leipzig, 1911, pp. 163 f.), Papyrus 13446e, line 8.

7:22 (p. 280). The verse is correctly rendered in our translation, "Besides, you know very well that many times you have reviled others" (p. 178). It should be added that this verse is an example of "anticipation," i. e., a syntactic usage in which part of a subordinate clause is moved forward and incorporated into the main clause. Here פְּעָמִים רַבּוֹת is logically part of the subordinate clause modifying קִלַּלְתָּ, but has been moved forward to the main clause. For a simple, classic instance of this usage, see Ehrlich, *Randglossen* on Gen. 1:4. For a more complex example, see Gordis, "A Note on *Joshua* 22:34" in *AJSL*, vol. 47 (1931), pp. 287 f. Another instance of "anticipation" may occur in our book in 5:19 (see the Commentary, p. 256 f. above).

7:24 (p. 280). The problems confronting Koheleth due to the absence of a philosophical vocabulary are highlighted in this verse among others. מַה־שֶּׁהָיָה lit. "what has come into being" is equivalent to "reality" or "the cosmos." The absence of a technical vocabulary is not, however, an unmitigated evil. Koheleth is compelled to use language of general discourse rather than have recourse to a jargon limited to a narrow circle of readers.

8:2 (p. 288). The reference at the end of par. 2, should be Hos. 14:9, not 12:9.

8:12 (p. 298). The elliptical use of וּמַאֲרִיךְ לוֹ for וּמַאֲרִיךְ אַף לוֹ "He is patient, long-suffering with him" is attested in Rabbinic Hebrew: שאני בית ראשון שהיה מאריך להם הקב"ה מימות רחבעם "The First Temple is different because the Holy One, blessed be He, was long suffering with them from the days of Rehoboam," *Kallah Rabbati, Perek Kinyan Torah*, ed. M. Higger, *Massekhtot Kallah* (Brooklyn, 1936), pp. 227 f.

9:2 (p. 300). We have rendered הַכֹּל כַּאֲשֶׁר לַכֹּל as "everything is like everything else, one fate awaits all men." This evidently idiomatic locution has its parallel in the old English proverb, "All in all, and all in every part," which means "total identity." It occurs in Shakespeare's *King Henry IV*, Part II, Act V, Scene v, line 29: " 'Tis all in every part," i. e., "it is all the same."

9:3 (p. 301). On the clause וְהוֹלֵלוֹת בִּלְבָבָם see the Supplementary Note above on 3:11.

9:9 (p. 306). Though Koheleth has his doubts regarding the character of women, as is clear from the famous passage 7:26–29, our observation in the Commentary (*ad loc.*) needs a modification in emphasis. While Koheleth was almost surely a bachelor and no apologist for the institution of marriage, he was not an advocate of promiscuity. This is clear from his admonition, "Enjoy life with the woman whom you love *through all the brief days of your life*, which God has given you under the sun."

10:1 (p. 313). שמן רוקח has a Ugaritic parallel, *šmn rqḥ*.

10:11 (p. 323). The present verse supplies additional evidence for refuting the theory of an Aramaic origin of Koheleth, on which see Supplementary Note A and the literature there cited. The paronomasia of נָחָשׁ and לַחַשׁ is characteristically Hebrew and cannot be reproduced in the Aramaic חִוְיָא "snake"; לַחַשׁ "charm".

10:15 (p. 324). On עָמָל, note other nouns common in gender, *kōs, šabbat, derekh, šemeš, maḥᵃneh*. The Mem of הכסילים may be a scribal error, or the enclitic Mem (which H. L. Ginsberg proposed for Isa. 10:1, ומכתבים עמל כתבו, and other passages. Cf. QHA, p. 100).

10:16 (p. 325). The rendering of נער as "youth, child," should be replaced by "slave," on the basis of the contrast with בֶּן־חוֹרִים in the next verse and Pr. 30:21 f. which declares that the earth cannot bear "a slave who becomes a king" — a reflection of the upper-class viewpoint of Wisdom.

10:17 (p. 326). The substantive בֶּן־חוֹרִים meaning "the son of nobles, nobly born" is semantically intermediate between the Biblical Hebrew חוֹרִים (Jer. 27:20; I Ki. 21:8, 11; Neh. 2:16) meaning "nobles" and the Mishnaic Hebrew בן חורין "free man." Thus it exhibits the same stage in the development of Hebrew as the noun חֵפֶץ, on the semantics of which see p. 364, n. 14. Similarly, the root רָעָה "desire" (cf. Hos. 12:2) still possesses its basic sense in Koheleth's use of רַעְיוֹן (Ecc. 1:17; 2:22; 4:16) and in רְעוּת (1:14; 2:11, 17, 26; 4:4; 6:9). In Mishnaic Hebrew and in Aramaic רעיון has lost its optative sense and simply means "thought" (Dan. 2:29, 30; 4:16; 5:6, 10). The Vav consecutive, which is a basic phenomenon of classical Hebrew, still occurs, though rarely, in Koheleth (1:17; 4:1, 7). It disappears completely from Mishnaic Hebrew. In all these respects the intermediate position of Koheleth between classical Hebrew and the Mishnaic stage is clear. (See chap. VII above for further details.)

On the semantic relationship between "control" and "strength," cf. also Hebrew *hithappeq*, "control oneself," from the root *'āfaq*, "hold, be strong," Akkadian *epêqu*, "solid, strong," Arabic *'afiqa*, "surpass, excel." Thus Targum Onkelos translates *hithappeq* by *ḥasan* (Gen. 43:31; 45:1).

10:18 (p. 327). The juxtaposition of two such rare verbs as *mkk* and *dlp* is paralleled in the Ugaritic text, III A B, A 17 (*mkk* parallel to *dlp*), as Ginsberg (*JAOS*, vol. 70, 1950, pp. 158 f.) is constrained to admit. The parallel does not prove Canaanite influence (ag. Dahood, p. 44), but it does serve to demonstrate the authentic Hebrew character of *Koheleth*.

10:20 (p. 328). The meaning of מדע as "bedroom" may have lain at the basis of the Midrash which cites our verse in rebuking David for taking many concubines. Cf. *Yalkut Shimeoni*, on *Samuel*, sec. 138; *Midrash Shoḥer Tob* 7:2 (private communication from Dr. J. H. Greenstone).

On בעל הכנפים cf. Pr. 1:17, בעל כנף, "bird," a phrase which occurs in Ugaritic in the cultic meaning "Baal of the wings." So, too, בני רשף, originally "sons of the god Rešeph," becomes a common noun in Job 5:7, whether its meaning be "bird," "bird of prey," "eagle," "spark," or "lightning dart." See the Commentaries on *Job* of Driver-Gray and Dhorme, *ad loc.*, for the various views.

12:1 ff. (pp. 338 ff.). In our analysis of "The Allegory of Old Age," after the principal views of the passage are presented, the conclusion is reached (p. 339) that no single line of thought is maintained throughout and that two metaphors, that of the deterioration of an estate and the decay of the bodily organs, are utilized by the author. The discussion ends with the statement, "Under other circumstances, the reader's inability to grasp the poem's precise intent at so many points, coupled with the author's failure to carry his metaphor through consistently, would have doomed the passage. It is a tribute to its greatness and vividness that nevertheless it casts a powerful spell upon the reader." This apologia for the author's literary inconsistency needs to be revised in view of the prevalence of mixed metaphors in literature. Thus in the Bible, Ps. 23 pictures God as both a shepherd and a host and Ps. 48 compares the trembling of the foreign kings before the majesty of the Holy City, Jerusalem, both to a woman in travail and to a mighty east wind. Mixed metaphors are characteristic of all writers, including poets like Shakespeare, Blake, Matthew Arnold and Dylan Thomas (see *BGM*, pp. 202 f. for a discussion of mixed metaphors, including our passage).

12:4 (p. 343). In addition to the Biblical parallels adduced in the Commentary for בנות השיר as meaning "daughters of song, songstresses," an epithet for "birds," cf. the Ugaritic *bnt hll snnt*, "daughters of joyful noise, swallows" (Ginsberg, *BASOR*, 72, 1931, pp. 13 ff.; Dahood, *op. cit.*, p. 47).

12:5, 6 (p. 345 f.). In stich e, the participle הֹלֵךְ should be taken as in the present progressive tense: "Man is going." He is not yet dead, but the professional mourners are already prepared for him! The force of עַד אֲשֶׁר לֹא "before," should not be lost sight of. The passage should therefore be rendered:

> For man is going to his eternal home
>   and the hired mourners walk about in the street,
> Before the silver cord is severed,
>   and the golden bowl is shattered
> and the pitcher is broken at the spring
>   and the wheel is shattered at the pit.

The ultimate tragedy of man's death dissolves in the ironic reflection that it represents simply one more professional engagement for the hired mourners, who wait impatiently for the call even before the dying man has breathed his last.

12:6 (p. 347). On נלת הזהב cf. the Ugaritic parallel *gl ḥrṣ*.

12:11 (p. 353). For בעלי אספות, "masters of assemblies," see Comm. Dahood, pp. 49 f., proposes that the suggested Phoenician vocable בנאספת, which occurs in the *Kranzinschrift* from Piraeus of 96 B. C. E. (Lidzbarski, 52;

Cooke, *North Semitic Inscriptions*, p. 94), should be read as בן אספת, lit. "sons,"
i. e., members of the assembly. He also cites the feminine proper name אספת,
which occurs in a bilingual, third-century inscription from Piraeus (*CIS*, 119).
However, since it is transliterated 'Ασεπι, it is not morphologically identical
with the Biblical *ᵃsuppoth*, but is closer to the very common Mishnaic Hebrew
אסיפה, "gathering" (e. g., Y. Taan. I, 64c, a. e.).

   12:12 (p. 354).   On להג, Dahood (p. 51) suggests that the Lamed should
be regarded as the preposition before the root *hg*, which occurs in Ugaritic in
the meaning "reckoning, counting," parallel to *spr*, "number" (Keret Epic A,
col. 2, lines 90, 91). However, the parallel infinitive עשות, which occurs in our
passage without the preposition, does not support this interesting suggestion.

   12:13 (p. 354).   כי זה כל האדם. To the parallels cited in the Commentary
for this usage, add Micah 5:4, והיה זה שלום, "This shall be the *sign of peace*."
The *theme* of our passage is expressed in Job 28:28, "And unto man He said:
'Behold, the fear of the Lord, that is wisdom; and to depart from evil is understanding.'" Both its form and its content are paralleled in Mat. 7:12: "So
whatever you will that men would do to you, do so to them, *for this is the law
and the prophets*."

SUPPLEMENTARY NOTES

A. The Theory of an Aramaic Origin of Koheleth

The view that the Hebrew book of Koheleth is a translation from a no
longer extant Aramaic original was first raised as a question by Burkitt, has
been seriously maintained by Zimmerman, and has been vigorously defended
by H. L. Ginsberg. The detailed evidence for not accepting this hypothesis is
presented in the literature cited above on p. 364, notes 12–16; ch. VIII adduces
the more general considerations. Several other lines of proof may be added:

I. *The phenomenon of paronomasia* which exists in the Hebrew and not in
the Aramaic. Thus in 7:1, the play on *šem* and *šemen* would be lost in the
Aramaic *šum* and *mišḥā*; note also the balancing of *tōbh šem* and *šemen tōbh*,
which is obviously original. The same paronomasia occurs in Canticles 1:3,
שמן תורק שמך. Other instances in our book are 7:6, *hassīrīm*, "thorns," and
hassīr, "pot"; and 9:5, *zēkher*, "remembrance," and *sākhār*, "reward" (rather
than the usual *yithrōn*).

Ginsberg's effort to counter these examples by supposing a paronomasia in
the alleged Aramaic of 3:4, *raqed*, "dance," and *'arqed*, "mourn," cannot be
pronounced successful. One instance of this rhetorical usage among fourteen
pairs of verbs in the Catalogue of the Seasons is hardly impressive. Cf., for
example, Isa. 5:7, where the play on words is carried out in both parallel stichs:
mišpāṭ and *mispāḥ*, *ṣᵉdākāh* and *ṣᵉ'ākāh*. The two other examples of paronomasia which he creates in the alleged "lost" Aramaic original are even less
convincing, resting, as they do, upon emended texts, over and beyond the
assumption of a translation.

II. *The rhythmic structure of various passages* in Koheleth, which are
characterized by parallelism and regular meter (cf. 1:2 ff.; 3:1–8; 9:8 ff.;
11:7 to 12:8; the proverbs 1:18; 4:5 f.; 5:9; and the collections in chaps. 7 and
10), creates a presumption (though not a proof) in favor of the originality of
the received text, for a translation would tend to blur the metric form of the
original. See *QHA*, pp. 107 ff.

III. *Ben Sira's verbal dependence on Koheleth* (see above, pp. 43 ff.) also
strengthens the originality of the Hebrew. It would surely be remarkable that
Ben Sira (c. 190 B. C. E.) could use the Aramaic "original" of Koheleth and
translate its phraseology into a Hebrew which resembles the independent
translation of Koheleth, not produced until much later!

IV. *The close approximation by Koheleth of the Hebrew of the Biblical
passages* which he utilizes (see pp. 43 ff. and *QHA*, pp. 106–107) points in the
same direction.

V. *The authentic examples of parallels to be found in Canaanite literature*,
which are discussed below in Supplementary Note C, do not prove Phoenician

influence; they do, however, reflect a common vocabulary shared by Hebrew-Canaanite. That the singularly inept translator whom the theory creates would render the Aramaic original into Hebrew, using words and phrases derived from a very ancient Northwest Semitic literary tradition, is another extreme coincidence difficult to accept.

The Aramaic theory has, accordingly, won no adherence from any scholar except its original proponents, and may safely be pronounced unacceptable. The originality of the Hebrew text has been affirmed by W. F. Albright (*Jewish Frontier*, Jan., 1952, pp. 30 ff.); H. H. Rowley (*Judaism*, 1952, vol. I, p. 279); O. S. Rankin (*Book List of the Society for O. T. Study*, 1952, p. 32); M. J. Dahood (in *Biblica*, vol. 33, 1952, pp. 30–52, 191–221); R. Marcus (in *Jewish Social Studies*, 1953, p. 174); E. Hammershaimb in *Vetus Testamentum* (1951), vol. 2, pp. 237–40.

B. On Scientific Method in Koheleth Research

All too often, modern Biblical scholarship is guilty of violating basic canons of scientific research. This is particularly true in dealing with a work as unique as *Koheleth*. Envying the certitude and exactness of the natural sciences, at least as it appears to outsiders, Biblical scholars sometimes forget that the phenomena with which the literary and historical disciplines are concerned are far more complex than those of the natural world, and that unilinear explanations can therefore rarely be true. Moreover, the conclusions of scholarship cannot be tested experimentally in the laboratory. Dogmatism is therefore particularly unjustified in these fields, and humility is more than a moral virtue — it is an indispensable trait of the truly scientific spirit.

These basic principles of method need to be restated, particularly with regard to the book of *Koheleth*:

A. *The prevalence of multiple factors in historical phenomena must be kept in mind.* The author of *Koheleth* is a complex, richly endowed personality. On the one hand, he is the heir of pre-Exilic Hebrew religion, as taught preeminently in the Torah and the Prophets. He is himself a devotee and practitioner of *Hokmah*, which possesses its own rich tradition. He is also the contemporary of the "proto-Pharisaic" period in the history of Judaism, with the basic ideas of which, such as that of the after-life, he is familiar. He has also absorbed some widely diffused Greek ideas, such as the doctrine of the "four elements" (1:2 ff.) and the "golden mean" (7:16–18), as well as the more general skeptical temper of the Greek way of life. Finally, he is more than a mere echo of his background, possessing a searching and original spirit. Hence it is a distortion to demand documentation at each point in his book through parallels in other cultures, and to interpret his meaning exclusively in terms of the usage of other writers.

The style of Koheleth reflects the complexity of his background and of his personality. This book exhibits: (a) many affinities with classical Hebrew;

(b) many points of contact with the Mishnaic era of the language, of which it constitutes an early stage; (c) countless instances of the powerful influence of Aramaic, which was the spoken language of his environment; and (d) unique modes of expression for his special ideas. In part he uses the accepted religious vocabulary of his day as a vehicle for his own unconventional ideas. In part, he is a pioneer in the attempt to use Hebrew for quasi-philosophic purposes, to express such ideas as "past," "present," "future," "recurrence," "moderation," etc.

B. *The comparative method, which has proved so fruitful in contemporary Semitic and Biblical studies, has two aspects, not one.* The discoveries of vast amounts of epigraphic material from the surrounding cultures of the Fertile Crescent, Sumerian, Akkadian, Syrian, and Egyptian, as well as the remains of Hurrian and Hittite civilization, have naturally absorbed the energies of scholars eager to illumine Biblical life and thought through parallels. However, this "horizontal" aspect of the comparative method, i. e., through space, has obscured the "vertical" aspect, i. e., through time, namely, the light shed on Hebrew life and thought by the later phases of Jewish religious and cultural development. The Hebrew Scriptures were written by a people which remained a recognizable religio-cultural-ethnic group for centuries, with an unbroken literary tradition. The Hebrew language never became extinct.

For various reasons, the methodological error is made of ignoring or belittling the evidence from post-Biblical Hebrew sources in favor of alleged parallels from non-Hebrew cultures, emanating from other geographical milieus and ethnic groups. This, in spite of the fact that the evidence adduced from the "vertical aspect" is, other things being equal, at least as significant as that of the "horizontal aspect," if not more so. For in the case of material emanating from non-Hebrew sources, the problem still remains (though it is often disregarded) of explaining when and how the contacts were established by the peoples involved and what the avenues were for the transmission of culture.

C. *There is need to distinguish carefully between parallels and borrowings,* when the two cultures are as similar in background and character as are the various peoples of the ancient Semitic world. This becomes an increasingly necessary — and difficult — procedure, when the peoples involved have an even closer physical and spiritual relationship, because they emanate from the same area, speak practically the same language, and share a similar background, as, e. g., the members of the Northwest Semitic culture-sphere. Here mere resemblance is insufficient to prove borrowing; it may simply reflect an independent, parallel development of elements going back to a common inheritance. Only an unusual combination or a special sequence of factors can serve to demonstrate direct dependency.

Careful adherence to all these three canons of methodology is essential, if we are to achieve results which will possess, not the mere thrill of novelty, but the abiding value of truth.

C. THE THEORY OF A PHOENICIAN BACKGROUND
OF KOHELETH

The suggestion, tentatively advanced by C. H. Gordon (*Ugaritic Litera-ture*, Rome, 1949, p. 123), that Koheleth shows Phoenician influence (see above, p. 362, note 47) was expanded into a monograph by Father M. J. Dahood, "Canaanite-Phoenician Influence in Qoheleth," published in *Biblica*, vol. 33, 1952 (pp. 30–52, 191–221), and subsequently appearing as a separate work (Rome, 1952). Dr. Dahood's thesis is that Koheleth wrote in Hebrew, not in Aramaic, that he employs Phoenician orthography and betrays strong Canaanite-Phoenician literary influence, and that he was a resident of a Phoenician city (*op. cit.*, cf. pp. 3, 5, 39).

The theory was examined and criticized in two papers read at the Annual Meeting of the Society of Biblical Literature held in New York on December 30, 1954, one by Prof. H. L. Ginsberg ("The Romance of Koheleth the Canaanite"), the other by the present writer ("Was Koheleth a Phoenician?"), to which the reader is referred for a full treatment of the subject. Only a few examples of the argumentation can be adduced here.

Dr. Dahood's treatment observes the first canon of methodology set forth above (see Supplementary Note B) and avoids the unilinear theorizing which has affected much contemporary research. He recognizes the existence of Aramaisms and Rabbinic locutions in the text. However, he violates the third canon. For Dahood fails to recognize the importance of "the vertical aspect" of the comparative method, postulating Phoenician influence where the Hebrew literary tradition itself offers a thoroughly satisfactory explanation.

Dahood's first argument is that the book exhibits "Phoenician" orthography, i. e., defective spelling, with few vowel letters. He overlooks the fact that the defective orthography, which was originally basic to Hebrew, was modified, under the stress of need, sporadically and irregularly by each scribe, who added *matres lectionis* at will. The early conservers of the Biblical text, who may fairly be called Masoretes, and whose labors began *before the destruction of the Temple* (70 C. E.), halted the process by selecting the most ancient and accurate Biblical manuscripts as the basis of the *textus receptus* (see *BTM*, pp. 29–33). The official codices which they adopted as normative already exhibited all varieties of spelling, defective, plene, and mixed, as the medieval Masorah noted (מלא, מלא דמלא חסר, חסר דחסר, etc.). The guardians of the text could not and did not reverse the process. The function of the Masoretes was to preserve the status quo and to prevent further inroads into the accepted text. Other, non-official, codices continued to show increasing numbers of vowel letters, as in the variants registered by Kennicott, de Rossi, and C. D. Ginsburg, and in the Biblical manuscripts found in Qumran. Yet even these Scrolls have no consistent orthography (cf. J. Muilenburg, in *BASOR*, Oct., 1954, pp. 23 f.).

This mixed orthography occurs also in the second-century C. E. bill of sale published by J. T. Milik (*Revue Biblique*, vol. 61, 1954, pp. 182 ff.), where the wife's name is written *defectiva* (שׁלם) on l. 12 by the scribe and *plene* by the lady herself on l. 16 of the same document (שׁלום).

The MT of *Koheleth* exhibits the same variations of orthography. To argue from the real or alleged defective spellings in the MT of Koheleth for a Phoenician provenance of the book is completely unjustified. As a matter of fact, many of the instances of variants in Hebrew manuscripts, as well as alleged divergences in the Versions (as, e. g., היו — היה in 1:10, 16; 2:7; 4:16), are not orthographic at all, but are syntactic in character (see, e. g., the Commentary on 1:10, p. 198).

The various other phenomena in morphology, syntax, and vocabulary, which Dahood assembles, do not demonstrate a Phoenician provenance. They are thoroughly explicable in terms of the various elements of Koheleth's style: (a) Biblical; (b) proto-Mishnaic; and (c) Aramaic influence. Only a few instances of each category can be given here, especially since a good deal of the evidence is cited in the Commentary at the relevant passages.

A. *Authentic Biblical Style.* Biblical Hebrew exhibits such phenomena as the non-syncopation of the article (6:10 Kethib; 8:10; 10:3 Kethib). It contains many nouns of the type מִשְׁלַחַת (8:8), like מִצְנֶפֶת, מִשְׁאֶרֶת, מִשְׁעֶנֶת. The conjunction גַּם אִם (8:17) needs no Phoenician parallel אַף אִם (*CIS* 3, 6), in view of the common Biblical locution גַּם כִּי (Ps. 23:4).

Similarly, the infinitive absolute with a pronominal subject (4:2) has authentic parallels in classical Hebrew in Lev. 6:7 and Deut. 15:2. (Est. 4:2, which Dahood cites [p. 20], is not an example.) In all these, and many other cases, there is no need to go to extra-Biblical sources, Phoenician or otherwise.

B. *Mishnaic Hebrew.* The preference for the masculine plural suffix הם over the feminine (p. 14) (2:6, 10; 10:9; 11:8; 12:1), already frequent in Biblical Hebrew, became absolute in Rabbinic Hebrew. The demonstrative זה, which occurs eight times in the Bible, six of them in Koheleth (p. 15), is the normal form in Mishnaic Hebrew (זו). The relative pronoun שׁ crowds out אֲשֶׁר completely in Rabbinic Hebrew. Koheleth's use of אשׁר 89 times and שׁ 67 times stands midway between classic Biblical and Mishnaic Hebrew.

C. *Aramaisms.* These include עַל־דִּברַת (3:18; 7:14; 8:2), which occurs also in Ps. 110:4, and כְּל־עֻמַּת (5:15). On בלא עתך in 7:17, see the Additional Note on the text. On the Aramaic character of the noun רְעוּת, see the Commentary on 1:14.

Dr. Dahood's study, it may be added, has revealed a few interesting parallels between Phoenician and Punic, on the one hand, and Biblical Hebrew, on the other. This is a situation to be expected in view of the close kinship of both languages and literatures. These parallels (10:18; 12:4) are most welcome exegetical aids, and although they do not prove Phoenician influence, they provide additional support for the authentic Hebrew character of *Koheleth*, if any were needed (see Supplementary Note A, V above). On these and other passages, see the "Additional Notes on the Text" at 3:17; 10:1, 18, 20; 12:4, 6, 11, 12.

D. On the Meaning of עָמָל in Koheleth

At the very beginning of *Koheleth* there occurs the important term עָמָל which we have generally rendered "toil, hard labor," in our translation. The twelfth-century Jewish commentator Rabbi Samuel ben Meir, in his comment on 2:24, renders the noun as "his money for which he toiled" (*māmōnō 'ašer ṭāraḥ bō*). A present-day scholar has extended this insight of his medieval predecessor and vigorously argued that this is virtually its only meaning in *Koheleth*. He writes: "It is not clear whether Rashbam recognized that *in the entire section 1:2–2:26 and throughout the book*, the noun *'āmāl* means *almost always* (*kim'at tamid*) 'possession and wealth' or 'possessing and acquiring', and the verb *'āmal* also has the meaning almost always of 'acquire and achieve' " (italics ours). (H. L. Ginsberg in his Hebrew commentary *Qoheleth*, Tel Aviv-Jerusalem, 5721 = 1961, p. 14). As our discussion will demonstrate, the restraint of the medieval scholar is far more justifiable than the extreme position adopted by his modern successor.

At the outset, it should be noted that the legitimacy of Rashbam's interpretation is validated by an important semantic principle in Hebrew, which possesses wide ramifications — the same term will be used in Hebrew to express both a quality or an act and the consequences of that quality or act. Thus the word חַיִל, "strength, efficiency," (so *BDB*) also means "wealth," i. e., "what is acquired through strength and efficiency," (cf. e. g., Gen. 34:29; Num. 31:9; Isa. 8:4; 60:5; Jer. 15:13; Mi. 4:13, and elsewhere).

The root יָגַע "toil, grow weary (through labor or trouble)" yields the nouns יְגַע (Job 20:18, on the rendering of which see Gordis, *The Book of God and Man — A Study of Job* (Chicago, 1965 = *BGM*, p. 265), יְגִיעַ (Deut. 28:33; Isa. 45:14; Jer. 20:5; Hos. 12:9; Hag. 1:1; Ps. 128:2, and elsewhere) and the Rabbinic יגיעה (B. Taan. 16a) יש לו יגיעה בשדה וביתו ריקן "one who has his possessions in the field and whose house is empty." (For the meaning, see H. Malter, *The Treatise Ta'anit of the Babylonian Talmud*, Phila., 1928, p. 113, n. 247.) All these nouns mean "wealth, possessions."

The noun אוֹן "vigor" also has the meaning of "wealth" (Hos. 12:9; Job 20:10) and may be related to הוֹן "wealth," frequent in Wisdom literature (so *BDB*, s. v. הוֹן p. 223b). So, too, כֹּחַ "strength" has the connotation of "riches" in Pr. 5:10; Job 6:22. Similarly, מַעֲשֶׂה "act, deed" develops the meaning of "consequence, reward" (Isa. 32:17; cf. also Hab. 3:17).

The same semantic principle explains how the various Hebrew terms for "sin" develop the meaning of "punishment," an observation that has significant philosophic and religious implications, which cannot be spelled out here. Thus, חֵטְא "sin" also means "punishment" in Isa. 53:12 (not "sin"!), in Lam. 3:39 and in the common idiom *nāsā' ḥē(t)'* "bear punishment" (Lev. 20:24; 24:19; Num. 18:22, 32; Ez. 23:49 and elsewhere). The same meaning inheres in חַטָּאת (Zc. 14:19).

The Hebrew verb אָשַׁם "offend, be guilty" develops the clear connotation of "be punished" in Judg. 21:22; Isa. 24:6; Jer. 2:3; Hos. 5:15; 10:2; 14:1;

Ps. 34:22, 23. As we hope to demonstrate elsewhere, in Lev. 4:4, 13, 22, 27, this meaning, which has not been recognized, is crucial to the understanding of the entire section. The synonym עָוֹן "iniquity, guilt" also has the meaning "punishment" in such passages as II Ki. 7:9; Isa. 53:6, 11 (see *BDB*, s. v., p. 731, a, b).

Because of the intimate bond between the act and its consequences, the Hebrew word employed may at times embrace both senses and the translator is unable to transmit the fullness of meaning intended by the original. (On the importance of the phenomenon of "double meaning" for literary style generally and for Biblical style in particular, see the discussion in *BGM*, chap. XIV, and esp. pp. 167, 196, 347, 357; also Gordis, *Lisegulloth Hamelisah bekhithebhei Haqodeš* in *Sepher Hamuggaš Likhebhod Doktor Moshe Seidel*, Jerusalem 5722 = 1962, pp. 253–63).

Thus, in Cain's complaint (Gen. 4:13) גָּדוֹל עֲוֹנִי מִנְּשׂוֹא both meanings are involved: "My sin — punishment is greater than I can bear," with perhaps a greater emphasis upon the second rather than the first meaning.

Similarly, both meanings are intended in the classical passage in Job 5:6, 7, where *'awen* and *'amal* include both evil-doing and its evil consequences:

כי לא־יצא מעפר און ומאדמה לא־יצמח עמל

כי אדם לעמל יולד ובני רשף ינביהו עוף

> Indeed, misfortune does not come forth from the ground,
> nor does evil sprout from the earth.
> It is man who gives birth to evil,
> as surely as the sparks fly upward.

(See *BGM*, p. 241 on the text and interpretation.)

In sum, there is sufficient basis in the semantic principle set forth to validate the meaning "wealth" for *'āmāl*. This offers no warrant, however, for the extreme claim that "wealth" is its invariable meaning in our book. It should be added that the word, which is by no means infrequent elsewhere in the Bible, has the meaning of "wealth, fruit of labor" in only one passage outside *Koheleth*, in Ps. 105:44, as *BDB* recognizes.

A study of the usage of *'āmāl* indicates that its use falls into five principal categories:

A. In some instances, similar to those adduced above, the noun *'āmāl* is freighted with both meanings, "labor — wealth." This was correctly felt by Rashbam when he rendered it in 2:24 ממונו אשר טרח בו "his money for which he toiled." As the context makes clear, the theme of the passage is man's obligation to enjoy both his activity and the wealth which is its tangible reward.

B. In a very few cases, the meaning "wealth" is preferable, as in 2:18, 19; 5:18. In the first two passages our translation reads "wealth" and "possessions" respectively, *supra* p. 152.

C. In some passages, the meaning "wealth" is possible, but by no means required, as e. g., 2:10, 20, 21; 6:7. Thus in 2:24; 3:13; 5:14, 17 the *Beth* in the phrase בַּעֲמָלוֹ or בְּכָל עֲמָלוֹ is the *Beth pretii* (of price or exchange); see Comm. *ad loc.*, and the vocable is best rendered "in return for his toil."

D. In other instances, the meaning "riches" is inferior to that of "labor." This is the case in 4:8 וְאֵין קֵץ לְכָל־עֲמָלוֹ, where both the succeeding clause and the second half of the verse suggest that Koheleth is referring to labor rather than to wealth.

E. In other passages the rendering "wealth" is impossible (as in 8:15, 17; 10:15). A case in point is afforded by the first instance of the use of ʿ*āmāl* in our book, in 1:3. This opening section deals with the monotonous regularity and lack of progress in the natural world, as seen in the recurrence of its phenomena. It thus underscores the uselessness and folly of all man's labors. The contrast between man's febrile activity and the unending repetition of the processes of nature is striking. A consideration here of man's wealth would be totally irrelevant to the theme of the section.

Similarly, in 3:1–15, Koheleth declares that all events are predetermined and that human activity is therefore ultimately useless. Hence in 3:9 a reference to wealth would be completely banal. The verse is to be rendered: "What profit then has the worker in all his toil?"

In other passages ʿ*āmāl* is characterized as הֶבֶל וּרְעוּת רוּחַ "vanity and a chasing of wind" (2:11; 4:6). The phrase "chasing of wind" is appropriate to an activity like labor, but not to an object like wealth.

Similarly, in 2:22 the juxtaposition בְּכָל עֲמָלוֹ וּבְרַעְיוֹן לִבּוֹ indicates that the meaning of the phrase is "labor and thought" (see the Comm. *supra* p. 225), not "wealth." In 4:4 the reference to hard work and skill (. . . עָמָל כִּשְׁרוֹן הַמַּעֲשֶׂה) is unmistakable. In the second half of 4:8, the juxtaposition once again אֲנִי עָמֵל וּמְחַסֵּר אֶת־נַפְשִׁי מִטּוֹבָה indicates that the meaning is "For whom am I laboring and depriving myself of joy?"

In 4:9 the reference is clearly to some form of activity, not to wealth. In 9:9, life with the woman a man loves is his reward for his toil, not for his riches.

It is therefore clear that the noun ʿ*āmāl* (and its verb) carry the meaning of "wealth" in a few instances, as Rabbi Samuel ben Meir recognized. It is also a possible rendering in a few other passages. But in most cases, it is either impossible or substantially inferior to its usual rendering as "toil."

In conclusion, a more general consideration may be advanced. The attempt to restrict ʿ*āmāl* in *Koheleth* to the meaning of "wealth" gravely reduces the scope and significance of the book. For it narrows its theme to some reflections on the paltry value of riches, instead of the larger concern with man's role and destiny in the world. For all these reasons, both specific and general, the contention that ʿ*āmāl* always, or nearly always, means "wealth" is to be rejected as unwarranted and unnecessary.

RECENT LITERATURE ON ECCLESIASTES AND WISDOM LITERATURE

AALDERS, G. C., Het Boek de Prediker (Kampen, 1948)

BEA, A., Liber Ecclesiastae (Rome, 1950)

BENTZEN, A., Praedikerens bog (Copenhagen, 1942)

DAHOOD, M. J., Phoenician-Canaanite Influence in Koheleth (Rome, 1952)

DUBARLE, A. M., Les Sages d'Israël (Paris, 1946)

DUESBERG, H., Les Scribes Inspirés (Paris, 1938–39)

GINSBERG, H. L., "Supplementary Studies in Koheleth," in PAAJR, 1952

LEOPOLD, H. C., Exposition of Ecclesiastes (Columbus, Ohio, 1952)

NEHER, A., Notes sur Qohélét (Paris, 1951)

PAUTREL, A., L'Ecclésiaste (Paris, 1948)

POWER, A. D., Ecclesiastes or the Preacher (London, 1952)

VAN DER PLOEG, J., Prediker (Roermond, 1953)

WEBER, J. J., Le Livre de Job, L'Ecclésiaste (Paris, 1947)

ADDENDA

P. 139. To the list of emendations proposed or accepted here, add the following minor modifications of the Masoretic text with regard to: (a) the vowels; or (b) the consonants, which are advocated in the Commentary (cf. S. H. Blank, in JQR, 1953, vol. 43, p. 94):

(a) 5:15 for כָּל־עֻמַּת read כְּלָעֻמַּת (not certain)

   8:10 for מִמָּקוֹם read מִמָּקוֹם

   12:5 for יִּרְאוּ read יִּרָא

   12:5 for וְתָפֵר read וְתָפֵר (not certain)

(b) 3:12 for טוב בם כי read טוב כי (not certain)

   5:9 for בהמון read המון

   7:25 for ולבי read בלבי

   9:2 for הנשבע read כנשבע

   11:3 for יהוא read יהיה or הוא (conflate)